WHAT THE THUNDER SAID

ALSO BY JED RASULA

Wreading: A Poetics of Awareness, or How Do We Know What We Know?

Genre and Extravagance in the Novel

Acrobatic Modernism from the Avant-Garde to Prehistory

History of a Shiver: The Sublime Impudence of Modernism

*Destruction Was My Beatrice: Dada and the
Unmaking of the Twentieth Century*

Modernism and Poetic Inspiration: The Shadow Mouth

Syncopations: The Stress of Innovation in Contemporary American Poetry

This Compost: Ecological Imperatives in American Poetry

The American Poetry Wax Museum: Reality Effects 1940–1990

ANTHOLOGIES

Burning City: Poems of Metropolitan Modernity coedited with Tim Conley

Imagining Language: An Anthology coedited with Steve McCaffery

POETRY

Hectic Pigment

Hot Wax, or Psyche's Drip

Tabula Rasula

WHAT THE THUNDER SAID

How *The Waste Land* Made Poetry Modern

JED RASULA

PRINCETON UNIVERSITY PRESS
PRINCETON & OXFORD

Published by Princeton University Press
41 William Street, Princeton, New Jersey 08540
99 Banbury Road, Oxford OX2 6JX

press.princeton.edu

Library of Congress Cataloging-in-Publication Data

Names: Rasula, Jed, author.
Title: What the thunder said : how the Waste Land made poetry modern / Jed Rasula.
Description: Princeton : Princeton University Press, [2022] |
Includes bibliographical references and index.
Identifiers: LCCN 2022006944 (print) | LCCN 2022006945 (ebook) |
ISBN 9780691225777 (hardback) | ISBN 9780691225784 (ebook)
Subjects: LCSH: Eliot, T. S. (Thomas Stearns), 1888–1965. Waste land. |
Eliot, T. S. (Thomas Stearns), 1888–1965—Influence. |
BISAC: LITERARY CRITICISM / Poetry | HISTORY /
Modern / 20th Century / General | LCGFT: Literary criticism.
Classification: LCC PS3509.L43 W3785 2022 (print) |
LCC PS3509.L43 (ebook) | DDC 821/.912—dc23/eng/20220421
LC record available at https://lccn.loc.gov/2022006944
LC ebook record available at https://lccn.loc.gov/2022006945

British Library Cataloging-in-Publication Data is available

Editorial: Anne Savarese and James Collier
Production Editorial: Lauren Lepow
Text and Jacket Design: Chris Ferrante
Production: Erin Suydam
Publicity: Jodi Price and Carmen Jimenez

Jacket images: (Top) Fernand Léger, detail of illustration from the cover of Blaise Cendrars's *J'ai tué*, 1918 © 2022 Artists Rights Society (ARS), New York / ADAGP, Paris. (Middle) Wood type letters from Gothic No. 50 type specimen by Hamilton Manufacturing Co., courtesy of Tool Case. (Bottom) Detail of the introduction from the score for *Le sacre du printemps* by Igor Stravinsky, 1921, courtesy of The New York Public Library Digital Collections.

This book has been composed in King's Caslon

Printed on acid-free paper. ∞

Printed in the United States of America

1 3 5 7 9 10 8 6 4 2

This book is for Suzi Wong,
who made the difference that made the book.

"There is no substitute for a lifetime."
(Ezra Pound, Canto XCVIII)

CONTENTS

WHAT THE THUNDER SAID

INTRODUCTION

By the time T. S. Eliot's poem *The Waste Land* entered public domain in the United States in 1998, it had been a staple of higher education for half a century. No teaching anthology could afford to omit it. Because Eliot succeeded in making the case that modern poetry had to be difficult, *The Waste Land* served as the paradigm of difficulty. More recently it has settled into its role as modernist icon, as every passing year brings a new round of centenaries commemorating modernism. Long canonized, Eliot's poem has acquired the demeanor of a scenic viewpoint, with its park service plaque and swivel mounted telescope.

Eliot's eminence as preeminent among poets ("king of the cats," as W. B. Yeats put it when he ascended to that role after Swinburne died in 1909) is not what it used to be. Yet because Eliot is no longer contemporary, his work is unencumbered by the reception accorded it on publication. And after a century of collage, of Dada and Surrealism, its disjunctive surface is less alarming. If it initially seemed a response to the late Great War, in its centennial year the poem's themes of drought and drabness sound immediate and foreboding to a generation facing climate disaster and the moral bankruptcy of the political class. The poem, straddling past and future, applies pressure on the present.

The Waste Land has a double legacy. It's the milestone that vaulted its author to considerable fame and influence, culminating with the Nobel Prize in 1948. It has held a permanent place in the pantheon of modern poetry since its publication in 1922. It has been an intimidating lump in the syllabus for generations of undergraduates, and a chastening puzzle to graduate students. But *The Waste Land* is not only a poem; it names an event, like a tornado or an earthquake. Its publication was a watershed, marking a before and after. It was a poem unequivocal in its declaration that the ancient art of poetry had become modern.

It's time to take *The Waste Land* out of the classroom, out of the text-books, to recover its force as explosive event, one that continues to emit an uncanny relevance a century later. In the centenary of its publication, *The Waste Land* merits recognition not as a poem—there's a mountain of

1

scholarship on that—but as a phenomenon. Eliot's poem is a component in a broader cultural revolution that led to abstraction in art, atonality in music, and an overall flouting of conventions by the international avant-gardes. *The Waste Land* partakes of collage as compositional principle in the arts; and it shares with Marcel Duchamp and others the notion that modernism convened a space in which every artwork could be a conceptual gambit, a wager like a throw of the dice, but in a game for which there's no table, and no croupier.

From Arthur Rimbaud's adamant exhortation in 1871 that one must be absolutely modern, to the international impact of *The Waste Land* half a century later, poetry was instrumental in making the modern an *ism*. But what was it about poetry prompting the thought that it needed to *become* modern? Was it something about modern life that seemed ripe for poetic treatment? And why poetry? Did poetry possess some symbolic currency unique among the arts? Or was it, rather, that modernist trends evident in other arts were felt to be lacking in poetry? Was it regressive? Did poetry need a makeover? And why did an art often associated with the adjective *timeless* feel the need to keep up with the times?

These are questions I asked myself a number of years ago and put to students in seminars. This book ruminates on the questions by tracing a line of poetry, spun out by Wagnerism and encompassing Symbolism, then given a differently ambitious torque as it was aligned with other arts in modernism. This is evident in the way *The Waste Land* is served up in lists of cultural bombshells from the early twentieth century. *The Rite of Spring* by Igor Stravinsky, Pablo Picasso's painting *Les Demoiselles d'Avignon*, Sergei Eisenstein's film *Potemkin*, and the architecture of Le Corbusier often fill out the roster. It might also include Joyce's *Ulysses*, Duchamp's *Fountain*, Kafka's story "Metamorphosis," Chaplin's tramp, the foxtrot, pictorial collage, the Bauhaus, Cubism, Tatlin's tower, Dada, quantum mechanics, and chance operations, and even Irving Berlin's best-selling "White Christmas." Because such lists have become familiar in part through *Time* magazine's curatorial relation to the twentieth century (*The Waste Land* was reviewed in *Time*'s first issue), it takes an effort to realize it's a triumphal parade of white men.

The Waste Land is Exhibit A of modernism in poetry, with its portentous use of the Grail legend and its generous helping of quotations and allusions from a range of historical sources. But Eliot's career began rather differently, with Prufrock, the mordantly comic figure introduced in the pages of *Poetry: A Magazine of Verse* in 1915. You know the guy: afraid to eat a peach. "The Love Song of J. Alfred Prufrock," with its varying moods and rhythms, had affinities with Charlie Chaplin's tramp, who combined a jaunty esprit with the down-and-out. It shared with the tramp certain characteristics of slapstick. The term *slapstick* comes from the clapper commonly used in the old commedia dell'arte with its stylized buffoonery. If the pratfall induces the belly laugh, there's also the chastened grin of the onlooker, not sure what will happen next. This was registered by Louis Untermeyer's first encounter with Prufrock. It was "the first piece of the English language that utterly stumped me," he reflected. "The other Sunday night there was a group at the house—a few poets, a lawyer, a couple of musicians and one psychoanalyst. I read it to them quite seriously—and no one," he recounts, "could keep a straight face."

As an undergraduate, even as he was studying philosophy and writing poems, Eliot reveled in American slang, the antic contraptions of Rube Goldberg, *Mutt and Jeff* comics, and the animal dances coming into vogue with ragtime, like the foxtrot, the bunny hug, the grizzly bear. He was inclined to combine *Krazy Kat* comics with Elizabethan revenge tragedies, merging highbrow with lowbrow the way Cockney pub talk concludes a Shakespearean episode in *The Waste Land*. Such passions and interests shape the person from whom a poem emerges, and poems are personal even if they refrain from personal declarations. As *The Waste Land* reveals, even the most abstruse phraseology and recondite references can be saturated with undisclosed privacy. It's also the case that a deep well of personal misery can provoke compositional adventures far removed from mere reportage. Poems can surreptitiously sustain a double focus, in which public and private imperceptibly change places, even in the flicker of an image. This enables readers to find themselves rather than the author entangled in a poem's words, rhythms, and images—even as they warily surmise a crafty magician at work behind the curtain.

The Waste Land spoke to a postwar generation, whispering its secret code into receptive ears of readers who found themselves awaiting it not only in England and America but around the world. It was a world contending with emergent mass entertainment industries, while an elite cultural consensus was beginning to dissolve. High and low, culturally speaking, were all mixed up, and Eliot had just the touch to make the confusion palpable, and the consequences appetizing. Although met with equal portions of dismay and enthusiasm, *The Waste Land* was recognizable as poetry's calling card to the twentieth century.

*

The Waste Land is not so much the subject of this book as its center of gravity. Because a number of topics are in its gravitational field, the poem's author (caveat emptor) does not make an appearance until halfway through. My approach to Eliot's poem is less that of a literary scholar than a cultural historian's. I'm more interested in how and why it made an impact than in what it "says." Like many cultural events, *The Waste Land* seemed unprecedented even as it had an aura of déjà vu. Its intimidating unfamiliarity seemed eerily familiar.

To approach Eliot's poem from this perspective means going back in time, tracing a foreground of instigations and influences, provocations and cultural resonances that contributed to its uncanny intimacy. It will take us back to the grandiose phenomenon of Wagnerism, which dominated Western culture for the second half of the nineteenth century, and still held sway into the twentieth. *The Waste Land* is a Wagnerian poem in that it shares Richard Wagner's vision of the remote past as a template for the future. Eliot, like Wagner, regarded modernity as the nightmare of history from which one could awaken only by baptism in the waters of myth. But Wagner revealed that the artist could not achieve this by simply adopting myth as subject matter. Method was as important as myth. Wagner sought to blend the separate arts into a collective enterprise, the *Gesamtkunstwerk*, or total artwork. This aspiration had enormous influence on practitioners in all the arts well into the twentieth century. It was a pipe dream, but it sanctioned dreaming as artistic prerogative.

Eliot, like most poets, found his calling in the provocations of his predecessors. In 1910, when he was a Harvard undergraduate, the state of English-language poetry was at a low point. It offered him nothing to work with, so he found what he needed, instead, in French Symbolist poetry of the nineteenth century. French Symbolism is Wagnerism through and through. It's easy to claim Wagner influenced the Symbolists, who in turn influenced Eliot. But there's no influence without receptivity, and receptivity arises in the creative spirit even before contact with any alleged influence. This is where it gets interesting, because that incipient creative wick is looking for a spark, not seeking a genealogy. *Wagnerism* is a term that speaks to the convulsiveness aroused by Wagner's operas. It was a swoon of almost debilitating identification, as Wagnerites discovered themselves in the mirror of the composer's work. Wagnerism was a kind of mania, and in fact it prompted the term *melomania* for an excessive idolatry of music.

In 1877 the English writer Walter Pater observed that music had become the art to which all the other arts aspired. In subsequent decades, artists were intent on incorporating musical sensations into their canvases. For a painter engrossed in Wagner, like Wassily Kandinsky, this was achieved through a turning away from mimetic representation by means of abstraction. For

Symbolist poets, it meant expanding the verbal resources of evocation to bypass naming altogether. "I say: a flower!" said Stéphane Mallarmé, who thought that out of "something other than the known bloom, there arises, musically, the very idea in its mellowness; in other words, what is absent from every bouquet." The poem would summon the vacant bouquet in all its paradoxical plenitude.

The lure of melomania was fading around the time Eliot was finding his way as a poet. He did not aspire to write the poetic equivalent of music, though he often made reference to the music of poetry. He didn't mean musicality, or anything like the mellifluous touches often presumed to provide the musical characteristics of versification. He was a Wagnerian in that he assigned to music a cognitive as well as a sensory dimension. A poem, for him, summoned a mood, a kind of mental sonority, in which one could think differently.

Another through line in my account goes back to melomania to trace a different order of mania. Modernism has often been linked to Freud's exposition of the unconscious. From the stream of consciousness pioneered by James Joyce to the dark peregrinations of the Surrealists, modernism has frequently tapped the limits of consciousness and explored the twilight zones of psychological affliction. The melomania stirred up by Wagnerism has an intriguing biographical profile in the case of the philosopher Friedrich Nietzsche.

Nietzsche composed music in addition to writing the incendiary works that made him a commanding force in modern thought. He was also devoted to Wagner. Their friendship was built on mutual admiration and lasted until Wagner's festival theater at Bayreuth became a posh tourist destination rather than the site for reviving mythic spectacle the composer had sought to create. Nietzsche then realized that Wagnerism was a kind of disease, diagnosing himself as one of the afflicted. During his remaining years he repeatedly wrote about Wagnerism as the characteristic affliction of decadence. He ended by succumbing to a syphilitic infection that left him nearly catatonic for his final decade. This terminal plight marked his own books in the public eye with an air of both clairvoyance and lunacy. Even the titles of *Beyond Good and Evil* and *The Anti-Christ* were enough to align Nietzsche with the dark side.

Around the time Wagner's cultural supremacy was peaking, a new diagnostic category began to circulate. It was named *neurasthenia* by Charles Beard, an American who thought it was a characteristic malady of America in that America embodied modernity, with its raw hustle and its social anxieties. It was concentrated in what he called "brain workers." It's no surprise that Eliot, suffering the repercussions of an ill-considered marriage and constant overwork, regarded himself as a neurasthenic. He completed *The Waste Land* while he was undergoing psychiatric treatment after a nervous breakdown. The poem itself can't be judged a product of mental illness, but it was written by a man who suffered years of trauma and despondency. Even earlier, however, Eliot had envisioned in a poem a madman shaking a dead geranium, scorching image of a mind adrift.

The Waste Land was not, in a technical sense, completed by its author. As its later dedication to Ezra Pound attests, a "finer craftsman" was needed to take a motley heap of drafts in hand, prune away, and envision a shape. Pound had pledged unquestioned support for Eliot since their first meeting in 1914, and regarded *The Waste Land* not only as Eliot's greatest work but as justification for what he called the "modern movement" in general. He eagerly gave Eliot's draft a thorough red-pencil treatment and, congratulating his friend on the result, confessed to being wracked with jealousy.

Pound was a passionate advocate for many others besides Eliot; but as years went by, he became obsessed with economics and politics. These obsessions affected his judgment, and he lost his way during World War II when he made broadcasts in support of the Fascist government in Italy. Filled with rancor directed at Roosevelt and the Allied war effort, smeared with anti-Semitism, the broadcasts resulted in the US government charging Pound with treason. He spent a dozen years in a mental hospital, a legal recourse designed to save the nation the ignominy of hanging a famous poet. If not certifiably "mad," he was manic and unrestrained.

The narrative arc of *What the Thunder Said* traverses the cultural complex indicated above, along with the various manias and debilities germane to the major characters. Part One begins with Wagner and Nietzsche, moving on to trace the impact of Wagnerism on modern poetry, particularly as pioneered by the French Symbolists. Ezra Pound then comes into the picture as a young American poet trying to make his mark in literary London, belatedly realizing that being modern entailed the effort to *become* modern.

Part Two concerns the challenge of becoming modern—personally, for Pound, then programmatically, as he embarked on the vanguard programs of Imagism and Vorticism. These initiatives reflect the post-Symbolist impact of Futurism, which flamboyantly sought to dispense with the burden of the past altogether. Futurism thrived on a martial rhetoric instructive to Pound and others emboldened by the cause of cultural revolution. Futurism jolted English artist Mina Loy into new life as a poet who became a much-respected ally of Pound. He was fortified in his commitment to "the modern movement" when he met T. S. Eliot, astonished that this fellow American had somehow modernized himself on his own.

Part Three brings Eliot into full view, chronicling his impetuous marriage in 1915 up to the publication of *The Waste Land* in 1922. These were years of hardship. The marriage was difficult, as Eliot's wife Vivien was ravaged by poor health, and his own health faltered as well. His literary ambitions—urged by both Vivien and Pound—were arduously pursued even as he worked full-time in a bank. Eliot was making a reputation, and by the end of the war he felt poised for a major statement. But he suffered a nervous breakdown, and only during convalescence did he manage to focus a heap of drafts into what emerged as *The Waste Land*. Pound helped finalize the poem, as well as strategizing the transatlantic publications that made it an international cause célèbre in 1922.

Part Three focuses not only on Eliot but on the ways his poem took on a life of its own. Translations into many languages parlayed its influence far beyond the usual contours of Anglo-American letters. Another element less evident at the time, but documented in recent years, has to do with women poets who responded favorably to Eliot's poem in similarly ambitious works. Without intending to, Eliot enfranchised the unorthodox, and it was certainly unorthodox for women of highly intellectual temperament and training to write book-length poems. These are vital artifacts in their own right and shed new light on possibilities convened by *The Waste Land*.

Part Four takes us to another postwar in the 1940s, when Eliot's eminence was figuratively crowned by the award of the Nobel Prize in Literature. This distinction was contemporaneous with the controversial award of the Bollingen Prize to Pound's *Pisan Cantos* while he was still facing the charge of treason. The famous line from *The Waste Land* about fragments shored against ruins is uncannily resurrected in this episode involving Eliot's ardent supporter and longtime friend, embroiled in the collapse of his own life and, to some extent, his mental faculties. The final chapter tracks *The Waste Land* undergoing pastiche, adaptation, and a legacy of overexposure as cultural icon.

*

For its author, a mood of despondency continued after publication of *The Waste Land*. He regarded it as the end of a phase going back to his early undergraduate poems: "To me it was only the relief of a personal and wholly insignificant grouse against life; it is just a piece of rhythmical grumbling."

This is probably the most dismissive remark a writer has ever made about a signal achievement, but in a way it was accurate, for it was an intensely personal poem, the relic of a troubled marriage and psychological distress. The poem was regarded as unusually erudite, but in fact the purportedly universal themes of the poem were the stuff of a sensibility formed by prep school and Harvard, engaging to those with similar backgrounds. But *The Waste Land*'s slipstream of haunting images ("bats with baby faces," "fear in a handful of dust") spoke even to those without an education in the classics. Its atmosphere of ruination resonated with many after the war, but Eliot's method also compelled attention, for his was the first major accomplishment in English-language poetry of a practice well established in the visual arts—namely, collage.

Thanks to its method—"fragments I have shored against my ruins," the poem famously indicates—*The Waste Land* was effectively sui generis, at least in English. It was a poem that fell afoul of framing categories like lyric, ode, epithalamium, elegy, epic. It was a collage poem, similar to the "simultanism" developed a decade earlier by certain French poets. The possibilities of collage were worked out by visual artists, but it was a German contemporary of Eliot's, Kurt Schwitters, who doubled as artist and author. His collages suggest something of what a poem like *The Waste Land* harbored.

Schwitters roamed the streets of his native Hannover as well as those in Prague, Berlin, or wherever he traveled, gathering litter from gutter and street. It was not all cut-and-paste like Cubist and Dada collages. Schwitters even mounted the big wooden wheel of a dray cart on one assembly. Trolley tickets, magazine advertisements, newspapers and wrapping paper, calendar pages, subway maps, playing cards, banknotes, even clippings from his own publications could be found in a milieu nudged into tactility with buttons and strips of wood, a bit of string, a coin, a piece of lace, a wire grid, chess pieces, even bowling pins. Schwitters's exorbitant spectrum of collage constructions proffers an urban tide pool of the early twentieth century. You can lean over one of his horizontal assemblages and feel a vertigo, realizing you're literally bending over a piece of 1922.

The Waste Land is, in a different register, itself such a window. Eliot, like Schwitters, rounded up a potpourri of raw materials, some of which he had written himself but was now handling like rubble. The rubble consisted of a growing heap of pages, refuse of an abortive effort to conjure a long poem (he initially imagined something more than twice the length of *The Waste Land*). These drafts sputtered to a halt, cradling one or two images so compelling that Eliot held on to them. The challenge was bringing them together in a poem of consecutive focus and forward momentum. How could they fit together?

Collage was the unintended but handy solution. It was a medium in which there need not be a mutual or transactional relation between one fragment and another. Two distinct items conjoined by their proximity did not have to combine. Instead, they could cohabit the space like people passing each other on a sidewalk. Seen from above, a flurry of movement would become evident, as if the streets were filled with pulsating arrows on a flow chart. Everything contributes. It's the overall prospect that convenes a unity. The principle of unity in collage is *multum in parvo*, much in little, a lot crammed into a small space. Add to this method an overlying thematic, "waste land," with scenes of sterility in both environment and human volition. For its first readers *The Waste Land* summed up the postwar ennui of 1919–1921, the years Eliot wrote the bulk of it.

The Waste Land has invariably been paired with *Ulysses*, both published the same year. James Joyce's novel belabored a single day in Dublin into a behemoth of nearly eight hundred pages, much of it certain to stump the most adept readers of the daily press, the intellectual weeklies, and the pretentious assumptions paraded as received opinion in such venues. Scarcely two pages into the text the reader is treated to the vision of "a new art color for our Irish poets: snotgreen." Polite society was being told to step aside, and those subjected to this treatment naturally felt the sting.

Being impolite was far from Eliot's character and demeanor. He wrote *The Waste Land* while working in a bank, assessing foreign assets during and after the cataclysm of the Great War (a time when no one yet thought of it as the First). He wore a suit and sported a bowler hat and a cane. He was associated with some

FIG. 0.1. T. S. Eliot at the publishing house Faber & Gwyer, a year after he started working there in 1925.

of the most flamboyant members of the London avant-garde, but did not adopt the manners or attitudes of the Bohemian demimonde. He published reviews and essays in prominent periodicals, and his views were respected. His poetry was known to be peculiar, but not offensive. Nobody anticipated *The Waste Land*. Or, to put it another way, no one anticipated that poetry could move to the forefront of modernism as a signal artistic phenomenon. Nor was it imagined that poetry could threaten polite decorum by so emphatically raising the artistic stakes.

As shorthand for the impact of modernism, the year 1922 encompasses a decade or more leading up to it. It was a threshold, revealing that modernism (1) was international in scope, (2) spanning all the arts; and (3) it was decisive in addressing modernity on its own terms. Previous and even prevailing practices in the arts were about to expire or had already become anachronisms. Crucially, this meant that one could no longer expect a poem, a ballet, or a painting to serve up a timeworn subject in a transparently accessible manner.

Until around 1910 (the date assigned by Virginia Woolf to mark a definitive change), the adjective *modern* could be a casual reference. We're modern, anyone could think, meaning we're at the latest stage of whatever human enterprise has yielded until now. The term *modern* was a modifier. Talking on a telephone or riding in a motorcar was modern. These were modern conveniences—and sometimes inconveniences, sources of novelty and indignation alike. But what did it mean to *be modern*, to emphatically adopt a program or belief about such a thing? The verb *to modernize* was an acknowledged claim of politicians and city planners. Did artists feel compelled to modernize their equipment, their outlook?

A word not much in use in Eliot's time but which has grown long theoretical legs ever since is *modernity*. It names the big picture, the agglomerative piling up and piling on of all the characteristics and consequences of the modern. It encompasses the haplessly modern—side effects of technology, like the way we're wrangling in the early 2020s with the impact of social media—as well as the determinedly modern, like the programmatic antiornamental claims of modern architecture, or the alienation effect in Brecht's theater. Then there's the broad mixture of the two, as in the music of Igor Stravinsky, who continued to compose ballets, but imposed motor rhythms on the dancers. Eliot heard his music bring "the rhythm of the steppes into the scream of the motor horn, the rattle of machinery, the grind of wheels, the beating of iron and steel, the roar of the underground railway, and the other barbaric cries of modern life." He was writing about *The Rite of Spring*, in which ultramodern music revisits the oldest of primitive rituals, the fertility rite. A dialectic of fertility and sterility runs through *The Waste Land*, and Stravinsky's ballet was like Eliot's poem enacted in another art form.

Modern, *modernism*, and *modernity* constitute an operative shorthand for explanatory books and articles on How We Got This Way. That prospect, however, is retrospective. It was not the case for the figures profiled in this book. For Wagner and Nietzsche, Baudelaire and Mallarmé, Loy, Pound, Eliot, and others who make an appearance, the modern was an experiential inevitability. It was challenging to ordinary citizens adjusting to a changing world, but it provided a more acute challenge to artists, for they had to figure out how to make art that took modernity into account. Was it enough to acknowledge the existence of a petrol pump? Or did one need to consider what the artistic equivalent of aviation might be?

T. S. Eliot was deeply attuned to the past, but he didn't want to replicate it. His idiom was, in its way, akin to scientific observation. He sets a scene and conjures a mood as recognizable now as it was a century ago:

> The winter evening settles down
> With smells of steaks in passageways.
> Six o'clock.
> The burnt-out ends of smoky days.
> And now a gusty shower wraps
> The grimy scraps
> Of withered leaves about your feet
> And newspapers from vacant lots

These lines are from the poem "Preludes," first published in the aggressively avant-garde journal *Blast*, with its taunting pink cover, published a month before the "guns of August" turned the world upside down in 1914.

The term *avant-garde* is generally used to refer to those artistic movements agitating for drastic overhaul of the arts. A military term for an advance scouting operation, it became shorthand for breakaway units in art. But modernism can't be conflated with the avant-garde. For many artists, the simple business of living in 1895, 1910, or 1922 could be exhilarating and dispiriting at the same time. They were the ones who couldn't ignore what each day heaved up. They resisted the nostalgia of those content to chirp bucolic themes out of ancient Greece, or paint idylls befitting a Roman villa. What confounded the general public in 1922 was that Eliot could somehow combine a "burnished throne" festooned in classical regalia with a vision of "rats' alley" and the blare of motorcars.

The prevailing figure in *The Waste Land* is Tiresias, "the most important personage in the poem," Eliot said, "uniting all the rest." In Greek myth, the prophet Tiresias is transformed into a woman for seven years, giving him a rare perspective on sexual difference. But with respect to modernity, such a figure imparts a bifocal Janus-like gaze on past and present. Inasmuch as he unites the other characters, he brings past and present together in a single vision that is the poem. This was not a theme, but a deeply held belief that Eliot articulated in 1919 in his essay "Tradition and the Individual Talent." In it, he offered a vision of European literature as a simultaneity of past and present, with every contemporary contribution affecting past works. From that perspective, *The Waste Land* is a poem that not only makes use of the past but is keenly aware of how its own originality flickers across the seemingly completed monuments of yore.

*

The trajectory of this book goes from a preliminary pair (Wagner, Nietzsche) to a later pair (Pound, Eliot), who get the most attention. Each pair is irrevocably bound by their alliance. They were cultural crusaders. Wagner and Pound were the most explicit, articulating outsized programs to restart civilization, as Pound put it. Eliot's aspirations were similar, but he was less demonstrative. In the end, he wielded far more influence in literary and cultural affairs than Pound, who was increasingly seen as a crackpot. Nietzsche proved to be a commanding figure in the early twentieth century. Wagner's megalomania became an institution in the form of his Bayreuth Festival Theatre. Nietzsche denounced the institution, even as he recognized himself as its victim. He took upon himself, he thought, the sins of the father—meaning Wagner—fancying himself crucified by the blight of decadence, which he saw in the Wagnerism to which he had once dedicated himself. Nietzsche's presentation of himself as a sacrificial figure was rhetorical, whereas Pound's manic righteousness literally put him in harm's way.

Wagner and Nietzsche were disposed to issuing dicta, spewing judgments from a rhetorical firehose, and presenting themselves—as persons and personalities—as inescapable agents of and in their works. Their rhetoric provided them with all the theatricality they needed. With T. S. Eliot and Ezra Pound it was different. They were men of masks and personae, the traditional equipment of the theater. In fact, Eliot spent much of his career from 1930 to 1960 writing plays, beginning with *Murder in the Cathedral.* (His greatest stage success was posthumous, with the Broadway adaptation of his book of light verse, *Old Possum's Book of Practical Cats.*) The mask—in an expansive, not exclusively thespian sense—is a topic that goes to the heart of modernism and modernity.

An actor borrows a persona and fabricates another person. But just as masks have always been with us, identity too has a history. In traditional status hierarchies, identity was social, not psychological. Our very names tell us not who we are but who we were consigned to be, once upon a time. Miller, Baker, Carter, Smith, Taylor, or Müller, Becker, Schneider, Meunier, Boulanger, and so on. But we have long since regarded psychology rather than social position to be a determining factor. The mask can be self-applied.

An early register of this psychological alignment can be found in the essays of Michel de Montaigne (1533–1592). Credited with inventing the essay as we've come to know it (*essayer* in French means to attempt, to try out), Montaigne said of his enterprise: "These are *my* humours, *my* opinions: I give them as things which *I* believe, not as things to be believed. My aim is to reveal my own self, which may well be different tomorrow if I can be initiated into some new business which changes me." The shift so crucial for modernity is from doctrine to experience, what *I* believe, not some dogma to be followed. Montaigne gives credence to identity as variable—self not only changeable but precariously weathering the inevitable pressure of change, the historical condition that has prevailed for centuries.

Another weathervane, closer to our time, is the author of *The Education of Henry Adams* (1907), whose forebears had been the second and the sixth presidents of the United States. In this autobiography, written at the dawn of the twentieth century, Henry Adams (1838–1918) speaks of himself in the third person to register the disorientation he felt confronting "a new universe which had no common scale of measurement with the old." The expectation of change as normative unsettled him. Human identity, he was dismayed to find, was the abiding trace of what does not abide.

Many generations have now lived lifetimes within the conditions so distressing to Adams. Most recently, the internet and the cell phone have transformed human enterprise across the planet. For modernists like Pound and Eliot, change was registered in the airplane, the automobile, cinema, electric lights, indoor plumbing, radio, recording technology, and much more, including two world wars. But even earlier, with the legacy of democratic revolutions, change insistently hung in the air.

Wagnerism was one response to the historical condition of constant change. But Wagner's vision did not engage the future. His own revolutionary political hopes of 1848 having been dashed, Wagner dreamed of resurrecting the past, a halcyon vision of ancient Greece. A very different prospect was envisioned by a French teenager, for whom weathering the maelstrom of change was not imposed by society but was the vision quest of poetic vocation. Being modern meant more than being born in such and such a year. This was the discovery made by Arthur Rimbaud.

At sixteen, after running away from home to Paris, Rimbaud had seen enough to envision a magisterial transformation demanded of the poet. A letter of May 15, 1871, lays it out. Poets of antiquity are not what we assume; they lack the disjunctive realization of the modern poet, for whom "*I* is someone else (*Je* est une autre)." The daunting task is to make oneself into a seer (*voyant*), and "the soul must be made monstrous: in the fashion of the comprachicos, if you will! Imagine a man implanting and cultivating warts on his face." The comprachicos were thought to kidnap and mutilate children to exhibit them as monsters, so Rimbaud's poet is a comprachico who exhibits the freak of himself. He saw it as a Promethean vocation: "The poet is truly the thief of fire." To this end, "the poet would define the amount of the unknown awakening in his time in the universal soul." The unknown, manifested in individual souls, would come under scrutiny by Freud, who called it the unconscious.

Rimbaud's discovery has borne consequences for many subsequent poets. He seems to have come upon the outlook of existentialism nearly a century before Jean-Paul Sartre launched it as an operative philosophy for the Cold War. Sartre's famous formula, existence precedes essence, is the natural philosophy for those not born into station, yet psychologically disposed to realize themselves in their actions. It was just the ticket for a generation that survived the Second World War, or so it seemed. But it was really a diagnostic reckoning with what had been common enough among modernists of the early twentieth century, grappling with an earlier calamity.

For Eliot's generation, the situation was described by E. M. Forster in 1920. "Our 'own' times," the novelist observed, "are anything but ours; it is as though a dead object, huge and incomprehensible, had fallen across the page, which no historical arts can arrange, and which bewilders us as much by its shapelessness as by its size." Eliot's friend and ally Wyndham Lewis took stock of the situation when he was in combat in the First World War. "I was present—I dimly recognized—at the passage of an entire people out of one system into another." German artist Franz Marc wrote, shortly before hostilities broke out: "The world is giving birth to a new time; there is only one question: has the time now come to separate ourselves from the old world? Are we ready for the *vita nuova*? This is the terrifying question of our age."

The years of the Great War were like a slow earthquake, grinding the previous system into rubble. Lewis's autobiography, *Blasting and Bombardiering*, is "about the war, with a bit of pre-war and post-war sticking to it, fore and aft." Or, as he elaborates, "This book is Art—War—Art, in three panels." From his perspective, "prewar" does not refer to a period of happy ignorance. The *blasting* of his title was personal, for Lewis was one of those artists exasperated with civilization even before 1914, for whom art was "waged" like war. "You will be astonished to find how like art is to war," Lewis confides; "I mean 'modernist' art."

Lewis was a truculent personality, like his friend Ezra Pound. Eliot was the opposite. When he turned to Rimbaud and the French Symbolists as poetic compass, he was not repudiating English poetry, but simply recognizing it offered no way forward. Eliot was an unwitting revolutionary. *The Waste Land* was incendiary, to be sure, but it was not meant to be. It was simply all that Eliot could muster at the time—and the time was ripe. The same poem, published in 1910, would have passed without notice because it would scarcely have qualified as a poem at all.

In 1922, the same year *The Waste Land* was published, Walter Lippmann's influential book *Public Opinion* also appeared. The late war was decisive for him in revealing how, at its outset in 1914, everyone was "still adjusted to an environment that no longer existed." He proposed that even in unexceptional everyday circumstances we create a pseudoenvironment, consisting of our own assumptions, expectations, and fabrications. This was the basis of personal opinions, which when shared swell into public opinion. We cannot individually process everything going on in the world around us, but nonetheless "we have to describe and judge more people, more actions, more things than we can ever count, or vividly imagine. We have to summarize and generalize. We have to pick-out samples, and treat them as typical."

The idiom that Eliot had forged in poems written before the war took on a different relevance after 1919, as if they were Lippmann's typical samples. The fleeting moods Eliot evoked in poems like "Preludes" and "Rhapsody on a Windy Night" could now be integrated in a more encompassing form—not by narrative or expository means, but as building blocks of what Lippmann identified as "opinion." In 1910, Eliot had found an idiom that worked for him, borrowing some of the insouciance of French Symbolism to liven up the drab scenarios he sketched. His favorite among the French, Jules Laforgue, cheekily wrote of the cosmic themes so pervasive in nineteenth-century poetry: "Infinity, show us your papers!" That sort of touch enabled Eliot to ruminate, in the person of

Prufrock: "I have seen the eternal Footman hold my coat, and snicker, / And in short, I was afraid."

For the most part, Eliot's early poems are descriptive, synthesizing disparate cities—Cambridge, Massachusetts, Paris, Munich, London—into the generic one that makes an appearance as Unreal City in *The Waste Land*, consisting of a "thousand sordid images." The setting can be nocturnal:

> Every street lamp that I pass
> Beats like a fatalistic drum,
> And through the spaces of the dark
> Midnight shakes the memory
> As a madman shakes a dead geranium.

—or it may be dawn, when

> The morning comes to consciousness
> Of faint stale smells of beer
> From the sawdust-trampled street
> With all its muddy feet that press
> To early coffee-stands.

Rare is the interceding sentiment, the observational nudge—so rare that when it occurs, it seems a final judgment:

> I am moved by fancies that are curled
> Around these images, and cling:
> the notion of some infinitely gentle
> Infinitely suffering thing.

Such first-person statement is rare in Eliot's early poems, unless ventured by a mask like Prufrock. They are dispassionate observations, registrations of scenic particulars closer to the descriptive realism of the novel.

So what animates such poems? What is it that comes across despite the air of neutrality and restraint? This may be best answered with a surprising but relevant comparison. Charlie Chaplin's film sets resemble the milieu of Eliot's early poems. Chaplin animated them with his acrobatic physical comedy, while Eliot's scenes are mostly devoid of human presence except by inference. But the inferences convey the familiar aura of low-level doom. They don't aspire to the grimness of a predecessor like "City of Dreadful Night," by James Thomson (1874), but Eliot sustains an air of menace.

The Waste Land compounds the menace even as it steers clear of anything menacing. The poem drifts through a series of locations—the Alps, a garden, the visiting chamber of a fortune-teller, London streets, a deluxe interior, a pub, the Thames embankment, a cheap apartment, a bone-dry netherworld, and the recurring Unreal City—but instead of being backdrops to stirring scenes of human action and emotion, they enlist the reader's suppositions and expectations.

As the movies developed (around the time Eliot began writing poetry), filmmakers used locations to establish atmospheric potential. A rainy street, like a windswept mesa, instantly summons narrative possibilities. Commercially driven film, however, rarely lingered in these settings, anxious as it was to hustle people into the frame. Eliot is resolutely cinematic in setting scenes, but then pans away, as it were, before the bustle makes itself known. This is not to say his scenes are vacant. Rather, they are meticulously prepared slices of cinematic mise-en-scène, into which readers project what a movie would otherwise provide. *The Waste Land* was like a Rorschach test, capable of harboring whatever was projected onto it. As the abundance of reviews greeting its publication attest, it accommodated a considerable variety of projections.

Such diversity is intrinsic to collage. *The Waste Land* abounds in snippets and glimpses. This was evident in the working title of the poem, "He Do the Police in Different Voices." It's from Charles Dickens's novel *Our Mutual Friend*, in which a widow says of her adopted son, "You mightn't think it, but Sloppy is a beautiful reader of a newspaper. He do the Police in different voices." Eliot's draft was heavily edited and rearranged by Pound, who specialized in donning the voices of historical figures. An early title was *Personae*, which he reprised for *Personae: The Collected Shorter Poems* in 1926. His most successful venture was *Cathay* (1915), in which he intuitively found his way into the heart of ancient Chinese lyrics.

Pound's personae ranged from the Roman poet Sextus Propertius to medieval troubadours. Even his most autobiographical poem has a fictive persona, Hugh Selwyn Mauberley. Eliot started out with Prufrock and went on to Sweeney, Gerontion, and the slipstream of voices in *The Waste Land*. These could be called speaking roles, as both poets repeatedly donned verbal masks. The mask was a prerogative of many other modern poets, of course, but *The Waste Land* was a decisive intervention, because it revealed that readers would likewise need to adapt to mercurial identities and shifting perspectives. They would have to become different readers to read *The Waste Land*. Being conversant with poets popular at the time, like John Masefield or Carl Sandburg, was no help.

The new outlook demanded of the reader is suggested by a brief prose poem by an Eliot contemporary, French poet Pierre Reverdy:

Without a Mask

The non-speaking roles in this play or drama are among the
    audience—there are no wings. The makeup is in your eyes and
    your expression. What a role!

The Waste Land's first readers found themselves in such a role. But only the most astute among them realized it was the form of the poem that imposed the role, not the subject matter. Readers in 1922, regardless of their estimation of the poem's worth, thought it reflected "the immense panorama of futility and anarchy which is contemporary history"—a phrase Eliot used, writing about James Joyce's *Ulysses*. Subsequent generations have had occasion to find the same panorama unfolding in their own time. In any case, there was no particular urgency after the war to have news of the calamity issued in a poem. *Ulysses*, for that matter, was set in Dublin on a summer day in 1904. A year after his poem was published, Eliot sized up the issue of contemporaneity: "The present consists of a great deal of the past and a little of the future; it contains a majority of people who are echoing the past, and a very small number of writers who will represent this time fifty years hence, but who are, at the moment, rather a part of the future." Eliot surely sensed himself one of the latter.

What made *The Waste Land* matter is what it enabled readers to do. It activated them, vaulting them beyond armchair consumers into coconspirators, as it were. "The makeup is in your eyes and your expression," it seemed to suggest. They were emboldened by Eliot's poem to embark on their own unorthodox literary ventures. It emancipated certain women in particular from the steady beat of traditional versification established by untold generations of men. *The Waste Land*, for them, was not intimidating; it was liberating.

*

In his amusing novel *The Anthologist*, Nicholson Baker remarks on the role poetry has often played in general publications like the *Nation* and the *New Yorker*:

if you hunt around for a while in some of those periodicals you'll find
that most of the poetry in them is just there as a decoration. It's a form of
ornament, like a printer's dingbat. A little acorn with a curlicue. Or the

scrollwork on a beaux-arts capital. It's just a way of creating a different look on the page, and creating the sense on the part of the reader that he's holding something that is a real Kellogg's variety pack.

The practice continues apace, although the very thought of *The Waste Land* defies such use, not only because of its length. Eliot's poem invested poetry with a different potential, life beyond the dingbat. What his poem did is best approached by way of Richard Wagner.

Wagner recognized that melody in opera was concentrated in arias, leaving vast expanses of musical composition of no interest to the audience, who seized on these extended passages between arias as opportunities to socialize. Incensed, Wagner determined to write music that would compel attention all the way through. No filler. This was what came to be known as endless melody. One of the practical incentives that Wagner provided to all the arts was his conviction that endless melody was natural speech, not cultural artifice. The aria was a socially imposed limitation on the free speech of music.

Wagner wrote not only the music for his operas but the librettos as well. As both composer and poet, he imagined the two arts working together to achieve the full measure of what that adjective *endless* suggests. Pragmatically, it meant extending a melodic continuum across the entire composition. Formal repetitions would be eliminated (refrains, repeated couplets, the periodic phrase), but it wouldn't be a free fall. This was ensured by Wagner's use of leitmotifs, miniature melodic cues that he lavishly applied in his Ring cycle. Often heard recessed in the orchestral mix, leitmotifs are sonic reminders of particular people, events, and themes—diminutive cue cards, as it were, reminding the audience of the bigger picture.

Wagner drew inspiration from Beethoven, who he thought had consecrated the orchestra as a kind of Greek chorus, possessing a "faculty of speech" (*Sprachvermögen*). The orchestra "speaks" without saying anything in particular. Its speech is the stuff not of meaning but of meaningfulness. Wagner also sees the orchestra as bearing the potential to rediscover or reanimate primal speech. Endless melody, says Wagner, is the natural expression of endless yearning (*unendlichen Sehnens*). It is the musical speech of speechlessness.

For Wagner, the poet contributes to the speechless by refraining from speaking or writing: it is "that which he does not say in order to let what is inexpressible speak to us for itself."

It is the musician who brings the great Unsaid to sounding life, and the unmistakable form of his resounding silence is *endless melody*. [In

Wahrheit ist die Große des Dichters am meisten danach zu ermessen, was er verschweigt, um uns das Unaussprechliche selbst schweigend uns sagen zu lassen; der Musiker ist es nun, der dieses Verschwiegene zum hellen Ertönen bringt, und die untrügliche Form seines laut erklingenden Schweigens ist die *unendliche Melodie*.]

Eliot is unlikely to have read much in Wagner's voluminous writings, but he, like many of his generation, sat through multiple performances of the operas. He experienced endless melody. And he intuitively grasped Wagner's directive that the poet keep clear of the domain of the speechless. He well knew the arduous yearning of nineteenth-century English poets to transcend speech in and by means of poetry. In one of them, Swinburne, Eliot thought "the meaning is merely the hallucination of meaning." Such was the plight of an urge to express the inexpressible. In a 1924 novel by Maurice Baring, a character attending a Wagner opera "felt he was witnessing a poem of Swinburne's in action."

But there would still need to be continuity in a poem, some rhythm that would span the discrete units. Eliot appreciated the way Joyce deployed leitmotifs throughout *Ulysses*. He also recognized a narrative solution Joyce had derived from one of the French Wagnerians, Édouard Dujardin, editor of *La Revue Wagnérienne*. Dujardin had pioneered interior monologue as a technical resource in his novel *Les lauriers sont coupés* (1887). In Joyce's hands, this meant that a continuous fabrication of words filled page upon page, while not being strictly attributable to a speaker. It's hard to find a passage in *Ulysses* one could identify as coming from a narrator. It is, to use a term of musical theorist Lawrence Kramer, a kind of "omnianonymous" expressivity.

If a whole city could speak all at once, it would be omnianonymous—or so we learn by reading Joyce, and even more distinctly by reading *The Waste Land*. The poem took on a life of its own, and it continues to emit what its first readers recognized as an uncanny music. For many, it was like hearing their own minds refracted in strange new patterns of sound and image. The overfamiliarity of Eliot's poem may make it harder now to access that first response, but my aim is to make the poem strange again, to reclaim its drama as a high-wire act, not a tourist destination. Selfies abound in the presence of the *Mona Lisa*, but what do you do with a poem? "The makeup is in your eyes and your expression. What a role!"

Part One

CHAPTER ONE

Wagnerism

While he was a student at Harvard, T. S. Eliot took in a few operas, including several by Richard Wagner. It was the thing to do, at least for a conscientiously cultured intellectual. He was aware of the emotional paroxysms associated with Wagner's works but found himself less susceptible to such extremes. One of the operas was *Tristan and Isolde*, with "love torturing itself / To emotion for all there is in it," he wrote in a poem that envisioned "the last / Limits of self-expression." The poem ends with a wizened appraisal of his own lukewarm response to such limits.

> Life departs with a feeble smile
> Into the indifferent.
> These emotional experiences
> Do not hold good at all,
> And I feel like the ghost of youth
> At the undertakers' ball.

But Wagner persisted like a nagging scratch at the door, making his way into *The Waste Land* with four italicized lines in German from *Tristan*:

> *Frisch weht der Wind*
> *Der Heimat zu*
> *Mein Irisch Kind,*
> *Wo weilest du?*

Many readers in 1922 would have recognized the source, which prolonged the timeworn "love-death" aria to unprecedented lengths. Eight lines further on, another quote from *Tristan* appears: "*Oed und leer das Meer*"—the dying Tristan's rueful vision of an empty and desolate sea as he hopes for the ship to arrive with his beloved Isolde.

Eliot was not done with Wagner. Twice in part 3 of *The Waste Land*, "The Fire Sermon," he quotes the lilting croon of the Rhine Maidens from the *Ring of the Nibelungen* cycle:

Weialala leia
Wallala leialala

There are many quotations in Eliot's poem, but these four passages set
a Wagnerian tone, borrowing moods from a legacy channeled for Eliot
through Symbolism, particularly in the poetry of Charles Baudelaire and
Jules Laforgue. He made this link explicit in 1926. "It would be difficult to
say what there is in common between Wagner and Laforgue," he admitted.
But as with Wagner, "in Laforgue there is continuous war between the feelings implied by his ideas, and the ideas implied by his feelings." Reprising
his lectures in America a few years later, Eliot added that Laforgue was
"surprisingly modern," in that "his critical intelligence was incapable of
drugging itself with emotion as Wagner seems to have done."

One might suppose that Eliot was fussing with inherited baggage from
the nineteenth century. But it's more accurate to say that he was tying up
loose ends. In 1927 he astonished family and friends by declaring his conversion to the Anglican Church. Wagner, and to a lesser extent Laforgue,
represented a modern tendency with which *The Waste Land* had struggled
in its use of the Grail legend and its hodgepodge of cultural guideposts.

It's easier to get a handle on what Eliot was leaving behind by way
of W. B. Yeats, the Irish poet misapprehended by Eliot in his youth as
merely "a minor survivor of the '90s." Yeats traced his own outlook back
to William Blake.

> In his time educated people believed that they amused themselves with
> books of imagination, but that they "made their souls" by listening to
> sermons and by doing or by not doing certain things. . . . In our time we
> are agreed that we "make our souls" out of some one of the great poets of
> ancient times, or out of Shelley or Wordsworth, or Goethe, or Balzac, or
> Flaubert, or Count Tolstoy . . . or out of Mr. Whistler's pictures, while
> we amuse ourselves, or, at best, make a poorer sort of soul, by listening
> to sermons or by doing or by not doing certain things.

Thanks to this vision of soul making as a prerogative of creative spirits, Yeats
forecast a convulsive shiver in the artistic body politic at the dawn of the
new century. "I believe that the arts lie dreaming of things to come," he wrote.
"The arts by brooding upon their own intensity have become religious, and
are seeking"—he surmised—"to create a sacred book."

The devotional outlook Yeats cites is sometimes thought of as a religion
of art, but that's misleading. Religion is a social institution, and what Yeats

has his eye on is an individual prerogative, a disposition, a reverence for the kinds of experiences that art and music and poetry can provide. The sacred books for this outlook were not scriptures. If they announced anything resembling commandments, it was in the idiom of interpersonal disclosure, like the last line of Rainer Maria Rilke's 1908 poem "Archaic Torso of Apollo": "Du mußt dein Leben ändern"—you must change your life. The dawn of the new century kindled this expectancy. Change was everywhere, and technological advances were spurs to individual self-reckoning. The great provocation to such reckoning had swept over the world during the decades leading up to the turn of the century. It was known as Wagnerism.

"Just look at these young men—stiff, pale, breathless! They are Wagnerians: they don't know a thing about music—and nevertheless, Wagner lords it over them. Wagner's art pressurizes like a hundred atmospheres: just bend down, you can do no other." This was Friedrich Nietzsche's characterization of the throng of devotees at the Bayreuth Festival, which he attended at its inaugural season in 1876. He acknowledged he'd been one of them, conceding of his subsequent aversion, "I only attack things I fundamentally know—that I have myself experienced, that I have to a certain extent myself *been*."

Bayreuth was the triumph of Wagnerism, the first and most consequential of that retinue of *isms* peaking in the heyday of modernism in the early twentieth century. Wagnerism was hatched from a name, Richard Wagner (1813–1883), composer of *The Flying Dutchman*, *Tannhäuser*, *Lohengrin*, the Ring cycle (*Rheingold*, *The Valkyries*, *Siegfried*, *Twilight of the Gods*), *Tristan and Isolde*, and *Parsifal*, among others. Eleven Wagner operas have long been permanent fixtures on the international stage, but during much of the composer's lifetime they were commonly experienced in concert extracts, piano transcriptions, and other print resources. Wagner's ascendancy to an *ism* unto himself is a testament to a tendency recognized by his contemporaries, like Thomas Carlyle in *Heroes, Hero-Worship, and the Heroic in History* (1841), and in *Representative Men* (1850) by Carlyle's American friend Ralph Waldo Emerson.

In his day, Wagner was commonly classed with Napoleon and Christ as a world-transforming personality—the "messiah of a new age," a writer proclaimed him in 1888. Wagner's eminence signals the elevation of music as the art to which every other art aspired, in Walter Pater's famous remark. Legendary virtuosi like Paganini and Liszt were megastars of the midcentury; and while Liszt was a notable composer as well, Wagner took the upper hand because his compositions were accompanied by influential theories belabored in his writings.

FIG. 1.1. Richard Wagner.

Wagner's musical inducements to reverie were spurred on by a steady crescendo of intoxicating slogans. These slogans—"leitmotiv," "endless melody," "music of the future," "total artwork"—like so many keys to unlock the mysteries of inwardness, accompanied and encouraged an aura of religious devotion, just as the music itself was a portent of some journey to the center of the heart's earth (from Venusberg, that inner sanctum of sex in Wagner's early opera *Tannhäuser* in 1845, to the Grail sanctuary in his last, *Parsifal*, in 1882). In the twilight milieu of Art Nouveau and Jugendstil, Wagnerism was the quintessential *ism*, gradually morphing into Symbolism. Dance pioneer Isadora Duncan spoke for many when she said that "the work of Wagner flows through every drop of blood in every artist of the world, and his mighty rhythm has become part of every heart-beat of each one of us."

FIG. 1.2. Cartoon of Richard Wagner conducting (1876).

Wagnerism was a formidable device, at once telescopic and microscopic, while acquiring the aspect of a distorting lens along the way. Adherents aligned themselves with a world-historical phenomenon that was not necessarily contingent on Wagner, while its opponents worried that the egotistic grandiosity of the man had besotted the world with pipe dreams. "Other men are lenses through which we read our own minds," Emerson wrote, and to no one does this seem more applicable than the man who, inflated to Wagnerism, was at once a lighthouse beacon for the artistic aspirations of the age and a mirror reflecting the longings of those who aspired to launch themselves into the infinite.

Wagnerism tended to be whatever its partisans fancied, encompassing decadence, socialism, vegetarianism, erotic indulgence, mystical transcendence. Wagner himself was inconsistent: as James Huneker said, the

maestro "was not always a Wagnerian." Wagnerism encompassed Christians and pagans, monarchists and anarchists, nationalists and cosmopoli-
tans. Among such diverse constituencies, the only common denominator
was devotion to a cause. "Wagner seems to have attracted people who
thrived on controversy. Perhaps it would not be overstating the case to
say that the typical Wagnerian was someone with a fight to pick," and
Wagnerism nourished a combative mentality even among neurasthenics.
Irish novelist George Moore reflects a common experience: "Wagner's
operas are now my great delight and relaxation. I daresay I do not understand but what does that matter?" Incomprehension was initiation. Little
wonder, then, that some resisted Wagner categorically: "Be assured that
I have far too much self-respect to honor this music with my attention,"
a Frenchman boasted in 1884. "I have never heard a note by Wagner,
and that is proof enough that I know he has no talent." Both cases reveal
a compulsive naïveté.

There were two camps: "The Wagnerite must learn theories and culti-
vate habits," whereas "the Tristanite only has to be overwhelmed" (meaning those bewitched by *Tristan and Isolde*)—a telling distinction between
scholastic dedication and mindless enthusiasm that defined Wagnerism for
decades. The composer Saint-Saëns, more scrupulous in musical matters,
and an advocate of Wagner when French hostility was at its peak, made
the pertinent observation: "For the Wagnerian, music did not exist before
Wagner, or rather it was still in embryo—Wagner raised it to the level of
Art." Tchaikovsky likewise had an illuminating encounter with a fellow
Russian "who assured me that he acknowledges Wagner alone in the field of
music." Pressed about comparison cases, this unabashed Wagnerite admits
he "had no idea about music but had the good fortune to be personally
acquainted with the Master and had been invited to his receptions. He was
very flattered by this and felt it his duty to deny everything which Wagner
himself did not recognize."

The Bayreuth Festival Theatre opened in 1876, its sole purpose being
the production of Wagner's operas, his "deeds of music made visible."
Bayreuth was a modest community in Bavaria, due north of Munich and
east of Frankfurt am Main. Alex Ross observes that "the site had to exist
outside of extant cultural networks; it had to be a blank slate"—blank
in order to absorb the outsized expectations and hopes visitors brought
with them. "No matter where one goes," complained Karl Marx (who had
other fish to fry), "one is plagued with the question 'What do you think of
Richard Wagner?'"

As soon as Bayreuth opened, it was the hottest ticket around, the world's top cultural tourist destination. But not just any tourists. "One could not walk three steps without giving elbow-room to some celebrity," carped one visitor in the inaugural season. Celebrities, high society, and royalty notwithstanding, the scene was rife with souvenirs like the "Nibelungen" cap, the "Siegfried" hat, and even a "Wagner cravat." Wagner's profile adorned cigar boxes, beer mugs, pipe bowls, and sundry gewgaws. Souvenirs aplenty, but where could one eat? "Cutlets, baked potatoes, omelettes," Tchaikovsky reported, "are discussed much more eagerly than Wagner's music." "The town is packed, like a World's Fair," Nietzsche heard from a friend, "with emperors, other bigwigs and a whole assortment of riffraff," including "Jewish infiltrators, who can be seen crawling around in swarms." Bayreuth forced Nietzsche to realize that Wagner's seemingly incidental anti-Semitism harbored darker prospects. The seeds were planted, and in time Adolf Hitler would organize his activities around the Bayreuth season, welcomed by the composer's even more virulently anti-Semitic heirs.

England's *Daily Telegraph* observed that a "faith in the 'Art Work of the Future' goes in company with spectacles, long hair, and funny head-gear." "The coiffures and dress of the future?" wondered another reporter, noting the preponderance of "long hair, disheveled beards, and exotic dress" at Wagner concerts. Even decades later, Virginia Woolf noticed those in "the cheap seats on a Wagner night; there is something primitive in the look of them, as though they did their best to live in forests." A character in George Moore's novel *Evelyn Innes* is drawn to Bayreuth "in spite of an unconquerable aversion to long hair and dirty hands." Moore, a dedicatee of the Festspielhaus, could go into a swoon of reminiscence later in life, personal hygiene notwithstanding: "The word Bayreuth comes upon me now like the scent of lavender from an old chest."

While his other operas continued to be performed elsewhere, *Parsifal* was restricted to Bayreuth (it was not until the copyright expired that major European cities saw their first productions in 1914 in tandem with the Great War, including London, Paris, Vienna, Berlin, Brussels, St. Petersburg, Prague, Budapest, Rome, and Barcelona). To have seen it was a badge of honor for the faithful. *Parsifal* precipitated a devotional cult after its premiere in 1882, conscripting a new cadre among Christians, as well as giving a franchise name to the nascent medievalism of the fin de siècle.

August Strindberg described the post-*Parsifal* mood of Paris in 1897: "Young men dressed themselves in monk's cowls, cut their hair in a tonsure and dreamed of the monastic life; they wrote legends and performed miracle-plays; they painted madonnas and sculpted figures of Christ, gaining inspiration from the mysteries of the magician who has bewitched them with Tristan, Parsifal and the Grail." This was the calamity Claude Debussy lamented "in which the French genius has lost its way among the sham Wotans in Hessian boots and the Tristans in velvet jackets."

James Huneker, although a dedicated Wagnerian, thought *Parsifal* was feeble bombast. His diagnosis of its appeal, however, is telling: "Parsifal will long remain a rare and stimulating spectacle to those for whom religious feeling must be dramatized to be endurable." Despite the observation by one attendee, that its audiences were "in an unnatural state of wild hysteria," penitential boosterism ensued. American Wagnerian Oliver Huckel solemnly declared it "one of the few great dramas of modern times,—a drama which unfolds striking and impressive spiritual teachings." As promotional jargon would have it, a masterwork for seekers of all ages.

In Oscar Wilde's novel, Dorian Gray listens "in rapt pleasure to *Tannhäuser*" and beholds in it "a presentation of the tragedy of his own soul." These souls exposing themselves to Wagner's operas as if they were spiritual tanning salons could be admired for their devotion, or draw puzzlement for the obvious sublimation involved. Arthur Symons recognized that while *Parsifal* exuded a devotional aura, "it is the music of a religion which had never before found expression." Wagner's unique accomplishment, Symons found, was "to render mysticism through the senses."

In fact, Wagner's music had a reputation for being deliciously transgressive, at ease in a world of necrophiles, love slaves, femmes fatales. "The music creeps and catches, and with cruel claws and amorous tongue it feeds upon my flesh." Wagner was "a master of thrilling tones, a magician who everywhere finds willing thrall," wrote Huneker. "And the music—how it searches the nerves." Nervous excitement, nervous disorder: these were the symptoms of a malady that needed only the sanction of a proper name. "At no time before or since has one figure so dominated the debate on pathological music," writes James Kennaway about Wagner.

In 1891, Dutch psychiatrist Jacob van Deventer regarded it as a "symptom of the times" that "a large number of the mentally ill are passionate lovers of Wagnerian music." American psychologist Aldred Warthin reported that test subjects in a state of quasi-hypnosis had been brought to orgasm on hearing Wagner's music. Women were often thought to be dangerously susceptible to Wagner's orgasmically endless melody, but perceptions of sexual deviance also thrived on the Wagner spectrum, as in *Richard Wagner und die Homosexualität* by Hanns Fuchs (Wagner and homosexuality, 1902). In his 1907 book *The Intersexes*, Xavier Mayne included a questionnaire as a courtesy for the reader to detect latent homosexual traits. "Are you particularly fond of Wagner?" Such a leading question suggests a threshold beyond which the maestro was no longer a vague cultivator of inwardness but a prognostic tool for the New Psychology.

One needn't be pathologically invested, however, to be tremendously moved by the experience of *Tristan and Isolde* or the Ring cycle. "On every side one heard the stifled sobs of women, and one saw men wipe away their tears." In 1900 the Art Nouveau journal *Die Jugend* published Pauline Eigner's sketch of a performance of *Tristan and Isolde*, depicting numerous figures overcome by music "so internal, so organic, so visceral, that [it seems] like the reprise not so much of a musical motif as of an attack of neuralgia" (as Proust put it). Jean Cocteau likewise attributed this music heard through hands gripping the head to an attack of nerves, induced by the "hypnotism of Bayreuth." For these astronauts of inwardness, *Tristan and Isolde* was a one-way ticket to the beyond.

*

On February 14, 1883, a former professor of philology at the University of Basel mails his publisher a manuscript, suggesting it is nothing short of a fifth gospel. Since resigning from his academic post in 1879 because of ill health, he's been leading a peripatetic life. Most recently, while living in Rapallo, Italy, he produced the manuscript during the month of January. It bears the auspicious title *Also sprach Zarathustra*. Its author, Friedrich Nietzsche, despite envisioning epic heights of human self-overcoming in this book, knows himself to be "human, all too human"—the title of his earlier book published in 1878. He had sent that book to Wagner, with whom he had a long and devoted friendship. A few months earlier, Wagner had sent him the score of *Parsifal*, presenting it as a clerical gift. Nietzsche, son of a Lutheran pastor and exponent of the "Anti-Christ," deplored the maestro's newfound Christian piety, while Wagner balked at *Human, All Too Human* with its startling dedication to the French rationalist Voltaire. On his way to the post office to send the manuscript of *Zarathustra* to his publisher, Nietzsche chanced on a headline reporting Wagner's death in Venice.

Nietzsche first met the composer in 1868. During a visit to Leipzig, Wagner heard of a young local known for playing piano renditions of scenes from his latest opera, *Die Meistersinger von Nuremberg*. Had it not been for family expectations, Nietzsche would have preferred a life in music over the schoolroom. His pianistic improvisations impressed everyone who heard

FIG. 1.3. Friedrich Nietzsche.

them. A composer found "Nietzsche's touch was of great intensity, without being hard, his playing eloquent, polyphonic, with most manifold gradations, so that here the horn, flutes, or violins, there trumpets could be heard clearly out of its orchestral sound." A friend revealed that when playing passages from Wagner's operas, "he always did from memory and very masterfully." Wagner warmly encouraged the awestruck young man to look him up in the future.

Six months later, at the astonishingly young age of twenty-four, Nietzsche was appointed to the chair of philology at the University of Basel, not far from Wagner's villa on Lake Lucerne. He became a welcome member of the household—"a pell-mell of Genius-work, children-confusion, people uproar, animal delight," in the words of Cosima, mother of two of the four Wagner children, though still married to Hans von Bülow, a devoted conductor of Wagner's music. Nietzsche was even given his own room in the house, visiting six times in the summer of 1869, with seventeen more visits over the next three years, becoming something of a son to Richard, confidant to Cosima, and roustabout companion to their children. They celebrated birthdays together, and Nietzsche was routinely expected during the Christmas holidays. "Certainly those were the best days of my life," he reflected.

"I was indescribably happy in those days, when I discovered Wagner!" Nietzsche recalled in 1882. "I had sought for so long a man who was superior to me and who actually looked beyond me." A father figure? Wagner was in fact the same age as Pastor Nietzsche, who had died when his son was only four. But there was much more to it on both sides. In the first flush of friendship, the young professor was unstinting in his pledges of devotion: "The best and loftiest moments of my life are associated with your name," he assures Wagner in a letter of May 1869, soon after the first visit. A year later, he greets the master on his birthday: "My thoughts always circle around you," he confided, "my mystagogue in the secret doctrines of art and life."

Nietzsche was also thrust into the role of family factotum, called upon to shop for household sundries, toys, candies, and more. He was even tasked with obtaining silk underwear for the maestro. Exchange of gifts was an important part of the relationship, as on the occasion of Cosima's birthday, which happened to fall on Christmas. In 1870 he gave her a manuscript, "The Birth of the Tragic Concept," published two years later as *The Birth of Tragedy*, with a dedication to Wagner. "On every page," Nietzsche confided, "you will find that I am only trying to thank you for everything you have given me." Wagner was exultant: "This is the book I have been longing for." Certainly there was vanity involved in Wagner's response, but there was more than that. Responding to an earlier draft of the book, Cosima noted in her diary that "in it one sees a gifted man imbued with R.'s ideas in his own way." The full title was *The Birth of Tragedy out of the Spirit of Music*. Why music? Nietzsche quotes a passage from the philosopher Schopenhauer that runs to nearly two pages, the gist being that music differs from the other arts in that it does not copy phenomena but is, instead, a direct manifestation of the will.

When they first met, Wagner and Nietzsche bonded over Schopenhauer, whose *The World as Will and Representation* was the guiding light. Wagner himself was not only a composer, but author of numerous books and pamphlets, including *The Music of the Future*. What Richard and Cosima found in Nietzsche was a standard-bearer for the maestro's music *and* his ideas. Everything in *The Birth of Tragedy* seemed, to them, gratifying confirmation of this hope as they read it "with solemn feelings and with ever-increasing pleasure." Wagner hurried off a note: "Dear friend," he wrote, "never have I read anything more beautiful than your book! How splendid it all is! I am writing to you quickly now because reading it has left me so inordinately excited that I must first await the return of reason before reading it *properly*"—pointedly adding, "I told Cosima that you are second only to her." Six months later he reaffirmed his high regard: "Strictly speaking, you are the only real gain that life has brought me, and second only to my wife in that respect." *The Birth of Tragedy* was welcomed as the ultimate pledge of friendship and devotion, particularly in its affirmation of Wagner's lifelong vision of the regenerative potential of art.

The halcyon days ended in 1872 when the family moved to Bayreuth, the Bavarian town chosen as the site of Wagner's Festspielhaus or festival theater. Nietzsche's health was on the decline—he would be relieved of

teaching duties in 1876—and travel was a burden, as it took a full day to
get to Bayreuth from Basel. The fund-raising and festival preparations took
up most of Richard and Cosima's time. Wagner hoped Nietzsche would
edit a newsletter for the cause, which he resisted, although he was ardent
enough in pledging support that Wagner had to persuade him not to resign
his university post. Yet Nietzsche had a growing awareness that the maestro's solicitous benevolence harbored something else, though he was not
privy to such private disclosures as Richard's comment to Cosima regarding
a similar acolyte: "He is one of those I formed in my own image so that I
could get something out of him"; almost contemptuously he added, "As a
person he has no value for me."

Things took a turn, finally, when the festival opened in 1876 with the premiere of *The Ring of the Nibelungen*, its four operas unfolding over five days.
Despite his close bond with Wagner, on this occasion Nietzsche was edged
out by kings and dukes and princes all vying for the composer's attention.
In a single day, five hundred calling cards were left at the house. Bayreuth,
Nietzsche ruefully observed, had become a tourist destination for "the entire
loafing riffraff of Europe." It was a scene he wanted no part of.

Nonetheless, Nietzsche dutifully complied with the composer's expectations, publishing a celebratory pamphlet to coincide with the festival. The
Wagners were gratified by *Richard Wagner in Bayreuth* but had no time to
give it the attention they'd lavished on *The Birth of Tragedy*. Otherwise,
they might have noticed certain backhanded compliments, certain impertinent observations. "Wagner as a *writer* is like a brave man whose right
hand has been cut off and who fights on with his left," wrote Nietzsche in
a startling image; "he always suffers when he writes, because a temporarily
ineluctable necessity has robbed him of the ability to communicate in the
way appropriate to him"—that is, in music. In fact, Wagner's prose has
been lamented ever since even by his most devoted readers. Nietzsche,
reappraising Wagner's famous phrase (the music of the future), found him
"not the prophet of a future, such as he would perhaps like to appear to us,
but the interpreter and transfigurer of the past"—as was the case with all
his operatic subjects.

Nietzsche envisioned Bayreuth providing a transformative spiritual occasion, predicting that "all those who attend the Bayreuth Festival will be
felt to be untimely men: their home is not in this age but elsewhere." He
also suggested that such untimely figures needed the direct ministration
of the composer: "He who gives must see to it that he finds recipients
adequate to the meaning of his gift." Clearly, the noble "riffraff" did not
qualify. Nietzsche's sister—notoriously unreliable about her brother, but

accurate on this account—observed that the "class of rich idlers had found a new pretext for idling."

The festival fell far short of Wagner's lofty aspirations. After all, he'd dreamed of a great democratic replenishment, a kind of aesthetic curative for *das Volk*, "the people." With tickets for the Ring cycle costing the equivalent of three thousand dollars today, such folk were nowhere to be seen. A few months after the season had concluded, Cosima notes, "Frequent thoughts of giving up the festival entirely and disappearing." "Richard says that his main feeling during the performances was, 'Never again, never again!'"

Nietzsche and Wagner never shared their dismay. For his part, the philosopher bolted after the initial festivities, fleeing to a small forest village in the mountains. There, he purged himself of the Bayreuth scene by starting a project that eventually became *Human, All Too Human*, a "monument of rigorous self-discipline with which I put a sudden end to all my infections with 'higher swindle,' 'idealism,' 'beautiful things,' and other effeminacies." After this mountain interlude, he reluctantly returned to Bayreuth, "and had the inner composure to bear the nearly unbearable—keeping *quiet* in front of everyone!" His regret was registered in a pun: the German for "regret" is *Bereut*, acoustic cousin of Bayreuth. A French Wagnerite who sat with Nietzsche recalled, "When we left the performance together he uttered not one word of criticism; he showed much more the resigned sadness of someone who had lost something."

What did he regret? And what had he lost? He saw it differently: he had found something. A way out, something beyond serving a composer's dream. There was a new friend, philosopher Paul Rée. He was a Darwinian, a "positivist" in the argot of the day, scientifically disposed. A veritable contra-Wagner, in other words. The two men traveled to Sorrento on the Bay of Naples where they stayed for six months. Frequently overcome with migraines, vomiting, and failing eyesight, Nietzsche managed to continue working on the book he'd started when fleeing Bayreuth. Having been subjected to such unwelcome palliatives as leeches, hydrotherapy, and dubious miracle cures, Nietzsche's condition had deteriorated to the point that his doctor stipulated complete avoidance of reading and even writing for years to come.

In November the Wagners stayed in a nearby hotel for a few weeks, during which they had their final encounter with Nietzsche. They were displeased with Rée, "whose cold and precise character does not appeal to us; on closer inspection we come to the conclusion that he must be an Israelite," Cosima speculated. Wagner's anti-Semitism was even more acute. He found Nietzsche's friendship with such a person worrisome, distasteful, injudicious. Despite their reservations about the company Nietzsche kept, they continued to ask mutual friends about the state of his health.

It was a solicitous intervention by Wagner that led to the rupture. Nearly a year after their encounter in Sorrento, as Nietzsche confronted his dire diagnosis, he mailed the composer an article on his music written by his physician, Otto Eiser. Naturally, Wagner reached out in gratitude to the doctor, also expressing his concerns about Nietzsche's health. Wagner hoped the doctor would convey to his patient a particular concern, as he would be "more likely to listen to the friendly advice of a medical man than to the medical advice of a friend."

Wagner was concerned about the philosopher's tendency to form close alliances with male friends. He would not have known that Rée went so far as to refer to the Sorrento days as "the honeymoon of our friendship," and sent his book *The Origin of Moral Sensations* to Nietzsche with the inscription "to the father of this writing, from its grateful mother." Wagner resisted the assumption of homosexuality, however. In Nietzsche's case, he confided to Eiser, "I have long been reminded of identical or very similar experiences with young men of great intellectual ability. Seeing them laid low by similar symptoms, I discovered all too certainly that these were the effects of masturbation. Ever since I observed N closely, guided by such experiences, all his traits of temperament and characteristic habits have transformed my fear into a conviction."

Had Wagner's concern remained confidential, nothing would have come of the exchange. But Eiser let it slip. "When, in the privacy of my own house," he recounted, "and with the most benevolent of intentions, I told Nietzsche about my letter, he began to rant and rave. He was beside himself and I dare not repeat the words he uttered about Wagner." But word got out, and during the second Bayreuth Festival in 1878 the gossip was all about Nietzsche, said to be going blind owing to excessive masturbation; or, in the view of one biographer, suspected of homosexuality.

The indignity of it all finalized his break from Wagner. He did not disclose details, though he came close in a letter to Peter Gast, referring to the composer's "*belief* that my altered way of thinking was a consequence of unnatural excesses, with hints of pederasty." For the most part, he spoke darkly of betrayal. In 1883 he wrote a friend, "Wagner was by far the *fullest* human being I have known, and in *this* respect I have had to forgo a great deal for six years. But something like a deadly offense came between us; and something terrible could have happened if he had lived longer." Bayreuth too was tainted beyond repair. "I cannot go there unnoticed," he realized, "but that is ruinous for me after what has happened."

Since its publication in 1878, the Wagners were indignant about the "Réelism" to which Nietzsche had succumbed in *Human, All Too Human*. For Cosima, "in Nietzsche evil has triumphed"—worse, he "has joined the ranks of a well-armed enemy," meaning the Jews. Wagner refused to allow Nietzsche's name to be mentioned in his presence. Yet he continued to fixate on his old friend. Looking back at *The Birth of Tragedy*, he fulminated to a nephew, "It was my lead that he followed, so no one can judge better than I how deeply my ideas have penetrated the mind of this man." "*My* ideas," he emphasized. On other occasions he could be cruelly dismissive. "I find the whole man repulsive," he spat out, "a miserable dandy."

Nietzsche quickly detected a cold silence emanating from the recipients of *Human, All Too Human*. "It has been practically banned by Bayreuth," he noted; "what is more, the grand excommunication seems to have been pronounced against its author too. They are only trying to retain my *friends* while losing me—and so I get to hear various things that are happening and being planned behind my back. Wagner has failed to use a great opportunity for showing greatness of character." Clearly, Nietzsche is establishing ground rules here. He knows Wagner well enough to know he'll fail the test.

As his notebooks reveal, Nietzsche's doubts were emerging as early as 1874, when he was working on *Richard Wagner in Bayreuth*. He speculated that Wagner was primarily an actor, more a theatrical than a musical genius. "Absurd as it seems," Nietzsche wrote, "I often have had doubts about whether Wagner has musical talent." Wagner's grandiose sense of mission also aroused suspicion. "Wagner gets rid of all his weaknesses by imputing them to his age and his adversaries," Nietzsche noted. The maestro's "domineering character" revealed a fatal flaw: when failing to get his way, Wagner became "immoderate, eccentric, obstreperous." Nietzsche even wondered about the effect Wagner's music was unleashing in the world, enumerating its excesses in an astonishing retinue cascade of adjectives: it was "entirely unrestrained, breathless, impious, greedy, formless, unstable in its very foundations, almost desperate, nonnaive, thoroughly conscious, ignoble, violent, cowardly." None of this was revealed in the pamphlet for the Bayreuth opening, of course, but the notes of a budding disavowal were privately registered.

By the time he was completing *Human, All Too Human* in Sorrento in 1877–1878, Nietzsche clearly felt himself pulling away. His book, he declared, has "something of the almost cheerful and inquisitive coldness of the psychologist, who retrospectively confirms for himself a multitude of painful things that he has *beneath* him, *behind* him." This recognition from his notebook made its way into the second volume of the book, published in 1879 as *Assorted Opinions and Maxims*. "As soon as we climb higher than people who have up until now admired us, we appear to them to have sunken and fallen lower: for they had in any case believed that they stood up until now *with* us (if also owing to us) *upon the heights*." To whom could this refer if not the Wagners?

Nietzsche remained indebted to Wagner's music as a touchstone of the highest in art, and to the family circle in Lucerne as a lost emotional homeland. But the reckoning he had tentatively jotted down in notebooks in 1874 persisted, culminating in the screed published in 1888 as *The Case of Wagner*. It's not long, under forty pages, but its apparatus suggests that everything about Wagner invited second thoughts, and those thoughts invited second thoughts of their own. It has a foreword, a postscript, a second postscript, and an epilogue. So many feints of the rapier!

By this point, Nietzsche had perfected the signature style of his *gaya scienza*: tremendous power concentrated in aphoristic elegance, with wit and grace in abundance, all of it applied with the precision of a whiplash. "Wagner's stage needs only one thing—*Teutons!*" he observes of the composer's growing Germanophilia (the exclamation point is self-congratulatory). "When a musician can no longer count to three, he becomes 'dramatic,' he becomes 'Wagnerian.'" Wagner the actor now has "a talent for lying," and his productions thrive in the "*haut-relief* of a gesture, a scene that *bowls you over*." Wagner is nothing less than "the greatest mime, the most astonishing theater genius the Germans have ever had, our *stage-manager* par excellence," a point recalling Nietzsche's first evening with Wagner in 1869, when the maestro regaled the young man with imitations of all the singing parts in *Meistersinger*. Wagner was not only "this old magician" but a "clever rattlesnake" as well.

There are many such welts raised in *The Case of Wagner*, but the diagnostic core is self-reckoning: "I am the child of these times as much as Wagner, in other words a *décadent*." The proof: "I was one of the most corrupt Wagnerians." "The effect of Wagner is like continual alcohol abuse," he writes. "If you want to be released from unbearable pressure, you need hashish. Well then, I needed Wagner." Nietzsche had to become the homeopathist of himself, measuring out doses of the poison in order to neutralize it. For he understood Wagner as a disease. "*Wagner est une névrose*," he wrote in the language most associated with the *décadence* of the age. His "total transformation of art into theatricality is just as clearly an expression of physiological degenerescence (more accurately, a form of hysteria)." No flesh on these bones, he found, just nerves: "Wagner's art is sick. The problems that he puts on stage—nothing but hysterics' problems."

"Sickness itself can be a stimulant to life: except one has to be healthy enough for this stimulus!" That was the challenge, Nietzsche recognized. But "Oh, the rattlesnake-pleasure of the old master, accustomed to seeing the 'little children' come unto him!" he exclaims of the wily predator. He also strikes a barb at the old charge of masturbation, giving as much as (and more than) he got in 1878: Wagner "perhaps provides the grossest example of self-violation in the history of art"—ah, that *perhaps*, another perfect feint.

Self-overcoming was the watchword of Nietzsche's emancipation. It meant vanquishing the self that had been susceptible to Wagner. In *The Case of Wagner* the solution beggars credulity. Nietzsche claims to have liberated himself by becoming a fan of Bizet's opera *Carmen*, seeing it twenty times. That was a story he felt he had to tell in 1888, by which point he was the famous (and infamous) author of *The Genealogy of Morals*, *The Gay Science*, *Beyond Good and Evil*, and *Thus Spoke Zarathustra*. But what was at stake had been clarified five years earlier, shortly after Wagner's death, in a letter to his friend Peter Gast.

> I was *violently* ill for several days, and my landlord and his wife were most concerned. Now I am all right again, and even think that Wagner's death brought me the greatest relief I could have had. It was hard to be for six years the opponent of a man whom one has admired above all others, and I am not built coarsely enough for *that*. Eventually, it was the old Wagner against whom I had to defend myself; as for the real Wagner, I shall be in good measure his heir.

Nietzsche knew he'd never be able to disinvest himself. Wagner and Nietzsche were forever joined like Siamese twins, morphed into a Janus figure with faces gazing in opposite directions.

Nietzsche's friends and acquaintances knew it too, though they had different ways of understanding what had happened. One observed that "the emotivity in his temperament struck me as strange. Especially his monologues on Wagner, which began calmly with rationally founded judgments, but soon accelerated into an avalanche of words that stirred up psychic depths and ended in tears." Another observed that "the break with Wagner was a deathblow for Nietzsche, at any rate he was afterwards a completely changed man." Or, in the most pithy of all such observations: "He died of Wagner."

In the decade following the break, his peripatetic life as self-declared Wanderer resulted in the books that have made him even more influential than the composer. In his final year of sanity (his long years of suffering were the result of a terminal syphilitic infection) he produced a spate of books and was meticulous about the order in which they should appear. *The Case of Wagner*—subtitled *Letter from Turin of May 1888*—was first, issued in September. In December he was juggling *Nietzsche contra Wagner* (dated Christmas 1888 in the foreword), *Ecce Homo*, *Twilight of the Idols*, and *The Antichrist.*

Nietzsche contra Wagner consists of extracts from previous publications, often revised, with a few new observations ("Ever since Wagner came to Germany he stooped down to everything I despise," reads one, "even to anti-Semitism"). And while he repeats some of the old charges—Wagner was "the most fanatic mimomaniac that ever existed, *even as a musician*"— the final six pages of this twenty-page booklet make no reference to Wagner at all. But they bring to a point themes taken up earlier in *The Gay Science*. Nietzsche versus Wagner now came down to Yes against No. "Regarding artists of any kind, I now avail myself of this major distinction: has *hatred* against life or *superabundance* of life become creative here?" Sounding the diagnostic note again, "My objections to Wagner's music are physiological objections: why disguise them first with aesthetic formulas? Aesthetics is just applied physiology."

The pathos of Nietzsche's decline is ripe material for a Hollywood melodrama. Even as he was busy sending manuscripts to his publisher, he fired off a volley of holiday greetings to friends and family, in missives revealing the onset of looming insanity. Many were signed either "The Crucified" or "Dionysus." To Cosima he wrote four words: "Ariadne, I love you." The vision of some grandiose transfiguration seeped through: "I have begun to be quite unprecedentedly famous," he wrote. He broke with his sister, warning her she had no idea whom she was dealing with: "I hold, quite literally, the future of mankind in the palm of my hand." The last was to his old friend and Basel colleague, the great historian Jakob Burckhardt. "Dear Professor," he began, "Actually I would rather be a Basel professor than God, but I have not ventured to carry my private egoism so far as to omit creating the world on his account." This one, at least, was modestly signed "With fond love, Your Nietzsche."

Two days earlier, on January 3, 1889, while out for a walk near his pension in Turin, he chanced upon a horse being beaten and rushed to embrace the poor beast while sobbing convulsively. He was somehow guided back to his residence, where he spent several days terrifying his landlord's family with belligerent howls, bellowing, singing, and stomping. Not until five days later did his friend Franz Overbeck arrive, alarmed by the disclosure he received on the 7th: "I am just having all anti-Semites shot." Through delicate maneuvers, Nietzsche was coaxed away to a series of asylums, finally ending up near his mother in Jena, where the institution's file records his admission statement: "It was my wife Cosima Wagner who brought me here."

Eventually released into the care of his mother, the philosopher lived until 1900, raving and whimpering, still capable of playing the piano but incontinent and robbed of rational awareness. Ignominiously, his sister became his caretaker after the death of their mother. Nietzsche had denounced her as an ardent anti-Semite, but now she set about creating an archive to promote the bowdlerized vision she extracted from her brother's writings, even as the author was kept out of sight, famous in circulated images for the immense moustache that helped conceal the manic contortions of his face. The Nietzsche Archive, like Bayreuth, became a destination site for Nazi pilgrims in years to come.

*

Writing his sister in 1882, Nietzsche admitted, "My Wagner mania certainly cost me dear. Has not this nerve-shattering music ruined my health? And the disillusionment and leaving Wagner—was not that putting my very life in danger?" After Nietzsche distanced himself from his former idol, Wagner became his voodoo doll, his aesthetic pincushion. Fixated on Wagner to the end, like an obsessed pop fan, Nietzsche bore the scars of self-diagnosis. Suffering acute symptoms of his syphilitic infection, Nietzsche was uniquely suited to realize the full *power* of disease—disease *as* power, to which only his fabled "will to power" could hope to summon a countervailing strength.

Wagner plagiarized every desire on behalf of *sickness*, Nietzsche thought. The question for him, confronting Wagner and his heckling *ism*, was *Where's the disease?* Was Wagner himself an affliction? Or was the illness confined to his followers? Was it the old affliction of idolatry? Could one be infected by the sheer longing agitated by Wagner's music-theatrical extravaganzas? The case of Nietzsche, as the nineteenth century neared its end, blended with the case of Wagner. Both men signified some broader malady.

The crude banner uniting them in infamy was *Degeneration*, an international best seller published in 1892. Its author was Max Nordau, a forty-three-year-old doctor and journalist from a German-speaking Orthodox Jewish family in Hungary. Most of his life he was a resident of Paris, where he had studied with Charcot, shortly before Sigmund Freud was an apprentice at the same clinic. He published many novels as well as nonfiction titles, but without *Degeneration* he would be best known as an influential advocate for Zionism later in his life. *Degeneration* followed Nordau's even more popular exposé, *Conventional Lies of Our Civilization* (1883).

Degeneration, at nearly six hundred pages, is a doorstop, replete with citations of medical and psychiatric literature, delivered with an air of imperturbable conviction. Despite the window dressing of unctuous authority, *Degeneration* is a barely veiled "J'Accuse" aimed at virtually all modern art, with Wagner and Nietzsche in particular pinioned on the rack of merciless scrutiny. Others singled out for prosecution include Baudelaire, Whitman, Tolstoy, Ibsen, and Zola, followed by a vast retinue of "vermin" and "parasites," expeditiously dismissed. The parade of insults is so steady as to suggest that the air of reasonableness is simply Nordau's way of working himself up to an expletive, declaring Zola a "sexual psychopath," Rossetti an "imbecile," and Baudelaire's writings evidence of a "mystically degenerate mind."

Nordau's scientific credentials and his posture of unimpeachable sobriety make an appeal to common sense. But then come the little taunts and barbs, the venomous rebukes steaming out of his paragraphs in unrestrained passages of purple prose. He scoffs at calling Nietzsche a philosopher. Rather, he is

> a madman, with flashing eyes, wild gestures, and foaming mouth, spouting forth deafening bombast; and through it all, now breaking out into frenzied laughter, now sputtering expressions of filthy abuse and invective, now skipping about in a giddily agile dance, and now bursting upon auditors with threatening mien and clenched fists.

At most, "here and there emerges a distinct idea, which, as is always the case with the insane, assumes the form of an imperious assertion, a sort of despotic command." Nordau confidentially adds that "Nietzsche wrote his most important works between two detentions in a lunatic asylum." Not true, although he accurately reports that the philosopher has been irrevocably insane since 1889.

It's ironic, then, to find that Nordau's treatment of Wagner closely follows Nietzsche's own views. "Wagnerism is the most momentous aberration of the present time," he writes. "The Bayreuth festival theater, the *Bayreuther Blätter*, the Parisian *Revue Wagnérienne*, are lasting monuments by which posterity will be able to measure the whole breadth and depth of the degeneration and hysteria of the age." As for the composer himself, Nordau, like Nietzsche, notes his persecution mania, his "craving for revolt and contradiction," his imperious grandiosity. But where Nietzsche knew him as a flawed man, Nordau sniffs out an etiology. "Richard Wagner is in himself alone charged with a greater abundance of degeneration than all the degenerates put together."

At the core of *Degeneration* is an unreflecting presumption of normality. The bland aside, like a wink and a nod, assures the reader of belonging to a fraternity of right-minded citizens. Compared with Nietzsche, Wagner, and the parade of "hysterics" and "ego-maniacs" Nordau summons, "let us imagine these beings in competition with men who rise early, and are not weary before sunset, who have clear heads, solid stomachs and hard muscles: the comparison will provoke our laughter." In his turn to Zionism, Nordau promoted the model of the "muscle Jew," and his own stalwart work ethic is a tacit counterpoint to the sloth he claims to find in degenerates. After all, in addition to his medical practice and career as journalist, he managed to publish nine volumes of fiction, seven plays, and fifteen works of nonfiction. Nordau may not have been a neurasthenic, but he was surely a workaholic.

Did *Degeneration* actually persuade its readers of the perfidy of Nordau's targets? It was an international best seller, and no doubt there were many who pounded their armchairs in emphatic agreement, but Nordau comes across as a know-it-all, so serenely self-assured and superior that one begins to wonder why he is picking on such undeserving losers. By the same token, the terms could be flipped. "Can any one with a grain of humor read Max Nordau's attacks on Wagner without imagining an irascible toy-terrier barking at the moon?" This was the question put by the author of the anonymous *Regeneration*, published hard on the heels of *Degeneration*.

Scholarly references to *Degeneration* commonly make it sound disreputable. But its impact reflects the air of sagacious superiority Nordau brought to it. Eruptions of intemperance are rhetorical ploys to beguile readers with their worst suspicions about Wagnerites, decadents, symbolists, and naturalists. Nordau's framing hypothesis is in fact quite prescient, aligning closely with the more scrupulous outlook of sociologist Georg Simmel in his essay "The Metropolis and Mental Life" (1903). "The psychological foundation upon which the metropolitan individuality is erected, is the intensification of emotional life due to the swift and continuous shift of external and internal stimuli." Simmel here compresses into a sentence Nordau's diagnostic opening chapter.

The problem with Nordau's thesis is his immunization of normality from the overall explanatory hypothesis. In his succinct synopsis: "Its own new discoveries and progress have taken civilized humanity by surprise. It has had no time to adapt itself to its changed conditions of life." Yet in his exposition, it seems that only artists suffer the stress of this historically induced "fatigue." How, one wonders, can a universal blight yield symptoms in only a select group of hypersensitive artists? Simmel, by contrast, recognized that the seismic changes wrought by modernity affected everyone.

Nordau fails to credit artists with giving voice to recognizable perceptions and fears, doubts and desires. If they seem objectionable to the bourgeoisie, it's because they're swaddled in received opinion and bowdlerized cultural products that reinforce the perception of "normality" as an unchanging universal, catnip for a newly established social class anxious about pedigree. It's a state of mind similar to that of Nordau himself, for whom the normal is de facto perennial, while the abnormal and the atypical are medical symptoms confined to individual cases. It was along these lines that George Bernard Shaw penned his devastating rebuke of Nordau shortly after *Degeneration* appeared. It was reprinted as *The Sanity of Art* in 1907.

Shaw proved surprisingly patient in approaching *Degeneration*, but in the end could not resist the cutting wit for which he was known. So presumptuous is Nordau's circular reasoning, he declares, that "I could prove Nordau to be an elephant on more evidence than he has brought to prove that our greatest men are degenerate lunatics." Shaw suggests that Nordau's criteria are absurdly general, as if incriminating degenerates on the grounds that "they all have heads and bodies, appetites, aberrations, whims, weaknesses, asymmetrical features, erotic impulses, fallible judgments." *The Sanity of Art* is, for the most part, a lucid response to a patently hysterical book, to which Shaw puts the sensible question "What in the name of common-sense is the value of a theory which identifies Ibsen, Wagner, Tolstoy, Ruskin and Victor Hugo with the refuse of our prisons and lunatic asylums?"

The answer has less to do with Nordau than with the zeitgeist. This was the moment, after all, just before Freud would usher in psychiatry, with its probing investigations of the role of the unconscious in human behavior. It was also a moment swirling with scientific theories of degeneracy and hereditary disease, theories that prompted corresponding models of cultural decline, culminating most flamboyantly in Oswald Spengler's *Decline of the West*, published in 1918 but completed before the Great War.

CHAPTER TWO

The Forest of Symbols &
the Listening Eye

The juggernaut of Wagnerism was self-propelling, and didn't need the support of artists and writers. But they soon realized Wagner was conjuring a future that would engulf them all. In 1850, French poet Gérard de Nerval—known for his habit of promenading the boulevards of Paris with his pet lobster on a leash—had an assignment to review Wagner's opera *Lohengrin* conducted by Franz Liszt in Weimar. Nerval didn't arrive until two days after the performance and had to get details from Liszt, which he then expanded into a breathless report for three Parisian publications. Insofar as Nerval favored imaginative reverie over actual experience, it's fitting that the performance itself did not impact his account.

Two key collections have pride of place in the origins of modern poetry: *Leaves of Grass* by Walt Whitman (published anonymously in 1855) and *The Flowers of Evil* by Charles Baudelaire (published in 1857 and promptly suppressed by French censors). Max Nordau reviled both poets. The American graybeard was "a reprobate rake." (Whitman is reported to have said, "So many of my friends say Wagner is Leaves of Grass done to music that I begin to suspect there must be something to it.") As for Baudelaire, "he loves disease, ugliness and crime; all his inclinations, in profound aberration, are opposed to those of sane beings; what charms his sense of smell is the odor of corruption; his eye, the sight of carrion, suppurating wounds and the pain of others; he feels happy in muddy, cloudy autumn weather." Baudelaire was in his element at a Wagner concert in 1861. A reviewer cast aspersions on Wagner by characterizing his audience as a group of "mediocre writers, painters, untalented sculptors, quasi-poets, lawyers, democrats, suspect republicans, false spirits, women of no taste, dreamers of nothingness."

This particular dreamer happened to be strolling by the Théâtre des Italiens on January 25 when he noticed a concert was about to begin. So Baudelaire ducked inside and was swept away. The opening bars of the prelude to *Tannhäuser* enraptured him, and he was overcome by "a joy almost sensual, like the feeling of rising into the air, or floating on the sea!"

45

That's what he wrote Wagner in a breathless letter of February 17, assuring him that his music was nothing less than "the final cry of a soul that has soared to a paroxysm of ecstasy." Such exclamations were a portent of twentieth-century fandom. "I am not including my address," Baudelaire concluded the letter, "for that might make you think I had something to ask of you." The gratified composer managed to track the poet down, inviting him to his soirees.

Baudelaire's essay "Richard Wagner and Tannhäuser in Paris" appeared in *Revue européene* in April 1861 and was issued the next month as a pamphlet. He lamented the ignominious dismissal of the German by fellow Parisians. Baudelaire felt Wagner's music to be an inordinate expansion of space—as in an opium dream, his favored milieu. He marveled at the "deeply-pondered, astonishingly skillful and poetically intelligent combination with which Wagner, *by means of several leading phrases*, has tied *a melodic knot* which constitutes his whole drama." His chaotic vitality, thought Baudelaire, was a salutary triumph of excess.

Baudelaire recognized the charge of *décadence* that was to suffuse Wagnerian circles in Paris, and he responded with a calculated reversal of values. "I admit that I am no enemy of extravagance," he said about art, and "moderation has never seemed to me to be a sign of a robust artistic nature. I love those excessive states of physical vigor, those floods of intellectual energy which write themselves on works of art like flaming lava on the slopes of a volcano." This terrestrial vigor, he felt, overflowed into other domains. Sounds could incite colors. Painting could absorb sensory infusions from other arts. Baudelaire predicted that in the wake of Wagner a massive adjustment of aesthetic ratios was at hand.

In "Richard Wagner and Tannhäuser in Paris," Baudelaire pointedly quoted a poem of his own, as if it heralded an aesthetic outlook he found validated in Wagner.

> La nature est un temple où de vivants piliers
> Laissent parfois sortir de confuses paroles;
> L'homme y passe à travers des forêts de symboles
> Qui l'observent avec des regards familiers.
>
> Comme de longs échos qui de loin se confondent
> Dans une ténébreuse et profonde unité
> Vast comme la nuit et comme la clarté,
> Les parfums, les couleurs et les sons se répondent.

Nature is a temple wherein living pillars
Sometimes let slip some muddled words;
Man passes there through forests of symbols
That observe him with familiar looks.

Like long echoes that distantly enfold
In a tenebrous and profound unity,
Vast as night and as clarity,
The scents, the colors and the sounds respond.

Baudelaire's "forest" provided a poetic weathervane for generations of poets.

Of one, Baudelaire observed, "I like that young man—he has all the vices." This was Catulle Mendès, another ardent Wagnerian. His wife, Judith Gautier, was the daughter of Théophile Gautier, whose verses Baudelaire prized, and who himself was an early enthusiast of Wagner. Accompanying her father to a concert, the then fifteen-year-old Judith defiantly told the skeptical composer Berlioz that he'd just witnessed a masterpiece. No wonder her nickname in the family was Hurricane. Judith adored Wagner's music, and her curiosity about the man was piqued by misleading reports from those supposedly in the know. "One authority reported that he had a seraglio of women of all countries and of all colors, clothed magnificently, but that no one ever crossed his threshold." In another account, he was rumored to be "an unsociable man, gloomy and disagreeable, living alone in strict seclusion, his only companion a great black dog." Such rumors were nothing more than whimsical suppositions published for effect.

Catulle and Judith visited Wagner in Lucerne in 1869, accompanied by Auguste Villiers de l'Isle-Adam, that curious author of the play *Axël* (1890) with its famously decadent line "As for living? our servants will do that for us." As Mendès recounted, the composer greeted them at the train station, "a bundle of energy, while the tension of waiting had apparently produced the almost convulsive trembling of a woman suffering from 'nerves.'" In their visits to Wagner's villa, Tribschen, over nine days, Wagner never stopped talking, and never sat down. "Now smiling ear to ear, now turning emotional to the point of tears, now working himself up into a prophetic frenzy, all sorts of topics found their way into his extraordinary flights of improvisation," Mendès recalled; "we felt like a cloud of dust stirred up by a storm, but also illuminated by his imperious discourse, frightful and delightful at once." And then there was the music. Villiers marveled at the way Wagner could summon an entire orchestral panorama out of his piano, and "what a piano! muffled, sonorous, deep, billowy, magical, a crystal gong, a storm, a thunderclap, and so gentle, a divine whisper when he wishes!"

Wagner was even more boisterous in the presence of Judith, by all accounts a beauty. During the visit, Cosima had a telling dream: "R. set his head on fire by carelessly turning up a gas flame." Wagner's capering response to Judith was a portent, as it turned out. Seven years later, during the first Bayreuth season, Judith renewed her contact with the composer. He gave her personal tours backstage, and during the performances the two sat in a box together, holding hands and shedding tears as the Ring unfolded before them. It was the beginning of a fine romance. Biographers are split on whether it was consummated, but his letters certainly burn with ardor. "Could it have been for the last time that I held you in my arms this morning?" he wonders on September 2, 1876.

Because Bayreuth was both a strain and a disappointment—*never again*, he insisted—his affair with Judith was "the only ray of love at a time that some people found delightful but I found so unsatisfying." He consoled himself with an outpouring of endearments, pointedly mixing languages as a simulated embrace (beloved lady, consult the dictionary):

Ma Judith! Je dis «*meine Judith!*
Geliebtes Weib!»
(voir le dictionnaire! Ah!!)

In his ardor, he yearned for the recently invented telephone to come into general use so he could hear her voice from afar. "Nowhere does reflected beauty shine with greater sadness or intensity than in the love letters of an aging man," observes a biographer.

Judith became one of the keepers of the flame after Wagner's death, beginning with *Richard Wagner et son oeuvre poétique depuis Rienzi jusqu'à Parsifal* while he was still alive in 1892. "This marvelously organized nature," she later recalled, "endowed with such exquisite sensibility, nervous and impressionable in the highest degree, suffered from terrible outbursts that left one wondering how he could possibly withstand them. One day of grief aged him ten years, but by the morrow he was even younger than before." It was this mercurial energy that fascinated her. It didn't hurt when he avowed that her embraces were "the most intoxicating and proudest events of my life."

Given the Wagnerian enthusiasm generated by Nerval, Baudelaire, Mendès, and Gautier, it's not surprising that the periodical *La Revue Wagnérienne* was published in Paris (1885–1888). Its contents were largely

literary. Its editor was the writer Édouard Dujardin, who wore his allegiance
to Wagner not on his sleeve but on his vest, which sported the emblematic
swans of *Lohengrin*. Dujardin pioneered interior monologue in his novel
Les lauriers sont coupés (1888), a technique made famous when James Joyce
adopted it as a signature feature of his own work. Dujardin wrote his novel
"with the crazy ambition of transposing Wagner's procedures to the literary
domain." He expected as much for poetry. Thanks to the rhythmic freedom
pioneered for music by Wagner, it was "necessary to win an analogous
rhythmic freedom for verse." Among the many poets who contributed to
La Revue Wagnérienne was Stéphane Mallarmé, then becoming a polestar
of the Symbolist movement.

Mallarmé's life was singularly uneventful, but sublimely rich in contacts. His career as an English teacher secured a modest but content home
life, while his engagement with the arts put him at the epicenter of all
that now seems enchanting about the Belle Epoque. His friends included
artists (Édouard Manet, James McNeill Whistler, Edvard Munch, Edgar
Degas, Berthe Morisot, Odilon Redon, Paul Gauguin, Auguste Renoir,
Claude Monet), composers (Ernest Chausson, Emmanuel Chabrier, Claude
Debussy) and of course writers (Émile Zola, André Gide, Paul Valéry, Joris-
Karl Huysmans, as well as Dujardin, and Villiers, among others). Thanks to
these associations, more people are acquainted with paintings and sketches
of Mallarmé by his famous friends than with his poetry. Debussy's musical
evocation of the poem "Prelude to the Afternoon of a Faun" has been a
fixture of concert halls since its 1894 premiere.

Many of these figures attended his famous Tuesday evenings, beginning
with his move to the rue de Rome in Paris in 1875 and continuing to his
death in 1898. Others from abroad also attended from time to time, including W. B. Yeats, Oscar Wilde, and German poet Stefan George who later
modeled his own legendary cenacle on Mallarmé's soirees. Walking up to
his fourth-floor apartment, visitors would find the master's intelligence
touching on myriad topics, from news of the day to esoteric theories about
poetry. In the memory of one acolyte, the Tuesdays were held "in the
discreetly lit salon whose corners of shadow gave off the atmosphere of a
temple." Among younger poets especially, he was regarded as a saint, a
prophet, a messiah—terms that had long accrued to Wagner.

In addition to his Tuesdays at home, other evenings were spent at similar
gatherings, with Mendès on Wednesday, Zola on Thursday, Fridays and
Saturdays with various others. The cleansing ritual was on Sunday. "I'm off
to vespers," he'd announce to the family as he left for the Concerts La-
moureux, which specialized in the music of Wagner and his contemporaries.

"Mallarmé left the concerts full of a sublime jealousy," recalled a friend. "He sought desperately ways of taking back for our art what too powerful Music had stolen from it."

Mallarmé, syntactically evasive about everything, could be frank about his rivalry with music. In the wake of "prodigious occasions like a Wagner," the poet still had the opportunity to arouse, "in writing, the Master of Ceremonies of everyone's private feast day." Invited to speak at Oxford, Mallarmé confided to the English (albeit in French, as his spoken English left much to be desired) the startling news that in Paris "verse is being tampered with." It was on this occasion that he came to terms with the prospect of poetry vanquished by music. How? Through a "volatile dispersal of the spirit, which has to do with nothing but the musicality of everything."

Mallarmé's remark about tampering with verse was a reference to *vers libre*, free verse. In the French context, it was a recent effort to emancipate poetic measure from the Alexandrine, the twelve-syllable line that commandeered French poets like military service. The example of music, he saw, just might provide poets a way of stepping out from under this metrical shadow. Addressing the question How does Literature exist? he answered, Only in dispersal, giving up the ghost, chastened into liberation by music. The result was a "truly extraordinary spectacle, unique in the history of poetry: every poet finds his own spot to play on his own flute whatever tunes he wants." In this defiant yet oddly tentative self-portrait, the poet's choice of instrument conforms to Greek pastoral, even as it counts for little amid the opulent forces of Wagnerian orchestration. In a pointedly diagrammatic equation: "Music joins Verse to form, since Wagner, Poetry."

Mallarmé's poetry is notoriously impenetrable. A critic quipped that it was untranslatable—even into French. Yet its difficulties have nothing to do with esoteric references. His poems may best be compared with aromas, like a flower you can barely whiff, just enough to know it's nearby. In fact, a floral reference provides his most famous evocation of poetry. "I say: a flower!" But out of "something other than the known bloom, there arises, musically, the very idea in its mellowness; in other words, what is absent from every bouquet." Lest we regard this as the *idea* supplanting the flower itself, it's worth reiterating the reproach he ventured to a friend: poetry is written not with ideas, but with words.

And words were what Mallarmé handled and dandled, aligning them with refined care to supple spasms of consonants and syllables. Consider the bubbling of *b* sounds in the opening quatrain of "Le Tombeau de Charles Baudelaire" (the very title opportunistically aligns the *beau* of the word for tomb with the first phoneme of the poet's name):

Le temple enseveli divulgue par la bouche
Sépulcrale d'égout bavant boue et rubis
Abominablement quelque idole Anubis
Tout le museau flambé comme un aboi farouche

Translations flicker like firelit shadows in their attempt to bring any of this over into English: "The buried temple via the horribly dribbling / sepulchral sewer-mouth loosening mud and rubies / divulges a kind of idol of Anubis / the whole muzzle fired up like a savage bark" (Peter Manson)—"The buried temple empties through its bowels / Sepulchral sewer spewing mud and rubies, / Abominably some idol of Anubis / Its muzzle all aflame with savage howls." (Henry Weinfield)—"The buried temple shits from its sepulcher's / Mouth—a sewer drooling mud and rubies— / Some rabid idol Anubis, / Its fiery muzzle a savage bellows" (Blake Bronson-Bartlett and Robert Fernandez). At least there's a thematic consistency heating up the images.

Mallarmé's masterwork, the epochal *Un coup de dés jamais n'abolira le hasard* (A throw of the dice will never abolish chance) raises the stakes for poetry by means of its astonishing typography. Semantic ambiguities are left unresolved by the way the lines hang in space, like wires in a Calder mobile. The poem summons the specter of a shipwreck even as it engulfs the reader with syntactic suspension in a kind of hyperspace. It convenes a virtual theater to supplant the greasepaint of the musical stage. Reading it is like turning over a snow globe and watching the flakes descend in absolute silence, a silence become strangely musical.

The poem appeared in the journal *Cosmopolis* in May 1897, in a drastically compressed typographic realization. Mallarmé subsequently worked with a printer to design a book publication, but died before it was printed, delaying publication until 1914. In both formats it was preceded by a preface, which purports to cancel itself: "I would rather that this note not be read, or, if glanced at, that it be forgotten." He goes on to acknowledge the unorthodox spacing, emphasizing that the "blanks" as he calls them are as much part of the poem as the words. Each page of text traverses two pages in the book, crossing the "gutter" to achieve its spatial dimensionality.

Mallarmé somewhat obscurely spoke of "prismatic subdivisions of the Idea" as having replaced conventional verse form in the poem, but he never forgot the musical provocation. Free verse and prose poem, he acknowledges, are behind *A Throw of the Dice*, but "they are joined under a strange influence, that of Music, as it is heard at a concert." Almost like waves lapping a wharf, this musical impetus should be understood as a

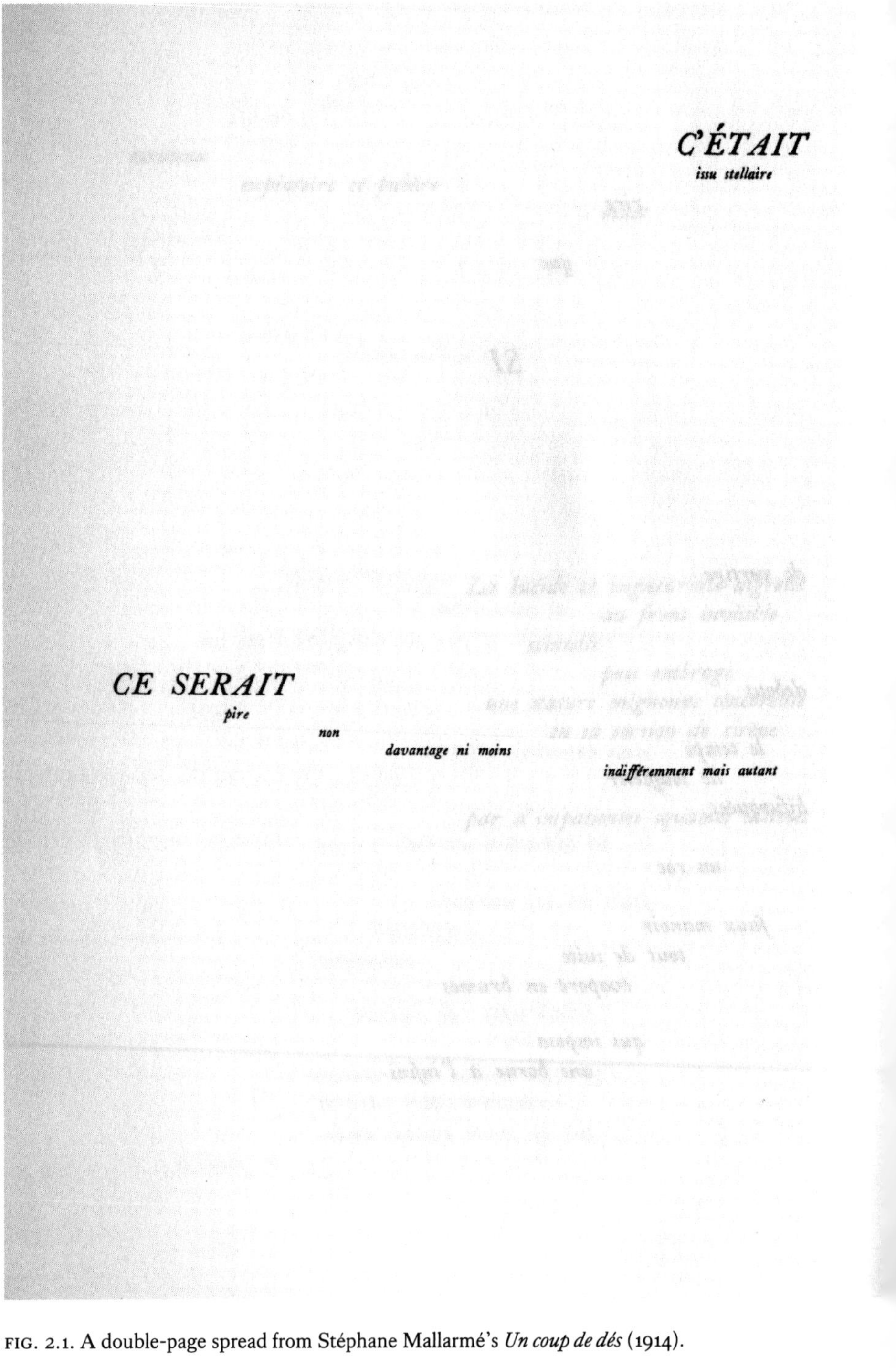

C'ÉTAIT
issu stellaire

CE SERAIT
pire

non

davantage ni moins

indifféremment mais autant

FIG. 2.1. A double-page spread from Stéphane Mallarmé's *Un coup de dés* (1914).

LE NOMBRE

EXISTÂT-IL
autrement qu'hallucination éparse d'agonie

COMMENÇÂT-IL ET CESSÂT-IL
sourdant que nié et clos quand apparu
enfin
par quelque profusion répandue en rareté
SE CHIFFRÂT-IL

évidence de la somme pour peu qu'une
ILLUMINÂT-IL

LE HASARD

Choit
la plume
rythmique suspens du sinistre
s'ensevelir
aux écumes originelles
naguères d'où sursauta son délire jusqu'à une cime
flétrie
par la neutralité identique du gouffre

contributing but not dominating factor. Little by little the poem blends into an unheard symphony.

Paul Valéry was the first to be privy to a reading (which, he gratefully recalls, was done in a normal quiet speaking voice, without theatrical or rhetorical fuss). Only after hearing the poem was Valéry allowed to *see* it. It was an experience still palpably vibrating a quarter of a century later. Suddenly, "I was looking at the form and pattern of a thought, placed for the first time in finite space. Here space itself truly spoke, dreamed, and gave birth to temporal forms. Expectancy, doubt, concentration, all were *visible things*." These included "silences that had assumed bodily shapes. Inappreciable instants became clearly visible: the fraction of a second during which an idea flashes into being and dies away." There, amidst a cascade of atoms in the void, "like some new form of matter arranged in systems or masses or trailing lines, coexisted the Word!" In his astonishment, Valéry discovered, "I was *now* caught up in the very text of the silent universe." Mallarmé had superimposed a "*spatial* reading" over the normal "*linear* reading," and words mobilized in space felt like intergalactic bodies. "*He has undertaken*, I thought, *finally to raise a printed page to the power of the midnight sky.*"

Valéry's response evokes the peculiar sensation experienced by readers of *A Throw of the Dice* ever since, being immersed in a dilatory space at once concrete and abstract, fixed and fleeting, simultaneously here and there—and, somehow palpably, nowhere. In his own way, Mallarmé had dodged the impending threat of (Wagnerian) music by creating a visual alternative to sonorous experience. The point was adeptly made by Belgian artist Marcel Broodthaers in 1969, when he produced a large-format folio of the poem with all the lines blacked out, printed on transparent sheets so the whole poem can be seen at once, like a receding X-ray. In his impenetrable if infinitely suggestive verses, Mallarmé had served notice that poetry had broken through some barricade: words really could sparkle in the mind like visual music, leaving the dictionary behind. Typography, he wrote in "The Book as Spiritual Instrument," is a rite—a prospect visualized in *Un coup de dés*. Mallarmé approached poetry as the administration of a sacrament. The corollary: "Verse is an incantation!" he exclaimed, as if just realizing what he had proposed.

*

Poetry of the fin de siècle aspired to the incantatory air of church rituals conducted in a language no one spoke. But how were poems to be uttered?

W. B. Yeats promoted the recitals of Florence Farr, who intoned poetry to great acclaim with her psaltery, the chromatic stringed instrument designed by Arnold Dolmetsch. Her method sought the melodic countenance of each word. Recitation was to follow intrinsic verbal melody, not mimic musical phrases. An accomplished actress—she starred in Shaw's *Arms and the Man* and Yeats's *Countess Cathleen*—Farr had also risen to the rank of chief adept in the Hermetic Order of the Golden Dawn (to which Yeats also belonged), possessing an initiate's understanding that "there were many ways of uttering 'words of power' in order to create moods of the soul or set in operation formative forces." Cambridge classicist Jane Ellen Harrison found Farr's voice "mesmeric": "'is it speech half asleep or song half awake'?" she wondered, quoting a line from Robert Browning.

Slumbering speech and somnambulistic song dissolve the distinction between conscious and unconscious. "The more closely I examine myself," wrote Symbolist poet Albert Samain, "the more I find that we do not live in the real, profound, and in some sort absolute sense of life except through the unconscious." The inner world was far vaster than the outer. A corollary, for Yeats, was to dispel the illusion of external abundance to awaken the sacred mission. "All art is, indeed, a monotony in external things for the sake of an interior variety, a sacrifice of gross effects to subtle effects, an asceticism of the imagination." A minimalist surface is all that's required if the goal of art is to draw imagination inward. For the Irish poet, this meant being conversant with symbols.

Most important was detachment from mundane preoccupations: "One is furthest from symbols when one is busy doing this or that, but the soul moves among symbols and unfolds in symbols when trance, or madness, or deep meditation has withdrawn it from every impulse but its own." This half-waking glimmer could be apprehended only indirectly. Arthur Symons evoked this ambiguous realm when he defined Symbolism as "a literature in which the visible world is no longer a reality, and the unseen world no longer a dream." Yeats suggested the function of rhythm was "to prolong the moment of contemplation, the moment when we are both asleep and awake, which is the one moment of creation, by hushing us with an alluring monotony, while it holds us waking by variety, to keep us in that state of perhaps real trance, in which the mind liberated from the pressure of the will is unfolded in symbols." The will specifies and individuates; the symbol concentrates the diverse into the singular.

The rhythmic trance Yeats sought had to be based on something more than individual caprice, for which *symbol* was the precise term. The word is from the Greek *symbolon*, meaning a token or pledge broken in half so that those possessing the halves could verify the fit and reaffirm the bond. Symbol is thus particular. But how can a symbol recur? How does typology come into play? It's the very principle of repetition that sanctions the power of sign and symbol to signify, and yet familiarity bred by repetition dulls the vision. Yeats's "secret rose" can feel attenuated. It's hard to detect the symbol through the stereotype.

The word *stereotype* was coined by eighteenth-century typographer Firmin Didot to refer to a metal printing plate, the use of which supplanted movable type and enabled the industrialization of print culture in the nineteenth century. Another printing term, *cliché*, applies to the same expedience (Mallarmé chose the Didot type font for his final version of *Un coup de dés*). The Symbolist movement is commonly understood as a repudiation of industrial economy with all its clichés and stereotypes; and yet the concept of the symbol is inherently caught up in repetition, with the potential to subside into stereotype.

Much of the paraphernalia of late nineteenth-century art and culture now seems a parade of clichés, like the stock-in-trade of Hollywood genre movies. This is evident in the stylistic and cultic consequences of Wagnerism. Take for instance Joséphin Péladan, who convened an aesthetic with religious trappings in Rose + Croix, founded in a fit of enthusiasm after he attended *Parsifal* at Bayreuth. "The essence of art is to figure forth the mystery, and not to explain it; to render it present and conceivable, to produce it and to unveil it," he proposed. Despite its initiatory esotericism, his Rosicrucian cult was a high-profile arts organization, mounting exhibits that were A-list events in fashionable circles.

Crowds attending the inaugural Salon de la Rose + Croix in 1892 were so huge the police had to stop traffic between the Opéra and rue Montmartre for much of the day, during which some 22,600 visiting cards piled up. Music for the occasion was by Erik Satie, who made his living as a pianist in Montmartre cabarets. Péladan's most vivid creation was himself. He coined a term for it, *Kaloprosopia*, the art of personality, or turning oneself into a work of art. This is distinct from "personality" in our public relations exposure to celebrities on the talk-show circuit. Péladan's cult of personality was about *depersonalization*. Opposing the thespian practice of actors personifying their roles, he imagined an alternative practice of hieratic gestures and calm rhapsodic articulation meant to evoke antique statuary. Posing in the garb of an ancient priest, Péladan (with tongue partly in cheek) called himself an adman for the beyond ("l'homme-affiche de l'au-délà").

Phenomena like Rose + Croix brandished a Symbolist stereotype: the elevation of art to ritual. But with Symbolism, the ritual was private transaction more than public occasion. A commentator on the paintings of a French Symbolist found that "the visible is only a grazing of the surface of the invisible. Like rocks that are slowly uncovered by the ebbing tide." The reader, the concert goer, like someone perusing pictures in a gallery, witnesses the ebbing tide. The model for this ritual of bearing witness was musical, and in music the distinction between natural and unnatural was becoming increasingly untenable in the wake of Wagner's chromaticism, in which the home key was forcibly severed from immediate resolution. Wagner's reference to his music dramas as "deeds made visible in music" had a riveting impact on his contemporaries, who often indulged in a conceptual slippage whereby a poem could be a symphony in words, the painting a beguiling aroma for the eye.

After Whistler's first solo exhibit in London in 1874, in which all but one of the canvases bore musical titles, painters started calling their efforts sonatas and fugues and symphonies. Paul Signac even applied tempo markings like allegro and adagio to his paintings. Critics adjusted their vocabulary accordingly, as in a review of a painting by Alphonse Osbert, said to evoke "a musical sensation of deftly orchestrated themes; the blues sing alongside the golds, which resonate like brass." Artists in each medium devoted themselves to blurring the material singularity of their means, while composers began to shed the foothold of tonal centers under the sway of Wagner. And then, from another quarter altogether, music was suddenly in thrall to Maeterlinck.

The abstract sets for Maurice Maeterlinck's plays, combined with the emphatic spirituality of his essays, infiltrated post-Wagnerian music. Fauré, Sibelius, Chausson, Dukas, Zemlinsky, and Stravinsky are a few of those who drew upon his work for compositions ranging from incidental music and song cycles to tone poems and operas. Most influential was Debussy's operatic version of *Pelléas et Mélisande* in 1902. Arnold Schoenberg wrote a symphonic score for *Pelléas* in 1905. Apart from the vogue for Maeterlinck, a considerable repertoire of songs composed by Debussy, Chausson, Ravel, Fauré, and others made abundant (even devotional) use of Symbolist lyrics. In Dujardin's estimation, "music revealed itself to Mallarmé and the symbolists, not as an art of virtuosity, piano or violin concerto, scales and acrobatics, but as the profound voice of things." That voice was not music, but *musicality*.

Maeterlinck was the master hypnotist of Symbolism. His was the voice of "all the divine that throbs in man," as he put it. "We all live in the sublime. Where else can we live?" he asked in his insinuating way, guiding fin de siècle souls to the homeland of exalted humility. Maeterlinck's outlook is epitomized by the title of a book of his essays, *The Treasure of the Humble*, in which he wrote:

> I have grown to believe that an old man, seated in his armchair, waiting patiently, with his lamp beside him; giving unconscious ear to all the eternal laws that reign about his house . . . motionless as he is, does yet live in reality a deeper, more human and more universal life than the lover who strangles his mistress, the captain who conquers in battle, or "the husband who avenges his honor."

Maeterlinck's plays and the precepts in *Treasure* synthesized various tendencies of Symbolism. The supreme goal of existence, he affirms, is "to bring to birth the inexplicable within ourselves." For him, the inexplicable is a portal to the unutterable. "It is idle to think that, by means of words, any real communication can ever pass from one man to another." What from another writer would seem ironic—explaining the inexplicable, saying in words that words fall short—passes muster coming from the sage of silence, advocate of "listening to another soul" by holding one's tongue. And so it is that, abiding by the hush, Maeterlinck suggests another order of audition in which might be heard "the solemn, uninterrupted whisperings of man and his destiny."

Maeterlinck's star has long since faded, but a similar temperament remains ever popular in Rainer Maria Rilke, who wrote in an early poem, "I feel myself more trusting in the nameless." It's not surprising to find him turning to Maeterlinck. "'The enigma suffices,'" the Belgian sage wrote, to which Rilke adds: "The artist's function is—to love the enigma." *Loving the enigma* sounds much like the soft-focus early Rilke that made him a steady stocking stuffer for New Age gift shops.

Symbolism as a movement was largely a Parisian literary affair, with many of its adherents contributing to *La Revue Wagnérienne*. But its more pervasive activity was by painters in many European countries, east and west, north and south. Symbolist painting exudes an air of compulsion, as if the subjects chose the artist and not the other way around. These scenarios of silence and absence seem on the verge of releasing some sound, like the skittering of dead leaves or a spooky flutter of pigeons. The cinematic trope of a solitary figure traversing a depopulated space—the camera framed tightly on the face, leaving the milieu ominously offscreen—may be indebted to this Symbolist *Stimmung*, or quivering moodiness. But it also suggests something about wiping the slate clean, convening a tabula rasa.

This can seem like a gesture of repudiation, though in many cases it was a matter of trying to draw a breath, find a moment of repose, a blank page or canvas, to start from scratch. So we have Mallarmé exclaiming over that spatial virginity he celebrated in the dance of Loïe Fuller, a quality sought by Maeterlinck in his fantasy of purging the theater of actors, or Gustave Kahn's desire to eliminate language altogether from the stage. Gauguin called it "abstraction," urging his followers to resist painting from nature. Mallarmé intimated the elimination of the author (almost a century before postmodern versions by Barthes and Foucault). Adolphe Appia wanted to strip the entire encumbrance of stagecraft from Wagner's operas. By the time Ezra Pound was making his mark by issuing slogans about what poets should do and not do, retraction and contraction had long since wound their way through all the arts.

For his productions of Ibsen and Maeterlinck at Théâtre de l'Oeuvre, Lugné-Poë had the actors deliver their lines in monotone; their gestures and movements were somnambulistic; and the audience strained to see the dimly lit production through a gauze scrim. Conventions of stagecraft persisted, but in a blur. His theater was like a skeleton key to modernism. Six weeks after the publication of his founding manifesto of Futurism in 1909—claiming to dispense with moribund cultural institutions, including Symbolism—Marinetti's own Symbolist play *Le Roi Bombance* was performed at Théâtre de l'Oeuvre. Marinetti was directly inspired by Alfred Jarry's *Père Ubu*, which was premiered by the same company in 1896, compelling Yeats to wonder about the advent of a "savage god."

Modernism repeatedly emerged from atmospheric extensions of Symbolism. Debussy's orchestral evocation of Mallarmé's poem *Prelude to the Afternoon of a Faun* prompted one of Nijinsky's signature dances with Ballets Russes. Before founding the company, the impact of which was continuous from 1909 to 1929, Serge Diaghilev edited the Symbolist journal *World of Art*. Walter Benjamin's fame has centered on his prescient essay "The Work of Art in the Age of Mechanical Reproducibility," but his sensibility was steeped in the nineteenth century like a teabag, forever doting upon the Berlin of his childhood and the books of his youth, about which he wrote at length—although *writing* in his case includes the copywork he indulged at exorbitant length for his *Arcades Project*, that stupefying *dossier d'amour* of a vanished Paris. Would Baudelaire now have the status of a Founding Father of modernism without Benjamin's discerning adulation? Even Edgard Varèse, enfant terrible of sound masses and electronics, collaborated in his youth on an opera with Joséphin Péladan.

Symbolism ran its course through different countries and cultures as an artistic and spiritual awakening. Unlike its modernist successors, manifestos brandished to rally the troops, the 1886 Symbolist manifesto by Jean Moréas was not a call to arms but a response to an invitation by the editor of *Le Figaro* to comment on recent trends in poetry. A few Parisians might call themselves Symbolists, but it was really an international mood (or *moodiness*) that rippled through all the arts of the fin de siècle—a "sphinx-like majesty of attitudes." So everything took on a penumbral Symbolist tinge: decadence and Wagnerism, nationalism and anarchism, Satanism and Catholicism, even Jugendstil and Art Nouveau. Its impact was such that early treatments of what's now called high modernism—Edmund Wilson's *Axel's Castle* (1931) and *The Heritage of Symbolism* by C. M. Bowra (1943)—took Symbolism as the unquestionable precondition.

Wilson and Bowra were not misguided. The essential point about Symbolism in its bearing on modernism was spelled out by Remy de Gourmont in the preface to his *Book of Masks* in 1896. "What is the meaning of *Symbolism*?" he asks.

> It may mean individualism in literature, liberty in art, abandonment of taught formulas, tendencies towards the new and strange, or even towards the bizarre. It may also mean idealism, a contempt for the social anecdote, anti-naturalism, a propensity to seize only the characteristic details of life, to emphasize only those acts that distinguish one man from another, to strive or achieve essentials; finally, for the poets symbolism seems allied to free verse, that is, to unswathed verse whose young body may frolic at ease, liberated from embarrassments of swaddling clothes and straps.

*

By the fin de siècle, artistic aspiration in general had been beholden to the rising eminence of music for fifty years. In the process, "music" had been diffused into an evocative, intersensory *musicality*. So the question—To what sense is music addressed?—would have prompted surprising responses in the twilight years of the nineteenth century. "We now *hear* undeniable rays of light," Mallarmé attested. Richard Wagner, under such auspices, was not the Saxon composer of "music dramas" but a code name for a vital reckoning with artistic destiny. Painter Maurice Denis compared the "orange motif" in a painting to "the seduction of the violins in the *Tannhäuser* overture" by Wagner. The luminous palette of his mentor, Paul Gauguin, reinforced Denis's conviction that the function of color was to prompt "musical sensations"—soliciting "the language of the listening eye."

The prospect that music might be induced by a visual image reflected a widespread aspiration in which every art form was thought to petition the sensations specific to another art. Denis came up with the staggering neologism "polichrophilharmonique." In this milieu, Arthur Farwell could designate a piano composition *Tone Pictures after Pastels in Prose* (1895). The full title given by Paul Signac to his 1890 portrait of anarchist, editor, and critic Félix Fenéon is typical: *Opus 217: Against the Enamel of a Background Rhythmic with Beats and Angles, Tones and Tints.* The turn of the century did little to quell such formulas, although this tendency took on an increasingly anachronistic aura.

In his introduction to Pound's *Certain Noble Plays of Japan* (1916), W. B. Yeats refers to "that curious game which the Japanese called, with a confusion of the senses that had seemed typical of our own age, 'listening to incense.'" Thanks to the incense, Yeats speculated that the Japanese "would have understood the prose of Walter Pater, the painting of Puvis de Chavannes, the poetry of Mallarmé and Verlaine." Mallarmé paid tribute to fellow symbolist Villiers de l'Isle-Adam as one who evokes "the sound of an hour missing from clock faces." Belgian artist Fernand Khnopff named his pastel evocation of Mallarmé's poetry *Listening to Flowers.* The same year as Yeats's essay, painter Max Weber embraced the slogan "To look is to listen to the silent," insisting that "the great worlds of colored matter in light must be *heard* through the eye." Such propositions envision a sensitized soul passing through some aesthetic switchyard where the audition of a sonata could provoke an aromatic mezzotint.

Richard Wagner, honorary godfather of these pipe dreams, scoffed at the simple arithmetic behind synesthesia, as if "in a picture gallery and amidst a row of statues a romance of Goethe's should be read aloud while a symphony of Beethoven's was being played." But the dream had staying power. Dancer and devoted Wagnerian Isadora Duncan spoke for all artists at the turn of the century: "This is what we are trying to accomplish: to blend together a poem, a melody and a dance, so that you will not listen to the music, see the dance or hear the poem, but will live in the scene and the thought that all are expressing." The pot of synesthetic gold at the mystic end of the modern rainbow started with music—or, to be precise, emerged like a mirage from an auditory rapture enticing artists and writers. For them, a concert was a ritual and they were the supplicants.

A memorable misadventure of synesthetic experiment occurred on December 11, 1891, at the Théâtre Moderne in Paris. The evening began with

Maeterlinck's play *The Blind*, an allegory of spiritual sleuthing in the author's "static theater" mode. With the stage plunged in gloom, a housebound family is disturbed by vague portents that only a blind man realizes presage an imminent death. *The Blind* was followed by Jules Laforgue's comic sketch *Le Concile féerique*, in which a moonlit idyll is disrupted by sightseers. The cause célèbre premiered at 1:00 a.m., the multisensory *Song of Songs* by Paul-Napoléon Roinard, one of those typically Parisian occasions known for fisticuffs, canings, and in this case even a few gunshots.

Billed as a biblical "symphony of spiritual love in eight mystical emblems and three paraphrases with music," the work emphasized the synchronization of effects, with each of the "emblems" or tableaux coordinating a musical key with a particular color, scent, and textual recitative. One, in C major, stressed the letters *i* and *o*; the scene was bathed in lavender, as young men (mostly Symbolist poets) spritzed perfumes throughout the audience. While some audibly sniffed, seeking the designated aroma, others just laughed—or sneezed. Raucous bemusement was the predominant mood, since the spectacle was supposed to induce a mood of religiosity. Vapor control proved impossible, and the cumulative scents became an olfactory mush.

Roinard's *Song of Songs* was not the only one of its kind. In 1902 Sadaki-chi Hartmann mounted a "perfume concert" in New York (reprised decades later for Hollywood tycoons). *A Trip to Japan in Sixteen Minutes Conveyed to the Audience by a Succession of Odors* featured two geishas and a dancer. "The affair came off at Carnegie Hall," James Huneker reported, "and we were wafted on the wings of song and smell to Japan—only I detected the familiar odor of old shoes and the scent of armpits—of the latter Walt Whitman has triumphantly sung." Huneker's evocation preceded his merry fantasy of an astral visit to Paris for the latest rage, a "synthesis of the seven arts." He evokes a potpourri of sensory jolts, and at one point the scenery "faded into a dullish dun hue, while the orchestra played a Bach fugue for oboe, lamp-post (transposed to E flat and two policemen) accordions in F and stopped-strumpets." A Jabberwockian recitation follows; "'This beats Gertrude Stein,' I thought, as the orchestra played the Galumphing motive from The Ride of the Valkyrs, and the lights were transposed to a shivering purple." Huneker concludes with bemused exasperation: "Talk about faculty of attention! When you are forced to taste, see, hear, touch, and smell simultaneously, then you yearn for a less alembicated art. Synthesis of the arts? Synthesis of rubbish! Only one at a time, and not too much time at that. I pressed my astral button and flew homeward, wearily."

These olfactory productions by Hartmann and Roinard were catnip to Alexander Scriabin, who, unlike Huneker, was serious about astral buttons. The Russian composer was convinced that "through music and color, with the aid of perfume, the human mind or soul can be lifted outside or above merely physical sensations into the region of purely abstract ecstasy and purely intellectual speculation." Kandinsky's *Blue Rider Almanac* included an enthused article on Scriabin's "sonar-chromatic correspondences," which the composer had scrupulously worked out in the score of *Prometheus, The Poem of Fire* with lighting specifications provided in bar lines atop each page. Unfortunately, the primitive mobile light projections used for a Carnegie Hall performance in 1915 were a dismal failure.

Undiscouraged, Scriabin forged ahead, preparing his grandiose *Mysterium* for a temple in India built for a single apocalyptic performance. But *performance* hardly applies to an event that was to last a week, transform humanity, and abolish space and time. Pragmatic details were bold but sketchy, involving a multitude of singers and dancers (including Isadora Duncan), and even a way to "modify the architectural contours" of the temple itself. To envision architecture that mutates in accord with atmospheric effects suggests nothing so much as virtual reality. Scriabin's project was thus not strictly a belated manifestation of Wagnerism.

Others inspired by Scriabin could be no less impetuous in their pursuit of hybrids. For pianist Katherine Heyman—Ezra Pound was her concert promoter in his youth—the musical note E was the very sound of mana-consciousness: "In its relation to the sky it is the wind; relating to the earth it is a tree; relating to man it is a mood," she wrote. "The corresponding color is green (chrome green). In taste, the nearest approach to its correspondence is the flavor of chicken liver. The gesture corresponding to E is from right to left." Heyman's book *The Relation of Ultramodern to Archaic Music* (1921) urged a revival of ancient cosmology. Accordingly, she inveighed against cheap tricks like the metronome. "Would you have your music comport with the clock, or be one with the motion of the stars?" She was confident that the ancient hermetic wisdom with its code of correspondences was being renewed by enlightened souls like Kandinsky, Yeats, Pound, Scriabin, and Claude Bragdon, architect and fourth-dimension theorist. For her, the metronome's ticktock rhythms were no match for galactic spirals.

In 1920, Cyril Scott (1879–1970) published *The Philosophy of Modernism—Its Connection with Music*, in which the English composer and concert pianist revealed himself to be a fellow traveler along astral byways. He regarded Scriabin as an adept in the spiritual world, who lacked only the assistance

of the highest astral forces to have overcome the blood poisoning that killed
the Russian composer at forty-three. But work like *Prometheus* manifested

> almost continuous *false relation*, i.e. "the occurrence of chromatic contra-
> diction in different parts" played simultaneously. And yet only through
> this device, which caused the pedagogues of an earlier period to shudder
> with righteous indignation, is it possible to obtain that sense of "between
> the notes" which is essential to the portrayal of Deva-music.

The Devas, Scott explains, are "those spiritual intelligences ranging from
smallest nature-spirits to loftiest cosmic archangel." For him, music is the
privileged medium allowing us to perceive this lofty realm "with its millions
of incorporeal denizens existing concurrently with the physical." In defense
of Scriabin's seemingly failed attempt to bring the senses together in *Prometheus*, "color, music, perfume, are all synthesized and not apportioned to
different senses as in the material world." A material failure in the concert
hall, in other words, testifies to the integrity of his grand vision.

Scott extended the same generosity to "the boys of sour chords," Stravinsky and Schoenberg. Their discords, he suggests, were needed not only
as a challenge to "undesirable obsessing thought-forms"; but also to unsettle
musical conventions that had, over time, been mistaken for rules. "Only
dissonances possess the power to alter the hard outlines of the *mental bodies*
of pharisaical or conventional people, and so render them more pliant and
receptive to new ideas." In the Deva Realm, the mental-body is part of an
ensemble with the sensation-body, emotion-body, and intuition-body.
In his traversal of musical history, Scott was attentive to the various ways
composers occupied one or more of these astral bodies.

Scott was an avowed occultist, and as with many of those in Symbolist
circles in the late nineteenth century, the *materia hermetica* of ancient lore
was part of his intellectual palette. He studied music in Germany in his
youth, where he was drawn into the circle of poet Stefan George, who had
attended Mallarmé's Tuesdays. Through George, Scott had been initiated
into esoteric doctrines. Thanks to his original yet perfectly elegant wardrobe
and his "advanced" compositions, around the turn of the century Scott
had a reputation as a modernist, and Debussy even wrote an adulatory
appraisal of his music.

"Why limit our inspiration by this hampering fetter of key?" Scott asks;
"why have any key at all? or why not invent new scales, or regard the whole
of tonality as chromatic? Thus some of us have abolished key-signature
altogether, and have bid farewell to an old convention." These principles

followed those set forth earlier by Ferruccio Busoni. In his *Esthetic of New Music* (1907), Busoni challenged the whole apparatus of Western music (tonic and dominant, major and minor, and the division of the octave). Above all, Busoni was an ardent champion of the future, drawing the vilification of Hans Pfitzner, musical conservative and future Nazi, who attacked him in *The Dangers of Futurism*. But what Busoni and Scott both advocated is best understood by way of a posture Scott picked up from physicist H. L. Hinton's portrait of the Unlearner. "Unlearning is one of the most important and difficult faculties for every creator to acquire," Scott summarized, "because, although it is tolerably easy to learn, yet to unlearn, it requires almost a genius: and certainly it requires an unlearner to create a genius."

Busoni was of an older generation, born in 1866 like Kandinsky, a year younger than W. B. Yeats. The Great War was a catastrophe for the cosmopolitan Busoni, fluent in five languages and at home everywhere. (He even found Americans agreeable—as well as the Dadaists in Zurich in 1916, and fellow exile James Joyce.) Among his students were Louis Gruenberg, one of the earliest to adapt jazz elements into classical compositions, and Kurt Weill. Though not a student, Edgard Varèse felt licensed by Busoni's advocacy of tonal emancipation to pursue experiments in emancipated sound. Busoni knew the cost of taking a bold leap into the future. Recognizing that the architectonic laws of harmony would have to be repealed to foster new developments in music, Busoni nonetheless suffered as loss what he himself advocated—an experience that's been called "the pathos of emancipation."

The pathos of emancipation revealed that, around the turn of the century, certain artists deemed the senses inadequate to their roles. While the organism perceives by means of a sensory manifold, the arts were understood in terms of distinct sensory inputs, as if painters were deaf and composers blind. Synesthetic aspirations reflected a desire to surmount the input/output ratio of sense-specific arts, provoking for visual artists the awareness that their work need not be strictly optical, while reminding composers that music might enrapture and arouse, but could neither prove nor openly declare. In the fin de siècle the allure of synesthesia ameliorated the pathos by shifting attributes of one art to the *potential* liberation of another. In this round of aesthetic hot potato, poets realized words lived secret lives; while novelists and playwrights discovered in the New Psychology that persons were incommensurate with themselves. Max Weber's dream of hearing through the eye needn't be taken literally: such propositions resembled mantras intoned in secret ceremonies. To mention synesthesia was a way of sounding the temple bell. The bell, having been rung, led back to music.

Modern theories of music as the pinnacle of human consciousness (Scott's Deva Realm notwithstanding) were beholden to German philosopher Arthur Schopenhauer. In music, he believed, "we like to hear in its language the secret history of our will and of all its stirrings and strivings." For Schopenhauer, music was at once preternatural and supernatural, maybe even supremely natural: "We can regard the phenomenal world, or nature, and music as two different expressions of the same thing." He is often said to maintain that music is an immediate copy of the Will itself, but his proposition is more deeply implicated in the vision made explicit in the title of his book, *The World as Will and Representation*: "Music is as *immediate* an objectification of the whole *will* as the world itself is." He spelled out the implications: "We could just as well call the world embodied music."

Schopenhauer thought music provided direct access to cosmic vibrations, such that "we ourselves are now the vibrating string that is stretched and plucked." After Schopenhauer, music would become a cosmic symptom rather than a particular art form, available to a mode of consciousness that would not be known as "subconscious" or defined as the *unconscious* until the end of the century. Still, the structure Freud elucidated is implicit in Téodor Wyzéwa's claim in the inaugural issue of *La Revue Wagnérienne* (1885) that "only music can express that deep-rooted emotional ground, at times situated beneath our ideas." Peel back consciousness and what you find is music.

The omnipresence of music in the fin de siècle brought to fruition a lingering trope of the Romantic legacy, concretizing what had hitherto been an analogy, as in Gustav Mahler's remark that "one is, so to speak, oneself only an instrument on which the universe plays." Others, like Jules Laforgue, even specified the instrument:

Each man is, according to his moment in time, his racial milieu and social situation, his moment of individual evolution, a kind of keyboard on which the exterior world plays in a certain way. My own keyboard is perpetually changing and there is no other like it. All keyboards are legitimate. The exterior world likewise is a perpetually changing symphony.

Nietzsche felt the need to develop "a few gay spirits in my own style," he wrote. "I must learn to play on them as on a keyboard." The metaphor served Russian writer Andrei Bely as well: "I saw my future as a keyboard, and it depended on me to play a symphony." Accordingly, he began to write symphonies, but not in music: Bely published four prose "symphonies" between 1902 and 1908.

Bely's *Dramatic Symphony* (1902) is called a novel in defiance of the theatrical and musical stipulations of its title. In fact, Bely's idol, Nietzsche, had called *Also sprach Zarathustra* a symphony. He was not the first. Melville applied the term *symphony* to the culminating chapters of the whale chase in *Moby-Dick*. Even earlier Ludwig Tieck offered his mixed genre *Die Verkehrte Welt* (Topsy-turvy world) as a symphony in prose. But Bely's practice was musical in a more systematic, less evocative, manner: "With phrases as my material, I wanted to do what Wagner did with the melody," he said. To that end, "the colors of the wallpaper, of a dress, of the sunset are not a chance digression from the semantic trend of the work but *musical leitmotifs* (our emphasis) painstakingly weighed and measured." Bely wedged himself in "the meeting-point of poetry, prose, philosophy and music. I knew that each was defective without the others, but as to how to combine them all within myself, I had no idea."

Romantic aesthetics, particularly as validated by the Hegelian doctrine of the world spirit fulfilling itself, privileged elasticity—play, or give, in the material. Cyril Scott, citing the "degree of incessant flux" pervading the universe, observed, "The modern tendency, then, is to invent new forms or structural designs, more subtle, more mystical, more flowing than heretofore." Yet, given the hyperbolic notions of music afoot, it was all too easy to conflate musical elasticity with the free play of unregulated desire. So it turns out not to be music as such but a fantasy of music as direct expression of inscrutable interiority that galvanized the moderns.

These motives prompted Jugendstil designer August Endell to realize that "we are not just at the beginning of a new period style, we're witnessing the onset of a completely new art, an art with forms that designate nothing and depict nothing and recall nothing, but will be able to stir our souls so deeply, so powerfully, as before only music has been capable of doing with sounds." Endell's vision appeared in the journal *Dekorative Kunst* (Decorative art) in 1897, when the urge to extend the principles of decor to all the arts was peaking, but this immodest tendency would end up knocking all aesthetic principles off their pedestals in coming decades—much as Endell's ex-wife, Elsa von Freytag-Loringhoven, would unsettle and reanimate the burgeoning Dada enclave in New York during the First World War.

Dada irreverence, ultramodern to bystanders and wags, had a hidden genealogy of which at least one participant, Marcel Duchamp, was aware. The Montmartre cabaret Chat Noir spawned a series of exhibits under the name *Arts Incohérents*—courtesy of which, Mona Lisa was blowing smoke rings out of a pipe more than thirty years before Duchamp added a mustache and goatee to Leonardo's enigmatic lady. One exhibition featured Alphonse Allais's *Album Primo-Avrilesque* (1897), with mono-chromatic paintings in different colors, each cleverly titled to explain the lack of pictorial content.

Hoaxes in one sense, such ventures bolstered a widespread incentive to resist artistic "expertise," and avoid the dictates of schools and academies. Paul Gauguin, incensed by state-sponsored meddling in the arts, scornfully reproached public indifference to "a whole Pleiades of independent artists whom the official painters have anxiously been keeping track of," while keeping their distance. "All of twentieth-century art will derive from them," he claimed. And he was right, allowing for the hyperbolic vigor of his "all."

The fin de siècle turns out to have been a threshold over which items were passed like contraband: what entered one side was unrecognizable when it emerged from the other. It was a rare moment when certain elders in every art conceded the field to their juniors, not in defeat but in rapt anticipation of what might happen next. Soon, as artists considered the potentiality of emancipating art, they were tempted to strike the "art" altogether, so nothing but sheer potentiality remained. The Dadaist rage for cancellation was a big *no* disguising an uninhibited *yes*. But even the fastidiously decorative exhibitions of the Vienna Secession movement greeted the new century with an invitational gesture. The uncluttered spaces in Joseph Olbrich's Secession building emphasize the vacancy as much as the artwork on the walls. Generously spaced, the paintings seemed to suggest the distance to be traversed as each art went in search of contact with another, like intergalactic travelers in search of other life-forms. The Secession rooms were inspired by the Wagnerian quest for a totalized solution, the *Gesamtkunstwerk*. But where Wagner sought an encompassing assimilation of all the arts into the grand spectacle of the music drama, the Secessionists (like modernists in general) aspired not to *summon* and *gather* but rather to reconfigure any work of art as an index to other arts.

CHAPTER THREE

Becoming Modern

Wagnerism—and, by association, Symbolism—were pronounced dead after the First World War. In December 1918, a month after Guillaume Apollinaire's death, *Mercure de France* published his lecture from the previous year, "The New Spirit and the Poets." In it, he resoundingly declared, "Il n'y a plus de wagnérisme en nous" (there's no more Wagnerism in us). Looking back on the oceanic swell that had brought poetry heaving and bobbing up to the present, he calmly surveyed the options and recognized that cinema, the telephone, the gramophone, and other modern appurtenances had put an expiration date on Wagnerism.

Apollinaire was himself a living rejoinder to the lingering past. After a decade fastidiously cultivating the old verse modes, he executed a quick turnabout in 1912 when, shortly before his collection *Alcools* was published, he eliminated all the punctuation. Yes, it's worth repeating: he deleted every comma, every period, colon, semicolon, exclamation point, even the question marks from the entire book. And there the poems stood, bare on the page with only the words themselves to speak their piece.

Alcools (not quite a pun, but not an accepted plural—it's tempting to render it as *Driiinks*) was quickly followed by *The Cubist Painters*, based on numerous articles Apollinaire published on the work of his friends. He had been a constant companion of Picasso's since 1903. His theories of art could sometimes perplex the painters themselves, but he was a gallant supporter and a man about town. Not only a journalist, poet, and gourmand, he was also an occasional pornographer in a venerable French tradition going back to the Revolution.

There was a troublesome patch in August 1911, when the *Mona Lisa* was stolen from the Louvre and Apollinaire was jailed as a suspect for nine days (guilt by association, for he did knew someone who lifted artifacts from the museum). Even this, characteristically, was grist for his creative appetite:

Avant d'entrer dans ma callule
Il a fallu me mettre nu
Et quelle voix sinistre ulule
Guillaume qu'es-tu devenu

Before I could enter my cell
I had to strip to the skin
A dire voice whimpered its spell
Guillaume what have you done

Picasso refused to vouch for Apollinaire in a deposition, wary of being deported as a foreign national. This did not deter Apollinaire from giving Picasso pride of place in *The Cubist Painters*. "Picasso studies an object like a surgeon dissecting a corpse," he pungently observed. Having followed the arduous expedition into the unknown carried out by Picasso and Georges Braque during the years when they refrained from exhibiting their Cubist explorations, Apollinaire recognized Cubism as a watershed, "not an imitative art, but a conceptual art." "These young painters are giving us works which are more cerebral than sensual. They are moving further and further away from the old art of optical illusion," he noted, "in order to express the grandeur of metaphysical forms." It was this final formulation that might have raised an artist's eyebrow. But they knew him as a wordsmith, prone to observations like "Most of the new painters are mathematicians without knowing it."

There would be no grandeur of metaphysical forms in Apollinaire's own creative work, which nonetheless abounded with variety and ingenuity, especially in the years following *Alcools* until his death from influenza in 1918. He resurrected the ancient art of pattern poems, included in the typographic bonanza of *Calligrammes* (1918). He called it "visual lyricism," a classic instance being "Il Pleut," in which the rain of the title is replicated in four slanting lines. It could have been hokey, but it works. And it's endearing.

He also pioneered what he called "conversation poems," like "Monday on Christine Street," consisting exclusively of bits of overheard conversation, the sort of thing you'd pick up at a café table, snagging phrases and sentences from passersby.

Bing bang bong
I owe damn almost 300 francs to my landlady
I'd rather cut off you know what than give them to her

I'm leaving at 8:27 p.m.
Six mirrors keep staring at one another
I think we're going to get into an even worse mess

Dear sir
You are a crummy fellow
That dame has a nose like a tapeworm

Apollinaire was a master of versification—"Le Pont Mirabeau" is still a staple of French education (my daughter had to memorize it in lycée)—but he was also highly adept at free verse, with its potential for conveying speech rhythms without artificially straining for lyricism: "Lyricism is only one domain of the new spirit in today's poetry, which often contents itself with experiments and investigations without concerning itself over giving them lyric significance." His *visual* lyricism followed in Mallarmé's footsteps, embracing typographic bravura as an open possibility. He was inspired by "catalogues, posters, advertisements of all sorts. Believe me, they contain the poetry of our epoch." He even fancied that someday cinema would become a prerogative of poets, who would then possess "a freedom hitherto unknown."

Thanks to his heterogenous enthusiasms and eclectic tastes, Apollinaire merits Roger Shattuck's inspired characterization of him as a "ringmaster of the arts." The illegitimate child of a Polish woman, he was born in Rome on August 26, 1880, and raised on the French Riviera. He had one of those jawbreaker names common at the time, so the name he published under was a selection from a list: Guillaume Albert Wladimir Alexandre Apollinaire de Kostrowitzky (his friend faced an even more extravagant menu: Pablo Diego José Francisco de Paula Juan Nepomuceno María de los Remedios Cipriano de la Santísima Trinidad Martyr Patricio Clito Ruiz y Picasso). Maybe loquacity is a natural outcome of such names; in any case, Picasso's lover said that Apollinaire's demeanor "made you listen to him when he started talking—and he talked a lot."

He wrote, as he talked, *a lot*. In addition to turning out potboilers and pornographic novels, he edited a series of reprints of classics of the genre, "Les maîtres de l'amour," from 1909 until his death. The series even included Baudelaire's *Les fleurs du mal* in 1917 when it passed out of copyright. For a year he wrote a column on literary women under the nom de plume Louise Lalanne. There was also a bounty of art criticism, and daily columns on miscellaneous topics for *Paris-Journal*. The sheer variety of poetic forms in *Alcools* provoked one reviewer to call it a junk shop, which may have pleased the poet, who was a devotee of such places in his Parisian peregrinations.

After enlisting in the war effort, Apollinaire continued to find welcome stimulation even in the trenches and under bombardment. Assigned to an artillery battery, he undertook a "theoretical and practical study in detail of the 75 [mm.] which is a beautiful piece, as beautiful, as strong, as tender as one of my poems." Overall, he found combat to be a theatrical affair with Wagnerian overtones. Writing to a friend in December 1915: "To my way of thinking it is an ascetic and theatrical life, and, strange to say, the legend and music of Parsifal come close to giving that impression of sublime abandon and watchfulness which never slacks off, of infinite chastity, of white metallic monotony."

The metal took a decidedly unmonotonous turn when, on March 16, 1916, while he was sitting in a trench, reading, a shell burst nearby. He thought nothing of it until blood started dripping onto the page, and he found that his helmet had been pierced. An operation was required to remove the shrapnel, resulting in the bandaged head sketched by Picasso, facing the title page of *Calligrammes*.

He was lionized in Paris. Several friends announced that the moment had arrived for them to gather around Apollinaire, the man who had opened up new horizons. They formalized their dedication with a new

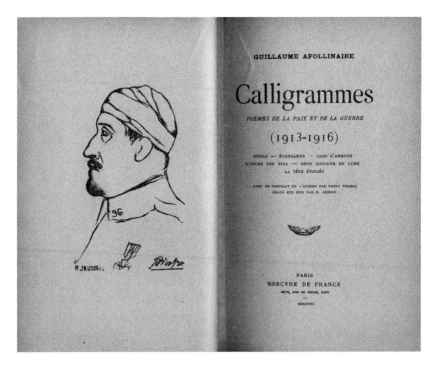

FIG. 3.1. From Guillaume Apollinaire's *Calligrammes* (1918), title page and sketch of the wounded poet by his friend Picasso.

journal, *Nord-Sud*, named after the subway line connecting central Paris with Montmartre (site of his early friendship with Picasso). In December, a huge feast for ninety guests was held in his honor, with the servings given literary titles like "Hors d'oeuvres cubistes, orphistes, futuristes," "Méditations esthétique en salade," "Café de Soirées de Paris," and of course plenty of "Alcools."

For a final flare that would light the sky of Parisian litterateurs in the years after his death, Apollinaire coined a word that inspired another *ism*. In a program note for the ballet *Parade*—a collaboration of Diaghilev's Ballets Russes with Picasso, composer Erik Satie, and Jean Cocteau—he described it as "a sort of sur-realism in which I see the point of departure for a series of manifestations of the new spirit." Seven years later, André Breton and Yvan Goll made simultaneous bids to don the mantle of Surrealism, with the Frenchman prevailing over his Alsatian rival.

Despite being a stage production, *Parade* was far from the raptures of Wagnerism. Satie made a point of calling his compositions *musique d'ameublement*—"furniture music," later known as elevator music. "It fills the same role as light and heat," he said, "as *comfort* in every form." *Background* agreeability. Of course it was an insult to audiences accustomed to paying for the foreground, but Satie was being impish. He also called a musical composition *Three Morceaux in the Shape of a Pear*. He never tired of pulling the long sober leg of Wagnerism. "The first time I got hold of a phonoscope," he quipped, "I examined a B flat of moderate scale, and I can tell you, I've never seen anything so repugnant." As for composing, "before writing a work I walk around it several times accompanied by myself." Only someone like Satie could have divided his time between performing as a pianist in a cabaret and playing organ in a church.

Furniture music makes a point of having nothing to say. There's no preaching, no emoting; it's just there, like something noticed or found by the wayside. It has a certain affinity with the conversation poem. But Apollinaire was still weaving strands of overheard conversation to make a poem. Blaise Cendrars took another audacious step with the found poem, the tenth of *Dix-neuf poèmes élastiques* (Nineteen elastic poems) titled "Dernière Heure" or News Flash. It has its own byline: "OKLAHOMA, *20 janvier 1914.*" It's a report of a prison break, just lightly touched up from a *Paris-Midi* article of January 21. The last line acknowledges source and method: "Télégramme-poème copié dans *Paris-Midi.*"

Cendrars had the audacity of Satie, combined with the ingenuity and fortitude of a grease monkey. His most formidable use of found materials is the book-length poem *Kodak (Documentary)* (1924), in which he adapted various descriptive passages from Gustave Le Rouge's pulp novel *The Mysterious Doctor Cornelius* in order to demonstrate that the author was indeed a poet. The Kodak company threatened legal action over the title. "Poetry isn't in a title but in a fact," Cendrars wrote in the preface to a second edition, "and since in fact these poems, which I conceived of as verbal photographs, form a documentary, I will henceforth title them *Documentaries*." It might even be a new genre, he added. As indeed it became, as in the extensive series *Testimony: The United States* by Charles Reznikoff, chronicling deaths and injuries documented in legal affidavits.

Cendrars is among the more inventive and lively figures in modern poetry. His pen name evokes fire and ash. A globetrotter from an early age, he was born Frédéric-Louis Sauser in Switzerland in 1887. He kept running away from school until he was apprenticed to a watchmaker in Russia in 1904. The next year he made a journey on the Trans-Siberian Express that led to his most famous poem, *La prose du Transsibérien et de la Petite Jehanne de France*, published in 1913 as a meter-long multicolored poster illustrated by Sonia Delaunay in an edition of 150 copies. Taken together, they would attain the height of the Eiffel Tower. The "prose" of the title is a nod to its break from standard modes of French versification (as is the case with all of his poetry). An endearing refrain throughout the poem is uttered by the poet's female companion, "Dis Blaises, sommes nous bien loin de Montmartre?"—tell me, are we a long way from Montmartre? Cendrars was someone always estimating his distance from the metropole.

Cendrars was much involved with other arts, with lovely ruminations on the art of his friends, including Picasso, Braque, Léger, Delaunay, Survage, Chagall. Some of them illustrated his books, with several by Fernand Léger being among the great collaborative publications of the twentieth century. He wrote of Léger, "His eye goes from the tin can to the zeppelin, from the caterpillar to the little spring in a cigarette lighter. An optical signal. A notice. A poster." Of Picasso, "He is the only man in the world who knows how to paint heat, cold, hunger, thirst, perfume, odor, fatigue, lust, envy, paralysis, palpitation, indecision."

American writer Henry Miller described Cendars's work as "written in blood, but a blood that is saturated with starlight." He elaborated: "Cendrars is like a transparent fish swimming in a planetary sperm; you can see his backbone, his lungs, his heart, his kidneys, his intestines; you can see the red corpuscles moving in the blood stream. You can look clean through him and see the planets wheeling." This risks making him sound like a mystic, but if he was one, he was a mystic of the everyday. He could be moved to compare the slow-motion film of a flower blooming with the flexing of a biceps. And he exclaimed that the lens of a motion picture camera was "more marvelous than the multi-faceted eye of a fly."

Cendrars's dedication to modernity meant taking the measure of "the optimistic pessimism of the man today." It took him to the cinema, where he worked with Abel Gance on his epic railway film *La Roue*, and to the stage, where he provided the script for *Le création du monde*, produced by the Ballets Suédois in Paris in 1923. Léger designed the sets and costumes, and Darius Milhaud wrote the music, which was among the first classical compositions to be informed by jazz. Not only jazz, but Black jazz that Milhaud had heard in Harlem. It was just the ticket for the scenario, which Cendrars cobbled together from African folktales he had researched and published in *Anthologie nègre* two years earlier.

Cendrars became a conduit between Latin America and the European avant-garde, frequently traveling back and forth across the Atlantic. Thanks to his provocation the 1922 Modern Art Week in Brazil registered the seismic impact of modernism for the continent, and Cendrars chronicled his voyages in several collections of poems illustrated by Brazilian artist Tarsila do Amiral. Nor did he neglect North America. His first poetry title, *Les Pâques à New York* (1912) recounts the Easter he spent in the city. He later went to Hollywood to write up a scoop on the studio scene, and his first novel, *Sutter's Gold*, was made into a silent film. It was also the first of his books translated into English. Next was *Panama, or The Adventures of My Seven Uncles* translated and with illustrations by John Dos Passos.

Dos Passos dubbed Cendars the "Homer of the Trans-Siberian," enticed by his panoptic vision.

> From Paris has spread in every direction a certain Esperanto of the arts that has "modern" for its trademark. Blaise Cendrars is an itinerant Parisian well versed in this as in many other dialects. He is a kind of medicine man trying to evoke the things that are our cruel and avenging gods. Turbines, triple-expansion engines, dynamite, high tension coils. Navigation, speed, flight, annihilation. No medicine has been found strong enough to cope with them; in cubist Paris they have invented some fetishes and gris-gris that many are finding useful.

Dos Passos's nod to Cendrars's African research also touches on the poet's self-portrait in "Profound Today," when he envisions himself "lost in the labyrinth of stores where you renounce yourself to become everyone," lounging there on the boulevard where "you are part of the great anonymous body of the café." "Profound Today" churns on through a whirlwind of phantom apparitions until his persona comes to rest: "Seated in my rocking chair I'm like a Negro fetish, angular beneath the heraldic electricity."

"Profound Today" is one of two major prose poems Cendrars published in illustrated editions. The other was *J'ai tué* (I have killed) in 1918. It was written in the wake of his combat experience, in which he lost his right arm. The severed limb evoked for him the cosmic figure of the Hindu god Shiva. The phantom sensation recurs for him not in the stump "but as an aura, someone opened like a fan, the bony web of more or less crushed fingers, the ultra-sensitive nerve endings finally imprinting on my mind the image of Siva dancing and being rolled under a circular saw that cut

FIG. 3.2. Cover of Blaise Cendrars's *J'ai tué* (1919) with illustrations by Fernand Léger.

off all his arms, one by one; then, I was Siva himself, the man deified. A bewildering sensation."

In *J'ai tué* he makes no mention of his injury in the combat scene he describes, except obliquely.

> Limbs fly through the air. A gob of blood hits me right in the face. We hear lacerating screams. We jump over abandoned trenches. We see heaps of corpses, vile as bundles of rags; shell-craters brimming like garbage cans; pots filled with nameless things, juices, meats, clothing, excrement. Then, in the corners, behind the bushes, in a sunken path, ridiculous dead men, frozen like mummies, making a little Pompeii.

J'ai tué ends on the note struck by its title. "I have the sense of reality: me, the poet. I acted. I killed. Like someone who wants to live."

Ernest Hemingway responded warmly to the combat veteran, often encountering him at the Closerie des Lilas. "The only poet I ever saw there was Blaise Cendrars, with his broken boxer's face and his pinned-up empty sleeve, rolling a cigarette with his one good hand," he recalled. Hemingway found Cendrars to be "a good companion until he drank too much and, at that time, when he was lying, he was more interesting than many men telling a story truly." Over time, the storytelling supplanted the poetry, which Cendrars left behind in the twenties.

Cendrars was a late master of the prose poem, given definitive credibility by Baudelaire in *Paris Spleen* (1869), though he noted the precedence of Aloysius Bertrand's *Gaspard de la nuit*. As he read Bertrand's minute historical portraits, Baudelaire says, "the idea came to me of attempting something in the same vein, and of applying to the description of our more abstract modern life the same method he used in depicting the old days, strangely picturesque." Pondering the expansive prospect at hand, he wonders,

> Which of us, in his moments of ambition, has not dreamed of the miracle of a poetic prose, musical, without rhythm and without rhyme, supple enough and rugged enough to adapt itself to the lyrical impulses of the soul, the undulations of reverie, the jibes of conscience?

A heady thought indeed, but his head was not in the clouds.

It was the specific circumstance of metropolitan modernity that tickled Baudelaire's fancy. "It was, above all, out of my explorations of huge cities, out of the medley of their unnumerable interrelations, that this haunting ideal was born." It remained a haunting ideal inasmuch as his prose poems were more like vignettes and anecdotes than the equally urban verses of *Flowers of Evil*.

After Baudelaire, another shadow was cast by the *Illuminations* of teenager Arthur Rimbaud, who thrust the manuscript on his former lover Paul Verlaine who had just completed a prison sentence for having shot Rimbaud in the hand. It was Rimbaud's farewell to literature. He then departed for Africa, leaving literature behind. Verlaine saw Rimbaud's collection into print in 1886. *Illuminations* is made up of forty-three titled prose poems, comparable in scale to those by Baudelaire. In the remaining years of the century, some of the Symbolists dabbled with the prose poem. And because Mallarmé was not a prolific poet, the dozen prose poems he wrote form a considerable portion of his legacy. A few post-Symbolist figures contributed to the genre, most notably Léon-Paul Fargue.

For all his eclecticism and formal explorations, Apollinaire refrained from writing prose poems. He may have sensed that his friend Max Jacob preempted the field. Jacob had befriended Picasso even before Apollinaire, but it was thanks to the latter that his work made its way into print in 1905. In 1915 Jacob published *Cornet à dés* (The dice cup), a title suggesting some alchemical affinity with Mallarmé's epochal "Throw of the Dice." But in fact these were all prose poems. In their easy proximity to unconscious impulses, they prefigure Surrealism.

Jacob repudiated Rimbaud's efforts as "le triomphe du désordre romantique" (the triumph of Romantic disorder). He thought the prose poem should aspire to the opposite, "balancing the elements that compose it" rather than igniting verbal fireworks. And it was not a matter of style. "Style is considered here"—he wrote in the preface to *The Dice Cup*—as "the deployment of materials and as the composition of the whole, not as the language of the writer." For Jacob, this meant "artistic emotion is the effect of the activity of thinking upon a thought activity (l'émotion artistique est l'effet d'une activité pensante vers une activité pensée)." It's an architectonic concept. The passion is in the construction, not the expression.

In 1939, Max Jacob looked back over more than thirty years of his writing, during which he was a constant witness to the mercurial transfigurations of his friend Picasso's art. What he enumerates deftly encompasses a range of practitioners and movements, private and collective initiatives. (I've broken his prose into lines to emphasize the distinctions he lists.)

complexity in form;

dominance of interior harmony over meaning;

speed in the association of images, ideas, and words;

love of words;

surprises, willed or not;

the appearance of dream or dream itself;

invisible rhythms

Far from being confined to Jacob's work, these are the features—call them symptoms, enticements, magnifications—of modern poetry in general as it emerged from that premonitory quiver of Baudelaire's forest of symbols. These were the terms by which Symbolism overcame itself, yielding a modernism that would find its distillation in *The Waste Land*. Becoming modern was a struggle; and struggle—difficulty, resistance—would in turn be the face of modernism.

*

Conrad Aiken had been a classmate of T. S. Eliot at Harvard. These old friends both lived in England and regularly got together for meals. Aiken reviewed *The Waste Land* when it was published in 1922, and recognized that its "emotional ensemble" superseded any pretension of an intellectual program. The next year, publisher Alfred A. Knopf provided a contextual note on the dust jacket of Aiken's book-length poem *The Pilgrimage of Festus*: "Festus is an Odyssey of the soul of modern man; it is *The Waste Land* set to a magical music, but sharing none of its bitterness."

Aiken's pursuit of a "magical music" in poetry culminated in *Festus*. In 1916 he published *The Jig of Forslin*, a book-length poem subtitled

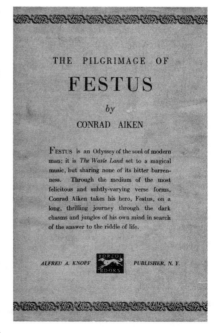

FIG. 3.3. Dust jacket of Conrad Aiken's *Pilgrimage of Festus* (1923).

A Symphony. The House of Dust (1920) bore the same subtitle. These two volumes were part of a longer sequence to which *The Pilgrimage of Festus* also belonged. Along with *Senlin: A Biography* and *The Charnel Rose*—issued in a single volume in 1918—the five "symphonies" were reprised as *The Divine Pilgrim* in 1949. It opens with a neo-pagan salute to the cosmos: "She rose in moonlight, and stood, confronting sea, / With her bare arms uplifted . . ." The raised arms in this belated and overripe product of the fin de siècle are a pervasive gesture in art of the time, from the calendars of Maxfield Parrish to the photographic movement known as Pictorialism. Ecstatic supplication was the signature of a century nearing its end—arms raised in total exposure, surrender, or was it petition?

In 1922 Aiken was asked by *Poetry* editor Harriet Monroe to review three of his own "symphonies" for the magazine. For this unusual assignment, he recalled his aspirations in terms that could have been plucked from a Symbolist credo of the 1880s.

> I flatly give myself away as being in reality in quest of a sort of absolute poetry, a poetry in which the intention is not so much to arouse an emotion merely, or to persuade of a reality, as to employ such emotion or sense of reality (tangentially struck) with the same cool detachment with which a composer employs notes or chords. Not content to present emotions or things or sensations for their own sakes—as is the case with most poetry—this method takes only the most delicately evocative aspects of them, makes of them a keyboard, and plays upon them a music of which the chief characteristic is its elusiveness, its fleetingness, and its richness in the shimmering overtones of hint and suggestion.

Traces of a long-vanished aestheticism are evident, but there's nothing to suggest Aiken thought it antiquated.

Aiken's appraisal of *The Waste Land* (in the same year as his self-review) owed less to his friendship with Eliot than to their shared debt to French Symbolism, in which the rage for music was prevalent. Aiken was not alone among poets of his generation in his pursuit of the musical analogy. When the first of his symphonies was published in 1916, another volume of poetry with comparable aspirations appeared: *Goblins and Pagodas* by the misanthropic John Gould Fletcher. It consists of eleven "symphonies" in various colors. For Fletcher, "Poems can be written in major or minor keys, can be as full of dominant motif as a Wagner music-drama, and even susceptible of fugal treatment."

These instances may seem like unwarranted extenuations of a moribund, or at best fanciful, aesthetic—subsiding pulses on the seismic spectrum of Wagnerism. But they raise a question. If Busoni and Scott, not to mention Schoenberg with his emancipation of dissonance, were venturing their revisionary programs soon after the dawn of the twentieth century, what was the state of poetry? An answer is provided in the case of overlooked English poet Edward Storer, born in 1880.

In 1908 Storer published *Mirrors of Illusion, With an Essay*, following a largely free verse collection, *Inclinations*, published the previous year. The seventy pages of verse in *Mirrors* displayed the rudimentary characteristics of verse in Georgian England. There were rhymes, if not altogether predictable, and the sentiments were what readers of the time expected from verse. The thematic material could disguise the absence of verse conventions. This tendency is brought to a head in two short poems in the book. Here's one.

Street Magic

One night I saw a theatre,
    Faint with foamy sweet,
And crinkled loveliness
Warm in the street's cold side.

The forty-page essay accompanying Storer's collection takes a leisurely but pointed stroll through prevailing assumptions about verse, debunking them one by one. He builds slowly in order to make certain points: "It is certain that incessant rhyming is barbarous, crude, monotonous, and truly unpoetic." Rhyme is a mold into which a predictable content is poured. No wonder poetry, by his time, was associated with the pablum of pulpit homilies and versified regurgitations of timeworn platitudes and decorous consolations. In the face of all this, he ventures that "most of the good poetry of the world has been written, as it were, by accident, in spite of colossal self-imposed difficulties and constrictions, such as the employment of forms."

Only near the end of Storer's essay do certain names arise, signaling where he's headed. These are, predictably, Wagner (Was art ever self-conscious before Wagner? he wonders) and Mallarmé. The phrase on Storer's horizon, intimated by his two short poems, is *vers libre*. He suggestively observes that English poets have always been "vers-librists, for we never insisted on such rigidity of form as the French did." Finally, in an aside, he recognized that "you can do almost anything you like in this country, provided it is not against the law, so long as you do not propound any reason, any philosophy for doing it." Ezra Pound, soon to meet Storer, would fail this test.

Storer was a member of a group of poets who met at the Tour Eiffel restaurant. The group was convened by T. E. Hulme, who reduced the finer points of poetics to a barnyard metaphysic: "I want to speak of verse in as plain a way as I would of pigs: that is the only honest way." He ridiculed Romanticism—still the prevailing poetic mode—as "spilt religion." "It is like pouring a pot of treacle over the dinner table." Hulme's bluntness forced the question: Was it possible to face reality head-on in poetry? Insofar as poetry could be direct, he thought, it was by way of images. Specifically, "new verse resembles sculpture rather than music." Another regular attendee was a workingman, Frank Flint, who later collaborated with Pound on Imagism. He eagerly followed these discussions in which the doctrine of the image was ground out to a pristine clarity.

At Pound's first appearance in Hulme's group he thunderously declaimed his newly published "Sestina: Altaforte," beginning

Damn it all! all this our South stinks peace.
You whoreson dog, Papiols, come! Let's to music.
I have no life save when the swords clash.

With this, the diners had a taste of a "gymnastic personality" (as E. E. Cummings later described Pound). On subsequent meetings, the proprietor placed a screen around the poets' table. Storer faded away, but *vers libre* began to stir the imagination of the young American, his head still in the clouds of romance where swords clashed and troubadours answered the call.

*

In these early years, Pound was blissfully ignorant of modern poetry, particularly the French. By the time he became aware of Cendrars, hoping to get him to contribute to Anglo-American periodicals, Cendrars had already left poetry behind. But there was an American Pound had not yet met, whose entire orientation to poetic possibility was indebted to the French.

T. S. Eliot began to write "The Love Song of J. Alfred Prufrock" as an undergraduate, around the time he discovered Laforgue in Arthur Symons's book *The Symbolist Movement in Literature*, published in 1899 (a second edition in 1908 is what he read). Laforgue was "the first to teach me how to speak, to teach me the poetic possibilities of my own idiom of speech." In 1917 Eliot recalled that "it was several years before I came across anyone who had read him or could be persuaded to read him. I do feel more grateful to him than to anyone else, and I do not think that I have come across any other writer since who has meant so much to me."

Symons characterized Laforgue's manner as pitched between "slang and astronomy." He chose words with the insouciance of fingers plucking petals off a daisy, as in these lines from "Avant-Dernier Mot" (Next-to-the-last word):

In fact, O my years, what to do	En vérité, ô mes ans, que faire
With this precious flesh?	De ce rich corps?
This	Ceci,
And that	Cela,
Here	Par-ci
And there . . .	Par-là . . .

For Symons, Laforgue marked the advent of the modern:

> The old cadences, the old eloquence, the ingenuous seriousness of poetry, are all banished, on a theory as self-denying as that which permitted Degas to dispense with recognizable beauty in his figures. Here, if ever, is modern verse, verse which dispenses with so many of the privileges of poetry, for an ideal quite of its own.

In his copy of the book, Eliot underlined the first sentence about old eloquence. The second sentence applies as much to "Prufrock" as to Laforgue. It was a poem that dispensed with "privileges" increasingly dubious to those, like Eliot, whose path into the modern would not follow English precedence.

Part Two

CHAPTER FOUR

The School of Images

In January 1908, a twenty-three-year-old instructor of French at Wabash College in Indiana was asked to resign his position after a female was discovered in his boardinghouse room. He had sheltered the penniless woman when he found her in a snowstorm. That an act of generosity could land him in hot water foreshadowed Ezra Pound's life in general. The Wabash administrators accepted Pound's explanation, and he was invited to continue teaching, but he took the occasion as an opportunity to abandon his budding academic career and go to Europe.

As a teen, Pound visited Europe with his parents in 1898 and 1902, and spent several months in Spain in 1906 on a fellowship from the University of Pennsylvania, where he completed his master's degree after his return. He concentrated on languages at Penn and at Hamilton College, including Latin and Greek, German, Anglo-Saxon, and a bevy of Romance languages: French, Italian, Spanish, and Provençal. Now, in 1908, he was facing the future in the guise (and garb) of a poet. A marriage proposal to one young woman was declined, and the father of another, Hilda Doolittle—whom he'd been seeing since 1905—sent him packing.

While in Venice, in 1908 Ezra privately printed a collection of poems, *A Lume Spento* (With tapers quenched). Despite its heft at seventy-two pages, it was in effect a calling card. By autumn he was in London, drawn to the presence there of William Butler Yeats and Henry James, whom he (and others) considered the greatest poet and the greatest novelist of the day. A penurious young American newly washed up in London could have found no more welcoming shelter from the storm than Elkin Mathews's bookshop on Vigo Street, centrally located near Savile Row and the Royal Academy of Arts. It was an establishment described as a throwback to the eighteenth century, with its precarious stacks of books among which "the genial proprietor should don a bob-wig and knee breeches to make the illusion complete." Mathews indulged the young American and was soon inviting him to his country house for weekends. It says much about Ezra's precarious fiscal situation that Mathews's young daughter thought the pale, slender young man was rather ill.

Mathews, who had been in the publishing trade since 1894, recognized the American's drive and put him in contact with literary circles. His authors included John Masefield, as well as such Rhymer's Club figures as Lionel Johnson, Ernest Dowson, and Yeats. More recently, he'd published a slim collection of poems by an unknown Irishman named James Joyce. In Mathews's shop Pound met several poets from an older generation, minor luminaries on his poetic star chart. He also saw to it that Mathews stocked *A Lume Spento* and a smaller book, also self-published, he assembled for the Christmas season, *A Quinzane for This Yule*. Mathews did well enough with them that he offered to publish future collections.

With this encouragement, the young poet promptly set to work promoting himself as a champion of the new and scold of moribund literary tastes. In his view, recent English poetry was "a horrible agglomerate compost." It was "not even baked, a doughy mess of third-hand Keats, Wordsworth, heaven knows what, fourth-hand Elizabethan sonority blunted, half-melted, lumpy." Insofar as he was an American, his brashness was tolerated, his relentless self-promotion only to be expected. He sought "giants & dragons I may devour." It was this sort of outsized bluster that actually saw him through, and of course ruffled feathers.

Pound quickly established himself in London not so much as a man to watch as a force of nature. By 1916 he had ten poetry titles to his credit. Adhering to Barnum's circus principle that being in the public eye is everything, Pound published in every outlet that would have him. And he was delighted when he was parodically announced in *Punch* as "the new Montana (U.S.A.) poet, Mr. Ezekiel Ton" (a geographical misdirection: Pound was born in Idaho). As he told a friend, he was becoming a typing volcano.

It was recognized that Pound's colorful wardrobe was selected with insolent exactitude, but even more distressing to some was the realization that his behavioral nonchalance added another layer of insolence. As a renegade in a milieu short on renegades, he was bound to agitate public opinion. Douglas Goldring (who became a great admirer) at first took him for "a bit of a charlatan" with "his whole operatic outfit of 'stage poet' stemming from Mürger and Puccini." Richard Aldington observed that he "dressed in imitation of Whistler," the American painter Ezra idolized and whose pince-nez he adopted.

His outfits were "most negligently worn but obviously far from negligently chosen," a friend observed. Witter Bynner characterized him as a "happily cuckoo troubadour" with his disconcerting outfits, which might include a bright blue shirt with an apricot orange tie, green trousers the color of billiard-table cloth, and a blazer with blue glass buttons. He affected a turquoise earring. Headgear ranged from a sombrero to a Panama hat. He sported an ebony cane, swirling, prodding, and poking at phantom opponents, indoors and out, leaving the impression that his clothes were always billowing, even while he was sitting down (not surprisingly, he was known for a tendency to demolish chairs, which led to a rebuke from Gertrude Stein).

Nancy Cunard, with whom he later had a love affair, was mesmerized. "His appearance was astonishing, as were his manner and mannerisms." She goes on to enumerate the features: the "green, lynx-like eyes, a head of thick, waving red hair and a pointed red beard. He was dressed at that time in black and white check trousers, black velvet jacket, with a large-brimmed black felt hat. He wore a sweeping black cape and carried yellow chamois leather gloves and a cane. Thus he looked singularly like Rodolfo in 'La Boheme.'" Nor was this an affectation of his youth: even living in Paris in the twenties, he donned "the large velvet beret and flowing tie of the Latin Quarter artist of the 1890s."

Pound's demeanor seemed to palpably emanate from his appearance. He'd burst into a room with his green eyes spinning it seemed under his high-massed red hair, making strangled and clucking sounds as he talked, all the while observing the social formalities. An older poet noted his "jerky manner as if afflicted with St Vitus' dance." T. S. Eliot found it "difficult to distinguish the energy from the restlessness and the fidgets." Ford Madox Ford described his exertions on the tennis court as those of "a galvanized agile gibbon" or, in another version, "an inebriated kangaroo"—but despite the marsupial evocation, he was winning tennis competitions in France into his late thirties.

Dance was another thing altogether. Brigit Patmore said that "Ezra danced according to no rules that I understood. New steps one may invent, but surely the music sets time and rhythm. But for Ezra, no; with extremely odd steps he moved, to unearthly beats." She was amused at the attitude of his fiancée, Dorothy Shakespear, who dreamily said, "'Ezra has a *wonderful* sense of rhythm.' Yes indeed," Patmore conveys with an almost audible clearing of the throat.

The most vivid depiction of his dancing is from his friend and publisher Caresse Crosby, who in 1930 took him to a club in Paris where Caribbean musicians held the stage.

As the music grew in fury Ezra avidly watched the dancers, "These people don't know a thing about rhythm," he cried scornfully, and he shut his eyes, thrust forward his red-bearded chin and began a sort of tattoo with his feet—suddenly unable to sit still a minute longer he leapt to the floor and seized the tiny Martiniquaise vendor of cigarettes in his arms, packets flying, then head back, eyes closed, chin out, he began a sort of voodoo prance, his tiny partner held glued against his piston-pumping knees.

After the other dancers cleared the floor, he grew even more passionate, until finally collapsing back in his chair. "The room exhaled a long orgasmic sigh—I too."

For all his quirks, Ezra Pound was tall and decidedly handsome. Soon after meeting him in March 1909, his future wife was smitten. Resentful that some would admonish him for his wardrobe, she wondered, "How could they look at his boots when there is his moving, beautiful face to watch?" Another Englishwoman noted that "Ezra never seemed conscious of the fact that his unusual looks were beautiful, not just the handsomeness permissible to a man in England." When he spoke at the Poetry Society in New York in 1911, one attendee thought nobody could have been "more charming, more boyish, more provocative than Ezra that night. Young and handsome, with his mass of golden-brown hair, his keen merry eyes, his careless ease of dress."

The plenitude of such observations is not incidental. It speaks to his visibility as a character, at a time in English society when being recognized as a character hummed with palpable consequence. What would this conspicuous American do? For several years to come, he complied with expectations. He might gobble flowers from a bouquet, while obstreperously proclaiming that poetry was no social frill, but an exalted art. His poems were pulsating time capsules, drawing readers far into ages of yore, much as *Tristan and Isolde* had captivated audiences with its Celtic setting.

Pound's first commercial collection, *Personae*, was published by Elkin Mathews in April 1909. At the end of the month, he got an invitation from Yeats, proudly informing his parents that the Irish bard had finally returned to London, "and I had about five hours of him yesterday." Soon he played host at the Irishman's Monday evening gatherings. By the end of 1910 he thought that "Yeats has found within himself spirit of the new air which I by accident had touched before him." Consequently, the brash younger poet presumed, "he and I are now as it were in one movement with *aims* very nearly identical."

In addition to Yeats, Pound spent time with another of his literary heroes, eminent American expatriate Henry James. Influential editor and novelist Ford Madox Hueffer also became a valued contact, through whom he met

FIG. 4.1. Ezra Pound, photographed by fellow American expatriate Alvin Langdon Coburn, probably around 1912 when they met. Coburn and Pound developed the Vortograph, a photographic technique said by Pound to take Picassos from nature. Coburn also provided the frontispiece photos for the twenty-eight volumes of Henry James's collected works.

an aspiring English writer his own age, D. H. Lawrence. Lawrence found Pound "rather remarkable, a good bit of genius," but quickly soured, resentful of being taken around like a "show dog." The American's response was mixed. "Detestable person but needs watching." The reason? "I think he learnt the proper treatment of modern subjects before I did." Pound was beginning—and only just beginning—to wean himself from his attachment to the past, which was all too apparent in his publications.

In October 1909 Mathews published a second collection, *Exultations*, once again serendipitously timed with a poem in *English Review* that caught the attention of the poetry community, "Ballad of the Goodly Fere," a jocular portrait of Jesus as a jolly good mate. Pound's poetry of these early years leaned in on the old pronouns, *ye* and *thou* and *thine*. Hard consonants were dropped (ne'er, o'er) and inversions typical of moribund versification were common ("Love makes me the poet play"). *Nay* and *yea* were plentiful, as were *durst*, *wast*, and *hast*. One does not prove, but *proveth*, like *moveth*. And of course *It is* must by these affectations become *'Tis*. In his first two books, self-published (*A Lume Spento* and *A Quinzaine for This Yule*), nearly half the poems have titles in other languages, and he continued to pepper subsequent collections with poems bearing titles in Greek, Latin, Provençal, Old French, French, Italian, and Old English. The books were diminutive in scale—7 by 4½ to 5 inches—comprising little more than fifty pages each. (In some there's more than meets the eye, as the print is so tiny.) But they were much reviewed, and Pound's name also circulated through the abundance of articles and reviews he produced, a needed side hustle at the time.

Personae was greeted in the press with no fewer than ten reviews. One thought the poet someone to watch, capable of "a thread of true beauty, which gives the book something of a haunting charm." But Pound's mannerisms could be irksome. Rupert Brooke, a rising star, complained of his "foolish archaisms." Another reviewer balked at "'ellum' for 'elm,' in a poem written not in dialect, and 'mine fashion' for 'my fashion,'" finding such mannerisms "merely silly." The eminent Edward Thomas noted the poet's penchant for archaisms but applauded his "vague large promise." Thomas may have been the anonymous reviewer for *Bookman*, for whom "no new book of poems for years past has had such a freshness of inspiration, such a strongly individual note, or been more alive with undoubtable promise." By the time he reviewed *Exultations* in November, Thomas would no longer countenance "the turbulent opacity of his peculiarities," regretting that he'd previously tolerated this "still interesting—perhaps promising—certainly distressing" young American.

Thomas was not alone. *Canzoni*—the third title published by Elkin Mathews in less than two years—revealed that the "development" expected of a young poet was hanging in the balance. Pound was found to be mired in exoticisms. One critic noted the ambition but judged that "he has produced little but balderdash." Of his Pegasus, another quipped, "only very rarely can we see the steed for its harness." "The heavy incrustations of verbiage"—the "linguistic fancy dress"—were tiresome. Despite such cavils, a reviewer in the *Observer* observed that "few new poets have so quickly become known to literary London."

Meanwhile there was America, where news of his English success finally resulted in *Provença* at the end of 1910, bundling his two most recent collections under one cover. Floyd Dell, future editor of the leftist journals *The Masses* and *Liberator*, welcomed Pound's "shocking vigor," declaring him "a very new kind of poet" for which the epithet Neo-Impressionist might apply, Dell suggested, by analogy with the incendiary "Post-Impressionist" exhibition recently held in London. The eminent H. L. Mencken of *Smart Set* hailed Pound as a force of nature capable of surmounting the "boudoir tinkle" of American versifiers. "The pale thing we commonly call beauty is seldom in them," he wrote of the poems in *Provença*. "They are rough, uncouth, hairy, barbarous, wild. But once the galloping swing of them is mastered, a sort of stark, heathenish music emerges from the noise. One hears the thumping of a tom-tom. Dionysos and his rogues are at their profane prancing. It is once more the springtime of the world."

What Dell, Mencken, and others recognized was the poet's ardor, though it was largely borrowed. *Personae* disclosed a favorite stance, donning the mask. Nearly all the poems in *Personae* are in voices from the past, troubadours above all. The book's epigraph (carried over from *A Lume Spento*) specifies the time frame: "Make-strong old dreams lest this our world lose heart." *Exultations* was an exclamatory title, but it too was another book of masks. Both collections poached extensively from earlier publications. Nearly half the poems in *Personae* were from *A Lume Spento*, and *Exultations* tapped five more from that book, and six from *Quinzane*. Clearly the young poet was eager to make a mark, but with his increasingly busy social life, he wasn't producing as much as his publications made it appear.

A quaint but oddly endearing trait was Pound's habit of addressing his poems as unruly offspring. He regarded them as a bestiary of "songs," urging them to go forth and multiply.

> Go, my songs, to the lonely and the unsatisfied,
> Go also to the nerve-wracked, go to the enslaved-by-convention . . .
>
> Come, my songs,
> Let us take arms against this sea of stupidities— . . .
>
> Come, my songs, let us express our baser passions . . .
>
> I have gone half cracked,
> I have talked to you so much that
>   I almost see you about me,
> Insolent little beasts, shameless, devoid of clothing!

Pound returned to America in July 1910 for six months. While much of his time was spent with family and friends (including H. D. and William Carlos Williams, his poet friend from Penn who was now doing his medical residency), he made a comparison study of New York to see whether it could hold water against London. It failed his test. After returning, he made a consequential visit to Ford Madox Hueffer. *Canzoni* had just been published, and unlike *Personae* and *Exultations* it included only two earlier poems. It was, in effect, Pound's first fully up-to-date book.

Hueffer responded to the poems by rolling on the floor, laughing and snorting at Pound's futile effort to make his antiquities pass for modern. Imagine this outburst by visualizing Hueffer as a "flabby lemon and pink giant, who hung his mouth open as though he were an animal at the Zoo inviting buns." Ezra then realized that *Canzoni* "displayed me trapped, fly-papered, gummed and strapped down" in "the stilted language that then passed for 'good English' in the arthritic milieu" of London tastemakers. "And that roll saved me at least two years, perhaps more," he recalled in 1939. "It sent me back to my own proper effort, namely, toward using the living tongue." Thanks to Hueffer, or "Fordie," Pound learned a lesson he would repeat over the years: poetry must be as well written as prose. He reprised the dictum in a review of *Love Poems* by D. H. Lawrence, who, "almost alone among the younger poets, has realized that contemporary poetry must be as good as contemporary prose."

In November Pound began writing for *The New Age*, a cultural review with a circulation of over twenty thousand, though it was unclear (to him) who read it. He later said the only subscriber he'd met was an admiral. For the next decade he wrote regularly for the journal, which provided both a steady income and a venue in which he could extend his interests at length. The first was "I Gather the Limbs of Osiris" in twelve installments from July 1911 to the end of February. Most featured translations with extended commentary. The series purported to illustrate "The New Method," a category he drummed up to arouse interest. Insofar as any method was concerned, it appeared to pertain to "luminous detail." *Luminous detail* has persisted in Pound scholarship ever since.

The first in the Osiris series would prove to be one of his most esteemed efforts, "The Seafarer." It begins,

> May I for my own self song's truth reckon,
> Journey's jargon, how I in harsh days
> Hardship endured oft.
> Bitter breast-cares have I abided,
> Known on my keel many a care's hold,
> And dire sea-surge, and there I oft spent
> Narrow nightwatch nigh the ship's head
> While she tossed close to cliffs.

And so it goes for six pages, in which the anachronisms suddenly become a benefit, taking us back in time to when they were not affectations but part of a living, thriving tongue. He was still adopting a persona, but by way of translation, a practice that would soon escalate dramatically.

Another installment of "I Gather the Limbs of Osiris" included "The Complete Poetical Works of T. E. Hulme," preceded by a disquisition on technique. Pound cautions the novice that "no one cares to hear, in strained iambics, that he feels sprightly in spring, is uncomfortable when his sexual desires are ungratified, and that he has read about human brotherhood in last year's magazines." The challenge is to find "some entanglement of words so subtle, so crafty that they can be read or heard without yawning." Hulme's poems then follow without comment.

Pound was at this point finishing up his next volume, *Ripostes*, which includes the Hulme poems. He offers them "for good fellowship" and "for good memory" of "meetings two years gone," by which he means those of the group over which Hulme presided. Hulme's poems were modest, dallying with imagistic scenarios in free verse, with some arresting lines, like "The old star-eaten blanket of the sky," "beauty like a scented cloth," and the opening of "Autumn":

> A touch of cold in the Autumn night—
> I walked abroad,
> And saw the ruddy moon lean over a hedge
> Like a red-faced farmer.

There were only five poems by Hulme, so the auspicious title "Complete Poetical Works" (also given on *Ripostes*'s title page) was an inside joke.

What's most intriguing about Pound's prefatory note is his reference to a "'School of Images' which may or may not have existed," compounded by a reference to "*Les Imagistes*, the descendants of the forgotten school of 1909." This framing note must have been added to the book at the last minute, since it was published in October 1912, only two months after his first use of the term *Imagiste* in a letter to Harriet Monroe in Chicago. Having convinced fifty people to commit fifty dollars annually in support of *Poetry: A Magazine of Verse*, she sought Pound's editorial input. Passing through London in 1910 en route to China on the Trans-Siberian Express, she'd visited Elkin Mathews's bookshop and been persuaded by the proprietor's enthusiasm to buy two of Pound's books, which she absorbed with delight while riding the rails.

Pound was at once enthused and skeptical. "Can you teach the American poet that poetry *is* an *art*," he wondered, mentioning that during his recent return to his homeland "I found no writer and but one reviewer who had any worthy conception of poetry, The Art." But, he prudently added, "I need not bore you with jeremiads." He mentions that the page proofs of *Ripostes* are on his desk, along with the only two poems he could offer that were not in that book. These were an appreciation of Whistler's painting, which he regarded as a touchstone, and "Middle-Aged," which he characterized as "an over-elaborate post-Browning 'Imagiste' affair." The quotation marks around Imagiste make it sound vaguely esoteric, and the terminal *e* points to France. He may have come up with the term while deliberating on the poems by Hulme. At this date, August 1912, it was a word in search of an application.

The opportunity arose the next month. Hilda Doolittle had moved to London the previous year, unsettled to find Ezra engaged to Dorothy Shakespear, daughter of Olivia Shakespear, who had once been Yeats's lover. After Hilda's father had found the Bohemian poet unsuitable, she nonetheless persisted in thinking herself still engaged to him. Looking back on their time together in Philadelphia, fifty years later, she felt the smart of Ezra's abandonment. The engagement was not broken off; he just left. Then she learned he'd been playing the field. After his departure for Europe, "a sort of *rigor mortis* drove me onward," Hilda recalled. "No, my poetry was not dead but it was built on or around the crater of an extinct volcano."

The poems emitted from that volcanic soil were like hothouse emanations. "Garden" begins:

You are clear
O rose, cut in rock,
hard as the descent of hail.

I could scrape the color
from the petals
like spilt dye from a rock.

If I could break you
I could break a tree.

A second part evokes heat as encompassing environment.

Fruit cannot drop
through this thick air—
fruit cannot fall into heat
that presses up and blunts
the points of pears
and rounds the grapes.

It's as if Hilda was working through the passion still smoldering from "first kisses," regarding which, "—what did one expect? Not this. Electric, magnetic, they do not so much warm, they magnetize, vitalize. We need never go back. Lie down under the trees. Die here. We are past feeling cold." On another occasion they climbed up into a tree in her family's yard. "We sway with the wind. There is no wind. We sway with the stars. They are not far." Ecstasy.

FIG. 4.2. H. D. (Hilda Doolittle).

"Why had I ever come down out of that tree?" She got over Ezra by having an equally incendiary erotic covenant with a woman, Frances Gregg, who followed Hilda to London and got involved with Ezra, writing of the plight in her diary: "Two girls in love with each other, and each in love with the same man. Hilda, Ezra, Frances." This triangular scenario set a pattern for Hilda in years to come.

It was while going over manuscripts of Hilda's recent poems with her in the tearoom of the British Museum that Ezra, eyebrows raised as he finished "Hermes of the Ways," scrawled "H. D. Imagiste" at the bottom of the page. In addition to bestowing a nom de plume upon Hilda, Imagisme had a cause, which Ezra promptly set in motion in the pages of *Poetry*. Earlier in the year he'd met an English poet, Richard Aldington, who at nineteen was too young to gain admittance to the British Library but possessed unusual self-assurance. He submitted to Ezra and Hilda's "almost insane relish for afternoon tea," so their discussions took place "in the rather prissy milieu of some infernal bun-shop full of English spinsters." Hardly the place to launch a vanguard movement. But it did spark a romance: Richard and Hilda were married in 1913. The marriage did not outlast the war, but they remained close confidants for the rest of their lives. "I have never known anybody," he wrote in his autobiography in 1941, "with so vivid an aesthetic apprehension."

Ezra had tossed off the adjective *Imagist*, but no movement was mentioned. Yet the newly launched *Poetry* was promptly associated with the cause. In the issue of November 1912, Aldington is identified in the contributor's notes as "one of the 'Imagistes,' a group of ardent Hellenists who are pursuing interesting experiments in *vers libre*; trying to attain in English certain subtleties of cadence of the kind which Mallarmé and his followers have studied in French." These Francophone Hellenists must have puzzled subscribers, but the reference signaled that this was going to be a venturesome periodical.

In the January 1913 issue H. D. made her debut. She was described as an American lady residing abroad (London unspecified); no more details were provided. Hence the description that fills most of the contributor's note: "Her sketches from the Greek are not offered as exact translations," we're told, "but as experiments in delicate and elusive cadences." To emphasize the *cadences* of both Aldington and H. D. suggests that Imagism was about cadence, and that cadence was a characteristic of free verse. It would take little time for pundits and prognosticators to align free verse with all the other emancipatory squawks afoot in the public sphere, like free love. Combined, they became "vers libertines," presumed to advocate "the Elimination of Corsets in Versifying."

The references in *Poetry* to Aldington and H. D. as "Imagists" naturally aroused interest in what this obscure clan was up to. Clarification was forthcoming in the March 1913 issue, with "Imagisme" by F. S. Flint (who rankled at being told by Ezra what to write) and "A Few Don'ts by an Imagiste" signed by Pound. Flint's article enumerated the three principles to which practitioners were presumed to adhere:

1. Direct treatment of the "thing," whether subjective or objective.
2. To use absolutely no word that did not contribute to the presentation.
3. As regarding rhythm: to compose in sequence of the musical phrase, not in sequence of a metronome.

These points were elaborated in "A Few Don'ts." "If you are using symmetrical form, don't put in what you want to say and then fill up the remaining vacuums with slush." Free verse relieved the poet from such temptations. "Go in fear of abstractions," Pound urged. "Don't retell in mediocre verse what has already been done in good prose," announcing a theme to which he would often return—namely, that prose set a standard poets should heed. In a quaint but optimistic formulation, "Let the candidate fill his mind with the finest cadences he can discover, preferably in a foreign language so that the meaning of the words may be less likely to divert his mind from the movement." This comes perilously close to suggesting that poems need not mean anything at all, so long as they sound alluring.

The most definitive of Pound's dicta was this: "An 'Image' is that which presents an intellectual and emotional complex in an instant of time." Short and to the point. But he adds a potentially intimidating qualification: "I use the term 'complex' in the technical sense employed by the newer psychologists." This was a signal that something called the New Psychology was in the air, and poetry might not arise from sentiment so much as from subterranean forces. Such forces were not evident in poems published by the Imagists, so it was assumed by interested readers that the new movement was pictorial. In fact, its antiquarian orientation shared much with a prevailing trend in photography, known as Pictorialism, promoted since early in the century by Alfred Stieglitz's journal *Camera Work*.

Pound consolidated the first fruits of Imagism with a dozen poems in the April 1913 issue of *Poetry* under the collective title "Contemporania." He had suggested to Harriet Monroe that she use her own discretion about printing them, urging her to begin with Aldington and H. D. "I don't know that America is ready to be diverted by the ultra-modern, ultra effete tenuity" of his recent poems. The first, "Tenzone," provocatively concludes:

> I mate with my free kind upon the crags;
> 　　the hidden recesses
> Have heard the echo of my heels,
> 　　in the cool light,
> 　　in the darkness.

This blends a visual image with an acoustic one in its reference to an echo. It also conveys the poet's ease in the modern idiom of free verse, in which the emergent image prompts a rhythm of attention that sidesteps the mechanical thump of conventional verse, straining against metrical braces like a show pony snorting its rounds.

The most audacious instance of what Imagism had to offer was reserved for the final poem in "Contemporania." The six words of its title are nearly half the length of the poem itself, presented in *Poetry* with open spaces that were closed up when the poem was reprinted in Pound's *Lustra*.

In a Station of the Metro

The apparition   of these faces   in the crowd   :
Petals   on a wet, black   bough   .

What sets off this poem from all the others by Pound or his recruits to Imagism is that here we feel the subterranean pressure of psychological "complexes." Of course, the setting, in the metro, already takes us underground, but to condense human faces into soggy vegetation has the smack of something beyond mere analogy.

With steady venues of publication at hand, his poetry reviewed and accepted, and literary circles opening up to him, Pound was emboldened to influence public taste. Flush on the heels of the launch of Imagism in *Poetry* he met Robert Frost, a fellow American living in England, pronouncing him "Vurry Amur'k'n." The New Englander learned of Pound through Flint, who put them in contact in January 1913.

Frost's correspondence was soon filled with references to "my dazzling friend Ezra Pound" and "Ezra Pound, the stormy petrel." In May he offered this profile:

And then there is my particular friend Ezra Pound the dazzling youth who translates poetry from six languages. Someone says he looks altogether too much like a poet to be a poet. He lives in Bohemia from hand to mouth but he goes simply everywhere in great society. A lot of the daffy duchesses patronize him and buy tickets to expensive little lecture courses he gets up when he has to raise the wind. It sounds peculiar, but he's really great sport <u>and</u> a yank, an expatriate.

Frost's contact high was about to expire.

In his review of *A Boy's Will* for *Poetry*, Pound wrote that Frost "has the good sense to speak naturally and to paint the thing, the thing as he sees it. And to do this is a very different matter from gunning about for the circumplectious polysyllable." Frost was gratified by the attention, and even allowed that "I don't mind his calling me raw. He is reckoned raw himself." But he was alarmed by Pound's indictment of American publishers and editors, and his suggestion that Frost had been driven into exile for lack of attention in his homeland. Of the editors Pound cited, Frost confided to a friend, "they are better ignored—at any rate they are better not offended. We may want to use them sometime."

Frost later recalled their six months' friendship as being a mere six weeks, though he continued to acknowledge Pound as "the most generous of mortals." Feelings were ruffled when Pound tried to place Frost's poem "The Death of the Hired Man" in *The Smart Set*, a venue Frost wanted no part of. What irked Frost most in the end was that Pound's support might tar him as a Bohemian renegade. "I want to be a poet for all sorts and kinds," he wrote a friend in November 1913. "I could never make a merit of being caviare [*sic*] to the crowd the way my quasi-friend Pound does." This episode—the meet, greet, praise, and flee—was one way of responding to Pound's promotional avidity. It was one thing to make up Imagism to boost his little circle of like-minded poets. It was something else to take a proprietary interest in the cranky New Englander.

Frost was wary about anything smacking of collective action, especially a vanguard. With Imagism consuming Pound's attention, he began to think in terms of groups, and left Frost behind. In England in 1913, an avant-garde movement was unheard of, which is why Imagism wasn't perceived that way. There may have been some shuffling of feet, nervous titters, and muffled coughs, but there was nothing incendiary about Imagism. Despite the pointed "Don'ts" in *Poetry*—which was in any case published far afield in Chicago—Imagism passed without notice in London.

To launch a poetry movement in 1913 would have struck many in England as sheer folly, given the exorbitant success of the *Georgian Poetry* anthologies, the first of which was published in 1912, followed by four more over the next decade. By the time Imagism made its debut, the first Georgian anthology had sold fifteen thousand copies, and the second would go on to sell nineteen thousand. Pound had in fact been asked to contribute two poems, but wanted to reserve them for his own books. Besides, this was not the company he longed to keep. From the first Georgian anthology, John Drinkwater's "I turned me from that place in humble wise, / And fingers soft were laid upon mine eyes" reveals by contrast the merits of Pound's medievalism as opposed to this warmed-over Victorian treacle. As a dedicated antiquarian, he knew the difference. Apart from Yeats, his sense of poetry probed deeper and deeper into the past. Apart from his enthusiasm for Yeats, the deep past was for Pound a wellspring, not a source of ornament.

"Ezra was a citizen of the world," Aldington observed, in stark contrast to the Georgians, who were "in love with littleness. They took a little trip for a little week-end to a little cottage where they wrote a little poem on a little theme." (As T. S. Eliot later observed, "the Georgians caress everything they touch" with effervescent pleasantries—"a rainbow and a cuckoo song.") Although Ezra did not expect his Imagists could rival the Georgians in popularity, an anthology was in order, and it would even be issued by the same publisher as the Georgian anthologies. *Les Imagistes* (with its characteristic flaunting of French) did not appear until 1914, and it's such a motley assemblage that group solidarity is undetectable. Although there was bona fide Imagist content by those already known as Imagists, any prospective focus is scattered by a miscellany of Ezra's unaffiliated friends, including Allen Upward, Ford Madox Hueffer, John Cournos, Skipwith Cannell, and William Carlos Williams, and a poem by James Joyce, whose fiction had yet to be published.

Imagism, like a magic potion, captivated the Boston poet Amy Lowell. A member of the fabled Lowell family (the eminent poet James Russell Lowell was a cousin, and her brother was president of Harvard University), she had recently seen her first book of verse fizzle. She saw a way forward with these new emanations from London. To her, Imagism didn't mean fine-tuning or modest adjustments: it was a way of flinging open the doors to the modern. And she had the means, crossing the Atlantic accompanied by her own automobile and chauffeur. She showed up in London ready to play, bargain, and cajole her way into the inner sanctum of the new poetic initiative.

"I have just met the erratic young poet, Ezra Pound," she wrote back home, fresh from the encounter. "He is the oddest youth, clever, fearfully conceited, &, at the same time, excessively thin-skinned; & I imagine that never, since the days of Wilde, have such garments been seen in the streets of London. He arrays himself like the traditional 'poet' of the theatre." Lowell herself was no stranger to idiosyncrasy. She was a florid smoker of cigars and scandalized a young man when she said that unwrapping her Manila was like undressing a woman. When the war broke out, she ordered a supply of a thousand stogies to ensure uninterrupted access.

In London, fired up by the Imagist publications in the recent issues of *Poetry*, she had hosted the authors in her hotel suite to the kind of meal none of them could afford on their own. She returned a year later, having forged a new idiom in her collection *Sword Blades and Poppy Seed*, hoping it would be acclaimed the latest triumph of Imagism. She recruited Lawrence, H. D., Aldington, Fletcher, and Flint to contribute to a series of anthologies under the seemingly innocuous title *Some Imagist Poets*.

Lowell's enterprise was not brought off without ruffling Pound's feathers. His main objection was to the editorial arrangement whereby the contributors would each select their own poems. For Pound, Imagism "stands, or I should like it to stand for hard light, clear edges. I can not trust any democratized committee to maintain that standard," he wrote Lowell. He hoped she'd consider a subtitle extending the focus to free verse or the modern movement. He wrote Harriet Monroe to suggest a pamphlet reprint of his "Few Don'ts" along with some supplementary material. "It would be much better than my writing new articles pointing out the various sorts of silliness into which neo-imagism or neogism is perambulating."

Even H. D., a contributor to Lowell's enterprise, nervously suggested dropping the Imagist label altogether. The situation wasn't helped when the American publisher advertised the anthology, identifying Lowell as a "foremost member of the 'Imagists'—a group of poets that includes William Butler Yeats, Ezra Pound, Ford Madox Hueffer." Lowell rebuffed Pound's pleas and went ahead unperturbed. "You have only yourself to blame for including me in the group," she told him, "and it is not agree-able to feel that you only wished the inclusion so long as I could be kept obscure and insignificant." Point taken, Pound dismissed the enterprise as "Amygisme."

By now Pound had come to regard (lowercase) imagism as a tendency in modern poetry generally, about which there could be little cause for concern. In the September 1914 issue of *Fortnightly Review*, he patiently laid out the precepts of a new movement, which he called Vorticism, through the lens of Imagism. The three principles of Imagism from Flint's *Poetry* article are dutifully reiterated, as if they were timeworn Mosaic doctrine, with no controversy implied. Indeed, "Nearly anyone is ready to accept 'Imagisme' as a department of poetry, just as one accepts 'lyricism.'" The risk of the image, he pointed out, was casual application, ornamentation rather than insight. "I once saw a small child go to an electric switch and say, 'Mamma, can I *open* the light?' She was using the age-old language of exploration, the language of art." That was not ornamental.

To elaborate on the exploratory potential of the image, Pound spent several pages outlining the background of "In a Station of the Metro," which had its origin in the Concorde station of the Paris subway, where his glimpse of lovely faces in the crowd converted them to petals on a dark log. This poem in its brevity approached projectile precision, paving the way for a decisive definition: "The image is not an idea. It is a radiant node or cluster; it is what I can, and must perforce, call a VORTEX, from which, and through which, and into which, ideas are constantly rushing." It sounds like a particle accelerator in physics.

Vorticism, as Pound explained, was a bundle consisting of "expression-ism, neo-cubism, and imagism gathered together in one camp and futurism in the other." Futurism, launched by F. T. Marinetti in 1909, had served as prototype for subsequent avant-garde movements, and Marinetti's periodic visits to London generated much commentary. Pound regarded Futurism as an "accelerated impressionism," a mere "surface art, as opposed to vorticism, which is intensive." This was just a rhetorical ploy. In fact, the procedures and rhetoric of Vorticism in the inaugural issue of its programmatic journal *Blast* were virtually indistinguishable from those of Italian Futurism. Cozying up to Cubism and Expressionism, with Imagism in hand, seemed the best way forward. But even Pound was inconsistent, characterizing the Vorticist periodical *Blast* as "a new Futurist, Cubist, Imagiste Quarterly."

In May 1915 *The Egoist* devoted most of an issue to a profile of Imagism. This was Aldington's doing, as he was then literary editor of the journal originally launched as a suffragist vehicle. There were articles on Pound, H. D., Flint, Fletcher, Lawrence, and Lowell, mostly by other Imagists, along with a few poems. The most substantive contributions were an article by the poet and editor Harold Monro, who had published *Les Imagistes*, and Flint's history of the movement. By then, Flint had soured on Pound, as had Fletcher (who reviled "that wretched little viper, Pound"). Flint wrote his history, however, with scrupulous attention to facts, refraining from any negative remarks about Pound. His account is much like the re-

FIG. 4.3. The old guard meets the young, January 18, 1914: (left to right) Victor Plarr, Sturge Moore, W. B. Yeats, Wilfred Scawen Blunt, Ezra Pound, Richard Aldington, F. S. Flint.

port Pound himself summarized in 1917, that Imagism was produced "on a Hulme basis" and was influenced by "the French groups catalogued by Flint in the P.R." (Monro's journal *Poetry Review*). This was a sore point for Flint, who observed that "before August, 1912, Ezra Pound used to say that he knew no French poetry after Villon. After August 1912, he became like a cat in heat." Not only that, but he published a series of articles in *The New Age* titled "The Road from Paris," without acknowledging Flint's precedent. Pound threw a fit when he read Flint's "History of Imagism." Flint was never conciliatory—he'd done a decent job, after all—while allowing, "You deserve all the credit for what you have done." But, he said, "you spoiled everything by some native incapacity for walking square with your fellows. You have not been a good comrade."

While Pound refrained from publicly giving Flint due credit for rousing his interest in modern French poetry, he was aghast at his own longstanding indifference to it. In the pages of *Poetry* in October 1913 he confessed to having wasted "about four years puddling about on the edges of modern French poetry without getting anywhere near it." In a letter, he marveled at what he was finding in the verse of Gautier, "and alternately bless & curse my education which has kept me from so much modern continental stuff." It was a mixed blessing, he admitted, for his ignorance "allowed me so much that I would never have bothered about if I'd known the modern stuff first."

Imagism had its greatest success in the United States, and the success was largely centered on Amy Lowell. T. S. Eliot dubbed her the "demon saleswoman" of poetry, an epithet she certainly earned. *Some Imagist Poets* sold over 1,300 copies in 1915, and the second collection sold 500 copies in a single month after its publication. Both were reprinted to meet demand. Lowell's own books rode the welcoming wave as well, with *Men, Women and Ghosts* selling most of its printing of 1,250 copies even before publication. Within a few months it was in a third printing. Her poetry was a success, and she was newsworthy. Lecturing to a large audience at the Poetry Society of America, she suggested that "the most national things we have are skyscrapers, ice water, and the New Poetry." It was a vision that consigned London to a small, distant island.

As it happened, Imagism spawned a double, better termed in this instance a stunt double. Witter Bynner (who had coined a cruel term for the large Amy Lowell: "hippopoetess") got together with fellow poet and lawyer Arthur Davison Ficke in February 1916 and, aided by abundant Scotch, concocted the Spectra movement as a spoof of Imagism. They invented two poets. Bynner was Emanuel Morgan and Ficke was Anne Knish. Both men had published books with New York publisher Mitchell Kennerley, who issued *Spectra: A Book of Experiments* by Knish and Morgan later in the year—albeit unaware of Bynner and Ficke's involvement. "When we invented the Spectric School, both of us were genuinely indignant at the charlatanism of some of the new 'schools' of poetry," Ficke recalled in 1939. "We who devoted our whole lives to poetry were angry and indignant on seeing apes and mountebanks prancing in the Temple." For Ficke and Bynner, the apes were the Imagists.

Where Pound's itemized credos in "A Few Don'ts" had been straightforward, the Spectrists decided that Anne Knish would preface the collection with obscurantist jargon more likely to have been gleaned from Pound's theory of Vorticism. "Spectric connotes the overtones, adumbrations, or spectres which for the poet haunt all objects both of the seen and the unseen world,—those shadowy projections, sometimes grotesque, which, hovering around the real, give to the real its full ideal significance and its poetic worth." This roused the popular poet Edgar Lee Masters to exclaim enthusiastically, "Spectrism if you must name it is at the core of things and imagism at the surface." Knish's preface also mentioned the role of humor, which was about the only thing going for the poems.

> If I were only dafter
>   I might be making hymns
> To the liquor of your laughter
>   And the lacquer of your limbs.

Morgan mainly wrote in verse forms, Knish in *vers libre*. All the offerings were given opus numbers instead of titles. Opus 200 by Knish:

> If I should enter to his chamber
> And suddenly touch him,
> Would he fade to a thin mist,
> Or glow into a fire-ball,
> Or burst like a punctured light-globe?
> It is impossible that he would merely yawn and rub
> And say—"What is it?"

Spectra was widely reviewed and discussed throughout the United States, contributing to the ongoing debates about Imagism, which elicited scorn and enthusiasm in equal measure. Alfred Kreymborg made room for a special issue of his journal *Others* in 1917, "The Spectric School," adding a third poet, Elijah Hay. A prose extract, "The Spectric Intention," was taken from a *New Republic* review by Bynner, when nobody knew of Bynner's role in Spectra. "The theme of a poem," the passage quoted in *Others* begins, "is a spectrum through which all the light there is separates into rays, then recombines or focuses into a certain concentrated point of something or other in the reader's brain." It's the "something or other" that nearly gives the game away, but this was Bynner as reviewer, not Morgan the Spectrist.

The self-reviewing had been bound to occur, because Bynner and Ficke were well-known poets and likely authorities on a new school of verse. Kennerley, who also published the journal *Forum*, engaged both of them to weigh in on the phenomenon. "The Imagists, suicidally advertised by a concerted reciprocal chorus of poet-reviewers, might once have been capable of employing this very theory in a tentative way," they wrote. But "the time is past." Not included in the *Others* quote was Bynner's suggestion in *New Republic* that Spectra "takes a challenging place among current literary impressionistic phenomena." Impressionism, although decades old by that point, had only recently come before the American public at the sensational Armory Show in 1913, so anything seemingly new was deemed Impressionist or Post-Impressionist. Although Cubism was not part of the Armory Show, it was familiar enough to Bynner that he could commend Spectra as being "to poetry what Cubism is to painting."

While the Armory Show was originally planned as a showcase for American art, its organizers made a belated trip to Europe, where they were astounded by hitherto unknown paintings by Van Gogh, Gauguin, Cézanne, Picasso, Matisse, and dozens more. By the time the show opened at the cavernous 69th Infantry Regiment Armory on Lexington Avenue in midtown Manhattan, the American contributions were completely overshadowed by "futurist," "fauvist," "expressionist," and "cubist" works exemplifying the latest European trends. The press had a field day, and cartoonists spoofed the "nuttists," "dope-ists," "topsy-turvists," and "toodle-doodle-ists" on display. Kenyon Cox, deemed an important arbiter of taste at the time, excoriated this "deification of Whim." The latest European art, he declared, was "no longer a matter of sincere fanaticism. These men have seized upon the modern engine of publicity and are making insanity pay." Another pundit, Frank Jewett Mather, Jr., thought the work "essentially epileptic," and said that the experience of attending the exhibit resembled "one's feeling on first visiting a lunatic asylum," acknowledging that its "inmates might well seem more vivid and fascinating than the everyday companions of home and office," just as "a vitriol-throwing suffragette

[is] more exciting than a lady." Confronted by the work of Picasso, Picabia, and Duchamp, Mather was unsure whether it was "a clever hoax or a
negligible pedantry."

The Armory Show traveled to Chicago and Boston. *Poetry* editor Harriet
Monroe found it a salutary lesson in hard knocks. "We are in an anaemic
condition which requires strong medicine, and it will do us good to take it
without kicks and wry faces," she observed. New York lawyer John Quinn,
soon to be a patron of Pound and Eliot, felt vindicated in his purchases of
ultramodern art. "When one leaves this exhibition one goes outside and
sees the lights streaking up and down the tall buildings and watches their
shadows, and feels that the pictures that one has seen inside after all have
some relations to the life and color and rhythm and movement that one sees
outside." What Quinn found salutary was what the genteel public held most
objectionable, preferring art to be a hothouse flower far removed from the
rough-and-tumble of the street.

A mock counterexhibition was mounted under the delectably named
Academy of Misapplied Arts (sponsored by Lighthouse for the Blind).
Behind it was humorist Gelett Burgess, famous for his ditty about a purple
cow and for coining the word "blurb." He came up with a sculptural device
intended "for the elimination of thought in all forms," capable of emitting
"nonsense in three dimensions." Later, in *Burgess Unabridged*, he coined
diabob as the term for "an object of amateur art" with the adjectival form
diabobical, meaning "ugly, while pretending to be beautiful." In a dig at the
Armory Show, Burgess writes:

> And yet, these diabobs, perhaps
>   Are scarcely more *outré*
> Than pictures made by Cubist chaps,
>   Or Futurists, today!

The greatest notoriety of the Armory Show accrued to Marcel Duchamp's
Nude Descending a Staircase, risibly renamed in the press with boundless
appetite, from "Food Descending a Staircase" to "Explosion in a Shingle
Factory." Duchamp arrived in New York two years later and spent much
of the rest of his life there.

With the great hoopla of the Armory Show still in the air, Spectra could
seem like a minor if equally preposterous application of artistic hoodwink to
the literary sphere. In January 1917, students at the University of Wisconsin
premiered a knockoff of Spectra, the school of Ultra-Violet poetry. They
contrasted normal states of consciousness with the new movement. Where

one sees "a tomcat on a back fence and thinks of brickbats and shotguns, which is banality and matter-of-fact prose," the other "sees the same cat and immediately associates it with false teeth and a lawn party in Chicago, which is genius and Ultra-Violet poetry." The next year, two young poets, Malcolm Cowley and S. Foster Damon, invented the poet Earl Roppel and sent his poems to Bynner, who shared them with others, including composer Arthur Farwell who set one poem to music. Roppel was discovered to be another hoax in due time, and his creators went on to long and distinguished careers. Spectra, Ultra-Violet, and Roppel reflect a newfound interest in poetry in America: call it poetry by any means.

Emanuel Morgan made an encore appearance in 1920 in the jaunty little collection *Pins for Wings*. There are caricature sketches of twenty poets scattered throughout, and the text consists of poets tagged in two- or three-line "wings" pinned into place in alphabetical order. So Conrad Aiken is "phosphorescent / plumbing," Stephen Vincent Benét "a pistol / of crystal," and Edgar Lee Masters "a graphophone / in the morgue." The perpetrators of Spectra are included, as are most of the prominent poets of the day. And of course the Imagists, who turn out to be exquisitely susceptible to the treatment.

RICHARD ALDINGTON
an Attic vase
full of tea

F. S. FLINT
the halo
of a street-lamp

H. D.
the Winged Victory
hopping

D. H. LAWRENCE
lovers
eating thistle-pie

EZRA POUND
a book-worm
in tights

CHAPTER FIVE

Pig Cupid

Wyndham Lewis's autobiographical account of the years 1914–1926 encompasses in its title, *Blasting and Bombardiering*, his combative attitude in both war and peace. The war, for him, was neither good nor bad, just "supremely stupid." And with his magazine's big pink cover seeking attention just weeks before the guns of August turned the world upside down, he found "a bigger *Blast* than mine had rather taken the wind out of my sails." Before he was called up, Lewis had been known as "the ringleader of 'les jeunes'" with "a personality *and* a BRAIN." While in the military, Lewis found it disconcerting when art came up for discussion, like the time he was approached by a senior officer who pulled him aside to ask, "What is all this Futurism about?" Pound offered to send a recent book of his to the officer.

It was a ticklish time for combatants and civilians alike. With the war effort providing a united front against an enemy, how would domestic affairs prove themselves of worth? Culture, viewed from the trenches, seemed pointless. Back in London, Pound persisted in his commitment to modernizing the arts. It had started with *Poetry* in Chicago. During the war he took on editorial commitments to *The Egoist* in London, and the American vanguard journal *The Little Review*. H. L. Mencken hired him as a talent scout for *The Smart Set*. He edited the two issues of *Blast* with Lewis, and edited the *Catholic Anthology* in 1915, mainly as a way of hustling his latest find, T. S. Eliot, into print. He was a kind of literary switchboard operator, channeling manuscripts hither and yon. Correspondence with the editors of these and other publications was a torrent of advocacy, invective, and flamboyant spelling.

Pound's advocacy resulted in the serialization of Joyce's *Portrait of the Artist as a Young Man* and Lewis's novel *Tarr*, both in the pages of *The Egoist*. Then chapters of Joyce's *Ulysses* began to appear in *The Little Review*, and finally the Irishman's early collection of stories, *Dubliners*, was published. With Joyce, Lewis, and Eliot in hand from his own generation, and the elder Hueffer and Yeats on board, Pound took on the demeanor of the commanding officer of a combat unit. The posture was not original. It was borrowed from the Italian Futurist F. T. Marinetti.

110

The son of a wealthy Italian family, raised in North Africa, Marinetti donned the role of vanguard ringleader and agitator with the sense of entitled ease that others might bring to the boardroom or a diplomatic post. He had the financial means to make things happen (Wyndham Lewis thought Marinetti's resources derived from his father's chain of high-class bordellos in Egypt). In 1909 he bought three and a half columns on the front page of the Paris newspaper *Le Figaro* to print the first manifesto of Futurism. It opens with a zesty account of running his car (he was among the first Europeans to own one) into a ditch, from which he arises reborn as a Futurist. A what? one can hear the idle *boulevardier* sipping his espresso, eyes widening in amazement as Marinetti declares the advent of a new beauty, the beauty of speed. A roaring automobile, he declares, is lovelier than the *Victory of Samothrace*.

He goes on to denounce "moralism, feminism, and every utilitarian or opportunistic cowardice." The rhetoric swells: "We intend to destroy museums, libraries, academies of every sort." To top it off, "We intend to glorify war—the only hygiene of the world." But Marinetti's bravado also reveals his roots in Symbolism, which until 1909 had been his literary mainstay. "We stand on the last promontory of the centuries!" he boasts. "Time and space died yesterday. We already live in the absolute." Only a former Symbolist could speak openly of the absolute.

Although Marinetti was cosmopolitan, and wrote in French, Italy was the target of his efforts. He wanted to shake his fellow Italians out of the complacency that had reduced the nation to little more than a tourist destination. He wanted factories, not relics of ancient Rome. A torrent of invective propelled further manifestos: "Let's Murder the Moonlight!" (1909), "Against Passéist Venice" (1910), "Destruction of Syntax—Radio Imagination—Words-in-Freedom" (1913), "Down with the Tango and Parsifal!" (1914), "The New Religion-Morality of Speed" (1916)—all these and more, well into the thirties. His agitation roused others to join, and they wrote manifestos too, concentrating on technical means by which painting, sculpture, music and sound, cinema, dance, and even clothing could be transformed into Futurist weaponry. He could dismiss Wagner's *Parsifal*, but would have shared the composer's confession that he harbored an "enormous desire to commit acts of artistic terrorism."

Marinetti was described as "a flamboyant personage adorned with diamond rings, gold chains and hundreds of flashing white teeth." Soon he was taking his show on the road. He and a phalanx of Futurists, dressed in tails and top hats, would roar through sleepy towns in their automobiles, horns honking; posters would go up announcing a *serate*, or Futurist evening.

FIG. 5.1. F. T. Marinetti.

At the appointed hour an agitated audience would find itself heckled from the stage with manifestos, free-word poems, noise concerts, and plays that lasted no more than a minute. Marinetti trained himself for maximum delivery and stoic persistence in the onslaught of fruit and vegetables pelting the stage.

After making the rounds of Italy, the Futurist painters waged their campaign in Paris—a somewhat abortive effort, as they were ignorant of the radical tendencies beginning to be exhibited after Picasso's and Braque's expeditionary excursions into the austerities of Cubism. The Futurists had to adjust their program when it was clear their own efforts were tepid by comparison. Meanwhile, Marinetti was embarked on a series of grand tours that took him from Moscow to London and stops between, a mobile piñata and showman extraordinaire.

Despite repeated visits to London (a Futurist city, he informed the English press) from 1910 to 1914, Marinetti was able to recruit only a single English adherent, the painter C.R.W. Nevinson. Nevinson was, with Lewis, a participant in the Rebel Arts Centre. Lewis described the Italian's performance at a favorite venue of the artists, the Cabaret Club at the Cave of the Golden Calf: "Marinetti declaimed some peculiarly blood-thirsty concoctions with great dramatic force." Lewis later found artillery bombardments at the front couldn't compare with Marinetti, whose favored text for these declamations was on the siege of Adrianople in the Italian campaign against Tripoli in 1912.

Edward Marsh, influential promoter of the Georgian poets and private secretary to Winston Churchill, found Marinetti's performances "full of force and fire, with a surprising gift of turgid lucidity, a full and roaring and foaming flood of indubitable half-truths." As an artistic presentation, Marsh decided, it was "about on the level of a very good farm-yard imitation—a supreme music-hall turn." It was not literature, though, "only an aide-mémoire for a mimic." Marsh was nonetheless inspired to attend a costume ball at the Albert Hall "as a Futurist picture designed by Wyndham Lewis!"

After one of his performances, Marinetti exclaimed, "You are a futurist, Lewis!" He insisted he wasn't, even after Marinetti said it didn't really matter, just pretend. But, said Lewis on the subject of the Futurist exaltation of machines, we English have had machines for a hundred years. He thought that the English, if anyone, should take the lead on the subject of modern civilization, not follow in the idolatrous footsteps of parochial Italy. Marinetti was no doubt disappointed not to sign up another recruit.

Prone to ruffling feathers, Lewis shared Marinetti's braggadocio. He even confessed to behaving rudely because it was easier than being polite. Aggressively confronting T. E. Hulme over a woman, Lewis was no match for the stolid Yorkshireman and found himself hung upside down on a park railing. He was tall, dark, and handsome, and had a cavalier way with women. There were children, and more children, and he could be cruelly indifferent to the mothers he abandoned. Lewis, in fact, far more than the Futurists, embodied their declared contempt for women. Despite his behavior, he managed to get several women artists involved with his new movement, Vorticism. Virginia Woolf loathed him but relished gossip about the "Wyndham Lewis pigsty." Pig cupid, cupidinous pug, artist, and sloganeer, Lewis was described by T. S. Eliot as "an orang-outan of genius" combining "the thought of the modern and the energy of the cave-man." As a consequence, Lewis found himself launched as a preening Neanderthal. It may have been his reputation, but Ernest Hemingway recoiled at his looks. "I had never seen a nastier-looking man," he said, describing Lewis's eyes as those of "an unsuccessful rapist."

FIG. 5.2. Wyndham Lewis.   FIG. 5.3. *Blast* (1914).

Lewis later realized "all this organized disturbance was Art behaving as if it were Politics." He was following the lead of Futurism, making a stink about art but in ways more familiar from the muckraking press and political dogfights. Only after several encounters with Prime Minister Asquith did he realize that the politician's interest in Vorticism was in fact a guarded attempt to detect some subversive propaganda effort. "I might almost have been the member of a powerful secret society," Lewis reflected. Meanwhile, the politician would have to puzzle out on his own the slogans printed in big bold type in *Blast*.

WE WHISPER IN YOUR EAR A GREAT SECRET.

LONDON IS <u>NOT</u> A PROVINCIAL TOWN.

Blast was a page-by-page manifestation of its own dictum, "The Art-Instinct is permanently primitive." It was avowedly and unambiguously insulting. Just turning the pages seems to presage a snarl. It was the definitive production of people willing to dishonor themselves in the public eye. Lewis was fine with that. Pound was more naive, and the taint of *Blast* marked the onset of dwindling opportunities in London's literary scene. Lewis and Pound had met long before but hadn't clicked until 1914. In his autobiography Lewis tells of when he and his friends were waiting to meet this "cowboy songster" getting attention in the press. He was rumored to be Jewish. "When Pound appeared I was mildly surprised to see an unmistakable 'nordic blond,' with fierce blue eyes and a reddishly hirsute jaw, thrust out with thoroughly Aryan determination." Lewis was taken aback, then, to learn of others' reaction: "Most of those present felt that he was indeed a Jew, disguised in a tengallon hat."

As Lewis got to know this peculiarly attired poet, "I discovered beneath its skull and cross-bones, intertwined with *fleurs de lys* and spattered with preposterous starspangled oddities, a heart of gold" and a friend for life. He was amazed that Ezra was both "a poet and an impresario, at that time an unexpected combination." And though Lewis could be skeptical of "Ezra's boyscoutery," he was a reliable partner in the cause of Vorticism and those artists to whom he gave unwavering support. These included Jacob Epstein, who had sculpted the extraordinary *Demon-Angel* for the tomb of Oscar Wilde in Père Lachaise cemetery in 1912. In 1915 Epstein exhibited *Rock Drill*, which paired an actual rock drill with a sculpted operator, a cyborg *avant la lettre*. "The whole effect is unutterably loathsome," wrote one critic. For another, "the incongruity between an engine with every detail insistent and a synthetic man is too difficult for the mind to grasp."

Pound visited Epstein's studio with his new friend, French sculptor Henri Gaudier-Brzeska, where they took in the astounding concoction. Pound began to yammer on about it, as was his wont, and Gaudier snapped, "Shut up, you understand nothing!" At issue was the role of the machine. It offended those who saw *Rock Drill* when it was exhibited in 1915, mainly because it was a found industrial object undisguised and used as itself, not symbolic of anything else. But machines were of interest to visual artists, who marveled at the structural integrity of their components. Marcel Duchamp and Fernand Léger were among those who avidly scrutinized industrial showrooms, which led to the chastening reflection that there was little an artist could add to such ingenuities. Pound honored Epstein's creation by naming one installment of his epic Cantos *Rock-Drill*.

Pound was willing to learn, if not from showrooms, in the studios of Lewis, Epstein, and Gaudier-Brzeska. Gaudier sculpted the *Hieratic Head of Ezra Pound*, complying with the poet's suggestion that it have a phallic contour. Much later, Pound wrote extensively on the virtue of machines for the modern imagination, stressing that "modern man can live and should live in his cities and machine shops with the same kind of swing and exuberance that the savage is supposed to have in his forest." He also shrewdly noted, "One can still think about the machine without dragging in the private life and personality of the inventor." Unlike practitioners in the fine arts, "they do not stir one to pathos by reasons extrinsic to their form." This perspective was brought to a fine clarity by Mina Loy in her poem "Brancusi's Golden Bird." Brancusi's masterpiece sparked a legal debate in America as to whether a sculpture should be exempt from import duties if it did not strictly resemble its subject. The poem concludes:

> The immaculate
> conception
> of the inaudible bird
> occurs
> in gorgeous reticence . . .

The ellipsis is Loy's way of suggesting immeasurable vistas.

*

Loy was one of the first female students admitted to Académie Julienne, the famous art school in Paris. She was English, and one of the great beauties of her day. Her mother warned her to stay away from men, but in short order she was engaged. Her husband, Stephen Haweis, was a fellow student, and though a mediocre artist he had social graces that kept him afloat. It was a misalliance from the start. The bride (having recently changed her name from the Jewish-sounding Lowy)—soon discovered herself to be in an "unfounded relationship with a mannikin." Never in love to begin with, she was "united in wedlock to the being on earth whom she least would have chosen," as she put it. Mina found herself becoming "an artificial monument of neurosis erected upon his nothingness." Nonetheless, the marriage persisted. The couple moved to Florence in 1907 and had a son and a daughter. The parents, being artists, consigned them to full-time nanny care. It was not long before Stephen, inspired by Gauguin in Tahiti, left for his own South Seas adventures. Mina, glad to be rid of him, took solace in her friends.

Soon after the couple moved to Florence, they had become frequent guests at the Villa Curonia, a mansion owned by American socialite Mabel Dodge, whose obliging husband (one of many—it could be called serial, but monogamy even during marriage was not to her taste) added a ninety-foot-long salon for her soirees. The couple met Gertrude Stein there, and Stein appreciatively remembered them as among her first readers. Stephen balked at Stein's lack of punctuation, but Stein approvingly observed that Mina "was able to understand without the commas." No doubt she would have been untroubled by Apollinaire's unpunctuated poems in *Alcools*. And when she began publishing her own poems, readers voiced their consternation about Loy's casual way with dots and dashes.

Mabel was so smitten with Stein's "Portrait of Mabel Dodge at Villa Curonia" that she had three hundred copies printed and bound in Florentine wallpaper. Mina found the floral cover delightfully incongruous for a text rich with seeming non sequiturs and sentence fragments. "A sap that is that adaptation is the drinking that is not increasing." "A plank that was dry was not disturbing the smell of burning and altogether there was the best kind of sitting there could never be all the edging that the largest chair was having." But Stein's portrait opens with a misleadingly straightforward sentence, "The days are wonderful and the nights are wonderful and the life is pleasant." This was a milieu of which Mabel reported that "the house is full of pianists, painters, pederasts, prostitutes, and peasants"—homing in on the letter *p*—adding incentive for a return visit by Gertrude: "Great material."

Mabel gave a copy of the pamphlet to her friend Carl Van Vechten, music critic for the *New York Times*. Charmed, he met Stein the next year and became a friend for life, editing *Selected Writings of Gertrude Stein* after her death in 1946. He met Mina Loy in Florence as well, their shared devotion to Stein making for a lasting bond between them. Van Vechten was soon placing Mina's writings in little magazines back in the States, including *The Trend*, which he edited. But it was Mabel who secured Mina's first publication, a poem appearing in *Camera Work*. The journal was edited by the eminent photographer Alfred Stieglitz, who had published Stein's abstract word portraits of Matisse and Picasso in 1912, and the portrait of Mabel Dodge in 1913. When he published Mina Loy's untitled poem beginning "There is no Life or Death," she had only recently taken up writing.

Introducing readers to Mina Loy in *Trend*, Van Vechten characterized her as "in sympathy with the Italian school of Futurists." This was a delicate way of putting it, as Mina was by no means a Futurist, but she was in fact embroiled in passionate affairs with two Futurists, while fending off advances from others. One of her lovers was Giovanni Papini, editor of the important Futurist journal *Lacerba*. Papini characterized his temperament as "like a cinema where the program changes hourly," which may explain Mina's exasperation with him. The second was none other than Marinetti.

Despite the stimulation of Mabel Dodge's salon and visits from Stein and Van Vechten, Mina had fallen into a funk. Listless and anxious at the same time, she was seeing a psychiatrist who emphasized "psycho-synthesis" as a way of addressing the scourge of neurasthenia. For him, neurosis arose not only from suppressed instincts, but also from repression of the sublime. Sublime, life force, jubilation: it was all about recovering joy. The treatment was well timed to coincide with Mina's encounter with Marinetti, who embodied the dynamism he preached. Attending a Futurist evening of manifestos, punchy skits, and recitations of *parole in libertà*, or free-word poems, Mina felt rejuvenated. Marinetti was accompanied by two other prominent Futurists, Carlo Carrà and Ardengo Soffici, when he met Mina. He conspicuously propositioned her, which she supposed was just to impress his colleagues. They kept running into each other, with Mina teasing the impresario of Futurism even as she warmed to him. She wrote Mabel, "He is one of the most satisfying personalities I ever came in contact with."

Mina finally succumbed to Marinetti's petitions, drawn to his ardor while becoming more and more immersed in Futurism. Clarifying the effect he had on her to Van Vechten, she insisted she was not a Futurist, but "you can say that Marinetti influenced me—merely by waking me up." He was the culmination of a long incubation involving "years of hard work—& Marinetti blithe fellow—was sent from heaven to put the finishing touch." She added, incredulously, "& they say he is a brute to women!" This woman, certainly, felt the benefit was all hers. She professed herself forever indebted to the Italian "for twenty years added to my life from mere contact with his exuberant vitality."

Mina Loy was roused by the encounter not only to life but to poetry. Literature as such had not been of particular interest to her—she was a painter and designer, after all. But Gertrude Stein kindled her interest in words. So when the exuberant Marinetti came prowling around her door, awakening a sexuality dormant during her decade with Haweis, she found herself "caught in the machinery of his urgent identification with motor-frenzy." After their affair ended, she was left with gratitude for the memory; but, more importantly, she came into her own as a writer, a vocation to which she had not previously aspired.

What Mina Loy got from Futurism was personal rejuvenation coupled with fearlessness. Many would see her as reckless, even obscene. The Futurists were never thought obscene. Dramatic yes, outrageous certainly, but they were *men*. Mina recognized the double standard and was struck by the realization that her response to Futurism was similar to that of men, not women. Why, she asked Van Vechten, did she respond that way? "Of course being the most female thing extant," she decided, "I'm somewhat masculine." This was more than a decade before Virginia Woolf pondered the man-womanly, woman-manly prospect in *A Room of One's Own*. Being "somewhat masculine" enabled Mina Loy to be explicit about sex, in print, in poetry.

Camera Work was not a literary journal, as its title makes clear. From 1904 to 1917 it was the leading venue for art photography. But Stieglitz had a little gallery, in which Americans had an opportunity to see work by Picasso firsthand in 1911. He evidently recognized Mabel Dodge's assertion that "Gertrude Stein is doing with words what Picasso is doing with paint," and was alert to literary corollaries. The poem he published by Mina Loy is unlike anything anyone else was writing.

> There is no Life or Death,
> Only activity
> And in the absolute
> Is no declivity.
> There is no Love or Lust
> Only propensity
> Who would possess
> Is a nonentity.
> There is no First or Last
> Only equality
> And who would rule
> Joins the majority.
> There is no Space or Time
> Only intensity,
> And tame things
> Have no immensity.

Parsed out line by line, the leading words—*absolute, intensity, immensity*—are the keys she sounds. But the moment also anchors itself in psychological reality: her husband registered as a nonentity in line 8, her Futurist lovers endorsed in the rhyme enabling a "propensity" beyond love or lust. Ending with a derisive gesture to "tame things," Mina claims immensity for herself.

Stieglitz took care not to leave Mina unduly exposed. Her poem is the second half of a double bill. Above it on the page is Katharine Rhoades's "Vision," addressing the "helpless, ecstatic, tearful atoms" stunned into arrest in amorous perplexity, "Held still a moment by a star or spark / And by a trick of time—inverted." Like Mina, she was bent on singular disclosures in the key of immensity. "When shall we demand enough?" she wondered on behalf of all women. "Reach intensity?"

Although the first appearance of Mina's poetry in print was in the April 1914 issue of *Camera Work*, it was preceded in the previous issue by three pages of her "Aphorisms on Futurism." Note that they're *on*, not *by* a purported Futurist. What could readers at the time have made of a text that now strikes us as unambiguously autobiographical? For a woman emerging from the suffocating cocoon of a loveless marriage to a "nonentity," striking sparks off the hot anvil of sexual affairs, the directional signals glow with the dazzle of an award show proscenium right from the outset:

DIE in the Past
Live in the Future.
THE velocity of velocities arrives in starting.

As it goes on, the rhetoric is borrowed from Futurist manifestos, but Mina accurately shaped her punch lines as aphorisms. Nonsequential, with often distractingly random targets, it lacks the consecutive force of a manifesto. Its truth in advertising is in the final line: "—Knick-knacks.—" in which the em dashes prevail, her favorite form of punctuation.

When she declares, "We shout the obscenities, we scream the blasphemies," she's touching on the exhilarating moment when she heard Marinetti specify his adoration of the vagina in a public occasion. Where some heard an obscenity, Mina was enthralled: "He had said one word—distinctly, unaffectedly; & it had crashed down the barriers of prudery. Such primordial pokes of simplicity might re-direct the universe."

Mina Loy put the face of enigma on Futurism, which till then had seemed so obstreperously and obviously a display of pugilistic masculine preening. Destroy the past, demand this, demand that, down with—and so on. Being confrontational and unapologetic about aggression was the modus operandi of Futurism. But what did it mean, and what did it *sound like*, when a woman took the platform? The nearest equivalent was the suffragette. But their slogans were in the news and bore little resemblance to Futurism. "MAY your egotism be so gigantic that you comprise mankind in your self-sympathy," Loy urged. How would the cause of women's suffrage be advanced by this genuflection at the shrine of Max Stirner's influential but *so* nineteenth-century book, *The Ego and Its Own*? In a few years, though, the suffragist periodical *The New Freewoman* would change its name to *The Egoist*, its literary focus guided by Aldington, Pound, and Eliot, while editor Dora Marcus reserved the opening pages of each issue for her Stirner-inspired philosophy.

Loy's Futurist aphorisms honor their Futurist roots with their reproachful demeanor, but they were also introspective. "FORGET that you live in houses, that you may live in yourself—": the conclusive em dash here has the force of an arrow. Will it find its mark? Was she getting restless in her domicile? "TODAY is the crisis in consciousness," Mina proclaimed, so she started looking to New York, the American metropolis emitting tantalizing vapors of modernity—and in which, thanks to Stieglitz, Van Vechten, and Dodge, Mina was already a presence in print.

Mina Loy's originality was evident, but what catapulted her to notoriety was a scandalously explicit poem, innocuously titled "Love Songs," published in the first issue of Alfred Kreymborg's free verse journal *Others* in 1915. The opening section immediately confronts the reader with

Pig Cupid   his rosy snout
Rooting erotic garbage

There was nothing leering about Loy's descriptions of what she tantalizingly named *love*. They were devoid of insinuation, but they were not clinical, either. Poetry took the lead. Her poems are the work of someone who declared, "THE Futurist can live a thousand years in one poem," and thought every aesthetic principle could be crammed into a single line. Her Futurism was short-lived. Later, in the manuscript of her "Aphorisms," Mina replaced "Futurist" and "Futurism" with "Modernist" and "Modernism" as she saw a bigger picture emerging.

The notorious reference to "Pig Cupid" became a minor scandal in American literary circles after its publication. Another of the four "Love Songs" by Mina was more explicitly sexual:

The skin-sack
In which a wanton duality
Packed
All the completions of my infructuous impulses
Something the shape of a man.

Near the end of the sequence the language partakes of an apocalyptic gesture:

Let them clash together
From their incognitoes
In seismic orgasm

It was scandalous enough that poets were now abandoning rhyme, rhythm, and reason (as was often quipped), but thanks to Mina Loy free verse suggested audacities with shocking intimacy.

Others would eventually supplement its title with a clarifying slogan: "The old expressions are with us always and there are always others." Kreymborg kept his faith in Mina, dedicating the entire issue of April 1917 to her work. It was a reprise of "Love Songs," now called "Songs to Joannes," its original four sections expanded to thirty-four, covering eighteen pages. It was the culmination of her enthused pursuit of "a crescendo & transcendo!" Loy's biographer, Carolyn Burke, perceptively sees these love songs as "a peculiar kind of war poetry"—war of the sexes, she means. In fact, Mina was doing hospital work in Florence, attending combat victims, and wrote to Van Vechten, "You have no idea what fallow fields of psychological inspiration there are in human shrieks & screams." Just imagine, she said, what poems she might write if permitted access to a combat zone.

In addition to the magazine, Kreymborg was also issuing annual anthologies under the Others imprint, taking the opportunity to reprint worthy material from other magazines, while including new work as well. These offered prime opportunities for readers to be exposed to ample selections by Mina Loy alongside Marianne Moore, William Carlos Williams, Wallace Stevens, Carl Sandburg, and T. S. Eliot. Mina would not have a book of her poems published until 1923, so in the decade leading up to it, her work was known exclusively through fugitive publications. It was a time when a network of "little magazines" published the most radical, and ultimately the most durable, contemporary writing.

Mina's work came to embody the maladjustments and improprieties that contemporaries attributed to *Others* and to little magazines generally. They were an "unaffiliated group of radicals, mood-jugglers and verbal futurists," judged Louis Untermeyer, a booster of Robert Frost. He singled out Loy's "falsetto radicalism" in particular. Untermeyer contemptuously found her typical of women who "having studied Freud, began to exhibit their inhibitions and learned to misquote Havelock Ellis at a moment's notice."

Mina, however, was hardly "typical" of anything. Futurism had encouraged her to try on for size the grand gesture, the explicit radical endorsement, the titillating insistence. But she added to it a kind of cosmic frankness. "LET the Universe flow into your consciousness, there is no limit to its capacity, nothing that it shall not re-create," she declares in a passage from her "Aphorisms on Futurism," echoing Ralph Waldo Emerson. The Concord transcendentalist had envisioned the poet "suffering the ethereal tides to roll and circulate through him," thereby becoming "caught up into the life of the Universe."

If Marinetti woke Loy up, it was Gertrude Stein who spurred her to write. A decade later, she published a lengthy essay in the *Transatlantic Review* that remains one of the most insightful and zesty treatments of Stein. It reflects the fact that, as Mina admits, "one must in fact go into training to get Gertrude Stein." The essay has as epigraph a poem.

Curie
of the laboratory
of vocabulary
   she crushed
the tonnage
of consciousness
congealed to phrases
   to extract
a radium of the word

This forceful analogy places Stein at the forefront of literary revelation and honors another woman inventor.

Mina was disposed to a cosmological outlook, confessing to a friend, "What I feel now are feminine politics, but in a cosmic way that may not fit in anywhere." But she recognized in Stein a phenomenon that transcended anything as socially pliable as gender. Reading Stein, she wrote, "I was connected up with the very pulse of duration." Her "continuous present" was nothing less than "the plastic static of the ultimate presence of an entity." To read her work was "to track intellection back to the embryo."

Mina discovered, and celebrated, that thin partition between profundity and simplicity. Stein was not a writer who expected of readers a formidable background in the classics. It's hard to imagine a body of writing less susceptible to being footnoted. Mina called it "a literature reduced to a basic significance that could be conveyed to a man on Mars." Yet she also knew it had affinities with Cubism, which Apollinaire had presumptively compared to the fourth dimension. For Mina, equally intent on evoking some superlative enigma, it was an "intercepted cinema of suggestion."

So where did the simplicity come in? "It is the variety of her mental processes that gives such fresh significance to her words," Mina wrote of Stein, "as if she had got them out of bed early in the morning and washed them in the sun." To be precise, she "scrubbed the meshed messes of traditional associations off them." Others availed themselves of similar analogies.

William Carlos Williams welcomed Stein's ability "to work smashing every connotation that words have had, in order to get them back clean." H. D.'s novel *Bid Me to Live* characterizes a writer "brooding over each word, as if to hatch it." Like Stein, "she wanted the shape, the feel of it, the character of it, as if it had been freshly minted." Novelist Sherwood Anderson saw in Stein an old-fashioned, down-home earth mother, "one who cares for the hand-made goodies and scorns the factory-made foods." Laura Riding, following Loy's lead, observed that "none of the words Miss Stein uses have ever had any experience. They are no older than her use of them," resulting in "pure, ultimate obviousness." Mina went so far as to compare Stein's work to the book of Job.

Readers even today would balk at the idea of anything obvious in Stein. Yet Stein is not a literary but a painterly writer. After all, Picasso was a fast friend from 1905 to the end of her life, and she followed him through his blue and pink periods, into Cubism, out into the neoclassicism of the twenties, and beyond. She described her own work in terms of comparable phases of applied study. Refraining from using words as signposts to extralinguistic phenomena, Stein applied them like patches from a color palette. The challenge for a reader is to apprehend the newly convened ensemble on the page as an emergent pattern, not a semantic program.

Practitioners of an art commonly begin as imitators, however unintentionally. Poets often disavow early work as derivative. Mina Loy's advantage is that she wasn't a writer. As a painter, she was disposed to recognize that Stein was doing what Picasso did, handling words in a "process of disintegration and reintegration." Add, subtract; precipitate and transform—these were the prerogatives of someone working a canvas. So when Mina started writing poems, she was not inclined to imitate Stein's voice, or style. After all, she had things to say, but thanks to Stein she saw that conventional expressions were a constant danger. Words had to be applied with exactitude.

Consider a basic precept of writing, the language in which it is written. To what tribe did Mina Loy belong? When she started writing, she had lived in Germany, France, and Italy for over a dozen years. Her tongue plied the native languages accordingly. Much later she told her son-in-law she subsisted in "a subconscious muddle of foreign languages" and was somewhat doubtful about whether (or where) English fit in. So she was "aiming at pure language." "I was trying to make a foreign language— Because English had already been used by *some* other people."

Loy's language can make English speakers doubt their competence in their native tongue when encountering the "eclosion" of an ego and "cymophanous sweat" in the "Love Songs," an "immediate agamogenesis" in "Lion's

Jaws," or "the carnose horologe of the ego" in "Die Blinde Junge." Real words or neologisms? Loy's reference to an "Etiolate body" dips into grammatical error, as the adjectival form should be *etiolated*. But she has a penchant for this formulation, as in "the theoretic elastic of your conceptions"—not *theoretical*—"Her eliminate flesh of fashion," "the inebriate regret," the "Diurnally variegate," and for elevating a potential adjective to a noun, "raw caverns of the Increate."

There's a parade of neologisms, some of which seem to be probes for words she can't quite locate, like "pornographist" for pornographer, or "elusion" for elision. There are wonderful inventions, like "flabbergastism," the "Omniprevalent Dimension" in "The Dead," and the "gong / of polished hyperaesthesia" prompted by "Brancusi's Golden Bird." The enticed reader will have a steady diet of plausible adjectives (*acolytian, satyric, incontrite, innubile, inconsummate, loquent, insentient, fluctuant*) and nouns (*incommensuration*). In "Apology of Genius," onomatopoeia agreeably swallows the neologism in "pulverous pastures of poverty." Evocative verb forms may also be absorbed ("Street lights footle in our ocular darkness," "jibber at each other," "Accoupling / of the masculine and feminine"), along with plausible adverbs ("quotidienly passed through," "flapped friezily"). All these mutations reflect Mina's outlook: "Poetry is prose bewitched, a music made of visual thoughts, the sound of an idea."

The persistence of such semantic peculiarities enhances the tone of Loy's poems. They are saturated with inventiveness, like the "broiling shadows" in "The Black Virginity," the "ilix aisles" in her poem on Poe, and the tawdry "shampooed gigolos" who "prowl to the sobbing taboos" in "The Widow's Jazz." Encountering the "bed-ridden monopoly of a moment" in one of the "Love Songs," or "the heinous absurdity / Of your street-corner smile," we're in the presence of a sharply focused satirical gaze. She delivers this heady language peremptorily and absolutely. "Our eyelashes polish stars" and "We splinter into Wholes" (in "The Dead").

A clue to Mina Loy's fertilization of the word is the way she squeezes proper names into anagrams. So she herself becomes Imna Oly, Nima Loy, and Anim Yol. Her lovers Marinetti and Papini are pretzeled into Raminetti and Bapini. Her affair with Papini undergoes a marquee makeover:

The Effectual Marriage

or

THE INSIPID NARRATIVE

of

GINA AND MIOVANNI

Finally, the famous Italian playboy author Gabriel D'Annunzio gets a five-page portrait as Danriel Gabrunzio.

*

Ezra Pound and T. S. Eliot would acclaim Mina Loy's work when it appeared in Alfred Kreymborg's anthology *Others* in 1917. From the vantage of London, though, they were unaware of her earlier publications in America. Thanks to the notoriety of her poems in cutting-edge magazines, Mina Loy's reputation preceded her arrival in New York in 1916. For a Sunday paper, Mina's friend Djuna Barnes profiled the milieu of a fashionable Greenwich Village bohemia with "yellow candles pouring their hot wax over things in ivory and things in jade":

> Incense curling up from a jar; Japanese prints on the wall. A touch of purple here, a gold screen there, a black carpet, a curtain of silver, a tapestry thrown carelessly down, a copy of *Rogue* on a low table open at Mina Loy's poem. A flower in a vase, with three paint brushes; an edition of Oscar Wilde, soiled by socialistic thumbs. A box of cigarettes, a few painted fans, choice wines.

Rogue was a modest but lively publication advertising itself as the "cigarette of literature," and "the new little journal de fun." Its pages offered a peculiar mix of fashion advice, avant-garde poetry, sketches in the style of Aubrey Beardsley, and other features resembling those of *Vanity Fair* but without its ads for the trendy set. It was a way station between the decadent nineties and the approaching roar of the twenties.

It makes sense that Mina was at the heart of it, even while living far afield in Italy. The links are instructive, and they can be traced back to Harvard. *Rogue* was financed by Harvard alumnus Walter Conrad Arensberg, a Harvard classmate of its editor, poet Allen Norton. Another classmate was Wallace Stevens, an insurance lawyer who also published poems in *Rogue*. They would not have encountered T. S. Eliot at Harvard, since they were about a decade older. Nor would they have met Carl Van Vechten there, who was of their generation but was a midwesterner who attended the University of Chicago. But Van Vechten, a columnist for the *New York Times* since 1909, was a member of their circle.

As editor of the final three issues of *The Trend*, Van Vechten published several of Loy's poems, including "Parturition," an extraordinary vision of childbirth as "lascivious revelation." He published his own article on "How to

Read Gertrude Stein." His advice: read her out loud, as she "drops repeated words upon your brain with the effect of Chopin's B Minor Prelude." This observation reflects his vocation as music and dance critic for the *Times*. It was through him that Stein's first book was published in America.

Tender Buttons was issued by Claire Marie Press in New York in 1914. This was a most unlikely alliance, as the press was dedicated to its publisher's affinity for the aestheticist primping of the nineties. Donald Evans, the publisher, was a poet and close friend of Allen Norton, the two of them known as "patagonians" thanks to Evans's collection *Sonnets from the Patagonian* (1914). Mabel Dodge urgently sought to dissuade Stein from being associated with Evans: "It would be a pity to publish with him *if* it will emphasize the idea in the opinion of the public, that there is something degenerate & effete & decadent about the whole of the cubist movement which they *all* connect you with." That Stein went ahead with Claire Marie anyway suggests that she thought it absurd that anyone would link Cubism with the weary aura of fin de siècle.

Now, with poems in *Trend* and *Rogue*, Loy could appear to be a denizen of New York, an association enhanced with the explosive appearance of "Love Poems" in *Others* in July 1915. It was Arensberg who bankrolled Alfred Kreymborg's magazine, though he withdrew from any public association with it before it appeared, as he was redirecting his attentions thanks to the arrival of French artist Marcel Duchamp, who knew no English and was in dire need of support. For some time he lived in the Arensbergs' apartment, until Walter rented a studio for him.

Duchamp was already a celebrity in America, thanks to the notoriety of his painting *Nude Descending a Staircase* in the legendary Armory Show in 1913 that had introduced the country to Impressionist and Post-Impressionist art from Europe. Duchamp's nude garnered the most attention, with its Futurist dabbling in simulated motion modeled on chronophotography. Reporters were beside themselves, devoting column space to this supposed "nude" nobody could make out. "Food Descending a Staircase," spoofed one. "The Rude Descending a Staircase (Rush Hour at the Subway)," chortled another. (When *Life* magazine profiled Duchamp in 1952, his offer to pose nude on a stairway was politely declined.)

By the time he arrived in New York in June 1915, Duchamp was on the verge of abandoning painting altogether. His studio was little more than a room to house objects he picked up, assigning them quizzical titles, like *In Advance of the Broken Arm* for a snow shovel. He busied himself learning English, while teaching French to starstruck young women. Beatrice Wood, who met him in 1916, recalled: "We immediately fell for each other.

Which doesn't mean a thing because I think anybody who met Duchamp fell for him."

In old age, asked what had been most satisfying in his life, Duchamp replied, "Having been lucky." Once he came to New York he was like the golden child who wanders unscathed through a labyrinth of perils, impervious to hazards and radiating a glow of immunity. But this seemingly innocent spirit harbored a dark, nihilistic core. He had above all a need to stay calm by doing as little as possible. He acknowledged that he was "enormously lazy. I like living, breathing, better than working."

With Duchamp in place as a resident deity, Walter and Louise Arensberg's apartment became the hub of lively social gatherings of artists and writers. Regulars included the composer Edgard Varèse, the Cubist painter Albert Gleizes and his wife, Juliette Roche (who documented the milieu in some strikingly original placard poems), the Dada artist Francis Picabia, American artists Man Ray, Charles Sheeler, Charles Demuth, and Clara Tice, and poets Wallace Stevens, Alfred Kreymborg, and William Carlos Williams, among others. It was the perfect setting to welcome Mina Loy to the New York arts world.

She lost little time in getting into the thick of things. In February 1917 she was profiled in the *Evening Sun* as exemplifying the "modern woman." At the same time, preparations were underway for an enormous exhibition sponsored by the newly formed Society of Independent Artists, with Arensberg and Duchamp leading the hanging committee. Mina had an entry in the show, but the exhibit became more famous for what it excluded than for the thousands of works exhibited by more than a thousand artists. The rules were clear: anyone paying an entry fee could be in the show, yet the hanging committee voted to exclude a piece of industrial porcelain. Duchamp promptly resigned. In fact, as a few others knew, it was he who had purchased a urinal and signed "R. Mutt 1917" on its rim. The phone number provided as contact was actually that of Louise Norton, editor, with her husband, of *Rogue*.

After its rejection from the Independent exhibit, Duchamp took the fabled object to Alfred Stieglitz's gallery, where it was photographed in front of a painting by Marsden Hartley. The photo appeared in the second issue of *The Blind Man*, a little magazine with contributions by Mina Loy in both of its issues. Beatrice Wood contributed the anonymous account, "The Richard Mutt Case," accompanying the photograph. Objecting to charges of obscenity, she pointed out that the offending object was on view "every day in plumbers' show windows." Concerning the charge of "plagiarism" or unoriginality, she fired back: "Whether Mr. Mutt with his

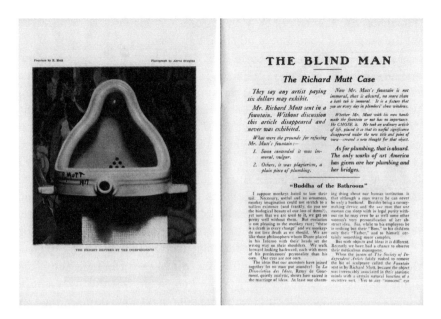

FIG. 5.4. Profile of Marcel Duchamp's *Fountain* in *The Blind Man*, no. 2 (May 1917).

own hands made the fountain or not has no importance. He CHOSE it."
She was, in effect, announcing the advent of conceptualism in art. The
artist ("Mutt"), by giving it a title and presenting it in an unfamiliar angle,
"created a new thought for that object." Finally, in a larger font in bold
italic type, the riposte concluded with a zinger aimed at the charge that it
was merely a piece of plumbing:

*As for plumbing, that is absurd.
The only works of art America
has given are her plumbing and
her bridges.*

This episode earned New York a place in the honor roll of cities that
accommodated Dada, the others being in varying degrees Zurich, Berlin,
Cologne, Hannover, and Paris. Duchamp and Man Ray moved to Paris
in 1920 and were there during the subsequent shenanigans in which Dada
thrived, tottered, and dissolved, giving way to Surrealism in 1924. Dada
learned brashness from Futurism but went far beyond Vorticism in originality.

Though as the *Fountain* of R. Mutt suggests, "originality" is an odd word for the sleights of hand and mind favored by Dada.

Another legendary episode in New York Dada involves Swiss-born Arthur Cravan (pseudonym of Fabian Lloyd), who had recently achieved notoriety by boxing heavyweight champion Jack Johnson, lasting six rounds before being knocked out. In Paris he had edited an incendiary magazine, *Maintenant* (Now), incurring the ire of Apollinaire among others for his calculated insults of artists. Arriving in New York in January 1916, he was welcomed by Duchamp and Picabia, who arranged for Cravan to deliver a lecture on modern art. He was so drunk for the occasion that he started to disrobe while shouting obscenities. The police intervened before he could achieve full exposure. "What a wonderful lecture," Duchamp appreciatively remarked.

There would be no point in mentioning Cravan here except for the fact that, after rebuffing unwelcome advances, Mina Loy fell for him. She felt an affinity for his undeniable vitality, while recognizing the frail inner core of a fellow neurasthenic. "Je suis brute à me donner un coup de poing dans les dents et subtil jusqu' à la neurasthénie," Cravan said (I'm enough of a brute to knock my teeth in and subtle as a neurasthenic). They fled to Mexico (he was avoiding military conscription), where hard times and poverty did little to damp their ardor. They planned to continue the journey down to Argentina, and to that end Cravan set sail, leaving a pregnant Mina behind. He was never heard from again.

She continued on to Buenos Aires, hoping for news of Cravan, and busied herself writing a curious little treatise titled "Auto-Facial Construction," urging prospective clients of her method to "become masters of their facial destiny." As if reflecting on the way Cravan's death or disappearance might affect her own peerless looks, she wondered, "To what end is our experience of life if deprived of a fitting esthetic revelation in our faces?" The previous year, while she and Cravan were together, Mina had composed another treatise, "International Psycho-Democracy." "Put yourself at your own disposal," it declared, proposing that the Psycho-Democratic movement "advocates the fulfillment of all Desire."

In the end, pregnancy compelled her return to England, where she gave birth to a daughter before rejoining her other children in Florence. She'd not seen them in three years. There was a period in Berlin, then a return to New York, before she settled in Paris from 1923 to 1937. During the years in Paris she was in her element among the avant-garde, as is evident in a group photo at the Jockey Club including Ezra Pound, Man Ray, and Jean Cocteau, among others (see figure 11.1). Her only collection of poetry, its title misspelled as *Lunar Baedecker*, was published in France in 1923. She wrote more poetry, designed fanciful clothing and furniture, and moved back to New York in 1937. She never forgot Cravan. He puts in an appearance in "The Widow's Jazz." In a club where "impish musics / crumble the ecstatic loaf," suddenly, the man known among his peers as The Colossus is at hand.

Cravan
colossal absentee
the substitute dark
rolls to the incandescent memory

of love's survivor
on this rich suttee

seared by the flames of sound
the windowed urn

holds impotently
your murdered laughter

Husband
how secretly you cuckold me with death

CHAPTER SIX

Enter Eliot

Ezra Pound's relation with William Butler Yeats developed into a fast friendship after their first meeting in 1909, and the elder Irishman was appreciative of the American he considered a "solitary volcano." He acknowledged Pound's obstreperousness and behavioral quirks. "He is a headlong ragged nature, is always hurting people's feelings, but he has I think some genius and great good will," Yeats recognized, comparing him to Hercules, who "cannot help seeming a little more than life size." Richard Aldington had a theory about it: Ezra had read Whistler's *Gentle Art of Making Enemies*, but "practiced it without the 'gentle.'" He even used Yeats's analogy: "In 1912 Ezra was great fun, a small but persistent volcano in the dim levels of London literary society."

For three consecutive winters beginning in 1913, Pound served as private secretary to Yeats at Stone Cottage, near Ashdown Forest in Sussex, south of London. His role was to handle correspondence and read to the eminent "eagle" after dark. Yeats respected what Ezra brought to poetry: "He helps me to get back to the definite and the concrete away from modern abstractions. To talk over a poem with him is like getting you to put a sentence into dialect. All becomes clear and natural."

The second winter Ezra was accompanied by Dorothy, his new bride. Yeats thought "her face was made out of Dresden China. I look at her in perpetual wonder. It is so hard to believe she is real; & yet she spends all her daylight hours drawing the most monstrous cubist pictures." Both men relished the companionship, sharing enthusiasms, fencing for exercise, and absorbed in their own work. For Ezra, these literary forays away from London took him far afield, to China and Japan.

F. S. Flint had perceptively observed that the poems of Pound's *Canzoni* were not translations but read as if they were. In 1914, striving to hone his skills as a self-proclaimed Imagist, Ezra looked beyond familiar European repertoire for models. In the February 1915 issue of *Poetry* he ventured, "It is possible that this century may find a new Greece in China." He had tinkered with examples of ancient Chinese poetry in Herbert Giles's *History of Chinese Literature* (1901). He was also familiar with *Le livre de jade* (1867, revised edition 1902) by Judith Gautier, translated before she became Richard Wagner's final heartthrob. It was her French renderings, translated again by Hans Bethge into German, that Gustav Mahler set to such heartbreaking music in *Das Lied von der Erde* (Song of the Earth) after the death of his four-year-old daughter in 1907.

A few of Pound's Imagist adaptations made their way into *Lustra* (published in 1916, but mostly completed in 1913), where "Ts'ai Chi'h" immediately preceded "In a Station of the Metro":

> The petals fall in the fountain,
>   the orange-colored rose-leaves,
> Their ochre clings to the stone.

Although this is an invention, not a translation, it was derived from his increasing immersion in Chinese poetry of the T'ang dynasty.

By the time it was published, *Lustra* was augmented by "Cathay," previously published by Elkin Mathews as a pamphlet in 1915. *Lustra* added a few more poems to the sequence. The 1915 pamphlet bore a lengthy identification of authorship on the title page. Although Pound was under the

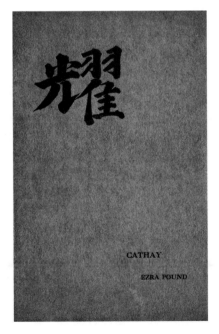

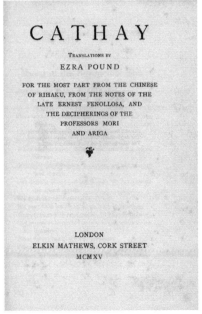

FIG. 6.1. Cover of Ezra Pound's *Cathay* (1915).   FIG. 6.2. Title page of Ezra Pound's *Cathay*.

impression that these were translations, there was more than met his eye at the time.

Ernest Fenollosa, Harvard grad, had gone to Japan at the age of twenty-five in 1878, immersing himself in Japanese art and culture. He helped found the Tokyo School of Fine Arts as well as the Tokyo Imperial Museum, and spent the rest of his life shuttling back and forth between Japan and the United States. He died in 1908, and in 1913 his widow identified Pound as the most suitable recipient of a trunk full of her husband's literary papers. He spent the rest of his life absorbing this windfall. It was not until November 1914, however, that he got started, reporting to his parents from Stone Cottage that he had "busted into" Fenollosa's notes and spent ten days relishing the contents.

Cathay's twenty-seven pages include fourteen poems (one with explanatory footnote), and two editorial statements. "Rihaku flourished in the eighth century of our era. The Anglo-Saxon Seafarer is of about this period. The other poems from the Chinese are earlier." But there is no poet named Rihaku. Pound got the name from Fenollosa's notes, which were dictated by Japanese tutors. Rihaku is better known by his Chinese name, Li Po. The Anglo-Saxon poem is mentioned because Pound included his translation of "The Seafarer," which had originally appeared in *The New Age* in 1911 in the first installment of "I Gather the Limbs of Osiris." The note explains the apparent anomaly of an Anglo-Saxon poem in a collection of Chinese lyrics.

The second note acknowledged "the personal hatred in which I am held by many," predicting that "the *invidia* which is directed against me because I have dared openly to declare my belief in certain young artists, will be brought to bear first on the flaws of such translation, and will then be merged into depreciation of the whole book of translations." Despite his expectations, it was well received. For Ford Madox Hueffer, *Cathay* was "like a door in a wall, opened suddenly upon fields of an extreme beauty, and upon a landscape made real by the intensity of human emotions."

Now, after a century of translations and scholarship, the intensity invested in landscape is a familiar feature of classical Chinese poetry, in which it is the figurative counterpart for human emotion. (T. S. Eliot would call it the "objective correlative," but without reference to Chinese poetry.) "Lament of the Frontier Guard" opens, "By the North Gate, the wind blows full of sand, / Lonely from the beginning of time until now!" "Poem by the Bridge at Ten-Shin" begins with an even more prolonged evocation:

March has come to the bridge head,
Peach boughs and apricot boughs hang over a thousand gates,
At morning there are flowers to cut the heart,
And evening drives them on the eastward-flowing waters.
Petals are on the gone waters and on the going . . .

The landscapes often involve exile and reports of distant war. *Cathay* was a fitting collection for 1915, with much of France being laid waste. And for those at the front, as for those at home, "There is no end of things in the heart."

In his introduction to Pound's *Selected Poems*, Eliot characterized him as "the inventor of Chinese poetry for our time." This is the opening of a long paragraph on mystifications of and assumptions about translation. It ends with Eliot suggesting that for future generations "it will be called (and justly) a 'magnificent specimen of XXth Century poetry' rather than a 'translation.'" The reason, he pointed out, was that "Pound's translation is interesting also because it is a phase in the development of Pound's poetry." Eliot regarded the fruit of translation for a poet to be "finding himself through the original."

It was clear this was Pound's China, not China per se. There were unavoidable errors. One of the translations actually consisted of two different poems in Chinese. Fenollosa's manuscript was a multilingual ping-pong in which Mori Kainan, a Japanese author of *kanshi* (poems in the style of old Chinese) provided oral glosses on the originals, while Ariga Nagao (adviser to the Japanese prime minister, and author of books in French, English, and Japanese) helped convey the information to Fenollosa, who scribbled notes in a kind of rapid trance. "If Pound's translations are in many respects mistaken," a scholar notes, "they are among the most generative mistakes in world literary history."

Pound translated from numerous languages during his lifetime, and has long been recognized as a great translator, not least because of "generative mistakes." As he learned from *Cathay*, any foreign source can prompt unanticipated originality. His next major venture along these lines was "Homage to Sextus Propertius," a long sequence consisting largely—and loosely—of translations from the Roman poet. Scholars howled (there was even an anachronistic reference to a Frigidaire), but Pound found that a translation can be a diving board, and the acrobatics of bounce and dive lend configurations of their own. With Propertius, he might as well have gleaned the results from informants, like an ethnographer doing fieldwork.

"I don't think I have consciously paid *any* attention to grammar anywhere in the 'Homage,'" he confessed. "Rendering is purely ideographic, i.e. whole thing rendered into Chinese and then into English." He was seeing thought forms, not words.

In two millennia, Latin had gone from being a living language to being a linguistic hobbyhorse in the classroom. Pound went in search of a living language. Propertius's "Nunc mihi, siqua tenes, ab origine dicere prima / Incipe: suspensis auribus ista bibam" became, in Pound's "Homage," "Out with it, tell it to me, all of it, from the beginning, / I guzzle with outstretched ears." The standard Loeb prose translation—"Now set forth thy tale to me from the first beginning, if thou rememberest aught; I will listen with eager ears"—sounds much like the early Pound of *Personae*. He recalled the eminent poet Robert Bridges who "carefully went through *Personae* and *Exultations* and commended every archaism (to my horror), exclaiming 'We'll git 'em all back.'"

As for translation, "My job was to bring a dead man to life, to present a living figure." Given that he had included references in the poem to Wordsworth and Yeats, Pound was incredulous that a Chicago professor (consulted by Harriet Monroe, who reluctantly published four of the sections in *Poetry* in 1919) accused him of mistranslating Propertius. Thomas Hardy kindly suggested that it be called "Propertius Soliloquizes" on the model of Browning, who was always ventriloquizing historical figures. Pound thought "Homage" a sufficient indication of what he was up to. The charges continued to nag him. In 1931 he figured, "I may perhaps avoid charges of further mystification and willful obscurity by saying that it presents certain emotions as vital to me in 1917, faced with the infinite and ineffable imbecility of the British Empire, as they were to Propertius some centuries earlier, when faced with the infinite and ineffable imbecility of the Roman Empire."

Speaking to the present through a mask, as the Propertius affair revealed, could be risky. In *Umbra* (1920), a selection from previous books, Pound provided a key to his "Personae and Portraits"—those being the categories to which most of his poems belonged. There were "Personae," historical figures donned as the speaker in a poem; "Sketches" of social types; "Etudes," which evoked the historical milieu of those treated in personae and sketches; and finally "Major Personae," the collective subjects of major poetic treatment, including Propertius and the poems of *Cathay*.

Two appraisals of Pound's practice are worth noting. Wyndham Lewis observed that "when he can get into the skin of somebody else, of power and renown, a Propertius or an Arnaut Daniel, he becomes a lion or a lynx on the spot." A similar assessment suggests a liability: "Pound has always to wear a costume, to enact some role proposed to him by other minds." Some element of volition is lacking, Paul Rosenfeld suggests here. Lewis saw this as well, even calling his friend an "intellectual eunuch." "He is never happy if he is not sniffing the dust and glitter of *action* kicked up by other, more natively 'active,' men." This would shortly be rectified by the appearance of someone Pound instantly recognized as a living person he was willing to back, like the personae he'd adopted for his poems.

*

After getting his bachelor's degree from Harvard in 1910, Thomas Stearns Eliot immediately commenced graduate studies in philosophy, starting with a year in Paris where he attended the legendary lectures of Henri Bergson at the Sorbonne. Back at Harvard the next year, he continued his studies, did a little acting, took dancing lessons, and wrote poetry. He returned to Europe in 1914 on a traveling scholarship. The day before his classes were scheduled to begin at the University of Marburg, war was declared, and a few weeks later Eliot found himself at Oxford.

He was on a professional track to become a philosophy professor, but poetry haunted him, not that he had much to show for it. While still in Germany he had sent some aborted pages to his Harvard friend Conrad Aiken—a reference to "Impatient tireless undirected feet" discloses his predicament and hopes—but already in September he was regretting it. "The stuff I sent you is not good," he wrote. "If only I could get back to Paris," he thought, maybe the juices would flow again.

The letter was dated September 30, 1914, and on that same day Ezra Pound wrote with enthusiasm to Harriet Monroe, "I was jolly well right about Eliot. He has sent in the best poem I have yet had or seen from an American. PRAY GOD IT BE NOT A SINGLE A UNIQUE SUCCESS." Tom had met Ezra ten days earlier, at Aiken's urging. The poem that got Ezra worked up was "The Love Song of J. Alfred Prufrock," begun while Tom was an undergraduate in 1909 and completed two years later. In his letter to Aiken of September 30, he lamented, "The devil of it is that I have done nothing good since J. A. P and writhe in impotence."

For Ezra, "Prufrock" was galvanizing, and Eliot was just the poet he was waiting for. "He is the only American I know of who has made what I can call adequate preparation for writing. He has actually trained himself and modernized himself *on his own.* . . . It is such a comfort to meet a man and not have to tell him to wash his face, wipe his feet, and remember the date

(1914) on the calendar." And how did Ezra strike Tom? "Pound is rather intelligent as a talker," he wrote Aiken, while "his verse is well-meaning but touchingly incompetent."

Monroe found the poem by Ezra's new protégé perplexing, and it took a good bit of coaxing to get her to print it in *Poetry*. (It had previously been rebuffed by London poet and publisher Harold Monro when Aiken pressed it on him.) There was certainly nothing like it. The reader is immediately immersed in a quaintly morbid atmosphere with its famous opening invitation.

> Let us go then, you and I,
> When the evening is spread out against the sky
> Like a patient etherised upon a table;
> Let us go, through certain half-deserted streets,
> The muttering retreats
> Of restless nights in one-night cheap hotels
> And sawdust restaurants with oyster-shells:
> Streets that follow like a tedious argument
> Of insidious intent
> To lead you to an overwhelming question . . .

(The ellipsis is in the poem.) The rhymes, being irregular, provide an insinuating insistence obscured by the variable meter. They help disguise a sudden transition between walking the *streets* and the *retreats* of lodging and food. It's like the transition in a dream: you start to go, then you're already there.

The images and scenarios of the poem are gradually infiltrated by a series of questions that are patently risible: "Do I dare / Disturb the universe?" "Do I dare to eat a peach?" These are interspersed with cautionary disavowals, "That is not what I meant, at all." Such tepid starts and stops reveal an embarrassed megalomania ("I am not Prince Hamlet," yet the speaker toys with the role of Lazarus returning from the dead). There are also the women coming and going while talking of Michelangelo, and the alluring mermaids at the end ("I do not think that they will sing to me"). This febrile mind that has "measured out my life with coffee spoons" is rendered with indelible futility.

Love song? The poem defiles the very notion, yet its adolescent equivocations are a reminder that love is confusing, desire disconcerting, and a happy outcome by no means assured. "I have seen the eternal Footman hold my coat, and snicker," we read in one arresting line, "And in short, I was afraid." The footman is a nod to Eliot's inspiration, French Symbolist poet Jules Laforgue, "one of those who come into the world with a ray of moonlight in their brains," remarked one of his peers.

Modern verse, dispensing with poetry's "privileges" to forge its own goal, is (in an observation by Arthur Symons) "a very self-conscious ideal, becoming artificial through its extreme naturalness; for in poetry it is not 'natural' to say things quite so much in the manner of the moment." This is the kind of moment disclosed by Prufrock's predicament:

> . . . when I am formulated, sprawling on a pin,
> When I am pinned and wriggling on the wall,
> Then how should I begin
> To spit out all the butt-ends of my days and ways?

"Prufrock" did not appear in print until the June 1915 issue of *Poetry*, serendipitously coinciding with Tom's marriage.

It was an impetuous affair. In March he had met Vivien Haigh-Wood at a garden party on the grounds of Oxford's Magdalen College. Mainly looking for a good time, he was struck by Vivien as a type rather than an individual: "charmingly sophisticated (even 'disillusioned') without being hardened." A few weeks after the wedding he wrote his Harvard professors to inform them of his marriage and to discontinue his graduate studies. To one he wrote, "Our marriage was hastened by events connected with the war," repeating the sentence to another with the verb changed to "accelerated." By January, Tom would write Aiken, he had "*lived* through material for a score of long poems, in the last six months."

A factor in this accelerated betrothal was the death of Jean Verdenal in combat on May 2. Verdenal was Tom's closest friend during his year in Paris. When he traveled to Italy and Germany in the summer of 1911, Verdenal wrote urging him to hear Wagner's music in Munich. He was in the throes of having just attended *Götterdämmerung*, which he found "sans doute un des points les plus hauts où l'homme se soit élevé"—undoubtedly one of the pinnacles of humanity. In another letter he anticipated *Tristan and Isolde* would flatten you with ecstasy ("vous laissent aplati d'extase"). The fourth section of *The Waste Land*, "Death by Water," is Tom's sweetly evanescent farewell to his departed companion ("once handsome and tall as you").

Taking a wife after the death of a close friend may have been a consolation, but Tom was evidently aware that such an impetuous alliance might be taken amiss. A scant month after the wedding he boarded an ocean liner to return to the States for a family visit. Vivien stayed behind for fear of the German torpedoes that made transatlantic crossings hazardous. The night before embarking he left a letter with Vivien to send his father in the event of his death. He asked that any inheritance be passed on to his wife. "I owe her everything," he explained. "I have married her on nothing, and she knew it and was willing, for my sake. She had nothing to gain by marrying me." What he didn't say is that this impetuous alliance was a clumsy attempt to solve the dilemma of being still a virgin at twenty-eight.

A precipitating factor in the marriage was Eliot's innocence. Near the end of his life he reflected that "I was very immature for my age, very timid, very inexperienced." On New Year's Eve, 1914, as if fortifying himself for a plunge into waters uncharted by Prufrock, he wrote Aiken about his quandary. "I have been going through one of those nervous sexual attacks which I suffer from when alone in a city." The visible presence of prostitutes in big cities exerted a constant pressure. A dedicated reader of Baudelaire, he had a heightened awareness of sexual temptations in the French metropolis. That demimonde was the world of *Bubu of Montparnasse* by Charles-Louis Philippe, which Eliot read during his first sojourn in Paris in 1910. It's a book, he recounted decades later, that remained for him "a symbol of the Paris of that time."

Tom confessed to Aiken, "I should be better off, I sometimes think, if I had disposed of my virginity and shyness several years ago: and indeed I still think sometimes that it would be well to do so before marriage." His outings on the dance floor where he met Vivien are evidence of his resolve. Short of prostitution, after all, social contact is a necessary prelude to erotic opportunity. By all accounts he was a good dancer. As an American, he found the English style of dancing stiff and old-fashioned, and "I terrified one poor girl," he informed his cousin Eleanor, "by starting to dip in my one-step."

Tom relished his role as American in a college debate at Oxford in 1914, when (writing a relative) he informed the English "how much they owed to Amurrican culchur in the drayma (including the movies), in music, in the cocktail, and in the dance. And see, said I, what we the few Americans here are losing while we are bending our energies toward your uplift." The great irony, he added, was that "we the outposts of progress are compelled to remain in ignorance of the fox trot," the latest dance craze back in his homeland.

Vivien struck most people as lively and attractive, while also being an odd match for Tom. Aldous Huxley was enthused to find "such a genuine person, vulgar, but with no attempt to conceal her vulgarity." Writing Lady

FIG. 6.3. Vivien Eliot (1930).

Ottoline Morrell after visiting the couple, he concluded that "it is almost entirely a sexual nexus between Eliot and her: one sees it in the way he looks at her—she's an incarnate provocation." Others remarked on her flirtatious nature as well. Ottoline characterized Vivien as "the 'spoilt kitten'-type, very second-rate and ultra feminine, playful and naïve."

At the time Tom met Vivien, she was with her friend Lucy Thayer, a cousin of Scofield Thayer, who had been Tom's classmate at Milton Academy and at Harvard. Unbeknownst to him, Thayer had been keen on Vivien for some time. They corresponded frequently, and Thayer's biographer characterizes Vivien's letters as "filled with a strange mix of flirtatiousness, condescension, wheedling, demanding, begging, and boasting." When Tom was back in America shortly after the wedding, he got a reproachful letter from Thayer, who felt blindsided by the precipitous nuptials. Tom replied, "You had never given me the impression that your interest in the lady was exclusive—or indeed in the slightest degree a pursuit; and as you did not give *her* this impression, I presumed that I had wounded your vanity rather than thwarted your passion." Thayer was touchy, but duplicitous. Reflecting on his relations with Vivien, "I might have had a breach of promise suit as it was if it hadn't been for Eliot stepping into the breach."

A year later Thayer was back in the States where he married Elaine Orr. His friend Estlin (E. E.) Cummings wrote a jubilant "Epithalamion" for the couple, who honeymooned in California, horseback riding, swimming, and reading Henry James to each other. Back in New York, Thayer suddenly decided Elaine was "banal" and set her up in a separate apartment, embarking on a series of erotic escapades. "I felt after E.O. the need to be in my sexual life messy because of my overlong virginity," a plight he shared with Eliot, who refrained from the escapades. Thayer's tastes inclined to increasingly younger women, with a penchant for "girls with arms as thin as sulphur matches; arms that can be broken between forefinger and thumb." As for Elaine, she and Cummings fell in love and had a daughter in 1919, though they separated not long after. In 1920 Thayer became co-owner and editor of *The Dial* (where we'll encounter him again in the next chapter), faithfully promoting Cummings's poems and drawings from the beginning.

Osbert Sitwell, a longtime friend of the poet, characterized the Eliot marriage as "an ambiance permeated with tragedy, tinged with comedy, and exhaling at times an air of mystification." Over the years, Sitwell was close witness to the predatory drama performed by the pair in public. There has been much speculation about the misalliance, but eyewitness accounts convey more about the psychological atmosphere than any physical details. Bertrand Russell, the philosopher, had a front-row seat. He had taught a term at Harvard where Tom was his student. After dining with the newlyweds in July, he confided in a letter regarding the bride, "I expected her to be terrible, from his mysteriousness; but she was not so bad. She is light, a little vulgar, adventurous, full of life," in striking contrast to Tom, whom

Russell found "exquisite and listless; she says she married him to stimulate him, but finds she can't do it." He concluded she would soon tire of him. He guessed correctly that she would be susceptible to stimulation outside the marriage.

In short order Russell became a patron of the Eliots, perceiving that their "pseudo-honeymoon" had been "a ghastly failure." Settled back in London, the pair found themselves in financially precarious circumstances. He helped them out with loans, and from September 1915 to the following March he put them up in his London flat. Much of the time Tom was away, teaching grammar school, and Russell's intimacy with Vivien had no practical obstacles. In January they even went away together on holiday.

Through all this, Russell was writing to his mistress Ottoline Morrell about the affair: "I want to give her some other outlet than destroying him." Ottoline was understandably dubious, warning that he risked his reputation. "Anyhow I don't think it would *help her* and help towards making the joint Eliot life happier to let her fall in love with you." For his part, Russell dedicated himself to "helping" her—while helping himself in the process—and it went on for much of 1916. Ottoline was exasperated. "I don't really understand her influence over him," she wrote in her diary. "It seems odd that such a frivolous, silly little woman should affect him so much, and she looks up to him as a rich god, for he lavishes presents on her of silk underclothes and all sorts of silly things and pays for her dancing lessons. It takes all his money."

By November 1915 Russell had grown quite fond of Tom and found him admirably devoted to his wife, who exhibited "impulses of cruelty to him from time to time. It is a Dostojevsky type of cruelty, not a straightforward everyday kind." Russell was both repulsed and fascinated by Vivien. "She is a person who lives on a knife-edge, and will end as a criminal or a saint," he decided. "She has a perfect capacity for both." Russell was off on both counts, which in any case point to her mental instability. It's intriguing that Evelyn Waugh registered a rumor in his diary as late as 1955 that "Mrs T. S. Eliot's insanity sprang from her seduction and desertion by Bertrand Russell."

It's improbable that Eliot didn't know of Russell's affair with his wife. It had started during Tom's American trip a month after the wedding. Vivien wrote somewhat coyly to Scofield Thayer that it was "unwise perhaps to leave so attractive a wife alone and to her own devices!" Vivien could hardly conceal her glee when she went on to inform him she was popular with Tom's friends: "No less a person than Bertrand Russell!!! He is all over me, is Bertie, and I simply love him."

Ottoline Morrell's assessment of the situation reflected her own claim on the philosopher, which went back to 1911. She also knew he was a Lothario, with his sequential affairs. In the end, that's what drew his attentions away from Mrs. Eliot when the next one came along. The affair was omitted from his *Autobiography*. Instead, he wrote of the Eliots, "I was fond of them both, and endeavored to help them in their troubles until I discovered that their troubles were what they enjoyed." While this glosses over his own role in the "troubles," it's an astute observation about the bond of misery Tom and Vivien shared—a "crucible of dysfunction" as her biographer put it. Irish writer Elizabeth Bowen saw them as "two highly nervous people shut up in grinding proximity."

At the heart of the crucible was Vivien's health. She had suffered from tuberculosis of the bone as a child, and medical issues of various sorts continued to plague her. In August 1916 Tom wrote apologetically to Aiken that his correspondence had fallen off owing to his wife's ill health during much of the past year: "It has been nerves, complicated by physical ailments, and induced largely by the most acute neuralgia." Vivien herself was more clinical: "The headaches are called hemicranial migraine, and they are really 'nerve storms' affecting one whole side of me—they make me sick and feverish and they always last 15–24 hours."

Tom's correspondence was taken up with chronicling these episodes, which were increasingly interwoven with his own bouts of fatigue and nerves. No sooner would one of them be up than the other was down. It went on for years, despite which Vivien kept Tom's literary aspirations in view. His abandonment of graduate study distressed his family. "I have absolute faith in his Philosophy, but not in the *vers libres*," his mother complained. (Bowing to family pressure, he submitted his master's thesis early in 1916.) Russell corresponded with her, and the best thing about Vivien's influence on Tom, he reported, was that "he is no longer attracted by the people who call themselves 'vorticists.'" Whether Russell believed this or not, it was patently untrue.

The second issue of the Vorticist journal *Blast*, with Eliot's "Preludes" and "Rhapsody on a Windy Night," was published in July 1915. Mindful of the incendiary inaugural issue of *Blast*, he had offered Lewis some of the ribald verses he'd shared with Aiken. But Lewis demurred, telling Pound he had a "naif determination to have no words ending in -Uck, -Unt, and -Ugger." In fact, this "war issue" of *Blast* was notably less aggressive than its predecessor. Even the columns of "Blast" and "Bless" were reduced to two pages (birth control was blasted, war babies blessed). Suddenly, with "Prufrock" and three other poems out in *Poetry*, two strong ones in *Blast*, and another in the American *Others*, all in the span of a few months, Eliot was someone to watch.

Pound put together *Catholic Anthology 1914–1915*, primarily as a way to get more of Eliot before the public eye. It was greeted with indignation. If "the unmetrical, incoherent banalities of these literary 'Cubists' were to triumph, the State of Poetry would be threatened with anarchy," warned one critic. It included "Prufrock," "Portrait of a Lady," and three shorter poems by Eliot (Yeats, Masters, Sandburg, and Williams were among the others included). Ezra was doing all he could to promote Tom's reputation, short of writing poems for him.

Once *Prufrock and Other Observations* appeared in 1917 (quietly subsidized by Pound), Eliot's focus turned to consolidating his reputation as a critic. As he informed his mother in early 1919, "everyone knows that anything I do write is good. I can influence London opinion and English literature in a better way. I am known to be disinterested." This was a bit of a stretch, as he was certainly known as an ally of Pound, Lewis, and Joyce, regarded by many as literary hooligans. Still, it was plausible to claim that "there is a small and select public which regards me as the best living critic, as well as the best living poet, in England." Whether or not he convinced his mother, he was trying hard to convince himself.

Eliot had an initial exposure to being an outsider when he was sent to Milton Academy in New England for his last year of high school in 1905. He grew up in St. Louis, in a neighborhood then giving way to a Black middle class. At the academy he found himself (employing the argot of his time)

> an American who wasn't an American, because he was born in the South and went to school in New England as a small boy [*sic*: he was seventeen] with a nigger drawl, but who wasn't a southerner in the South because his people were northerners in a border state and looked down on all southerners and Virginians, and who so was never anything anywhere and who therefore felt himself to be more a Frenchman than an American and more an Englishman than a Frenchman.

Eliot was a real nowhere man, determined to achieve the improbable as an American arbiter of English taste. In the process, he would eventually have larger ambitions. "It is the final perfection," he wrote, "the consummation of an American to become, not an Englishman, but a European— something which no born European, no person of any European nationality, can become."

FIG. 6.4. T. S. Eliot and Virginia Woolf.

A key factor in consolidating Eliot's cultural authority was access to the Bloomsbury group, which was anathema to his associates. Thanks to Russell, he was introduced to this exclusive circle of cultural sophisticates. The most important contact proved to be Virginia Woolf. Their first meeting was in November 1918, when Virginia found "a polished, cultivated, elaborate young American, talking so slow, that each word seems to have special finish allotted it." He had strong views, which she respected. She reported to Roger Fry, "We've been having that strange young man Eliot to dinner. His sentences take such an enormous time to spread themselves out that we didn't get very far; but we did reach Ezra Pound and Wyndham Lewis." She hadn't met either of them, and while she admitted she hadn't read Pound at all, her "conviction of his humbug is unalterable." Pound, for his part, distrusted the "Bloomsbuggars," known for their easygoing homosexuality.

Virginia decided she had an aversion to Americans. "The more I see of that race the more I thank God for my British blood, which does at any rate preserve one from wearing 3 waistcoats; enamel buttons on one's over-coat, and keeping one's eyes perpetually shut—like Ezra Pound." As for Tom, she flinched at his tendency to pounce on her figures of speech and demolish them. "But at my time of life," she complained to Fry, "I begin to resent inhibitions to intercourse; and these poor damned Americans so respect them."

Because Virginia liked his poems, she persisted in getting to know this strangely reticent creature. She and her husband, Leonard, decided that Eliot would be one of the first authors of their new Hogarth Press, an enter-prise intended in part as therapy for Virginia, whose periodic breakdowns punctuated her life. Tom was mindful of the fact that he and Leonard bore the custodial weight of sick wives. "We know what constant illness is," he told Leonard, "and I think very few people do." Virginia thought Vivien "a washed out, elderly & worn looking little woman"—an odd character-ization of a thirty-year-old (by a woman approaching forty). It's possible that Virginia's mental trials gave her an instinctive aversion to someone with similar struggles. She never warmed to Vivien, and later cruelly character-ized her as a bag of ferrets around Tom's neck.

Eliot's own mood swings were noted by many who knew him, even if they didn't know anything of his actual neuroses. Aldous Huxley, for instance, on first meeting Tom in 1916, found him "overwhelmingly cul-tured" yet somehow expressing his enthusiasm for French literature "in the most uninspired fashion imaginable." A year later he observed Eliot was "as haggard and ill-looking as usual." But in late 1918 he found him "very remarkable. Also very charming." In the end, as Huxley told Ottoline Mor-rell, "Eliot has created a character for himself—a sort of wooden artificial armor." Ottoline called him The Undertaker, wondering "Where does his queer neurasthenic poetry come from?" Like many others, she was stumped by his way of speaking slowly and tried French to free him up. But despite his impeccable command of the language, it was no use.

Virginia's friendship with Tom developed despite his reserve. "Pale, marmoreal Eliot" she called him, with a "sepulchral voice." "A mouth twisted & shut; not a single line free & easy; all caught, pressed, inhibited; but great driving power some where—& my word what concentration of the eye when he argues." He could be intimidating, and it was only in late 1921 that Virginia confided to her diary, "I am disappointed to find that I am no longer afraid of him." Yet she continued to find him "sardonic, guarded, precise, & slightly malevolent, as usual."

There was always a hint of snobbery in Virginia's estimations of people (Joyce she took to be a typically vulgar plebe). But Tom struck her as inscrutable. "He is a consistent specimen of his type, which is opposed to ours," she decided after he came for an overnight visit in 1920, though that didn't mean "unacceptable." She continued to observe and speculate about "the sinister & pedagogic Tom." He could be "peevish, plaintive, egotistical," she thought. Mindful of his penurious circumstances, she decided, "What it amounts to is that poverty is unbecoming. He nibbles at cherries." His contradictory nature was unavoidable: "He elaborates & complicates, makes one feel that he dreads life as a cat dreads water. But if I hint so much he is all claws."

Perhaps the most accurate of Virginia's many assessments of her friend was in early 1923, after the extraordinary impact of *The Waste Land*. She wished that "poor dear Tom had more spunk in him, less need to let drop by drop of his agonized perplexities fall ever so finely through pure cambric. One waits; sympathizes, but it is dreary work. He is like a person about to break down—infinitely scrupulous, tautologous, & cautious." Maybe he was Prufrock after all.

T. S. Eliot was undoubtedly a *persona*. Writing his brother in July 1919, he contrasted the English to slaphappy Americans, whom he found appalling. He also mentioned "some notoriety" connected with a small book "some friends of mine" had recently published, namely, the Woolfs' Hogarth Press *Poems*, a slim presentation of thirteen pages. Three of the seven poems were in French, written in an effort to break the impasse that had slowed his poetic output to a trickle.

As early as 1916, a year after the marriage, Tom confessed to his brother his inability to produce any new poetry. "I often feel that 'J.A.P.'"—meaning "Prufrock"—"is a swan-song but I never mention the fact because Vivien is so exceedingly anxious that I shall equal it, and would be bitterly disappointed if I did not." She was much absorbed with Tom's artistic potential, and he correctly surmised that it would be a blow to her as well as to himself if he failed to live up to it.

Prufrock and Other Observations consolidated his reputation as a poet in the summer of 1917. At thirty pages it was a modest production, cheaply printed, but it accomplished two things. It impressed other poets, and in conservative quarters (where most of the reviews came from) it bordered on the scandalous. "His 'poems' will hardly be read by many with enjoyment," the *Times Literary Supplement* imperiously scoffed. At best, an anonymous reviewer in *Literary World* acknowledged the poems were "interesting experiments in the bizarre and violent." *Prufrock* set Eliot up as a man to watch. But the years ticked by with decreasing prospects of a follow-up.

The strain of Eliot's domestic situation, combined with the ongoing challenge of making a living and sustaining a behavioral front, remained the great obstacle to the production of poetry. The poems Eliot published in 1915 were four or more years old. In October 1915 he had four short poems published in *Poetry*, all written earlier in the year. Two more from 1915 appeared in *Poetry* in September 1916 under the general heading "Observations," along with two earlier ones from 1909 and 1911. So he was scraping the barrel, and writing almost no poetry. Only eleven poems were completed from 1916 to 1918, all short, most in quatrains. The two longest barely exceeded forty lines.

Two sets of four poems in *The Little Review* in July 1917 and September 1918, and three more in other little magazines in 1919, were barely enough to keep his name as a poet before the public. That year he wrote "Gerontion," a return to the old mode and mood of "Prufrock" and "Preludes." And that was it. The well had run dry, and in the lead-up to "The Waste Land" Eliot produced nothing of note, publishing no poetry at all in 1920 and 1921.

A testament to the pressures inhibiting his production of poetry is the sheer quantity of prose he was churning out to pay the bills and maintain the level of presentability Vivien expected. In the first four years of his marriage he produced over seventy book reviews and some twenty articles. The pace slowed in 1920–1921, with few reviews but with another fifteen articles. He had transitioned from the grunt work of reviewing to the more prestigious role of critic, directing his energies to the production of *The Sacred Wood: Essays on Poetry and Criticism*, published in 1920.

With his literary ambitions in mind, and making the best of his meager output, Eliot realized that modest but impeccable publications were consequential (it's a mark of his exactitude that, once published, his poems were never revised). Scarcity proved to be a formidable advantage. The print runs of *Prufrock* (500 copies) and the Hogarth *Poems* (fewer than 250) ensured that only a select cadre of readers would see them. This association with

THE LOVE SONG OF J. ALFRED PRUFROCK

S'io credesse che mia risposta fosse
A persona che mai tornasse al mondo,
Questa fiamma staria senza più scosse.
Ma perciocche giammai di questo fondo
Non torno vivo alcun, s'i'odo il vero,
Senza tema d'infamia ti rispondo.

 ET us go then, you and I,
When the evening is spread out against the sky
Like a patient etherized upon a table ;
Let us go, through certain half-deserted streets,
The muttering retreats

Of restless nights in one-night cheap hotels
And sawdust restaurants with oyster-shells :
Streets that follow like a tedious argument
Of insidious intent
To lead you to an overwhelming question . . . .
Oh, do not ask, "What is it ?"
Let us go and make our visit.

In the room the women come and go
Talking of Michelangelo.

The yellow fog that rubs its back upon the window-
    panes,
The yellow smoke that rubs its muzzle on the
    window-panes,
Licked its tongue into the corners of the evening,
Lingered upon the pools that stand in drains,
Let fall upon its back the soot that falls from
    chimneys,
Slipped by the terrace, made a sudden leap,
And seeing that it was a soft October night,
Curled once about the house, and fell asleep.

E   33

FIG. 6.5. Page from T. S. Eliot's *Ara Vos Prec* (1920).

coterie publishers was enhanced by the more deluxe *Ara Vos Prec*, issued
by John Rodker's Ovid Press in 1920 (264 copies).

Most of the work in *Ara Vos Prec* and *Poems* broke with the precedent
of *vers libre* in *Prufrock*, as if to reproach critics who ventured that the
earlier volume had consisted not of poems but of "observations." Rhymed
quatrains were the rule, with corkscrew syntax openly taunting readers.
That wasn't all. The poems were riddled with arcane vocabulary. "Mr. Eliot's Sunday Morning Service" opens with "Polyphiloprogenitive" and
soon moves on to "Superfetation of το εν," Greek for *the One*. Young men

appear, "Clutching piaculative pence." Other poems offer up "Defunctive music," "anfractuous rocks," a "maculate giraffe," and "phthisic hand," compared to which the straightforward "protozoic slime" is a relief.* Such gambits with the dictionary inspired the composer Virgil Thomson to quip in a couplet, "between the idea & the creation / falls the shadow of his education."

An anonymous reviewer of the Hogarth pamphlet may have known something of Eliot's domestic plight, or had at least gleaned some sense of his personality, warning that he was "fatally handicapping himself with his own inhibitions; he is in danger of becoming silly." Another hazard was "writing nothing at all, but merely thinking of all the poems he has refused to write." Eliot was in fact thinking of a poem he was unable to write.

New York publisher Alfred Knopf expressed interest in doing a commercial collection of Eliot's poems. Having read *Prufrock* with "immense enjoyment," Knopf confessed that "I do not know whether it is great poetry or not. I do know that it is great fun and I like it. I surely hope that he writes some more of it so that we can make a book of him." For a while, Eliot dutifully tried to assemble a book combining poems and prose, but it didn't take. Meanwhile, Knopf published his monograph *Ezra Pound, His Metric and His Poetry* that year, albeit anonymously owing to his friendship with Pound. It was only in 1920 that Knopf issued the plainly titled *Poems*, which, like *Ara Vos Prec*, combined the contents of *Prufrock* with a dozen later poems.

Ara Vos Prec and the Knopf *Poems* garnered substantial reviews on both sides of the Atlantic. The antecedent of Laforgue was often noted, prompting Aldington's wry observation, "When the syllables 'T. S. Eliot' are pronounced, the reply 'Laforgue' is elicited as invariably as an automatic machine produces a very small piece of chocolate when pressed with a penny." Aldington wrote the most positive review. He was tartly acidic in his dismissal of certain protestations. "Mr. Eliot's English poetry is often attacked as incomprehensible and heartless, which is simply another way of saying that it is subtle and not sentimental," he observed. "His desire for perfection is misrepresented as puritan and joyless, whereas it is plain he discriminates in order to increase his enjoyment."

---

* *Polyphiloprogenitive* means very prolific; *superfetation* refers to the formation of a second fetus in an already impregnated womb; *piaculative* means expiatory; *defunctive* means dying; *anfractuous* is winding, maze-like; *maculate* is the opposite of *immaculate*; and *phthisic* means tubercular (pronounced *tisic*). These only begin to scratch the surface of helpful glosses. In the annotated scholarly edition of Eliot's poems, twenty-two pages of *Poems* are accorded eighty pages of commentary.

American poet Babette Deutsch was another avid supporter of Eliot's "Weird and Brilliant Book." She was one of the few who mentioned that the contents of *Prufrock* were included in the new title(s), characterizing the more recent poems as just "a few additions." She took them to be "intellectual curios," but "fortified by a dictionary, an encyclopedia, an imagination, and a martyr's spirit, even these may be enjoyed." For her, "Prufrock" and "Portrait of a Lady" were the highlights, as they were for many. Eliot, reading such reviews, may have winced at the thought that his prize specimens were now a decade old.

He might also have found it disconcerting that his recent work was characterized as "documents that would find sympathetic readers in the waiting-room of a private sanatorium." The irascible Louis Untermeyer, champion of Robert Frost, remained dubious of Eliot and thought the rhymed quatrains were in a "vein that tempts him most—and is his undoing." A majority of the poems in the book, in his estimation, "attain no higher eminence than [being] extraordinarily clever." Untermeyer derogated Eliot's work as being little more than "a species of mordant light verse." Even an approving reviewer, American poet Mark Van Doren, made Eliot out to be a meritorious buffoon: "He is now the uncanniest clown, the devoutest monkey, the most picturesque ironist; and aesthetically considered, he is one of the profoundest symbolists." Being called a "symbolist" in 1920 was a backhanded compliment.

The most intriguing response was by Clive Bell, Bloomsbury writer and Virginia Woolf's brother-in-law. He took the extraordinary step of comparing Eliot with Igor Stravinsky, then at a pinnacle of musical fame. "Mr. Eliot is about the best of our living poets, and like Stravinsky, he is as much a product of the Jazz movement as so good an artist can be of any." Jazz movement? It was a double entendre, given Bell's title, "Plus de Jazz"—a phrase from the Parisian circle of Jean Cocteau, who had embraced the music at the end of the war but declared *no more jazz* in 1921. Bell recognized that there was an affinity interconnecting jazz (and ragtime) syncopation, *vers libre*, and the motor rhythms of Stravinsky. The jazz movement "has given us a ragtime literature which flouts traditional rhythms and sequences and grammar and logic." He also found it in Joyce, and recommended the "jazz poetry" of Cocteau, Blaise Cendrars, and Dada artist Francis Picabia.

Rodker's edition of *Ara Vos Prec* is one of a number of fine press publications of the vanguard. The Ovid Press published the drawings of Gaudier-Brzeska, Wyndham Lewis, and Edward Wadsworth, as well as poetry titles by Rodker, Pound, and Eliot. His enterprise culminated with

Joyce's *Ulysses*, "published for The Egoist Press, London, by John Rodker, Paris, 1922." The Parisian coordinates of these robust small presses were plentiful. They included Robert McAlmon's Contact Editions, Caresse Crosby's Black Sun Press, and Nancy Cunard's Hours Press. In London there was the Hogarth Press, and in Majorca the Seizin Press of Robert Graves and Laura Riding. These presses produced a remarkable amount of now-canonical modernism: *Lunar Baedecker* by Mina Loy, *Spring and All* by William Carlos Williams, *Three Stories and Ten Poems* by Ernest Hemingway, Gertrude Stein's *The Making of Americans*, Hart Crane's *The Bridge* with Walker Evans's photographs; plus titles by H. D., Mary Butts, Nathanael West, Kay Boyle, D. H. Lawrence, William Faulkner, Ezra Pound, and others.

Eliot seems an unlikely participant in the coterie side of publishing, and *Ara Vos Prec* was the exception. He did not have the aestheticist leanings of Wallace Stevens, an insurance executive and closet dandy, who was delighted to have limited editions of several poems by Cummington Press (*Notes Toward a Supreme Fiction* in 1942 and *Esthétique du Mal* in 1945), as well as the Gotham Book Mart's *A Primitive Like an Orb* illustrated by German Surrealist Kurt Seligman in 1948. But, little as it's known, Eliot had a sustained collaboration with illustrators, many by his American friend in London, McKnight Kauffer. These were in Faber's "Ariel Poems" series: *Journey of the Magi* (1927), *A Song for Simeon* (1928), *Animula* (1929), *Marina* (1930), *Triumphal March* (1931), and after a couple decades *The Cultivation of Christmas Trees* (1954). In a draft sketch for *Marina*, Kauffer depicted a Tiresius figure writing "DATTA DAMYADHVA DAMYATA" from *The Waste Land* on his/her torso.

Pound was the most notable beneficiary of coterie publishing, which he welcomed because his commercial opportunities were dwindling during the war. The earliest venture along these lines was *Certain Noble Plays of Japan*, derived from the Fenollosa manuscripts, published by Cuala Press in Dublin. Cuala was started by Yeats's sister in 1908, and a majority of its titles were by the Irish poet and others associated with the Irish Literary Revival. Pound's was relevant in that his Noh translations reinvigorated Yeats's interest in writing verse drama.

Pound was further motivated to steer clear of commercial publishers because of his frustrations with *Lustra*. Elkin Mathews was concerned about potential censorship of several poems, and ended up producing an edition of two hundred intact copies for private circulation in 1916 and a regular print run with nine poems omitted. The American edition by Knopf

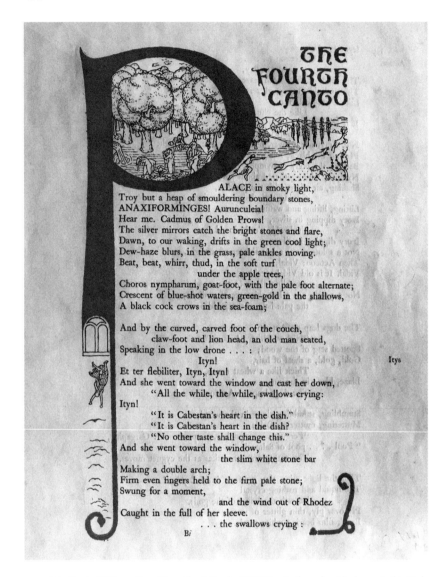

FIG. 6.6. Canto IV from Ezra Pound's *A Draft of XVI Cantos* (1925) with decorated initials by Henry Strater.

in 1917 added more poems, including "Three Cantos of a Poem of Some Length," in early versions.

The Egoist Press published *Quiva Pauper Amavi* (Love on the dole) in 1919 with a tipped-in color frontispiece of Picasso's *Boy Leading a Horse* (1907–1908), albeit not credited in the book. Its contents were the major sequences Pound worked on during the war: "Langue d'Oc," the contemporary social satires of "Moeurs Contemporaines," the three Cantos from the American *Lustra*, and "Homage to Sextus Propertius." Minus the Cantos, the contents appeared in *Poems 1918–1921* in America, a commercial edition by Boni and Liveright to which was added "Hugh Selwyn Mauberley."

Early installments of the Cantos received the most spectacular treatment of any book of modern verse in English. William Bird printed *A Draft of XVI Cantos* for Three Mountains Press on Îsle Saint-Louis in Paris in 1925. Fewer than a hundred copies were produced of this portfolio-sized volume. Each Canto has a large black and red illustrated initial letter. The design format was continued in *A Draft of the Cantos 17–27* by John Rodker in 1928, also in a tiny print run. There's something about the antiquarian format—along with the generous type size and layout—that allows the poems to ventilate and appear more welcoming than in other compressed printings. As Pound readily acknowledged while writing them, the Cantos grew more impenetrable with each installment—"too too too abstruse and obscure for human consumption." Reading them requires commitment and time, of course, but entering into their enigmatic atmosphere is paramount.

Hugh Selwyn Mauberley appeared in a limited edition by Ovid Press in 1920: two hundred copies, with square Vorticist decorated initials by Edward Wadsworth for each poem. The sequence, Pound said, was "an attempt to condense the James novel." It was his farewell to London after he'd struggled for years to elevate literary standards. "I'm no more Mauberley than Eliot is Prufrock," he insisted. But the sequence does begin with "E. P. Ode pour l'Election de son Sepulchre":

> For three years, out of key with his time,
> He strove to resuscitate the dead art
> Of poetry; to maintain 'the sublime'
> In the old sense.

The difference is in the years: Mauberley's three to Ezra's fourteen.

To call it a farewell poem is misleading, for it's just as much a reckoning with dismissal.

> Non-esteem of self-styled 'his betters'
> Leading, as he well knew
> To his final
> Exclusion from the world of letters.

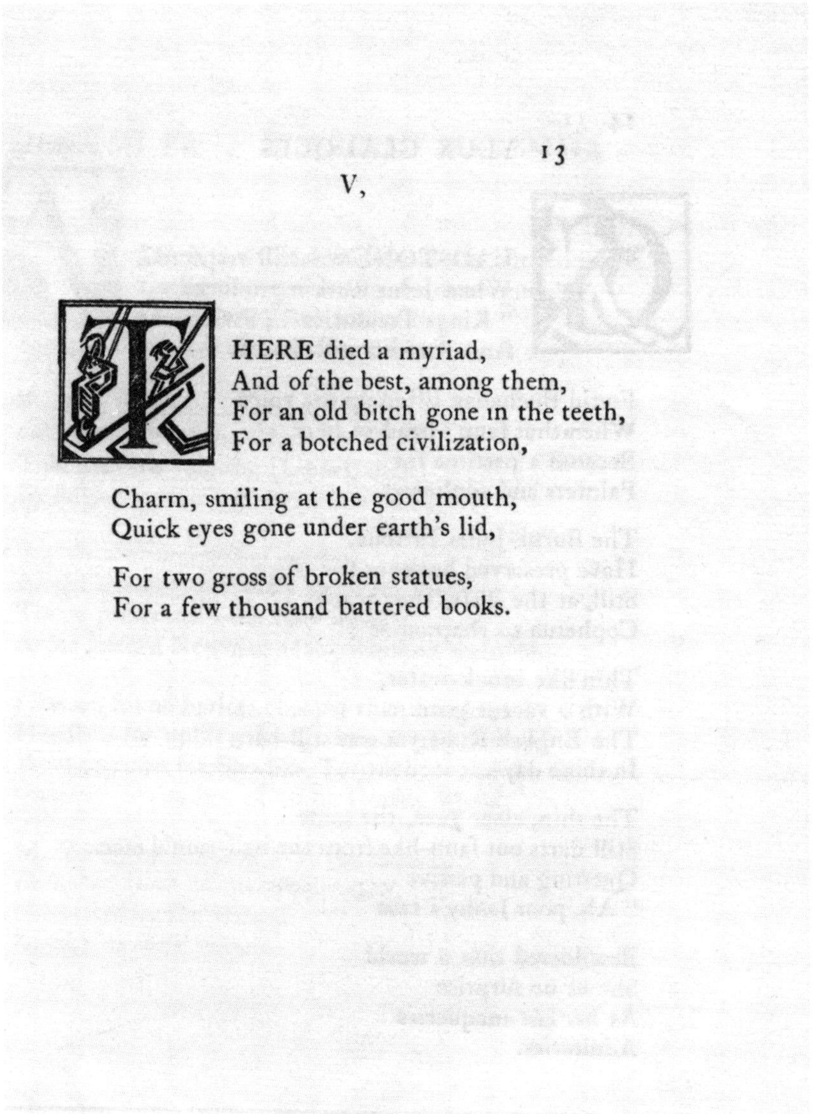

13

V,

HERE died a myriad,
And of the best, among them,
For an old bitch gone in the teeth,
For a botched civilization,

Charm, smiling at the good mouth,
Quick eyes gone under earth's lid,

For two gross of broken statues,
For a few thousand battered books.

FIG. 6.7. Page from Ezra Pound's *Hugh Selwyn Mauberley* (1920).

It's not as if he hadn't been warned. "Mr. Nixon" is a portrait of one of the "betters" in the literary market, who confides to the younger Mauberley/E. P. "I never mentioned a man but with the view / Of selling my own works." He then tenders the advice "give up verse, my boy, / There's nothing in it." Passages like this justify the stark lines "The age demanded an image / Of its accelerated grimace."

Aldington, as an Englishman, was acutely aware of the menace of figures like Mr. Nixon. During the war he suggested Eliot as a suitable subject for an article. The editor objected: "Eliot's a wild man." Around the same time another editor solicited a profile of one of the younger writers. Aldington listed Joyce, Eliot, Lawrence, Huxley, H. D., and Proust, only to be met with exasperation: "For God's sake, Richard, can't you think of somebody who has been heard of or is ever likely to be heard of?" In this environment, Pound's irascibility was simply "Ezra's form of defense against a none too considerate world. I should say Ezra has had to put up with far worse annoyances from other people than they ever have from him."

"Mauberley" was also a reckoning with the war, in which a friend of Pound's, the French sculptor Henri Gaudier-Brzeska, was killed in combat, as was T. E. Hulme. Wyndham Lewis and Ford Madox Hueffer served at the front, but they survived. The cost reverberates in the poem.

> There died a myriad,
> And of the best, among them,
> For an old bitch gone in the teeth,
> For a botched civilization,
>
> Charm, smiling at the good mouth,
> Quick eyes gone under earth's lid

The moral collapse registered with such acuity leads to a passage culminating in a word (usury) that would preoccupy Pound for years to come.

> Died some, pro patria,
>   non 'dulce' non 'et decor' . . .
> walked eye-deep in hell
> believing in old men's lies, then unbelieving
> came home, home to a lie,
> home to many deceits,
> home to old lies and new infamy;
> usury age-old and age-thick
> and liars in public places.

Yeats found in Pound's poem "that quality that makes ones hair stand up on end as though one saw a spirit." And there were spirits presiding. Hulme blown to bits by a direct artillery hit, Gaudier shot through the head. Men Pound knew and would continue to revere. Two among millions.

Part Three

CHAPTER SEVEN

"My nerves are bad tonight"

In the summer of 1917 *Prufrock and Other Observations* was issued by the Egoist Press around the time Eliot became assistant editor of the journal, replacing Richard Aldington, who had been conscripted by the military. During Eliot's tenure, until it shut down at the end of 1919, *The Egoist* was the literary organ of "the Men of 1914," a slogan Wyndham Lewis coined for the Pound-Eliot-Joyce-Lewis group. Its dwindling circulation registers the extent to which Pound's defiantly avant-garde efforts had become anathema in wartime England. Poems by Aldington, H. D., and Williams were frequent, along with fiction by Lewis and the earliest installments of Joyce's *Ulysses*. Pound and Eliot were prominent in most issues, the latter with a running series of "Reflections on Contemporary Poetry," followed by several "Observations" under the preening pseudonym T. S. Apteryx. In one installment of May 1918 he singled out Marianne Moore and Mina Loy as plausible heirs of Laforgue, and soon solicited contributions from Moore.

In the November 1917 "Reflections" he reviewed Harriet Monroe's anthology *The New Poetry*, observing that the role of such a compendium was not only to single out quality work but "to embalm a great many bad poems (but bad in a significant way)." By this means, "the reader's vision [is] clarified and his mind instructed, when bad poems of totally different types are set off against each other." Eliot was working his way to the perspective elaborated in a two-part essay published in the final issues of *The Egoist* in 1919, "Tradition and the Individual Talent." In it, he makes the case that all art is contemporaneous, identifying "the historical sense" that "compels a man to write not merely with his own generation in his bones, but with a feeling that the whole of the literature of Europe from Homer and within it the whole of the literature of his own country has a simultaneous existence and composes a simultaneous order."

In the July 1919 issue he made a curious observation that, for those in the know, was a kind of self-portrait.

> It is not true that the development of a writer is a function of his development as a man, but it is possible to say that there is a close analogy

between the sort of experience which develops a man and the sort of experience which develops a writer. Experience in living may leave the literary embryo still dormant, and the progress of literary development may to a considerable extent take place in a soul left immature in living.

One of those in a position to recognize this as self-portrait was Conrad Aiken.

Eliot's column (the passage above is its opening) addressed books by Herbert Read and Aiken, with an interlude on the Dadaist Tristan Tzara, whose work has "the odd distinction of being neither verse nor prose nor prose-poem." Whatever it was, though, was "agreeably competent." After quoting a bit of sound poetry—"Bonjour sans cigarette tzantzanza / ganga / bouzdouc zdouc nfounfa mbaah"—Eliot admits, with a straight face, "The only way to take this sort of thing is very seriously." Acknowledging that "at least it is a symptom of 'experiment,'" he advises that it "ought not to be put in the hands of the young." In any case, he added, it was very French and would be of no service in England.

Reviewing *The Charnel Rose*, Eliot praised Aiken for having "the distinction of believing in the long poem," while acknowledging that older models of narrative in poetry had been more or less outdated by the prose accomplishments of Chekhov and Henry James. Aiken recognized the challenge, though Eliot thought he "has gone in for psycho-analysis with a Swinburnian equipment." Consequently, "the effect is of immaturity of feeling." Nonetheless, Eliot found the attempt "more impressive than many English successes."

Aiken's poems were unambiguously fixated on psychosis. For him it was personal. At age eleven he heard sounds of argument from his parents' bedroom, then his father's voice counting off "one two three" followed by a gunshot. "One two three" once more and a second shot was fired. Young Conrad went in to find both parents dead. This murder-suicide took place in Savannah, Georgia. He and his siblings were taken in by relatives in Massachusetts; there he eventually became Tom Eliot's friend at Harvard where they coedited the school's literary journal. They reveled in a shared enthusiasm for Krazy Kat, Mutt and Jeff, and Rube Goldberg's "elaborate lunacies." Tom was particularly fascinated with slang, which exponentially blossomed with the throng of immigrants in the early years of the century.

The friends shared poetry and even adopted similar idioms. There's much in Aiken that sounds like Eliot. Not the other way around? Based on the early writings posthumously available, as well as drafts of "Prufrock" and other poems published later but dating back to undergraduate days, it's likely that Aiken followed Eliot's lead. Yet Aiken was the one who got off to a quick start, with three books to his name before Eliot's *Prufrock* was published in 1917, and more in the pipeline. *Senlin* was one of five long narrative poems Aiken published between 1916 and 1923, gathered into one volume as *The Divine Pilgrim* in 1949. By the end of his life, Aiken's *Collected Poems* exceeded a thousand pages—despite omitting most of the poems from his first and third collections—while Eliot's final tally barely exceeds two hundred pages. Eliot had learned the art of brevity the hard way, by entering into a punishing marriage that deprived him of the opportunity to produce much in the way of poetry, but in the end it proved a more approachable body of work for readers.

Echoes of Aiken's parental tragedy haunt his poetic narratives in a recurring refrain. In *The Jig of Forslin* we meet a Prufrockian figure: "he was oldish," and "he sat in a small bare gaslit room." "I am spread upon a fog, and know no place," he ruminates, as "The widths of puddles wedged his brain apart." Forslin's jig returns again and again to a murder, but "I do not know / If this is I," he reflects, who "stabbed my lover." "Who am I? Am I he that loved and murdered?" It's an unanswerable question in the misty delirium of Forslin's brain as he merges into the convulsions of multitude.

> We lift our faces to the sun.
> We flow together; we rage, we shout, we sing;
> Pour and engulf; recoil, disgorge, and spring.

Prufrock heeds the mermaids "Till human voices wake us, and we drown," while Aiken's Forslin submits to a comparable submersion: "That was a somber sea-pool to explore— / Strange things are on that floor."

When Eliot's *Poems 1909–1925* was published, Conrad Aiken marveled at his friend's preciosity. "How the devil did you manage to discover your identity so early?" he wondered, ruefully aware that he himself was still searching. Eliot responded with a cutout from the *Midwives Gazette* providing advice for those pursuing a nursing certificate.

> T. S. E. had underlined the words *Model Answers.* Under this was a column descriptive of various forms of vaginal discharge, normal and abnormal. Here the words *blood*, *mucous*, and *shreds of mucous* had been underlined with a pen, and lower down also the phrase *purulent offensive discharge*. Otherwise, no comment.

Aiken responded in kind. "Have you tried Kotex for it?" When Eliot visited a few days later, Aiken was "prepared for anything: and expected a permanent rupture." He was understandably bewildered, and embarrassed for both of them, though the encounter passed without reference to this epistolary exchange. "Was I the fool or was he?" Aiken wondered. "No, we were both fools."

The episode speaks volumes, revealing a misogynistic streak in Eliot's troubled relation to Vivien, with whom he had then endured a full decade. The "offensive discharge" also implicates the verse for which Aiken sent his congratulations, and may have been a swipe at Aiken's ongoing gusher of versified psychosis. Afflictions were ascendant all around. More than half of Eliot's *Poems 1909–1925* were written before his marriage, and the collection ends with the only poem he'd written since *The Waste Land*, "The Hollow Men," with its famous line about the world ending "*Not with a bang but a whimper.*"

From 1916 to 1919 Eliot was teaching and doing lecture courses in the evening, even after he started working full-time at Lloyd's Bank in spring 1917. He was also churning out a steady stream of book reviews and articles for periodical fees, and was assistant editor of *The Egoist* from spring 1917 through 1919. He was constantly on call tending to Vivien, who in turn was nursing him during his own relapses. It was a masochistic demonstration of devotion; it was also a concession to lifestyle expenditures barely affordable but deemed necessary for their social station, as both Tom and Viv were natty dressers, and liked cottage rentals in the country and having a live-in maid. Above all, the effort involved was disguised by the impassive persona Tom adopted for the public: don't blink, don't let them think anything is amiss.

Eliot sustained his visibility in literary London, but that was another kind of servitude. Lytton Strachey gives a riotous report of the Anglo-French Poetry Society in 1920, held in the house of novelist Arnold Bennett (who wisely avoided the occasion).

> There was an address (very poor) on Rimbaud etc. by an imbecile Frog; then Edith Sitwell appeared, her nose longer than an anteater's, and read some of her absurd stuff; then Eliot—very sad and seedy—it made one weep; finally Mrs Arnold Bennett recited, with waving arms and chanting voice, Baudelaire and Verlaine until everyone was ready to vomit. As a study in half-witted horror the whole thing was most interesting.

Eliot surely felt the same repulsion. At a similar soiree, he evidently looked bored. Asked if he didn't find it interesting, "Yes," he replied, "it is interesting if you concentrate on the essential horror of the thing."

Pressures escalated with the arrival of the Eliot family for a visit of several months in summer 1921, literally displacing Tom and Vivien, who rented a cramped attic for themselves. Before their arrival, he'd hoped to complete a poem, now in abeyance. The arts were his counterweight to distress. In late June Eliot attended a performance of *The Rite of Spring* and dedicated his regular London column for *The Dial* to "the greatest success since Picasso." Igor Stravinsky, "Lucifer of the season," had applied ultramodern music to a primitive ritual. "The effect," wrote Eliot, "was like *Ulysses*, with illustrations by the best contemporary illustrator." This was not intended as a compliment to illustration, for he felt that the prehistoric and the modern should be subject to "interpenetration and metamorphosis," a strategy he would undertake a year later in *The Waste Land*. It was not the ballet that thrilled him but the music, which transformed "the rhythm of the steppes into the scream of the motor horn, the rattle of machinery, the grind of wheels, the beating of iron and steel, the roar of the underground railway, and the other barbaric cries of modern life."

Earlier in the year Eliot had met Lady Rothermere, whose husband owned the *Daily Mail*. At society functions in her home he met Arthur Symons, whose writing had led him to Laforgue, and others including the composer Frederick Delius. He also attended a séance there, presided over by Russian guru P. D. Ouspensky. Lady Rothermere suggested Eliot edit a journal. He was keen on the prospect, as he and Pound had hoped to launch their own journal, but nothing had come of it. He endured months of fretting as she dithered. Finally, at the end of August, he received her formal offer to back a new intellectual quarterly, to be called *The Criterion* at Vivien's suggestion. The first issue was to appear early the next year.

In the later months of 1921 Eliot was doubly occupied, working days in the bank and nights planning the journal. This meant not only the editorial work, but the practical business of printing. Facing an exponential expansion of correspondence, he had to hire two typists. Despite Lady Rothermere's pledge, travails over *The Criterion* continued. At the beginning of November—at which point the first issue was in production—Vivien wrote in desperation to Pound, saying that Lady Rothermere was pelting Tom with "three offensive letters." Ezra came up with his permanent nickname for his friend: the possum, adept at playing dead. Dismayed that Eliot was producing not a fashionable arts journal but a sober literary review (an English *Dial*, not a *Vanity Fair*), his patron was already threatening to pull the plug.

So there he was, under duress, and in a country in which "one remains always a foreigner," he wrote his brother Henry. "It is like being always on dress parade—one can never relax. It is a great strain." Henry thought Tom "seemed a man playing a part." A friend observed, "He gives you the creeps a little at first because he is such a completely artificial, or rather, self-invented character," but admittedly "he has done such a perfect job with himself that you often end by admiring him." Nonetheless, certain behavioral symptoms unsettled others. Virginia Woolf heard that "he uses violet powder to make him look cadaverous." Osbert Sitwell, seated next to him at a dinner, was "amazed to notice on his cheeks a dusting of green powder—pale but distinctly green, the color of a forced lily-of-the-valley. I was hardly willing, any more than if I had seen a ghost, to credit the evidence of my senses." Sitwell decided this "must express a craving for sympathy in his unhappiness." In his view, Tom "seemed anxious to carry the whole weight of the marriage on his shoulders." The strain finally became intolerable, and in the fall of 1921 he was granted three months' leave from the bank to seek treatment. Under the care of Dr. Roger Vittoz in Lausanne, Tom pulled together the "heap of broken images" in manuscripts he'd brought with him and cobbled together a draft of his long poem.

On October 3, 1921, Tom informed his brother that he had seen a nerve specialist who told him that "I had greatly overdrawn my nervous energy." He told Aldington he didn't want to impose on Richard's generosity in offering rest and relaxation in his "cottage for neurasthenics." Aldington loaned him a book he read shortly before embarking on the rest cure. *La Poésie d'aujourd'hui: Un nouvel état d'intelligence* by Jean Epstein, Franco-Polish writer and filmmaker. Calling himself a neurasthenic was not necessarily pejorative, inasmuch as Epstein envisioned a "neuropathic aristocracy" of poets, a distinguished company Eliot was happy to join. Quite apart from considerations of actual disease, Epstein, wrote, "an *imperfect physiology increases coenesthesia which increases the sensitivity of the individual and consequently his artistic disposition*." (Coenesthesia—also cenesthesia—is the aggregate sense of bodily awareness.)

Poetry Today: A New State of Mind advanced the daring thesis that neurasthenia was the driving force of creativity in modern artists. For Epstein, "It is not a question of a malady but a modification of the organism." Summarizing his findings for an article in Le Corbusier's journal *L'Esprit Nouveau*, Epstein wrote:

Spatial speed, mental speed, multiplication of intellectual images and the deformation of these images, extension of auto-observation and of the importance given to the interior life, cerebral life and the fatigue that results from it. Such are the most important conditions under which the contemporary literary phenomenon comes into being.

A translated excerpt appeared in Harold Loeb's expatriate journal *Broom*, with its premonitory use of the title Eliot would decide upon later in the year: "Waste lands become populous, cheap tracts quintuple in price because a tramway, and that feed wire from which it licks up the sap of amperes and volts, now passes through a suburb." Epstein's thesis enabled Eliot to suspect neuroses in unlikely places. He detected a certain "neurotic carnality" in the poems of H. D., for instance (a prescient reading, given her subsequent role as hysteric in the film *Borderline*, starring Paul Robeson). Epstein's perspective helped him recognize that personal neuroses were not strictly personal, but sociocultural. Epstein's book corroborated Eliot's thesis in "Tradition and the Individual Talent" that art is not the expression of personality but the release of something transpersonal.

He read *La Poésie d'aujourd'hui* while preparing his essay "The Metaphysical Poets," summarizing Epstein's perspective in a famous passage: "Our civilization comprehends great variety and complexity," Eliot wrote, "and this variety and complexity, playing upon a refined sensibility, must produce various and complex results. The poet must become more and more comprehensive, more allusive, more indirect, in order to force, to dislocate if necessary, language into his meaning." It's almost as if Eliot is conceding that poetry is akin to stammering, like some aesthetically advantageous speech defect. Objecting to the timeworn dictum "Look into thy heart and write," he tellingly specified other body parts. "One must look into the cerebral cortex, the nervous system, and the digestive tracts." But mind ultimately registered bodily distress, inducing psychosomatic afflictions of its own.

Word got around. On December 3, Conrad Aiken revealed some news to a friend: "Tom Eliot has had some sort of nervous breakdown and is at present in Lausanne: hybrid difficulties, I suppose, or else the severe strain of being an Englishman." Tom had been nurturing the aspiration to write a long poem. But the "chief drawback to my present mode of life," he realized, "is the lack of *continuous* time, not getting more than a few hours together for myself, which breaks the concentration required for turning out a poem of any length." He'd been considering a poem of eight hundred to a thousand lines, a pipe dream for someone whose recent poems rarely exceeded a page. During therapy, other prospects emerged.

Dr. Vittoz was the author of *Traitement des psychonévroses par la rééducation du contrôle cérébral* in 1911. Eliot owned (and annotated) a 1921 edition of the book, which was coincidentally translated into English that year as *The Treatment of Neurasthenia by Means of Brain Control*. Vittoz's methodology involved getting patients to take charge of their mental expenditures. Therapeutically, he would lay hands on the patient's head to detect nervous energy, and assign exercises like concentrating on a rudimentary shape or a simple thought. Vittoz's approach had some influence in the profession. Matthew Gold notes that a therapeutic recommendation by W. Charles Loosmore in *Nerves and Man* (1921) "reads more like an assignment for a college literature class than a course of treatment." The passage he quotes begins, "Take a paragraph from Ruskin," and prescribes a basic cognitive analysis as a way of settling the agitated mind. Welcome treatment for a man like Eliot who did this all the time for his book reviews.

In Gold's suggestive reading, *The Waste Land*'s "disjointed narration leads the reader to experience a neurasthenic state of mind." That is, the perplexity of the reader facing a chaotic medley of voices without a guiding thread is precisely the state of mind of the frantic neurasthenic, unable to focus on anything. This is not a bizarre reading, but an accurate rendering of statements Eliot made about the nature of his therapy and the benefits he expected from it. From his perspective, he had been prone to losing focus, dithering, or otherwise wasting time. In an almost military sense, Vittoz pricked his conscience and got him standing to attention. Gold adds another observation, which acutely turns the screw a bit further: "Vittoz may not have realized it, but he was treating both poet and poem." As it happened, the poem benefited more immediately and consequentially than the man, whose despondency resumed after therapy.

*

When Eliot referred to himself as a neurasthenic in 1921, it was a diagnostic term about to expire. But was a sensible reference, inasmuch as it linked his malady with his homeland. The term *neurasthenia* was coined by American physician George M. Beard in 1869. In his influential books *A Practical Treatise on Nervous Exhaustion (Neurasthenia)* (1880) and *American Nervousness: Its Causes and Consequences* (1881), he appraised it as a uniquely American affliction. It was attributable, he thought, to America's pioneering role in the grand developments of modern life. He enumerated five in particular: steam power, telegraphy, the sciences in general, the periodical press, and the "mental activity of women."

Beard offered this synoptic formula for his findings:

American nervousness is the product of American civilization. All the other influences—climate, nervous diathesis, evil habits, worry and overtoil—are either secondary or tertiary. The philosophy of the causation of American nervousness may be expressed in algebraic formula as follows: civilization in general + American civilization in particular (young and rapidly growing nation, with civil, religious, and social liberty) + exhausting climate (extremes of heat and cold, and dryness) + the nervous diathesis (itself a result of previously named factors) + overwork or over-worry, or excessive indulgence of appetites or passions = an attack of neurasthenia or nervous exhaustion.

For Beard, it was a by-product of civilization, and "where there is no civilization there is no nervousness, no matter what the personal habits may be." The kicker was that "All our civilization hangs by a thread; the activity and force of the very few make us what we are as a nation." The few were the brain-workers, who were predominately white and had the greatest concentration of neurasthenics. "Modern nervousness is the cry of the system struggling with its environment," he wrote, and it was the system that induced the telling affliction.

Neurasthenia was coined to address the physical and mental cost of modern business, indoor living, sedentary ways. Just as fanciful as Beard's thesis of longevity was his identification of those most likely to exhibit neurasthenic symptoms. These were, he supposed, white, Anglo-Saxon, and Protestant. Rural folk, southerners, Catholics, Native Americans, and African Americans were exempt. It was a Yankee affliction, but also a *distinction*—with racist assumptions. Beard thought neurasthenia was not so much a scourge to be eradicated as a sign of American exceptionalism. Too much of a good thing, in a way. Another physician, Charles Dana, concurred, calling neurasthenia "our one great national malady" and even a "distinctive and precious pathological possession."

S. Weir Mitchell was also active in propagating the diagnostic relevance of neurasthenia. In *Wear and Tear* (1871), he asked, "Have we lived too fast?" and pointed to constant change as the typical American condition. At issue was whether cultural norms exacted a mental and physiological cost. Attributed to the precipitating cause of modernity, symptomatized by *Brain-Work and Overwork* (the title of a book by Horatio Woods in 1882), and combining sedentary habits with capitalist excitability, neurasthenia was (as the advertising nostrum has it) *widely available.*

Once established, neurasthenia quickly became a diagnostic catchall, a "contagious diagnosis" in the words of one historian, owing to its elasticity. It accommodated the most diverse set of symptoms. It could apply to fatigue as well as excitability. It was known in synonyms like "nervous exhaustion," and "nervous breakdown." And yet, as a mark of distinction, it also served as a portent of great things to come. The diagnosis prompted Teddy Roosevelt to make himself over as outdoorsman, adventurer, and military hero. Much as it was associated with despondency and inertia, it was the opposite of a wasting disease like tuberculosis: it was not fatal, as it had no particular corporeal location, and it could be an inducement to behavioral modification.

Neurasthenia has been called "a cacophony of complaints that replicate 'real' illnesses" without any observable injury. As such, it became "an incessant orchestration of physical analogies," according to Anson Rabinbach, "not simply a malady, but frequently an unstable mimesis of other maladies." Medically speaking, this could have been a liability. Soon after Beard identified neurasthenia, it was validated not only by scientific scrutiny but by popular demand. For one thing, it facilitated the spread of patent medicines. This market had grown with the exponential rise in newspapers and printed circulars—a by-product of the Civil War, when families across the nation tried to keep abreast of military developments. Some fourteen thousand men served as medics in the war, recruited from all walks of life, and many continued working in medicine after the war. Medications, therapies, and treatments all became tools of the trade for a rising class of practitioners for whom treating neurasthenia was a lucrative specialty.

Neurasthenia was called "the blues," a term also familiar from the musical accompaniment to traveling medicine shows. *The Blues: Causes and Cure* was a popular title on neurasthenia by Dr. Albert Abrams (1904). Such books, which were plentiful, fueled a burgeoning self-help market. The pharmaceutical industry issued booklets instructing prospective customers to diagnose their own symptoms and order medications by mail. This practice persisted until it was outlawed in the United States in 1922—a convenient date, as that's when a self-diagnosing poet's *The Waste Land* appeared. Self-medication was a commercial boon for the industry, of course, but it was made possible by the way neurasthenia had been marketed as a condition susceptible to those worn down by modern life.

The invasive power of today's pharmaceutical industry goes back to the Civil War. In 1859 industry profits were $3,500,000. By 1904 that figure was a whopping $74,500,000. But patent medicines constituted only one of the treatments for neurasthenia. Once it took off, neurasthenia became a lifestyle option for the upwardly mobile class. After Beard let it be known that the majority of his patients were from the "higher orders" of American society, it became fashionable to be diagnosed with some neurasthenic disorder. Moving in "neurasthenic circles," as William Marrs wrote in *Confessions of a Neurasthenic* (1908), was a status symbol. An article in 1898 archly noted a "vast army of up-to-date neurasthenia victims."

Treatment of this mercurial and ever-present malady varied, but it was sensibly understood that activity was an effective antidote. Office work could bring it on, but getting out and about was a corrective. Modern sports arose in part as antidotes to neurasthenia. These included basketball (1891) and volleyball (1896), as well as sporting organizations like the Rowing Association of America (1871), the National Bowling League (1875), and the National Association of Amateur Athletes of America (1879). The Young Men's Christian Association was formed to promote "muscular Christianity" with swimming pools, gyms, and organized sports in urban settings. Beard recommended camping and horseback riding, sailing and other outdoor adventures for those with the means to travel to the appropriate locations. Also promulgated by the rest cure was the pursuit of hobbies to combat neuropathic lethargy.

Neurasthenia could hardly remain confined to America, and in fact it became one of the more successful pre–World War I American exports. Unlike American physicians, those in Europe were far more inclined to identify neurasthenia with hereditary traits. And that meant no treatment or corrective could be offered, and certainly no patent medicines. In a rich biographical coincidence, one of the most eminent French specialists in neurasthenia was Achille-Adrien Proust, whose *L'hygiène du neurasthénique* was published in 1887. His six-year-old son Marcel was then about the same age as the autobiographical character of his epic novel *In Search of Lost Time*, which begins with a neurasthenic lad having trouble falling asleep.

Literary works of the late nineteenth century were filled with neurasthenic characters. Henry James's fiction would be depopulated without them. Charlotte Perkins Gilman's story "The Yellow Wallpaper" (1892) was written in defiance of her recent diagnosis as a neurasthenic, when the doctor recommended she read no more than two hours a day and cut out writing altogether (Eliot received the same recommendation). The story reportedly made the doctor reconsider his views on the disease. *The Magic Mountain* by Thomas Mann (1924) is an epic of neurasthenic treatments, with life itself depicted as a never-ending rest cure in an Alpine sanatorium.

German Dadaist George Grosz had a nervous breakdown in response to his military service during the war, and his poem "Kaffeehaus" (1917) reflects his experience:

Herr Ober!!—bitte Selterwasser—
Ich bin eine Maschine, an der der Manometer entzwei ist—!
Und alle Walzen spielen im Kreis—
Siehe: wir sind allzumal Neuartheniker!

Waiter! A glass of seltzer please—
I'm a machine whose pressure gauge has busted—!
And all the cylinders are spinning—
See: we're one and all neurasthenics!

Grosz was one of many writers who recognized that being modern meant inheriting a roster of liabilities. Being modern roused the sensibility but also agitated the nerves. Arriving in Paris in 1894, Swedish writer August Strindberg wondered, "What is happening to me? Are my nerves undergoing an evolution towards over-sensitivity and are my senses becoming much too delicate? Am I shedding my skin? Am I becoming a modern man?"

Nerves became the privileged medium of sensory awareness in the age of telegraph and telephone. In 1891 Viennese cultural critic Hermann Bahr observed that "when classicism says 'man,' it means reason and feeling. And when Romanticism says 'man,' it means passion and the senses. And when modernism says 'man' it means the nerves." A 1908 tally of occupational diseases in Germany found correlations between nervous illness and new technologies, catapulting neurasthenia from bourgeois affliction to a general condition. Risk became a nagging menace at the heart of modern life. Even going to sleep could be perilous, as in Franz Kafka's memorable tale of Gregor Samsa, the traveling salesman who wakes up in his bed one morning to find himself turned into a bug. Ruminating on Kafka, Walter Benjamin observed that "the invention of motion pictures and the phonograph came in an age of maximum alienation of men from one another, of unpredictably intervening relationships which have become their only ones," adding to emphasize his point, "Experiments have proved that a man does not recognize his own gait on film or his own voice on the phonograph." This technologically administered disorientation, Benjamin suggests, is what Kafka called "seasickness on dry land."

T. S. Eliot was another victim of this seasickness. For him, it was a personal affliction as well as an intellectual pedigree. Eliot was an heir of Baudelaire, who celebrated the rapture of nerves the French poet found in his American hero Edgar Allan Poe—nerves as multipliers of sensation, just as English writer Walter Pater commended "a quickened, multiplied consciousness" as aesthetic benchmark. Eliot's aesthetic sensibility harkened to this legacy, even as his personal crises cast a darker pathology over "nerves."

Spelling out his wife's condition, Eliot asked a friend, "Have you ever been in such incessant and extreme pain that you felt your sanity going, and that you no longer knew reality from delusion? That's the way she is." Vivien enumerated her symptoms for Pound, including colitis, temperatures of over 100°F (37.8°C), exhaustion, insomnia ("This has been going on for eight years"), migraines, and what she called "increasing mental incapacity." But, Tom reminded Ezra, "I have made a great many mistakes, which are largely the cause of her present catastrophic state of health." To Vivien's credit, "it must be remembered that she kept me from returning to America where I should have become a professor and probably never written another line of poetry, so that in that respect she should be endowed."

*

Pound's support of Eliot and others was unparalleled. Contributing to the largesse he extended to many was his own impecunious standard of living. He made his own furniture, did his own cooking, and scrabbled together bits of income from the freelance trade. Although he never had regular employment, he not only thrived but managed to be a behind-the-scenes benefactor of Eliot and Joyce in particular.

The most consequential of his ministrations to Eliot was the editorial finesse he brought to *The Waste Land*, for which Eliot dedicated the poem to "il miglior fabbro," the better craftsman. It was a role Pound had eased into from the beginning, as his beleaguered friend welcomed his attention to drafts of poems, however few and far between, in the years after their meeting when Ezra became Tom's number one booster.

The Waste Land was a transactional venture between the poet and his wife. It was, in a way, the seismograph of a shared neurosis. As he said later in another context, "We have all to choose whatever subject matter allows us the most powerful and the most secret release; and this is a personal affair." But the poem was also a media event—long before our current understanding of that phrase meant anything. Commercial radio was in its infancy, and television was in the distant future. Telephones were a novelty. The appearance of Eliot's poem was, in its way, a YouTube phenomenon in the slowest medium imaginable, print culture.

Eliot plugged away at drafts during much of 1921 and had shown Pound a version of the poem on his way to Lausanne. Pound's response spurred Eliot to continue working on it, writing the final section, "What the Thunder Said," "in a trance—unconsciously." When his rest cure in Switzerland was over, he visited Pound. "I placed before him in Paris the manuscript of a sprawling chaotic poem called *The Waste Land* which left his hands, reduced to about half its size, in the form in which it appears in print." On January 24, 1922, Pound wrote Eliot, "Caro mio: MUCH improved," adding in husky man-to-man palaver, "Complimenti, you bitch. I am wracked by the seven jealousies."

Pound added some verses to his letter, delighting its recipient with a tale of the poem's creation:

> These are the poems of Eliot
> By the Uranian Muse begot;
> A Man their Mother was,
> A muse their Sire.
>
> How did the printed Infancies result
> From Nuptials thus doubly difficult?
>
> If you must needs enquire
> Know diligent Reader
> That on each Occasion
> Ezra performed the Caesarian Operation

To John Quinn he wrote, "About enough, Eliot's poem, to make the rest of us shut up shop." In the summer he explained to his old college teacher in America, "Eliot's *Waste Land* is I think the justification of the 'movement', of our modern experiment, since 1900." By that point Joyce's *Ulysses* was being typeset, and the nearly simultaneous appearance of the two jewels of the "modern movement" elevated the year 1922 to its celebratory status as an annus mirabilis.

The path to notoriety was different for the two titles. *Ulysses* had been serialized in *The Little Review* for several years, though certain issues had been seized and destroyed for offenses to public morals. However, enough of the novel was available to have enshrined it in the imagination of many before its appearance as a fat blue tome. Because it was published in Paris, readers elsewhere needed luck and tenacity to get hold of it, as it was deemed inadmissible by customs agents. Of course, that only added to its reputation. It would not be legally available in Britain and America until more than a decade after its publication.

Unlike the trajectory of *Ulysses*, there was no gradual preview of *The Waste Land*. No preliminary excerpts were circulated or even considered (it was, after all, a scant 433 lines in five sections). But the preparations for its release were complex, extending through most of 1922. So the poem's impact differed from that of Joyce's novel in that, on publication, it was suddenly and unalterably *there*. And "there" was multiple, its impact compounded by two periodical appearances, followed by two book publications: a transatlantic debut in both England and the United States. Eliot had made a name for himself with his previous poems and essays, but there was no intimation in his earlier work of anything remotely like *The Waste Land*.

The preparations leading to the publication of the poem were long and labored. As Pound suggested in his playful verse, in the "accouchement," or lying-in, he was the midwife. While Tom was in Paris in early January 1922, on his way back to London from the clinic at Lausanne, he and Ezra had dinner with James Joyce and Horace Liveright. The New York publisher had recently arrived, looking to sign up various authors for his firm. He'd recently published Pound's *Poems 1918–1921*, and tried on this occasion to get contracts for *The Waste Land* and *Ulysses*. He knew the value of Joyce's book but could only take Pound's word for the potential of Eliot's poem.

Revisions of the poem continued to the end of January. Eliot started casting about for publishing opportunities in February, in both periodical and book formats. He had recently been engaged by Scofield Thayer to write occasional profiles for a "London Letter" in *The Dial*. Tom fancifully imagined his role in public relations terms, "Studies in European Literature, by one on the SPOT!" The contract also granted *The Dial* right of first refusal on any poems he wrote. In January, Thayer offered $150 for the poem, sight unseen, but Eliot dithered. A month later he insisted on $250, but the editor stuck to his original offer. There was even a bungled telegram in which Eliot appeared to be asking for the astronomical sum of £856. Finally, in March, he testily withdrew the poem, under the mistaken impression that George Moore was paid £100 for a short story, "and I must confess that this influenced me in declining $150 for a poem which has taken me a year to write and which is my biggest work." As Sibley Watson, co-owner with Thayer, ruefully reflected, Eliot failed to distinguish between the rates of the old *Dial* before they'd bought it and the rates under the new regime, which was hemorrhaging money.

Watson and Thayer were losing tens of thousands of dollars annually as they struggled to make *The Dial* both culturally and financially successful. Although Thayer was listed as the journal's editor, their ownership agreement stipulated that both were empowered to solicit and retain work. Watson welcomed Pound's advice and was an enthusiast of modernism in general. While Thayer idolized Picasso and collected modern art, his literary tastes did not follow suit. He was also put off by Pound's bluster, though on a visit to Paris he was relieved to find the bark worse than the bite. Of this "queer duck," he found that "at close quarters he is much more fair in his judgments than his correspondence and his books warrant one to believe." The two men visited Gertrude Stein, and Thayer was astonished to find Ezra reduced to silence in her presence as she held forth without the possibility of interruption.

Pound had previously secured John Quinn's pledge of support for taking over an existing journal, but nothing had come of it. Quinn then worked out with Thayer and Watson a position for the poet to become foreign agent for *The Dial* at $750 a year, enough to cover his living expenses. With characteristic gusto, he threw himself into his role. Advising the co-owners about how to manage payments, treat authors, and solicit contributions, he was clearly following the operational protocols he had planned for his own abortive periodical. By the end of its first year under new management, *The Dial* was largely a reflection of Pound's initiatives and contacts. He was earning his keep, even as he feared the journal might become yet another of those "mortuaries for the entombment of dead fecal mentality."

Thayer found it necessary to explain what he was up against, "With many apologies for your country and mine." Even something so apparently innocuous as reproducing a painting by Cézanne, he reported, was taken as an attack on "the very heart of patriotism, Christianity, and morality in general." Or, as an influential but unnamed "gentleman of some position in artistic circles hereabouts" declared, *The Dial* was "a dastardly attack upon 'all that the good and wise of every generation have lived and died for.'" Even his hometown newspaper in Worcester, Massachusetts, dismissed *The Dial* as an "intellectual sewer." Pound got the point, conceding that material like *Ulysses* was beyond consideration.

From the beginning, Pound's Cantos were eligible for inclusion in *The Dial*. Owing to the hostilities he outlined, Thayer was apologetic about having sent back a batch, suggesting that suitable placement in a section dedicated to "Modern Forms" might make innovative work more palatable. By the time three Cantos appeared in August 1921, that category had been abandoned (but not before featuring a play by Mina Loy, poems by H. D. and William Carlos Williams, and translations of Rimbaud and Paul Morand, and inaugurating Pound's monthly letter from Paris). But modern forms persisted as a bogey in Thayer's imagination, with the Cantos being most irksome. When negotiations over "The Waste Land" stalled at one point, and the text had yet to be seen by anyone at *The Dial*, Thayer consoled the staff: "If Eliot's long poem was anything like Pound's Cantos, perhaps we are unwittingly blessed." Later, after Eliot's poem had appeared in *The Dial*, Thayer said he wanted to wipe his editorial hands of "such matter as the silly cantos of Ezra Pound and as the very disappointing 'Waste Land.'"

While the prospect of "The Waste Land" appearing in *The Dial* was on hold, Pound set to work placing it elsewhere. Also in play was the glossy *Vanity Fair*, whose editor, the poet John Peale Bishop, would soon be in Paris. Meanwhile, Tom and Ezra met on vacation in Italy to strategize. By then, final arrangements had been made for Eliot's journal, *The Criterion*. The inaugural issue, in which he planned to include "The Waste Land," would appear in the fall. There remained the question of an American periodical publication.

The Little Review was an option, but it could hardly match Thayer's offer. Because it had serialized *Ulysses*, the association would reinforce the impression that Eliot's poem was a companion text to Joyce's already legendary opus. This would continue to be an association encouraged by the poet himself. Despite Eliot's stalemate with *The Dial*, that avenue was now being reopened thanks to Sibley Watson. Arriving in Paris, he promptly convinced Pound of his determination to break the deadlock. The solution was to give the annual Dial Award to Eliot for distinguished service to literature. The first had been awarded to novelist Sherwood Anderson. This would be the second (the editors had previously considered E. E. Cummings a potential recipient). It was a decisive gesture, as the award came with $2,000.00—and Eliot would still get $150 for the poem.

Most remarkable in all these negotiations is that no one but Pound had seen the manuscript. Eliot kept all the possibilities in play as long as he could, including *Vanity Fair*. Its immense circulation made it tempting, but it couldn't pay the equivalent of the Dial Award. It's also the case, as Lawrence Rainey suggests, that Eliot was carefully estimating the degree of his success. That is, he had made his reputation carefully through elite circles, avoiding overexposure. Publishing "The Waste Land" in *Vanity Fair* would look like commercial opportunism, whereas the Dial Award would generate an image of disinterested parties settling a laurel crown on the poet's head.

Liveright won his bid to publish the poem as a book for the American market, but delicate negotiations followed once *The Dial* was on board. It was all about timing, as the book couldn't precede the periodical. Quinn worked out the contractual arrangements. *The Dial* would purchase 350 copies of the Liveright book at market rates, ensuring that the publisher would break even. The poem would appear in the November issue of *The Dial*, along with an announcement of the award, which would also grace the dust jacket of the book,

FIG. 7.1. Ford Madox Ford (left), James Joyce, Ezra Pound, and John Quinn in 1923.

to be published a month later. The first publication, chronologically, would be in the October issue of *The Criterion* in England. Eliot, grateful to Quinn not only for this latest labor but for previous support as well, sent him as a gift the poem's manuscript. After the lawyer's death in 1924 it disappeared into his archive, not to resurface until after Eliot had died more than forty years later.

Quinn had been a regular benefactor of Pound as well as Eliot. Pound had first met him on an excursion to Coney Island with W. B. Yeats's father in 1910. Contact resumed a number of years later, and Ezra quickly became an art dealer for the American, who already had an extensive art collection. Being a firsthand witness to—as well as recipient of—Quinn's beneficence, in 1922 Pound came up with a scheme to institutionalize such efforts in order "to restart civilization." Called Bel Esprit, its purpose was to free artists from employment that infringed on their creative output. Eliot was chosen as the model case and prospective first beneficiary. A subscription flyer was circulated. Its pitch was to liberate the poet from his duties at the bank, where his work environment, the financial sector, or The City of London, gets an airing in *The Waste Land*. A refrain in the poem depicts this "Unreal City" where a crowd

Flowed up the hill and down King William Street,
To where Saint Mary Woolnoth kept the hours
With a dead sound on the final stroke of nine.

By the summer of 1922, Eliot had been five years at the bank. Pound informed him of the purpose of Bel Esprit, but it was not until he saw the draft of the flyer that Eliot objected. To say he worked at a bank was all right, but "If it is stated so positively that Lloyds Bank interferes with literature, Lloyds Bank would have a perfect right to infer that literature interfered with Lloyds Bank." Late in the year, after *The Waste Land* had been published, Ottoline Morrell started the Eliot Fellowship Fund. The existence of two such initiatives piqued curiosity, and in November 1922 the *Liverpool Daily Post* reported that Eliot had received £800 yet decided he would keep the money and stay with the bank anyway. None of it was true. This libelous claim led to a carefully worded rebuke the *Post* was obliged to publish. But the notoriety surrounding the alleged behavior of the author of the recently published *The Waste Land* hung in the air.

CHAPTER EIGHT

"I have heard the mermaids singing"

Early in his bid to stake a claim as a critic of note in London, Eliot published an article titled "The Borderline of Prose" in *The New Statesman*. It began with what, for its author, was a rare foray into journalistic wit and esoteric bravado.

> In the days when prosperous middle-class chimney-pieces were decorated with overmantels and flanked by tall jars of pampas grass; when knowing amateurs began to talk of Outamaro and Toyakuni; in the days when Mrs. Pennell's friends found source of laughter in feeding peacocks with sponge-cake soaked in absinthe; when Mr. George Moore was wearing a sugarloaf hat with a flat brim; then, or perhaps a little later; in the age of music-halls and cabmen's shelters; in the long-forgotten 'Nineties when sins were still scarlet, there appeared a little book called *Pastels in Prose*. It was mostly, if not altogether, translations from the French—from Ephraim Mikhaël, Judith Gautier, Mallarmé, and many less-remembered names. This book introduced to the English reader the Prose-Poem.
>
> It was after the time when Gautier had written the *Symphonie en blanc majeur*, and Whistler had painted symphonies in various colors, and program music was not unknown. So that several serious critics took alarm at the confusion of the genres, cried out upon an age of decadence and charlatanism. Charlatanism, no doubt, still exists; but decadence is far decayed; and it is now a little late to assume this motherly perturbation. Time has left us many things, but among those it has taken away we may hope to count *À rebours*, and the *Divagations*, and the writings of miscellaneous prose poets.

The attitudinizing here is exactly applied. Characteristic touches of judiciousness—"perhaps," "not altogether," "no doubt," "we may hope"— are deftly inserted, consolidating the air of casual authority. But Eliot's dismissal was premature. Huysman's *Against Nature* has remained the canonical novel of Symbolism, as has Mallarmé's sui generis collection of essays, notes, and what are worth calling *prosings* in *Divagations*.

Eliot penned this essay in response to the publication of two prose poems by Aldington in *The Little Review*. Eliot had himself written one prose poem, "Hysteria," included by Pound in his *Catholic Anthology* in 1915. The setting is a café, and it opens abruptly: "As she laughed I was aware of becoming involved in her laughter and being part of it, until her teeth were only accidental stars with a talent for squad-drill. I was drawn in by short gasps, inhaled at each momentary recovery, lost finally in the dark caverns of her throat, bruised by the ripple of unseen muscles." In the end the speaker resolves that "if the shaking of her breasts could be stopped some of the fragments of the afternoon might be collected, and I concentrated my attention with careful subtlety to this end." The piece was written in 1915, the year of his marriage; the psychosomatic affliction named in its title registers the sexual panic of a man engulfed by female laughter. Eliot's repudiation of the prose poem as genre, scholastic as he tries to make it sound, was a disavowal of the personal discomfort registered in his one and only prose poem.

Eliot later dismissed "Hysteria" as a mere prose notation for a possible poem and discouraged his Italian translator from taking it on. But it remained part of the canon. He acknowledged the legitimacy of the prose poem as a historical phenomenon, but mistakenly consigned it to the past despite the fact that its masters were Baudelaire, Rimbaud, and Mallarmé—figures of utmost consequence for the moderns. (Eliot would be astonished at the booming market in prose poems since his death.) He had undoubtedly heard Pound's insistence that modern poetry had to be as well written as prose; both men idolized Henry James and were transfixed by James Joyce. In a journalistic piece like "The Borderline of Prose," Eliot could be flippant, obsequiously clever, inattentive, or simply wrong. Mindful of the authority to which he aspired, however, he was careful about which publications of criticism to reprint. His judiciousness paid off. For some, even after the notoriety over *The Waste Land*, it was Eliot the critic who counted most.

In 1925, Scottish poet Edwin Muir (translator, with Willa Muir, of Franz Kafka) wrote an overview of Eliot, favoring his criticism over the poetry. As a critical intelligence, he found, Eliot "exercises continuously the faculty, rare in our time, of always saying more than he appears to say." Muir anticipated a sustained and broadening influence of Eliot the critic. "As a poet," on the other hand, "Mr. Eliot lacks seriousness. He is bitter, melancholy, despairing, but he is not serious." As evidence, Muir went back to "Prufrock," where "everything is underlined, every word is written for effect, and we are intended to know it." Muir put his finger on something nearly everyone recognized, but few regarded as an impediment. It might have been the case, as Hugh Gordon Porteus saw it, that "Eliot weighed his words as for an urgent cable addressed to posterity but liable to interception by the *Zeitgeist*." Those like Muir expected a harsher judgment from posterity while failing to account for the zeitgeist.

What spoke to many was the *Geist* as it was mercurially delivered in *The Waste Land*. But Muir's perspective is an important reminder that the poem gained authority from its author's critical acumen. *The Sacred Wood* was published in 1920, when the Knopf *Poems* also appeared. These two titles together generated a readership for *The Waste Land*. Although it was produced under great pressure, owing to Eliot's ongoing marital and professional burdens, *The Sacred Wood* was a shrewdly calculated culling from recently published essays and reviews. Its broad historical coverage and esoteric references prepared readers for comparable effects in *The Waste Land*; his readers were not surprised that the poem had notes, nor were they surprised by their scope. More than two hundred names found their way into *The Sacred Wood*, a text of fewer than two hundred pages of sparsely set type. It can at times seem like a blizzard of name-dropping.

A cluster of the names Massinger, Marlowe, Middleton, Kyd, Webster, Tourneur signals that the subject is Elizabethan drama. A very different roster—Harrison, Tylor, Levy-Bruhl, Cooke, and Cornford—points to the recent anthropological turn in scholarship on the classics. Eliot rarely uses first names, implying that those in the know are his audience, and can therefore congratulate themselves. For the intellectually aspirational, it was delectably intimidating.

The Sacred Wood had other fish to fry, foremost of which was Eliot's subtle but repeated suggestion that criticism as a higher calling was the prerogative of practicing artists. Professional critics, he said, were prone to misplaced envy. He was preparing a coup d'état of the critical establishment, the "Squirearchy" as it was called, after J. C. Squire, antimodernist editor of *London Mercury*. The genius of Eliot's approach in gathering material for his book was to avoid any appearance of partisanship on behalf of his allies. Pound, Joyce, H. D. are mentioned only in passing. Apart from the subjects of chapters (Euripides, Marlowe, *Hamlet*, Jonson, Massinger, Swinburne, Blake, Dante—a decidedly unmodern topic list), the most frequently cited figures in the book are Mathew Arnold, Coleridge, Milton, and Shakespeare.

The contents were carefully arranged. The book opens with nearly fifty pages devoted to "The Perfect Critic" and "Imperfect Critics," offering a cogent profile of practitioners both contemporary and historical. Only after that does "Tradition and the Individual Talent"—Eliot's most personal statement and a veritable manifesto—make an appearance. Its precepts were soon taken up as guides to reading his poetry. Poems, he insisted, were not the expression of personality but an escape from personality. The mind that suffers and the mind that creates are two different species, and the authentic creative fount is impersonal. Eliot regarded poetry as an arduous exercise in depersonalization. Whatever emotional content is detected in poetry is there by way of an "objective correlative," which is the assemblage of resonances that translate or transpose a personal emotive stimulus into concrete equivalents. Freud (unmentioned by Eliot) called such strategies *condensation* and *displacement* in the psychic economy of the unconscious.

For those mindful of the theoretical nuances of Eliot's prose, *The Waste Land* could seem like the objective correlative run amok. Everything in it reeked of condensation and displacement, obscuring any big picture expected of a work steeped in the Grail legend and its Wagnerian associations. Nonetheless, despite much perplexity Eliot's poem succeeded not least

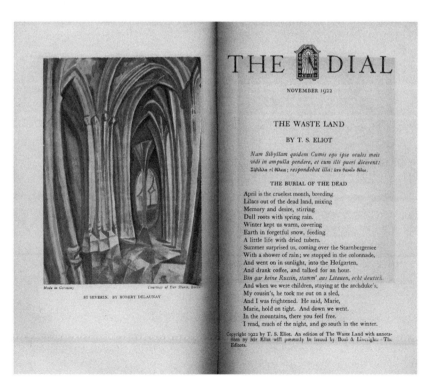

FIG. 8.1. T. S. Eliot, "The Waste Land," in *The Dial* (November 1922), with tipped-in plate of Robert Delaunay's *Saint-Severin* (1909).

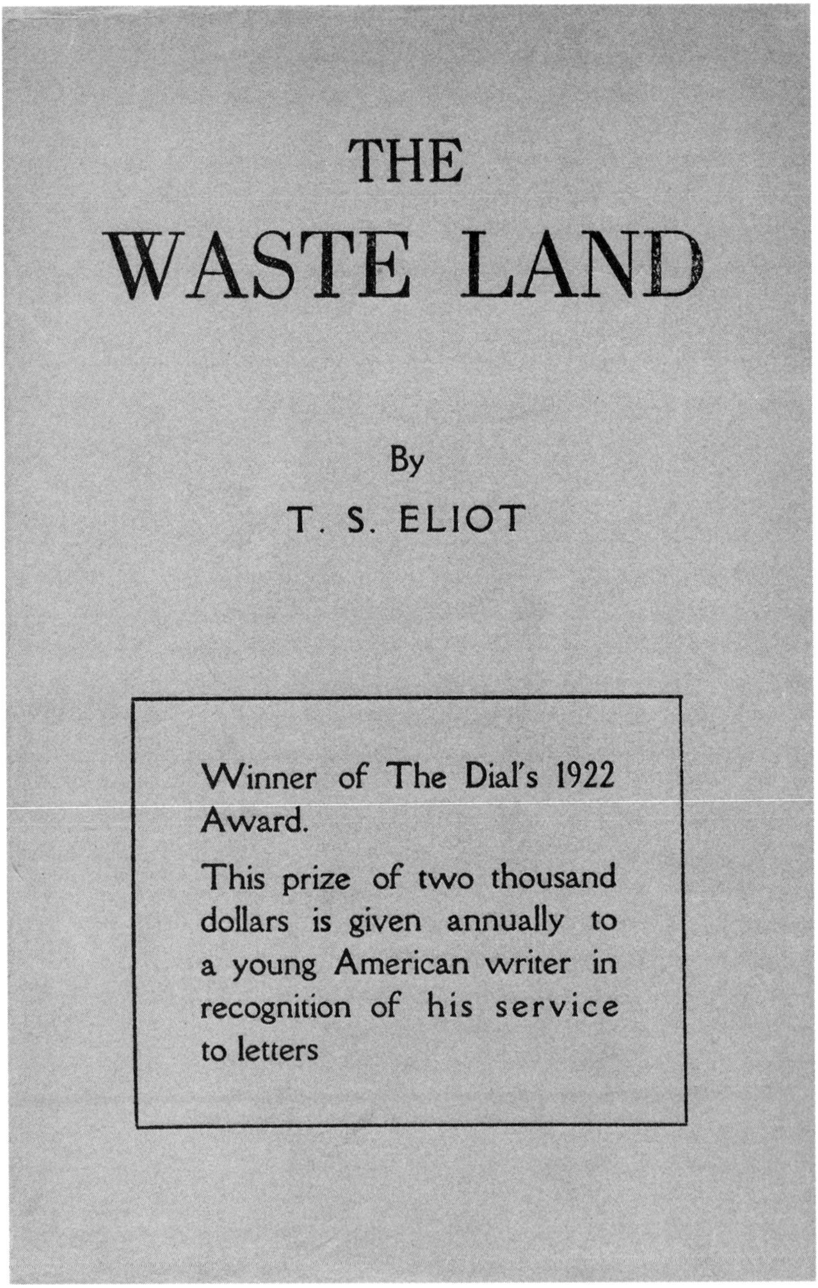

THE
WASTE LAND

By
T. S. ELIOT

Winner of The Dial's 1922 Award.

This prize of two thousand dollars is given annually to a young American writer in recognition of his service to letters

FIG. 8.2. Dust jacket of T. S. Eliot's *The Waste Land* (Boni and Liveright, 1922).

because of its carefully coordinated debut, straddling the Atlantic with two periodical and two book publications. In England, some reviewers addressed both the poem and the inaugural issue of *The Criterion*, while in America the Dial Award was commonly mentioned (sales of *The Dial* rose dramatically for the November 1922 issue in which "The Waste Land" appeared, to 4,500, increasing to 6,200 for the December issue—nearly double the monthly average).

Other reviews were based on the book, which was padded out with several pages of notes, adding talking points while exacerbating the general consternation about the poem. The distinction between the book and the periodical versions was reflected in basic orthography: "The Waste Land" or *The Waste Land*. An unfortunate preview of future bungling of the poem's title was in Boni and Liveright publicity announcements for "*The Wasteland*"—an error all too often perpetrated today. Even before it was published, Eliot felt it

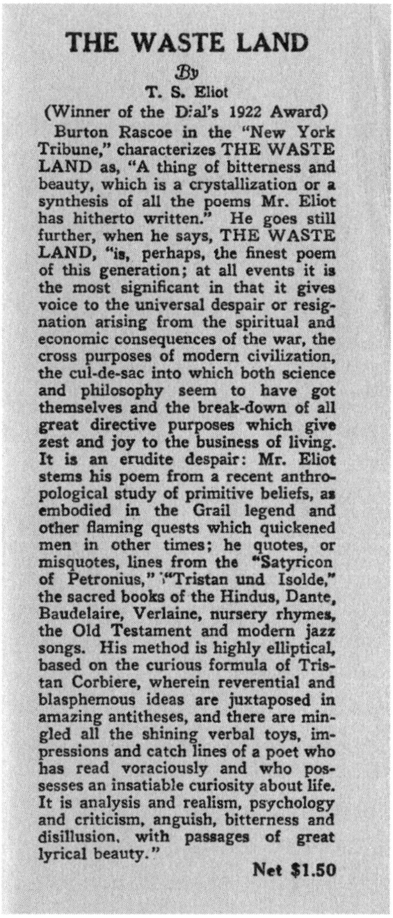

THE WASTE LAND

By

T. S. Eliot

(Winner of the Dial's 1922 Award)

Burton Rascoe in the "New York Tribune," characterizes THE WASTE LAND as, "A thing of bitterness and beauty, which is a crystallization or a synthesis of all the poems Mr. Eliot has hitherto written." He goes still further, when he says, THE WASTE LAND, "is, perhaps, the finest poem of this generation; at all events it is the most significant in that it gives voice to the universal despair or resignation arising from the spiritual and economic consequences of the war, the cross purposes of modern civilization, the cul-de-sac into which both science and philosophy seem to have got themselves and the break-down of all great directive purposes which give zest and joy to the business of living. It is an erudite despair: Mr. Eliot stems his poem from a recent anthropological study of primitive beliefs, as embodied in the Grail legend and other flaming quests which quickened men in other times; he quotes, or misquotes, lines from the "Satyricon of Petronius," "Tristan und Isolde," the sacred books of the Hindus, Dante, Baudelaire, Verlaine, nursery rhymes, the Old Testament and modern jazz songs. His method is highly elliptical, based on the curious formula of Tristan Corbiere, wherein reverential and blasphemous ideas are juxtaposed in amazing antitheses, and there are mingled all the shining verbal toys, impressions and catch lines of a poet who has read voraciously and who possesses an insatiable curiosity about life. It is analysis and realism, psychology and criticism, anguish, bitterness and disillusion, with passages of great lyrical beauty."

Net $1.50

FIG. 8.3. Front flap of the original dust jacket for *The Waste Land*.

necessary to remind people it was not "Waste Land" but *The* Waste Land: three words, not two.

Reviews were often pitched at nonspecialist general interest readers, coasting along on a soft carpet of unexamined assumptions about the arts, culture at large, civil discourse, and acceptable behavior. To come to Eliot's poem with a few platitudes about decency, intelligibility, and ease of access to poetic chestnuts was to be brutally confronted with something not only unknown but perilously close to the unknowable. Eliot originally wanted to use, as epigraph to the poem, Kurtz's gasp "The horror, the horror!" from Conrad's *Heart of Darkness*, but Pound talked him out of it. Had it remained, some reviewers would surely have flung it back at the poem itself.

Two notable omissions color all the reviews of *The Waste Land*. First, there was no reference to (nor any suppositions concerning) the nervous breakdown suffered by its author. In fact, several of those who wrote the most probing reviews—including Aiken, Wilson, and Seldes—knew of Eliot's personal plight. The second omission concerns the role of Pound in editing and shaping the original heap of fragments shored against the author's ruins. The famous dedication to Pound was not added until the poem was reprinted in *Poems 1909–1925*. Lacking awareness of the role Pound had played in convening a certain intelligibility for a heterogeneous ensemble, reviewers were left to speculate about the poem's disorderly conduct.

So plentiful were reviews and notices that there were reviews of other reviews, as in Christopher Morley's "Apollo and Apollinaris," which appeared in the *New York Evening Post* of January 9, 1923. He capped off his report by observing,

> Eliot is a mighty clever chap, and *The Waste Land* is unquestionably a highly sophisticated and cathartic bolus of cynical humor. But it has almost crazed some of the more advanced critics, who try with lamentable gravity to find Deep Meanings in some high-spirited spoofing.

For Morley, the poem was of negligible interest, and he may not have bothered to read it. The real news was the gossip, not the verse.

There was some derision in the reviews, understandable given that many metropolitan papers felt obliged to cover a newsworthy event. But even positive reviews tucked in a few throwaway barbs. In a sampling of characterizations meant to raise eyebrows, *The Waste Land* was charged with being an affront to literary values, as well as

> a hodge-podge of grandeur and jargon
> a parade of pompous erudition
> deliberate mystification
> a phantasmagoric fade-out of God
> the altar of some fantastic Mumbo-Jumbo
> one of the most insubordinate poems in the language

If some found the poem of negligible interest—one critic, punning on the title, called it "waste paper"—many found Eliot overly cerebral. He was thought flippant, pompous, and presumptuous by some, withdrawn and unresponsive by others. Some tried to have it both ways: Eliot was "a dandy of the choicest phrase"—a figure at once derogatory and laudatory.

Reviewers puzzled over what the poem was about. "It is an erudite despair," opined Burton Rascoe, and "the sardonic grin which suffuses it is a rictus which masks a hurt romantic with sentiments plagued by crass reality." For Edmund Wilson, Eliot depicted "the human soul as a mess." The poet Elinor Wylie came up with the most exceptional characterization. The author was "a cadaver, dissecting himself in our sight." "If this is a trick, it is an inspired one," she added.

Critics were either perplexed by or resentful of the multitude of references and quotations, especially if they were nagged by the notes, which some perceived as insolent. J. L. Lucas complained, "A poem that has to be explained in notes is not unlike a picture with 'This is a dog' inscribed beneath"; while Gorham Munson imagined a reader for whom the notes appeared to be an invitation to higher learning. Munson foresaw a reader's resentment when he "discovers that after all his research he has not penetrated into some strange uncharted region of experience but has only fathomed the cipher of a quite ordinary and easily understandable state of mind"—namely, despair.

Because *The Waste Land* was unorthodox, many were befuddled about the subject. It's remarkable how few realized that the title named the topic, and that the poem concluded with a reference to its method ("these fragments I have shored against my ruin"). Initial impressions were duly registered as a way of dipping a toe in purportedly turbulent waters. For the antimodernist J. C. Squire, it was little more than "a vagrant string of drab pictures which abruptly change, and these are interspersed with memories of literature, lines from old poets, and disconnected ejaculations." Others found the poem "a collection of flashes" "boiling in the nozzle of the whirlwind," amounting to "a cross-section of the human consciousness of a single specific human being."

Harriet Monroe, who had published "Prufrock" in *Poetry*, found *The Waste Land* "kaleidoscopic, profuse, a rattle and rain of colors that fall somehow into place." Reference to a kaleidoscope is telling, in that Baudelaire used the same figure when evoking the experience of urban crowds. The modern artist, he wrote, "enters the crowd as though it were an immense reservoir of electrical energy. Or we might liken him to a mirror as vast as the crowd itself; to a kaleidoscope gifted with consciousness." Herbert O. Gorman also applied the kaleidoscopic analogy to Eliot's poem, suggesting that there were two approaches: one that doted on detail (which he compared to a viewer examining palette daubs and brushstrokes in Whistler and Monet) and a more holistic apprehension. "One may easily isolate a passage and call it chaff from a spinning mind, just as one may isolate a bit of colored glass in a kaleidoscope and note that it is nothing more than glass. But the ensemble becomes a thing of magic."

Louis Untermeyer criticized the poem's "kaleidoscopic movement in which the bright-colored pieces fail to atone for the absence of an integrated design." The presumption of a dialectic between part and whole was the interpretive reflex many readers brought to the poem. For some it was a casual assumption, and insofar as it remained casual, they could be unperturbed. But the lure of "hidden form" was too tempting for others. "I am compelled to reject the poem as a sustained harmoniously functioning structural unit," wrote Munson. "On the other hand, it is amazing how simple is the state of mind which these broken forms convey." The broken forms, he suggests, are the fruit of a method "which is to take ancient beauty by the neck and twist it into modern ugliness." Given such savagery, another critic sneered, "a grunt would serve equally well."

Forms and formalism persisted as terms of reference. American poet John Crowe Ransom found the poem "the apotheosis of modernity" because it "seems to bring to a head all the specifically modern errors." These included "an extremely free verse which we know as the medium of a half-hearted and disillusioned art"; but the worst offense was Eliot's conflation of form with "formula"—though Ransom refrained from specifying what the formula was. Conrad Aiken offered a more audacious take on the question of form or design: "If it is a plan, then its principle is oddly akin to planlessness."

The most receptive readers of *The Waste Land* were those (to use a later idiom) who could go with the flow. The issue of plan or underlying unity was moot, thought Harriet Monroe, when one sees that, for the poet, "it is a condition, not a theory, which confronts him." The condition was manifestly chaotic—an unfamiliar sensation in poetry—but self-identified moderns among Eliot's readership recognized that the poem approximated a contemporary bedlam. Mood and emotion precipitate an atmosphere in which the wasteland shimmers like a mirage.

There was a medley of details, evocations of discrepant moments and events, but as a poem it had a sequence. The five numbered parts prompted some to conclude it was not one but several poems. Aiken speculated that it "originally consisted of a number of separate poems which have been telescoped—given a kind of forced unity." (Although he was Eliot's friend, he had not been privy to its composition.) Clive Bell identified in Eliot an engine "in perpetual want of grist." Unable to gush, he could only scavenge for material: "Birdlike he must pile up wisps and straws" to fill out the poem. An insistent concern was how such a hodgepodge could make an impact. There was a "rhythm of alteration," Gilbert Seldes observed, "between the spoken and the unspoken thought" in the poem. This touched on psychological matters most reviewers shied clear of.

Rhythm was key, suggesting a receptivity below conscious awareness. Helen McAfee, like Seldes, detected it through the lens of psychology and the way consciousness can serve "the bidding of the subconscious." In Eliot's poem, she discerned, "the parts move with a certain rhythm—the rhythm of daydreams—and, dream-fashion, resolve one into another and so achieve a whole. It is mood more than idea that gives the poem its unity. And that mood is black." Harold Monro likewise appealed to the model of the dream, going so far as to suggest that "this poem actually is a dream presented without any poetic boast, bluff or padding; and it lingers in the mind more like a dream than a poem, which is one of the reasons why it is both obscure and amusing." He also compared it to a cloud "which, though remaining the same cloud, changes its form repeatedly as one looks."

Music was also commonly used to explain the poem's unusual aura. One reviewer found that it lingered in the mind as "a sound of high and desolate music." Aiken, himself a seasoned recipient of the lingering provocations of Wagnerism, thought it merited description as program music. "We 'accept' the poem as we would accept a powerful, melancholy tone-poem." To *accept* is not the same as to *understand*.

Musical references could be used to suggest a more sinister turn. A reviewer for *The Double Dealer* found the poem an "agonized outcry of a sensitive romanticist drowning in a sea of jazz." "Sometimes it turns suddenly and shockingly into the jazz of the music-halls," noted Edmund Wilson. Untermeyer, incensed by the lack of any apparent governing pattern, derisively itemized "Eliot's jumble of narratives, nursery-rhymes, criticism, jazz rhythms, 'Dictionary of Favorite Phrases' and a few lyrical moments." Jazz was a largely disreputable reference at the time, redeemed only slightly by Clive Bell's use of the term to characterize what was most distinctive in modern art, literature, and music.

An infamous allegation concerning Eliot's poem was in the very first issue of *Time* magazine in a column provocatively titled "Shantih, Shantih, Shantih: Has the Reader Any Rights before the Bar of Literature?" In the final paragraph, "It is rumored that *The Waste Land* was written as a hoax." This incendiary statement was compounded by the erroneous assertion that the Dial Award was "for the best poem of 1922." No other print source refers to a hoax, but this suggestion does attest to the notoriety surrounding the poem's publication.

A concern raised in several reviews was the suspicion that, if not a hoax, *The Waste Land* was the result of some unsavory cabal, foisting undercooked fare on a gullible public. In his regular column for the *New York Herald Tribune*, Burton Rascoe reported a rumor that "a group of us are conspiring to mislead the public." His was a literary gossip column, which he stoked by recounting a meeting with Edmund Wilson and Elinor Wylie, who shared his excitement about *The Waste Land*. Wilson wrote two of the first reviews of the poem, Wylie wrote one, and Rascoe penned numerous salutes. But he insisted there was no group effort involved.

The source of the rumor of a cabal, Rascoe surmised, was Untermeyer, whose damning review of Eliot's poem had appeared a week earlier. The poem's "mingling of willful obscurity and weak vaudeville," Untermeyer wrote, "compels us to believe that the pleasure which many admirers derive from 'The Waste Land' is the same sort of gratification attained through having solved a puzzle, a form of self-congratulation." Wilson in his earlier review may have provided grist for the reference, when he suggested that some would suspect that "Eliot has written a puzzle rather than a poem."

In London's *New Statesman*, F. L. Lucas lamented that "at present it is particularly easy to win the applause of the *blasé* and the young, of the coteries and the eccentricities." This at least has the virtue of forecasting the avidity of the young and impressionable for Eliot's poem in the following years. Untermeyer had made a similar assertion about the American response, suggesting that the Dial Award and the poem "have occasioned a display of some of the most enthusiastically naive superlatives that have ever issued from publicly sophisticated iconoclasts."

A more reasoned take on the promotional incentives behind Eliot's poem was by Mary M. Colum, wife of Padraic Colum, who was a regular contributor to *The Dial*. She cited Rascoe and Wilson, and mentioned Gilbert Seldes as another enthusiast—an important reference, as he was assistant editor at the journal during the publication of "The Waste Land" (and would soon publish his influential celebration of popular culture, *The 7 Lively Arts*). Born in 1884, Colum was just old enough to refer to these "Saint Pauls of the new literary gospel" ten years her junior as "astonishingly bold and assertive young persons, to whom the editors of the intellectual publications give plenty of space for the adumbration of their ideas." Rascoe had his "Bookman's Daybook" column in the *New York Herald Tribune*, but the others were also in commanding positions, with Seldes at *The Dial* and Edmund Wilson the editor of *Vanity Fair*.

Colum's concern was not about the merits of Eliot's poem, but about "group-criticism," which she found lacking in subtlety, possessed of "the assertiveness and all-inclusiveness of a patent-medicine advertisement." As for Eliot, he deserved respectful attention, but his was an "assimilative mind and not the creative mind at all." For the latter, she recommends Joyce, "a universal artist." In fact, she and her husband were close friends and supporters of their fellow Irishman.

In the wake of the debates around *The Waste Land*, few would consider Eliot any less universal than Joyce. So thoroughly were the two men bound together in the public imagination, it was rare to find references to one without the other, whether positive or negative; they were presumed to be working in tandem. Seldes, in his review, proposed that Eliot as introvert and Joyce as extrovert together formed the nucleus of modernism. Wylie figured Joyce as the sea from which fisher-king Eliot snagged his catch. For many others, however, there was little concern to distinguish between the two. They were simply the Eliot-Joyce combo, avatars of the Men of 1914.

It was sensible to combine them, since they were hyped by Pound and published in the same little magazines. It was also the case that both were working their materials beyond the norms of their genres. In his review of *Ulysses* in *The Dial* (November 1923, exactly a year after the *Waste Land* issue), Eliot hailed Joyce's book as a step beyond the novel ("The novel is a form which will no longer serve"). He meant it as a compliment, mindful that there were those who disqualified *The Waste Land* because it failed to mimic verse conventions.

Eliot's review concluded with a vision of *Ulysses* that reads much like a description of his own poem. Having been paired with Joyce by the critics, he would now take it a step further and disclose the unity. What poem and novel shared was the "mythical method," deploying "a continuous parallel between contemporaneity and antiquity." The continuous sounding of the bells of antiquity is overt in *The Waste Land*, with its quotes and references. Joyce makes the mythic parallel explicit in his title (which only by inference points to his main character, Leopold Bloom). While teachers and students commonly refer to the chapters by way of Homeric parallels (Scylla and Charybdis, Oxen of the Sun, Calypso, Penelope, etc.), these are not given in the text.

A measure of the challenge faced by critics reviewing *The Waste Land* is how infrequently references were made to other poets or poems. A few mentioned Laforgue; one thought it could be chalked up to Tristan Corbière; and another recognized affinities with James Thomson's long London poem *The City of Dreadful Night* (1874). Eliot's alliance with Pound was noted, usually at the expense of the latter (Wilson referred to "his imitator Mr Ezra Pound"). Apparently Eliot's poem thwarted comparison, whether positive or negative.

Mina Loy was one of the few who took a broader view, concerning which the eternal battle of the sexes was once again registered strictly from a male perspective: "Practically the whole of our psychological literature written by men might be lumped together as the unwitting analysis of the unsatisfied woman." Eliot's typist, she noted, was observed in her sordid affair with the carbuncular clerk "with the same disrespectfully acute ray of observation that he turns on classicism and pessimism alike."

Inasmuch as there *were* comparisons to be made, Eliot was often compared to himself. Was this new poem an advance on earlier work? Did it contravene principles and practices evident in what preceded it? Or was it the culmination of a developmental trajectory? Many weighed in, but it was a hung jury. Another comparison was Eliot the poet and Eliot the critic. He had carefully formed his public image along these parallel tracks, so it was only sensible to wonder whether they worked in concert. In *The Dial* statement of its award, the editors tried to skirt the issue: "We hope not to be asked whether it is his criticism or his poetry which constitutes that service to letters which the award is intended to acknowledge." Untermeyer took "the absence of any verbal acrobatics from Mr. Eliot's prose" as evidence of a sound mind, proof therefore that the poem was an aberration.

Eliot's brother Henry kept him abreast of the American coverage ("undoubtedly the literary sensation over here, outstripping, I think, *Ulysses*— which derives part of its fame from the fact that nobody can get hold of it"). Henry liked the poem but complained it was dragged down by "considerable 'spoofing.'" It was like a practical joke overly prolonged. He bristled at the allusions and quotations as well: "I do not like a poem to be a scrap book." His mother wrote to Eliot's uncle to explain how the poet's domestic circumstances had resulted in the shattered ideals of the poem; and she hoped that he would follow it up with "its natural sequence 'The coming of the Grail.'"

Eliot was pleased to have created a sensation but confessed to a growing disgruntlement, finding *The Waste Land* "merely a kind of consummation of my past work, not the initiation of something new, and it will take me all my courage and persistence, and perhaps a long time, to do something better." In fact, it was two years before he produced another poem, "The Hollow Men," which reads like an appendix to *The Waste Land*. It was not until several years after his conversion to the Church of England that the altogether different *Ash Wednesday* appeared in 1930.

The eminent French poet Paul Valéry wrote Eliot to express his gratification at "un étrange monde lyrique" in *The Waste Land*. In particular, "La combinaison singulière de l'antique et du moderne donne des effets que je n'ai trouvé nulle part encore" (The curious combination of ancient and modern produces effects such as I have never seen anywhere before). Actually, Pound's Cantos had previously engaged this dialectic, with its hunt for resonances between motifs and episodes across time. Edmund Wilson, despite his swipe at Pound, recognized this as a core principle of *The Waste Land*, pitched between the temporal zones of history and the present moment. Eliot "loves to make its oracles as deep as the experience of the race itself by piling up stratum upon stratum of reference," so he "hears in his own parched cry the voices of all the thirsty men of the past." This vision of time as the echo chamber of history adhered to Eliot's own formula in "Tradition and the Individual Talent."

For aspiring young writers like Wilson, Gilbert Seldes, Gorham Munson, and Allen Tate, the advent of *The Waste Land* offered a welcome occasion for demonstrating their advanced tastes and critical acumen. For most other reviewers, the poem was a perplexing and sometimes alarming phenomenon, confirming their worst suspicions. Many among those assigned the task of placing the poem or the poet were simply newsmen on a beat, and why should they submit to the arcane enigmatic puffery of a nonsensical poem? I make this point because there are no winners or losers in the gambit created by *The Waste Land*. It only seems that way in retrospect, though retrospect commenced right away in Eliot's case in his role as editor of *The Criterion*. For that was an ambitious taste-making gambit, and he was at the helm until it ceased publication in 1939.

Yvor Winters, despite his adoption of Imagism for his early poetry, repudiated modernism generally and Eliot in particular. He ridiculed *The Waste Land* as merely "broken blank verse interspersed with bad free verse and rimed doggerel." And, in a telling analogy, he proposed that "the method is that of a man who is unable to deal with his subject, and resorts to the rough approximation of quotation; it is the method of the New England farmer who meets every situation in life with a saw from *Poor Richard*." This is just peevishness. Writing during the Second World War, when Eliot's authority seemed invincible, Winters knew he had little chance of prevailing in the court of public opinion.

More revealing than the reviews—which, after all, were intended as public notices—were private exchanges in conversation or correspondence. Everyone was expected to have an opinion. Edmund Wilson was invited to contribute an essay review of Eliot's poem to the December issue of *The Dial*, a month after its appearance in the November issue. He had recently become editor of *Vanity Fair*, succeeding his friend John Peale Bishop. The two had collaborated on a themed collection of poems, *The*

Undertaker's Garland, published earlier in 1922. Bishop had moved to Paris, so correspondence was the only way the friends could share their experience of Eliot's bombshell.

Wilson had access to advance page proofs of the book, writing Bishop in early September: "I am much excited about Eliot's *The Waste Land*, which I have just read," he reported. "It will give you quite a thrill, I think; it is certainly his masterpiece so far. He supplements it with a set of notes almost as long as the poem itself." Wilson was among those who knew about Eliot's breakdown, which he disclosed to Bishop, finding the poem "nothing more or less than a most distressingly moving account of Eliot's own agonized state of mind during the years which preceded his nervous breakdown. Never have the sufferings of the sensitive man in the modern city chained to some work he hates and crucified on the vulgarity of his surroundings been so vividly set forth. It is certainly a cry *de profundis* if ever there was one—almost the cry of a man on the verge of insanity." Given the urgency of his appraisal, it's all the more striking that Wilson published two reviews of the poem without any reference to Eliot's state of mind.

Bishop took the bait. By December, he found that "the chief difficulty is to eradicate T. S. Eliot from all future work." Wilson urged him to lay off: "For heaven's sake do read somebody besides Eliot for a little while—he is enslaving your style and your imagination." A month later Bishop confessed to being still obsessed with Eliot, but "I assure you I no longer want to go on in that direction which is aside from questions of individuality, an unsatisfactory one. I suspect that even Eliot thinks so. If Eliot succeeds, it is only because of his superlative technique and the intensity of his suffering." Despite his resolve, two years later Bishop was still struggling to get out from under Eliot's thumb. He wrote fellow poet Archibald MacLeish, "The problem is what to do about Eliot. Now with me, the pernicious influence has largely been Eliot's rhythm." It might be overcome, he surmised, "if only we were surrounded by enough bottles and the appropriate books." In the end, Bishop achieved a more analytical appraisal. "If only we can contrive to get rid of the Eliotic indirection, the left handed indication, the gaps that are more eloquent than said, references that are more profound than the content," then and only then might autonomy be achieved.

A dinner Bishop had with Ezra Pound in Paris provides a revealing glimpse of Eliot mania. This was during the height of his swooning letters to Wilson. Bishop was plying Pound for personal details of his new idol, with Pound deep in his cups and dishing out tall tales spiced with actual details.

Eliot is tubercular and disposed toward epilepsy. On one occasion he decided to kill himself in Pound's house but funked at the final moment. The psychological hour in *Lustra* gives E. P.'s reaction to T. S. E.'s wedding which was substituted on the spur of the moment for a tea engagement at Pound's. It seems that Thomas and Vivienne arrived in the hallway and then turned back, went to the registrar's and were wed, to everybody's subsequent pain and misery.

None of this is repeated in other sources. Pound was probably tickled by the young poet's credulity.

The Eliotic elixir did not affect everyone the same way. As soon as he read "The Waste Land" in *The Dial*, Hart Crane wrote Gorham Munson, editor of the little magazine *Secession*, "What do you think of Eliot's *The Wasteland*? I was rather disappointed. It was good, of course, but so damned dead. Neither does it, in my opinion, add anything important to Eliot's achievement." A few weeks later he acknowledged that for two years his poetry "has been more influenced by Eliot than any other modern." But he clarified the impact. "I take Eliot as a point of departure toward an almost complete reverse of direction." Crane wanted to retain the lesson of Eliot's poetry while divesting himself of the pessimism, striving instead for something positive, even ecstatic. He did concede one intriguing point, noting that Eliot "has outclassed Baudelaire with a devastating humor that the earlier poet lacked."

The scale of Crane's debt preceded "The Waste Land" by several years. In 1918 he wrote to Vanderbilt undergraduate Allen Tate, congratulating him after his first exposure to "Prufrock." "You will profit by reading him again and again," he expected, adding, "I must have read 'Prufrock' twenty-five times and things like the 'Preludes' more often." Even at this early point in his development, Crane did not feel constricted by Eliot. "Having absorbed him enough we can trust ourselves as never before."

Tate, for his part, was gobsmacked in a typically undergraduate way. He and a friend drafted "The Chaste Land," festooned with footnotes. He was immensely gratified when his younger roommate, "Red" (Robert Penn) Warren, painted mural scenes from the poem on their dorm room wall. Tate was an active member of the Fugitive group of poets in Nashville, and elder Fugitive Donald Davidson warned that he was limiting his potential as a poet "by the Eliotish manner." Tate persisted, sending poems to *Vanity Fair*. Edmund Wilson saw the debt right away. "I look forward to something extraordinary from you," he told the young poet. "But do try to get out of the artistic clutches of T. S. Eliot," reprising his advice to Bishop. Wilson's own career proceeded without the shadow of Eliot looming over him, mainly because he stopped writing poetry and concentrated on nonfiction prose. He wrote the first influential account of modernism in literature with *Axel's Castle: A Study in the Imaginative Literature of 1870–1930* published in 1931, with chapters on Yeats, Valéry, Eliot, Proust, Joyce, Stein, French symbolism, and Rimbaud.

Tate's fixation on Eliot nearly terminated his relationship with his teacher and mentor John Crowe Ransom. Shortly after "The Waste Land" appeared in *The Dial*, Ransom wrote Tate to express his incredulity. One speculative remark was sure to get Tate's goat: "Have you been struck with any resemblance between Vachel Lindsay (of all people) and Eliot?" Ransom wondered with faux innocence, knowing Tate was smitten with the poem. "The latter is a kind of burlesque or reductio ad absurdum of the former, carries three or four times as many tunes forward at one time, and repeats with unholy mock-unction things that Vachel gets out of his system with revival fervor. Funny."

American poets, transfixed as they were by Eliot's poem, had the advantage of geographical distance to insulate them from the man's shadow. The English were not so lucky. When Edgell Rickword reviewed Eliot's *Poems 1909–1925*, he reflected that "if there were to be held a Congress of the Younger Poets, and it were desired to make some kind of show of recognition to the poet who has most effectively upheld the reality of the art in an age of preposterous poeticizing, it is not possible to think of any serious rival to the name of T. S. Eliot." The reason, according to Rickword, was that "Eliot has been able to get closer than any other poet to the physiology of our sensations (a poet does not speak merely for himself), to explore and make palpable the more intimate distress of a generation for whom all the romantic escapes had been blocked." Among such escapes, "even 'Satanism' at its 1890 naughtiest had suddenly acquired a hangdog, old-fashioned air," mused American poet Horace Gregory.

W. H. Auden, who would emerge as the foremost poet of his generation, later penned lines acknowledging Eliot's role. When things got dark, he wrote,

> Blank day after day, the unheard-of drought, it was you
> Who, not speechless with shock but finding the right
>   Language for thirst and fear, did most to
>   Prevent a panic.

Auden famously renounced his juvenilia the moment he read *The Waste Land*, but it's important to recall that the Waste Land generation extended from those like Bishop and Wilson born in the early 1890s to those like Auden who went to university in the mid-1920s. During the 1930s, that generation was succeeded by the Auden generation, a phenomenon sanctioned in part by Eliot's role in publishing the poetry of Auden, Stephen Spender, and Louis MacNeice at Faber. Not every member of this cohort was beholden to Eliot, however. Cecil Day Lewis was dismissive of *The Waste Land*, deeming it "chiefly important as a social document." That was certainly the role it played in Evelyn Waugh's novel *Brideshead Revisited*, as an Oxbridge undergraduate declaims the poem on a campus quad: "After luncheon he stood on the balcony with a megaphone which had appeared surprisingly among the bric-à-brac of Sebastian's room, and in languishing tones recited passages from *The Waste Land* to the sweatered and muffled throng that was on its way to the river."

Eliot's own generation was captivated by the amplitude of the poem's aesthetic soundings, and by a reverence accorded the filchings from the classics that outweighed the irreverence of the music hall and Cockney pub chatter. But for the younger generation, *The Waste Land* was not high lament but high camp. The flippant posturing of the Bright Young Things of Auden's generation was a bad-boy attitude adopted in elite circles for the choreographed scandal of the matrons and public school officials. It was a voguish petulance.

In retrospect, Auden valued the tacit instruction provided by Eliot's example. As he reflected, it "made it possible for English poetry to deal with all the properties of modern city life, and to write poems in which the structure is musical rather than logical." In more personal terms, he recalled that "the provincial England of 1907, when I was born, was Tennysonian in outlook; whatever its outlook the England of 1925 when I went up to Oxford was the Waste Land in character. I cannot imagine any other single writer could have carried me through from the one to the other." More pungently, combining Tennyson and Eliot, he quipped, "If it is a natural preference to inhabit a room with casements upon Fairyland, one of them at least should open upon the Waste Land."

"However sheltered our young lives, however rural our normal surroundings, however pre–Industrial Revolution our education, we knew in our bones," wrote Irish-born MacNeice, "this which Eliot expressed so succinctly and vividly, this was what we were up against." Thanks to Eliot, MacNeice, like so many others, romanticized an urban squalor remote from their own rural upbringing. Slumming, they would "paddle along the evil-smelling canal through the slums," languishing in "an idle world of oily sunlit water," in search of "a sense of things worn out, scrap-iron and refuse, the shadow of the gas-drum, this England."

Poet (and later Blake scholar) Kathleen Raine, a year younger than Auden, thought of Eliot as "the poet who had taken upon himself the burden of experiencing the world for his generation." But for *her* generation ("a generation saturated in Atheism, Freudianism and Marxism") Eliot "enabled us to know our world imaginatively. All those who have lived in the Waste Land of London, can, I suppose, remember the particular occasion on which, reading T. S. Eliot's poems for the first time, an experience of the contemporary world that had been nameless and formless, suddenly received its apotheosis." For the young in general, "the modern world came into focus for the first time," wrote Norman Nicholson. One of them was Cyril Connolly, who recalled that "we were like new-born goslings" for whom Eliot served as a handy eraser. "Houseman, Flecker and the Georgians all melted away overnight."

James Reeve recalled entering Cambridge as an undergraduate. "The stranger who enters an Anglican church at service time is handed two books, *Hymns Ancient and Modern* and *The Book of Common Prayer*," while university proffered "in much the same spirit, two little books, the one in prose, the other in verse. They were *The Sacred Wood* and *Poems 1909–1925*." The mystique surrounding the man behind these breviaries was deftly conveyed by Aldington:

> He is a cosmopolitan, but he enjoys the flavor of nationality. He writes for an audience equipped to understand him, and is indifferent to popular success. His mind is exceedingly complex and moves with a rapidity incomprehensible to sluggish wits. He is perilously balanced among the rude forces of a turbulent mechanical age; he walks the tight-rope over an abyss and he knows it. His work has the gusto of peril.

Prospective readers, like Reeves, relished the tightrope. As he admitted, "So deeply has Eliot's poetic world sunk into my unconscious that I find myself continually remembering his images as if they were my own memories."

The feeling of being haunted and instructed was shared by William Empson: "I feel, like most other verse writers of my generation, that I do not know for certain how much of my own mind he invented, let alone how much of it is a reaction against him or indeed a consequence of misreading him." Empson bore the stamp of *The Waste Land* in his decision to append notes to his early poems. In a 1935 defense of his notes, he argued, "It is impertinent to suggest that the reader ought to possess already any odd bit of information one may have picked up," particularly given that "there is no longer a reasonably small field which may be taken as general knowledge."

In fact, as Empson recognized, the educational background, the classical learning, of Eliot's and Pound's generation had vanished even before the Great War. Yet the discourse of intellectual outlets, with their air of knowledgeable acculturation and ready access, continued to mislead readers with the sense that the references were a handy scorecard, practical aids to sagacity. This, in turn, spawned an obsequious snobbism in which ignorance was masked by the knowing glance and the handling of a cigarette. Such behavior was reinforced by such explicit expressions in the dailies as "we all know" and "it is surely the case that . . ." For the young, wary of class pretensions, *The Waste Land* was a welcome alternative.

MacNeice wondered, "How did we schoolboys come to read Eliot at all? The answer, I am afraid, is largely snobbery; we had seen reviews proclaiming him a modern of the moderns and we too wanted to be 'modern.'" His is a searching account, recognizing that the impact of poetry is not strictly coordinated with conventional assumptions about influence. "What we wanted was 'realism' but—so the paradox goes on—we wanted it for romantic reasons. We wanted to play Hamlet in the shadow of the gas-works. And this was the opening we found—or thought we found—in Eliot." Prufrock, he felt, gave the alienated adolescent a voice, while *The Waste Land* proffered something more profound: "To have painted the Waste Land so precisely that those who had never to their conscious knowledge been there could so fully recognize it at first sight and at every subsequent meeting could find it still as real or more so, was the feat of a great poet."

A revealing perspective on the Eliot generation makes no reference to Eliot, nor does it need to. It's in the autobiography of Donald Friede, who with Pascal Covici ran the American publishing firm bearing their names. While their greatest success was John Steinbeck, among the poets they published were Pound, Aldington, Cummings, Muriel Rukeyser, Horace Gregory, and Joseph Moncure March. In the twenties, Friede recalls, "I ran with the pack that ran ahead of those who ran with the pack. Most of the things I did, I did not quite understand. But that did not bother me too much. I was certain that many of my companions did not understand them either." This outlook, more than anything, made the reception of *The Waste Land* what it was.

Younger poets were more likely to ascribe greatness to one whose seniority set him apart. For his peers, it was different. For Aiken, who had known Eliot all his adult life, *The Waste Land* sparked a keen sense of rivalry. Well aware of his own derivations from Eliot's Prufrockian idiom, Aiken was gratified to find that in *The Waste Land* Eliot was finally indebted to him. Writing to a friend soon after the poem appeared, he wondered,

Am I cuckoo in fancying that it cancels the debt I owed him? I seem to detect echoes or parodies of Senlin, House, Forslin: in the evening at the violet hour etc, Madame Sosostris etc, and in general the 'symphonic' nature, the references to music (Wagner, Strawinsky) and the repetition of motifs, and the 'crowd' stuff beginning 'Unreal city.' However, that's neither here nor there: it's the best thing I've seen in years.

Aiken's review of *The Waste Land* was titled "An Anatomy of Melancholy," to which Eliot sternly responded: "There's nothing melancholy about it— it's nothing but pure calculation of affect"—a telling acknowledgment of the cold, imperturbable mask he'd assumed as a way of shielding himself from unwelcome intimacy.

Eliot was overplaying the calculation involved, but he was surely aware that some of his generational peers would be keenly attentive to a poet-critic as fastidiously self-conscious as he was. One of them was English writer Mary Butts, who felt that Eliot's presence had a preemptive effect not only on her own work but on the spirit of the time. On Christmas Day 1927 she wrote in her diary:

> T. S. Eliot, with his ear on some stops of english speech which have not been used before, the only writer of my quality, dislikes me & my work, I think. But what is interesting is that he is working on the Sanc-Grail, on its negative side, the Waste Land. Up to now, he has been before me with my titles. *The Sacred Wood*; *The Waste Land.*

Ten years earlier she had presciently registered her recognition that a "new imagination" was underway, "a new synthesis," listing as its avatars Joyce, Eliot, and Wyndham Lewis. She was, in 1917, among Eliot's first readers, and she continued to be attentive to his poetry, frequently copying out passages in her journal, and twice (a decade apart) transcribing the whole of "Gerontion."

The first published book on Eliot was by Hugh Ross Williamson, in which there is a reference to Mary Butts. In fact, the author was convinced that Butts was the more important writer, forecasting that by 1950 her reputation would prevail in her synthesis of "Eliot's intellectual classicism with Lawrence's emotional romanticism." She did in fact have some contact with Eliot. She tried to get him to write a preface to a revised English edition of her novel *Ashe of Rings* (it had been published by Robert McAlmon's Contact Editions in Paris in 1925). Eliot politely begged off, citing his edition of Pound's poetry as the exception to a principle to which he professed to adhere with regard to living writers. (Nonetheless, a few years later he wrote an introduction to Djuna Barnes's novel *Nightwood*.) Yet Eliot admired her stories, and welcomed a selection for Faber and Faber; sadly, his letter was in the mail when she died in 1937.

The most consequential link between Butts and Eliot is thematic. They were nearly the same age, and both derived much from Frazer's *Golden Bough* and Jessie Weston's *Ritual and Romance*. Butts's novel *Armed with Madness* (1928) is a compelling reenactment of Grail motifs set amid the casual dissipations of the twenties generation. As a resident of Paris during that decade, she was particularly attuned to an underworld of drugs, White Russian exiles, and homosexuality. Jean Cocteau was a close friend and contributed illustrations to her work. But her fiction is unusual in combining that netherworld with the England she knew best, both urban and rural.

Butts was raised in Dorset near the coast at the family estate, Salternes. Her great-grandfather was the patron of William Blake, and there was a Blake room in the house filled with his artwork (now part of the Tate collection). Mary's father guided her receptivity to Blake and much else that kindled her childhood imagination. Above all, the family environs provided a sense of *temenos*, or sacred enclosure.

In a letter of 1923 she described Salternes:

> There is no road to us from the top of Kimmeridge hill, but two miles of turf & a track down to the place where a wood shaped like a narrow fan runs up from the sea. That's called the Sacred Wood. Most people are afraid of it & say it is full of ghosts, & it is . . . I walk all day & at night, when the Sacred Wood dances, I dance too. And all the while, the wild life presses in.

Mary's sense of the sacred took many forms throughout her life, from pagan tree worship to the Anglo-Catholicism that she, like Eliot, later embraced.

Butts's pursuit of exaltation was founded on a continual self-reckoning, which in turn extended to the tenor of her time and its potential for a "new synthesis." "I have not got it yet, but I am beginning to know what is wrong with the time," she ventured in 1927. "And many of the things we do are not wrong, it is our way of doing them. They are very good things—Paederasty & jazz & opium & research." This odd list is a precise barometer of Mary Butts's unique outlook. Marianne Moore characterized her as "the frog that jumps twenty times his own length."

She was a clairvoyant of self-scrutiny, an outlook that informed her fiction. However dissimilar her lifestyle was to that of Eliot, she was one of the few to really relate to the sacramental pulse of his poetry—and, what's more, to have channeled that same aura in her fiction. "Why catch up with the Holy Spirit when He is hovering over Asia and saying 'Shantih'? He is in a nut in a Glastonbury thicket," she decided, ten years after *The Waste Land*. And as for human vitality, "There's more divine life in me than in any man I've known."

Butts explored something further that was inimical to Eliot, sexual passion. "Polyandry a most natural affair," she recorded in her journal. Immersed in the psychoanalytic theories of Freud and Jung, "I think that I am a fair example of libido rising freely into the conscious." Her exploration of libidinal matters could take unexpected turns. In January 1920 she found Wyndham Lewis to be "the first man I have met whose vitality equals, probably surpasses mine." In her fantasy, "A pleasure to be raped by him. Yes, that's true." In fact, nothing came of it, though he was a notorious womanizer. A few weeks later she ponders how men are fools at love. "Go away & flirt with Wyndham Lewis. Bim will come prowling after. I shall let myself be won back. How often! Do I care a pin for either of them? Or for some idea of love for which they are funnel? Flesh loves flesh. What does the mind love?" "Bim" was her husband, John Rodker. Together they ran the Ovid Press, which published Lewis's *Fifteen Drawings*, Pound's *Hugh Selwyn Mauberley*, and Eliot's *Ara Vos Prec*, among other titles. These were most likely typeset by Mary, who also provided much of the financial support for the press.

Mary Butts was one of several women who were inspired, befriended, or helped by T. S. Eliot, a story continued in chapter 10. But as I have suggested here, Butts felt herself uniquely to be a rival. Eliot may have been poaching her (privately held) titles, but she felt herself attuned to an ancient poetic wisdom from which both of them drew, a subject she addressed in a poem published in 1924, "Pythian Ode":

> The mind of the priests of the oracle. A delicious enquiry
> into the next event but one.
> A game of chance, a game of chess, a guess-game.

There was one reader of *The Waste Land* for whom the game was personal. Part II of the poem, "A Game of Chess," includes lines that Pound recognized as a glimpse into the Eliot household.

> 'My nerves are bad to-night. Yes, bad. Stay with me.
> 'Speak to me. Why do you never speak. Speak.

'What are you thinking of? What thinking? What?
'I never know what you are thinking. Think.'
I think we are in rats' alley
Where the dead men lost their bones.

The poem compounds the neurotic impasse: "What shall we do tomorrow?" and "What shall we ever do?" Humming throughout the passage are those nerves—bad, yes bad. More explicitly than any other part of *The Waste Land*, "A Game of Chess" documents the Eliot marriage—in one case too explicitly for Vivien, who asked Tom to delete the line "The ivory men make company between us." But she let stand the next one: "Pressing lidless eyes and waiting for a knock upon the door."

Vivien recognized the toll her afflictions imposed on her husband. "You know I am ill and an endless drag on him," she confided to Richard Aldington. In her diary at the end of 1919 she morbidly wrote, "Glad this awful year is over. Next year probably worse." And yet it went on, grinding the marriage into a miasma of misery. Ottoline was shocked at Vivien's treatment of Tom. "She spoke to him as if he was a dog." The chess match spilled out of the chessboard. In 1925 Eliot wrote, "In the last ten years— gradually, but deliberately—I have made myself into a *machine*. I have done it deliberately—in order to endure, in order not to feel—*but it has killed* V." Reflecting on his marital calamity much later he wrote, "To her the marriage brought no happiness," but "to me, it brought the state of mind out of which came *The Waste Land*." This is a stark reckoning, this disclosure about the price exacted by a poem.

CHAPTER NINE

Other Voices

The immediate response to *The Waste Land*, documented in the previous chapter, indicates that while many hedged their bets, the poem was a distinctly high-profile literary event. Left generally unspoken was the question What did it portend? Reviewers were unsure. But many others—men of letters, fellow poets—were more confident that Eliot's poem was a game changer. This chapter offers a closer look at those who were encouraged by *The Waste Land*, and even found that it opened new horizons for their own work.

The Waste Land was unique in how swiftly its impact spread abroad, deliberated upon and translated by major writers in other languages. Here's the familiar opening followed by translations:

> April is the cruelest month, breeding
> Lilacs out of the dead land, mixing
> Memory and desire, stirring
> Dull roots with spring rain.

> Avril est le plus cruel des mois, qui lève
> Les lilas de la terre morte, mêle
> Le souvenir et le désir, éveille
> Les racines assoupies sous la pluie du printemps.
> ("La terre mise à nu" 1926, translated by Jean de Menasce)

> April ist der grausamste Monat, er treibt
> Flieder aus toter Erde, er mischt
> Erinnern und Begehren, er wecket
> Dumpfe Wurzehln mit Lenzregen.
> ("Das wüste Land," 1927, translated by Ernst Robert Curtius)

> Abril es el mes más cruel; engendra
> Lilas de la tierra muerta, mezcla
> Memorias y anhelos, remueve

204

Raíces perezosas con lluvias primaverales.
(*Tierra Baldía*, 1930, translated by Angel Flores)

Abril es el mes más cruel: arbustos de lila engendra sobre yermos
    muertos, mezela al deseo con el recuerdo, agita incoloras raíces con
    las lluvias de primavera.
("El Paramo," 1930, translated by Enrique Munguía, Jr.)

April är grymmast av månaderna—driver
syrener fram ur de döda markerna, blandar
begär och minne, kittlar
dova rötter med vårregn.
("Det öde Landet" 1932, translated by Karin Boye and Erik Mesterton)

Aprile è il più crudele dei mesi: genera
Lillà dalla morta terra, mescola
Ricordo e desiderio, stimola
La sopite radici con la pioggia primaverile.
("La Terra Desolata," 1932, translated by Mario Praz)

As these passages reveal, Eliot produced a translatable poem. His first
three lines end with verbs, and the translations follow accordingly. (Early
translations into Chinese, Japanese, and Urdu could be added, but I can't
read them.) The defining feature of the poem was image, without complicated syntax. With little in the way of traditional verse forms—the aura
of which is elicited through quotation and reference—the poem adheres
to spoken cadences. It's rare for translators to introduce inversions of the
image sequence. In a rare exception, involving the clerk typist, Eliot writes
of the evening hour that "brings the sailor home from the sea. / The typist
home at teatime, clears her breakfast, lights / Her stove, and lays out food
in tins." A period separates the sailor from the typist. But Curtius uses a
comma instead: "heimwärts drängt und den Seefahrer heimbringt, / Das
Tippmädchen. Teezeit." The sense is the same, but the freestanding teatime, "Teezeit," punctuates the scene rather differently.

Two Spanish translations were simultaneously produced. The one in
prose is more ornamental. The other is by Angel Flores, a native of Puerto
Rico who went to New York University for a BA (1923), and later received
a PhD from Cornell. By the time he translated *The Waste Land*, he had
benefited from a decade in the United States. He undertook the translation
to test his proficiency in English, and at the same time he was translating a

novel from Spanish into English, the extraordinary *Cinelandia* by Ramón Gómez de la Serna. Translating both texts at the same time may have honed his perception of Eliot's poem as cinematic. "Su poema es una película erizada de accidentes. A menudo gestos y gestas se acumulan en una imagen, en una frase, y entonces el poeta se asfixia"—His poem is a movie bristling with accidents, its actions concentrated in an image or a phrase, and then the poet "suffocates." That is, the breath stops, and a borrowed phrase from Dante or another source comes to the rescue. Flores also recognized that the poem's length was deceptive: despite the "miraculous economy" of its 433 lines, "the germ of an epic can be discerned." I. A. Richards made precisely the same point: "Allusion in Mr. Eliot's hands is a technical device for compression. *The Waste Land* is the equivalent in content to an epic."

Dealing with Eliot's numerous borrowings could be a challenge. Most leave untranslated the lines and phrases in other languages, though often they're rendered in italics. The couplet from Webster's play *The White Devil* at the end of the first section, just prior to Baudelaire's French ("Hypocrite lecteur") is translated into Italian by Praz and Spanish by Flores, but left in English in Curtius's German translation and by Menasce in French. Menasce also leaves intact the song lyric ("O O O O that Shakespeherian Rag"), while Curtius gives us "dieser Fetzen Shakespeare." Overall, *The Waste Land* wielded a formidable international influence because it was pitched in a translatable idiom. In some languages it could be seen as deviating from norms of versification, but its deviations were those of the author, not the translators.

It's instructive that some of the earliest translations of *The Waste Land* were by scholars. Curtius (1886–1956) wrote extensively on modern literature, but his major work of scholarship was *European Literature and the Latin Middle Ages*. Praz (1896–1982) taught literature in England and in his native Italy, and wrote on literature (*The Romantic Agony*), visual art (*Mnemosyne*), and interior decoration. Flores (1900–1994) was a prolific scholar, translator, and editor, and spent his academic career at various American institutions. Jean de Menasce (1902–1973) was a Jewish-born Catholic priest who studied at the Sorbonne and at Oxford, and was a personal friend of Eliot and those in the Bloomsbury circle.

What is it about Eliot's poem that compelled scholars to translate it? Curtius suggests a plausible allure: In *The Waste Land*, "ages and styles coalesce into magical substance." As someone routinely immersed in the study of historical periods, sensitized to how differently styles and genres behave at different times, Curtius found in Eliot's poem a unique crystallization of

European literature. He later reflected how "even on the first reading, years ago, it captivated me with sudden dazzling flashes of mystery and music, with a resonant happiness." It's the mystery, the music, and above all the *happiness* worth recalling.

Translations of *The Waste Land* proliferated soon after publication, beginning with the French (1926), German (1927), two in Spanish (one in Barcelona and the other in Mexico City, both 1930), Swedish (1932), Italian (1932), Greek (1933, another in 1936), Chinese (1936), Russian (1937), Urdu (1937), and Hebrew (1940). There were partial translations early on, Part V in Italian in 1926, Part III in Czech in 1930, Part II in Japanese in 1939. Other complete renderings appeared in the late forties, suggesting delayed publication due to the war: in Polish (1946), a new French version (1947), Danish (1948), Dutch (1949), Norwegian (1949), and Finnish (1949).

Japan was unique in having at first prioritized Eliot the critic: collections of his criticism were published in Tokyo in 1931, 1933, and 1938, having been preceded throughout the twenties by many essays in periodicals. Studies of Eliot also proliferated, and several contained passages from *The Waste Land*. Interest in the poem was enhanced when Yvor Winters came to Japan to teach in 1931. In 1939, when foreign literature and modernism incurred official disapproval in Japan, Nobuo Ayukawa launched the literary magazine *Arechi*, meaning "waste land." Soon shut down by authorities, it was resurrected in 1947. "The only common subject for us is the modern waste land," wrote Ayukawa. "We, who lived in the years between the wars, and once staked our lives in the battlefields, still cannot free ourselves from the dark reality and the torn consciousness, and now must watch the course of the cold war." For this generation of Japanese, "without 'Civilization' to defend, war was nothing but an accidental misfortune like natural disaster." Spurred by Arechi, three translations of *The Waste Land* appeared in Japan in the early fifties. The first was by Junzaburo Nishiwaki, who had lived in England in the twenties, one of many major poets around the world who played a significant role in transfusing their native languages with Eliot's idiom.

Lucky as Eliot was with notable translations by scholars, the same can be said of the similar role played by poets. Two early translations of *The Waste Land* were by younger poets who would follow Eliot into the ranks of Nobel laureates: the Greek George Seferis and the Polish Czesław Miłosz, who translated the poem during the Nazi occupation of Warsaw in 1943, the pages lit by the glow of the burning ghetto. In the 1944 uprising, while carrying a copy of Eliot's poems, he had to throw himself to the ground to avoid a round of machine-gun fire.

Seferis had a diplomatic appointment at the Greek Consulate in London when, shopping for Christmas cards in 1931, he came across Eliot's "Marina," one of the illustrated Ariel Poems. It spoke to him with its evocation of a landscape that took the Greek poet back to his homeland.

> What seas what shores what grey rocks and what islands
> What water lapping the bow
> And scent of pine and the woodthrush singing through the fog

Seferis had already published a book of poems, but Eliot helped him change course. In "Reflections on a Foreign Line of Verse," dated Christmas 1931, the boat of "Marina" becomes Odysseus's vessel.

> He tells me of the harsh pain you feel when the ship's sails swell with
>   memory and your soul becomes a rudder;
> of being alone dark in the night, and helpless as chaff on the
>   threshing-floor;
>
> of the bitterness of seeing your companions one by one pulled down
>   into the elements and scattered;
> and of how strangely you gain strength conversing with the dead
>   when the living who remain no longer meet your need.

Odysseus and other figures from Greek legend often appear in Seferis's work as consultants, revenants, and harbingers of the contact points between ancient and modern. He found this mythic dimension vividly conveyed in *The Waste Land*, which he promptly set out to translate. "I wanted to test the resistance of my own language." It was published in 1936, with an introduction, and substantially revised in 1949.

Seferis's introduction reflects the literary roots he shared with Eliot, as both men found their poetic vocation through Baudelaire, Laforgue, and French Symbolism. He therefore had a special affinity with Eliot as a model of how to replenish one's own language by way of another. He was responsive to Eliot's moods of "chilled ashes within a sensation akin to voluptuousness." His sensitivity as a poet to what actually goes on in poems enabled Seferis to grasp something essential in Eliot. Because poetry is a combination of words and silence, "it sculpts silence in some sort of way." Especially in a poem as multifaceted as *The Waste Land*, an entire spectrum of silences slowly arises along and within the patterned words. Interpenetrating past and present, speech and silence, it was "the epic of a pivotal feeling of a moment in history," instantly recognizable to those living through it.

Seferis recognized in 1936 (before any of Eliot's plays were available) that his was not a lyrical but a dramatic poetry. "The difficulty inherent in poetry of this kind is that behind the drama that seems to unfold, there is another drama unfolding, parallel to the first but on a deeper level." He also noted that Eliot understood history not as that which was past; rather, it consisted of ways the past persisted into the present. This proved immensely fruitful for the Greek poet whose very language was an artery of ancient mythopoesis. Another difficulty he identified concerned the foreign languages, names, and allusions so plentiful in *The Waste Land*. These were, he pointed out, "foreign elements plain and simple." They were there not as blinking signs soliciting special consideration, but rather as the concrete residue of history. No different (though Seferis does not say this) from an old statue in a public square. As any visitor to Rome can see, young couples snuggling on a pedestal are probably clueless about what the statue represents.

"These days there are poets who use the word 'truth' or the word 'freedom' with the same indifference with which they say to a stranger 'I am pleased to have met you,'" complained Seferis, for whom "we have entered for good a period of mechanized stupidity, mechanized falsity and mechanical self-destruction."

> After the outburst of Dadaism and the experiments of surrealism which I had witnessed in France, after these tremendous excavations and explosions of the ego which had brought into the atmosphere of that time the sort of electrical tension one finds in tropical climates just before the advent of the rains, the renewal of the dramatic tradition which I found in Eliot brought me back to a more temperate zone. I feel it may be surprising that I talk in this way of a poem like *The Waste Land*, which, more than any other, gives the sensation of thirst among the dry cactuses, a sensation with which we were so familiar in those happy-go-lucky days.

Such a response is quite unlike those registered in the Anglo-American milieu and helps clarify how Eliot's poem spoke to many others around the world.

Although he didn't translate *The Waste Land*, Nobel laureate Eugenio Montale reveled in the miracle of "*an inner reading performed aloud*" in Eliot's poem. Mario Praz loaned Montale a few of Eliot's Ariel Poems, which he then translated into Italian. Praz translated some poems by Montale into English, which Eliot published in *The Criterion*, where a review of Montale's first book also appeared (*Ossi di seppia*, Cuttlefish bones, 1925, was published before he read Eliot). "Like the cubist painters, he attempts to construct objects which will emit feeling without declaring it," Montale recognized, and his own poems are similarly devoid of personal declaration, though they positively swell with an atmosphere accessible only through emotional intensity. It's an intangible mood that, thanks to Eliot, Montale, Seferis, and others, was beginning to be thought of as a music *of* poetry as distinct from any music to be found *in* poems.

The music of poetry: a vague attribution, casually but frequently used. It's also the title of a 1942 essay by Eliot. In the present context, though, it's a code that testimonials tend to adopt, particularly among those of the Waste Land generation, who came of age as Eliot's poem was published. For the young, an uncanny music surmounted the intellectual severities of the poetry, all too puffed out in the bibliographic dungeon of the poem's notes. It was a vision of their world as they felt it but had not imagined words capable of evoking it. Fifty years earlier they might have been Wagnerians.

Curtius found that "its music carried me over its obscurities." Like a sonic summons, whatever he meant by music dissolved the ostensible obstacles. "He is the discoverer of a new tone which can never be forgotten," Curtius judged. "He has heard the mermaids singing." Montale discovered in Eliot's idiom "the sense of an interior and personal fount of music vibrating all possible harmonics lying below common words." Praz approvingly quoted an Italian writer who found in Eliot "not an absence of music, but a new sense of it, which does not reject cacophony and dissonance, a music which, according to Eliot, is the function of the whole poem, not of isolated lines." English don I. A. Richards summed up Eliot's technique in three words: it was a "music of ideas." Not that such music tells us something, he cautioned, but it somehow conveys "a coherent whole of feeling and attitude."

These are honorific appeals to music. A more pungent reference cuts to the quick of the Waste Land generation: "The poetry got into your head like a song-hit," one recalled. An earworm: once heard, impossible to shake. When Eliot read the poem to Virginia Woolf soon after its completion, "He sang it & chanted it rhythmed it," she exulted in her diary, uncomprehending but thoroughly impressed with a poem she would soon be setting by hand for its Hogarth Press edition.

When Clive Bell identified Eliot as a "jazz poet" in 1921, the musical affinity was in place. The analogy was even more evident once *The Waste Land* appeared. Burton Rascoe, recalling the prolonged season of invention

in American arts in the early 1920s, made an intriguing comparison between Eliot and George Gershwin. "The mood of 1924 was that of romantic
melancholy," he recalled. "'The Rhapsody in Blue' expressed that mood
as definitely in native American idiom as did T. S. Eliot's *Waste Land* in
poetry. Like that poem, it mixed classico-heroic themes with barrel-house
wails of sorrow with a brooding overtone of lost loveliness."

Eliot distinguished the music of poetry from metrical schemes, sound
patterns, or anything superficially beguiling to the ears. We can relish the
sound of poetry in a language we don't understand, he said, but if we're
then informed it's just random sounds without meaning, we conclude that
"this was no poem, it was merely an imitation of instrumental music." He
did not acknowledge the existence of "sound poetry" as developed by the
Dadaists during the Great War. A singular example, on the scale of Eliot's
poem, is the *Ursonate* or "sonata in primal sounds" by Kurt Schwitters.
With four movements and a finale, its composition spanned the years 1922
to 1930. It's considerably longer than Eliot's poem, but it uncannily serves
as a phantom obverse of *The Waste Land*, and even its opening lines have
the signature memorability of "April is the cruelest month":

> Fümms bö wö tää zää Uu,
> > pögiff,
> > > kwii Ee.

Schwitter's *Ursonate* epitomizes Eliot's insistence that the music of a poem
is not incidental to certain lines or passages but emerges from the entire
poem: "I know that a poem, or a passage of a poem, may tend to realize
itself first as a particular rhythm before it reaches expression in words, and
that this rhythm may bring to birth the idea and the image." The *Ursonate*
is perched just before this parturition.

The idiom Eliot pioneered in his earlier work persisted in *The Waste
Land*, despite the constant interruption of quotations and esoterica. Stephen
Spender marveled over the fact that "despite its intensity the line of Eliot's
poetry is relaxed and natural. It is near to conversation made rhythmic."
The rhythm, importantly, resists the hobbyhorse of versification. *The Waste
Land*, noted Riding and Graves in their *Survey of Modernist Poetry*, "had
to invent its metrical changes as it went along." Montale observed that
"Eliot is one of the few for whom a line-break is not signaled by the bell
of the typewriter or by the intimidating *non possumus* of the last syllable
of the iambic pentameter." As Eliot himself told John Quinn, "the line
punctuates itself."

It may also be the case that a poem writes itself. Eliot said he wrote "What the Thunder Said" in a kind of trance, meaning he was carried along by a rhythm that yielded the idea (parched sterility) and the images (desiccated mountains, unreal cities). Spender, whose career benefited from Eliot's support at Faber, has an intriguing anecdote that supplements the trance experience.

> Once, after having followed a radio performance of *Das Rheingold* with the score, I asked him whether, when he wrote *The Waste Land*, he had been studying the libretto. He looked at me slyly and said: "Not just *Rheingold*—the whole of the Ring."

Spender pointedly adds, concerning an affinity between Wagner and Eliot, Nietzsche's remark that Wagner's strength was as a miniaturist. Likewise Eliot. "The most real horror that Eliot conveys in his work is also in the isolated phrase suspended between commas," Spender observed. "Eliot, a poet of fragments skillfully dovetailed into wholes, is a miniaturist." Alex Ross suggests that *The Waste Land* "is at least in part the interior monologue of an aesthete who came of age in Wagnerism's heyday." "Eliot's Wagner nostalgia was apparent," Igor Stravinsky speculated, "and I think that *Tristan* must have been one of the most passionate experiences in his life."

The music of *The Waste Land* rises up in wisps, much like the coiling tone of the bassoon that opens Stravinsky's *Rite of Spring*, its languid vegetal pulse gradually joined by peeps of flute and other woodwinds like an insect chorus in a bog. The first verse stanza of Eliot's poem, in eighteen lines, sounds notes of spring and winter, rain and sun, being frightened and feeling free, childhood memories and adult encounters. That's a lot to pack in, but it makes a music, and music sets a mood.

Many who felt compelled to read *The Waste Land* because of its notoriety were not interested in poetry as such but were intrigued by news of a poem that some doubted was a poem. It was a familiar charge, in fact, from other arts. When Arnold Schoenberg pioneered his tone row in Vienna, critics howled with indignation: this was not music but "a bomb in a poultry-yard." It was "methodische Negation bisher geltender Musikelemente" (a systematic negation of all hitherto accepted elements of music). Schoenberg was deemed "the cruelest of all composers for he mingles with his music sharp daggers at white heat, with which he pares away tiny slices of his victim's flesh." But the composer had an answer: his music engaged the "emancipation of dissonance." Sheer sound had a value apart from scales and keys.

Closer to literature were the sound poems pioneered during the war by the Dadaists at Cabaret Voltaire in Zurich. Hugo Ball's famous recitation while dressed in his "magic bishop" costume (which the Tin Man in *The Wizard of Oz* would resemble decades later) is one of those signal events like Eliot's poem. Ball went into a kind of trance as he intoned

gadji beri bimba
blandridi lauli lonni cadori
gadjama bim beri glassala
glandridi glassala tuffm i zimbrabim
blassa galassasa tuffin i zimbrabim

Those five minutes on a small Swiss stage cast Ball as the century's poster boy for the avant-garde. It was a role David Byrne embraced fifty years later when his band Talking Heads performed a musical version, "I Zimbra." What Hugo Ball discovered was that words without meaning still offered auditory and typographical experiences. At the end of *The Waste Land* a reader confronts similarly liturgical words. They happen to be Sanskrit, but for readers of the poem in *The Dial* and *The Criterion*, where there were no notes, "Shantih shantih shantih" meant little more than *gadji beri bimba*.

In art, Pablo Picasso and Georges Braque set a precedent with Cubism, which retarded mimesis and dislodged perspectival privilege. Picasso said a Cubist canvas was more like a perfume you might detect without knowing its source. What *The Waste Land* shares with Cubism and dodecaphonic music is that they've all abandoned the role of art as reassurance, especially the familiar platitudes expected by the bourgeoisie. Art was now becoming an exploratory medium, not a mimetic one. Readers of Eliot's poem and Joyce's *Ulysses*, conversant with similar initiatives in music and art, realized that similar explorations could now be a prerogative of the printed page.

In 1922, Joyce's novel and Eliot's poem were taken to be portraits of the modern world, charged with obscurantism, and purportedly incomprehensible. Yet they were also recognized as possessing a strangely insinuating music, a resonance emanating from words on the page. In this respect at least, they carried forward or perhaps culminated initiatives set in motion by Wagnerism half a century earlier. Obscurities there indubitably were, yet both made a show of musicality. Where Eliot gestured to Wagner via the "weialala leia" of the Rhine Maidens in the *Ring*, Joyce more expansively broke apart the surface of his prose in the "Sirens" chapter of *Ulysses* to propel an ad hoc oratorio.

Jingle. Bloo.
Boomed crashing chords. When love absorbs. War! War! The
   tympanum.
A sail! A veil awave upon the waves.
Lost. Throstle fluted. All is lost now.
Horn. Hawthorn.
When first he saw. Alas!
Full tup. Full throb.
Warbling. Ah, lure! Alluring.

The Waste Land contributed to the perpetuation of Wagnerism, which
had served as incentive to generic incertitude and interarts animation for
half a century. Smarting under the shadow of Wagner, Mallarmé yearned
for a way of transposing music onto the printed page. This was not strictly
a poetic aspiration; it had been a swelling preoccupation of philosophers
as well. Schopenhauer characterized music as "an unconscious exercise in
metaphysics in which the mind does not know it is philosophizing." Nietzsche
and Wagner bonded over their shared debt to Schopenhauer, and Nietzsche
even thought of *Also sprach Zarathustra* as a "symphony."

The role of music as the accreditation standard of all the arts had somewhat subsided early in the twentieth century, but it was notably revisited
in the aesthetic theories of painter Wassily Kandinsky, which had a considerable impact on Pound. *The Blue Rider Almanac*, coedited by Kandinsky
with Franz Marc (1912), was a studiously orchestrated array of all the arts
in pointed interaction. The volume culminated in Kandinsky's stage work
bearing the telling title *The Yellow Sound*.

In 1910, Harvard professor Irving Babbitt attacked the legacy of blended
arts in *The New Laokoon*. Eliot was a student in his class on French literature at the time, and at the end of his life acknowledged that among his
teachers at Harvard it was Babbitt who wielded the greatest influence on
him. Babbitt regarded the entirety of Western culture from the eighteenth
century into the twentieth as overly beholden to "Romanticism," to which
he attributed "a growing discredit of the will to refrain." Self-restraint became, for Eliot, the touchstone of his classicism.

In his poetry, this will had its test run in the persona of Prufrock, for
whom the slightest temptation augurs cosmic doom. *The Waste Land* lets
loose a veritable flood of pitfalls, and the havoc of its key words at the
end begs (in Sanskrit) for some regulating psychological sedative: "Datta.
Dayadhvam. Damyata"—give, sympathize, control ("beating obedient / To
controlling hands"—the hands of kindly Dr. Vittoz in Lausanne?). Once

Eliot revealed his newfound religious faith in 1927, many were inclined to revisit *The Waste Land* for premonitions of what, in 1922, nobody had foreseen—not even Eliot himself. Yet the will to refrain extolled by Babbitt consistently colored Eliot's essays; and, despite its provocativeness, maybe *The Waste Land* was another exercise in restraint. Certainly the tenor of Pound's handling of the manuscript was to rein in Eliot's excesses, like his indulgent pastiche of eighteenth-century verse couplets.

There was another kind of will afoot in the early twentieth century exemplified by *The Waste Land*. In her diary, Mary Butts copied a passage from Yeats in which he noted "a new naturalism that leaves man helpless before the contents of his own mind. One thinks of Joyce's *Annalivia Plurabelle*, Pound's *Cantos*, works of heroic sincerity, the man, his active faculties in suspense, one finger beating time to a beat sounding & echoing in his own mind." The Cantos were Yeats's compass for a new kind of poem, "a poem in which there is nothing that can be taken out and reasoned over, nothing that is not a part of the poem itself." Prefacing his play *Fighting the Waves*, Yeats continued his rumination, probing the question he asked in his poem "Among School Children" in 1928: "How can we know the dancer from the dance?"

> Certain typical books—*Ulysses*, Virginia Woolf's *The Waves*, Mr. Ezra Pound's *Draft of XXX Cantos*—suggest a philosophy like that of the *Samkara* school of ancient India, mental and physical objects alike material, a deluge of experience breaking over us and within us, melting limits whether of line or tint; man no hard bright mirror dawdling by the dry sticks of a hedge, but a swimmer, or rather the waves themselves.

Samkara refers to an eighth-century nondualist philosopher from India, and the mirror is Stendhal's famous figure for realism, which Yeats took to be the outmoded mechanical model of nineteenth-century aesthetics overcome by these modernist swimmers.

The mirror was a sturdy model for a rising bourgeois class that yearned to see itself depicted in art. The panoramic portraits of George Eliot's *Middlemarch* and Leo Tolstoy's *Anna Karenina* were feasts for the inner eye gazing on that reflective surface. When Joyce began to write *Ulysses*, the mirror had cracks, and by the time he completed the novel it was a rubble of glittering shards, pieces of a kaleidoscope. The outer world piles up in a blizzard of notations that add up—not into a clear picture, but into an overall mood. Following Leopold Bloom's peregrinations around Dublin during a summer day, you gradually get the picture, but not *the picture*. That was what got Yeats's attention. He could have added *The Waste Land* to his list.

Reviewing *Ara Vos Prec* when it was published in 1920, John Middleton Murry made the intriguing observation that its author "is like the chameleon who changes color infinitely, and every change is protective." Was *The Waste Land* yet another protective disguise? Or, as many were forced to wonder, what *was* this sensational entry into the field of letters anyway—incendiary device, certainly, but was it a poem? And, if so, what did it mean for the future of poetry? Although Eliot's poem was not a primary focal point in *A Survey of Modernist Poetry* by Robert Graves and Laura Riding in 1927, the authors were well aware of its implications.

Survey was commercially published in London and New York, and had a formidable impact, although reviewers—reflecting the sexism of the time—tended to attribute the book to Graves while disregarding Riding. But as the authors insisted, their collaboration was truly fifty-fifty—maybe more, inasmuch as the last chapter drew heavily on Riding's previously published article in *Transition*, "The New Barbarism and Gertrude Stein." Anyone paying attention at the time would have noted the overlap when Riding included an expanded version of the article in her own essay collection *Contemporaries and Snobs* (1928)—a banner year, when she also published *Anarchism Is Not Enough* and, with Graves, *A Pamphlet against Anthologies*.

In *A Survey of Modernist Poetry*, the authors document a dumbing down of reading habits. They observed that pundits called on Shakespeare to chastise unruly moderns, but "the reading public has been so undertrained on a simplified Shakespeare and on anthology verse generally, that modernist poetry seems as difficult as Shakespeare really ought to seem." As for the charge that "obscure" modern poetry was removed from life, they turned the tables with their suggestion that the reading public itself "gets its excitement from literature and literary feelings instead of from life," because "ordinary modern life is full of the stock-feelings and situations with which traditional poetry has continually fed popular sentiments." Nothing could be further from *The Waste Land* than stock-feelings. "The appearance of freakishness generally means: poetry is not in a 'poetical' period, it is in a psychological period. It is not trying to say 'Things often felt but ne'er so well expressed' but to discover what it is we are really feeling." This was a pertinent observation. The platitudes of yore no longer served. The freakish was the unfamiliar, and what was most unfamiliar was the content of other people's minds in a "psychological period."

The plain reader, in short, was "afraid of the infringements that poetry may make on his private mental and spiritual ease." This was especially distressing in the case of the moderns, when the mind of the poet "puts in a personal appearance; and it is the shock of this contact that the plain reader cannot bear." The casual reader, nurtured on anthology nuggets, "does not want to understand poetry so much as to have poetical feelings," and was predictably alarmed when familiar signs of uplift were withheld. Simply put, "the plain reader does not really want to be left all alone with poetry." Certainly some of the discomfort registered by readers of *The Waste Land*, now as well as then, is the feeling of being *left alone* with unsettling insinuations in rats' alley.

Eliot held similar views. Speaking at Harvard in 1933 on the difficulty of poetry, he envisioned a reader who, "warned against the obscurity of a poem, is apt to be thrown into a state of consternation very unfavorable to poetic receptivity." The result, he supposes, is a "desire to be clever and to look very hard for something, he doesn't know what—or else by the desire not to be taken in. There is such a thing as stage fright," he adds, "but what such readers have is pit or gallery fright." Eliot goes on to confess that some of the most consequential poetry for him is work he didn't understand at first, and that may continue to elude understanding.

The view of poetry that Graves and Riding embraced actually had its roots in Germany before 1800—not that they traced a particular genealogy back to the Romanticism theorized by Friedrich Schlegel, Novalis, and others. The Germans had been stirred by the French Revolution to envision a corresponding cultural revolution, in which inherited protocols of genre could be cast aside; they foresaw a world in which every genuine creative work could convene its own genre. It would be, by definition, sui generis. Likewise, modern poetry for Riding and Graves "is groping for some principle of self-determination to be applied to the making of the poem—not lack of government, but government from within." The modernist poem is nothing less than "a newly created thought-activity: the poem has the character of a creature by itself." The unavoidable characteristic of modern poetry, therefore, is "a declaration of the independence of the poem."

What Riding and Graves recognized about *The Waste Land* is that, while clearly declaring its independence, it also manifested the self-determination of "government from within." It preceded "not only from episode to episode, but from passage to passage. It is just at these delicate transitions from one atmosphere to another, where the separate parts are joined into a single continuous poem, that the poetic quality is to be looked for." They didn't use the term *collage*, but that's what they describe: an art form in which the ligatures and junctures between contributing parts are not eased by rhetorical flourishes, nor are they in any way disguised. It's in your face, but it's also an invitation to negotiate the transitions.

The Waste Land is a para-cinematic endeavor. It's full of jump cuts, requiring of the reader what German culture critic Walter Benjamin called tactile reception. We might think that cinema is all about looking, but "Tactile reception comes about not so much by way of attention as by way of habit," he observed. Learning how to watch movies is formed by habit, and movies were becoming the touchstone of perceptual education. *"Reception in distraction—the sort of reception which is increasingly noticeable in all areas of art and is a symptom of profound changes in apperception—finds in film its true training ground,"* Benjamin wrote in 1936. He contrasts perception in a state of distraction with the traditional posture of studious concentration before artworks. To concentrate on a poem means being absorbed by it, getting *into* it like entering an architectural space. "By contrast," he says, "the distracted masses absorb the work of art into themselves." Eliot's poem can be studied, but by this analogy it may be more successfully absorbed, imbibed. Neither rebus nor intellectual cipher, the work transmits a flavor, with an aftertaste.

The state of poetry convened by *The Waste Land* can be clarified by way of another American poet, Wallace Stevens. Like Eliot, he spent his life in office work, albeit as an insurance executive. In 1940 he wrote a poem, "Of Modern Poetry," that lays out the new predicament. It begins with a rumination on how the modern poet is engaged in "the act of finding / What will suffice." In the past, the stage was set, the script provided, and the poem merely "repeated what / Was in the script." But then the theater changed, Stevens goes on. The poet now "has to find what will suffice," which he can do only by constructing a new stage, a new presentational apparatus.

Stevens's theatrical scenario rehearses the predicament of modernism. There is no longer a playhouse or civic center where whatever is written on the page, played on musical instruments, painted or sculpted or danced or performed can meet a code of expectations. It's the scenario first broached by the German Romantics, as they theorized an open-ended prospect for art, destined for constantly new and ever revitalizing combinations, which they called *Mischgedicht*, or mingled composition. That prospect was worked out instinctively over the next century as music ascended to the status of the art to which all the other arts aspired. The compulsion waned at the dawn of the twentieth century, but the consequences permeated everything.

"Of Modern Poetry" spells it out. Once the preordained ancestral script recedes into the past, the figure on the stage has no recourse but to begin again, to find "what will suffice." A new stage can be constructed, but here's the kicker: it has to be constructed with each outing, each performance. What does this mean for poetry? Taking *The Waste Land* as compass, it means there's no discernable or reliable "speaker" addressing a reader. There is, instead, a field of operations open (and exposed) to a spectrum of consciousness surpassing any putative individual perspective.

Readers of Eliot's poem, then as now, face a discomforting polyphony. *The Waste Land*'s working title named the method: "He Do the Police in Different Voices." In drafts of the poem, Eliot consistently had a multitude of voices in play. How many? The tally will vary according to the reader, but I estimate a plausible count of sixty-six. The poem has 433 lines, so that computes to a different voice every six lines (I include as "voices" the poem's thirty or so quotations and direct allusions). If we think back to Apollinaire's poem "Monday on Christine Street" with its transcription of overheard bits of conversation, the snatches abruptly follow one another without any particular order, just as you'd experience it on the boulevard. Eliot's poem gives us no single locale from which his voices come tumbling, but the aesthetics of parataxis are the same as Apollinaire's.

Parataxis is the principle of collage, setting one thing next to another without propositional sequence. It's the opposite of hypotaxis, with its organization of sentence and paragraph, building toward an end point. Parataxis, on the other hand, allows the muddle of circumstance to leave its trace, like a footprint. And reading such prints is different from discerning what's intended by a syntactic arrangement. Hunters following animal tracks piece together directional coordinates from unintentional deposits. The deer, after all, is not leaving hoofprints and snapping twigs as invitations to be followed. Rather, these are the accidental by-products of physical motion. But they can be read. And where parataxis is concerned, attributing *intention* to the signs is not helpful.

To emphasize the paratactic aspect of *The Waste Land* is not enough, because there's also intelligible discourse to be considered. The presence of foreign languages adds a pertinent dimension to a cosmopolitan poem, replicating as they do the normal street-level experience of the modern metropolis. The voices are voices, whether intelligible or not. Some are past, some present; some spoken, others quoted from books; they can be collective or individual. Modes of voicing in the poem include performance, confession, exclamation, exhortation, conversation, incantation, recitation, and plea or petition. They range from the interpersonal domain of conversation to the private realm of prayer and spiritual supplication.

Eliot has been counted among those who ripped up the old playbook of the arts, convening a different proscenium like that given by Stevens in "Of Modern Poetry." But he was not a conceptualist like Marcel Duchamp, much as he too wrangled "found" objects. *The Waste Land* is not, to poetry, what Duchamp's urinal bearing the signature R. Mutt is to visual art. Eliot's *findings* are integrated into an overall composition. But they remain provocative, raising the sort of question put to the poet Robert Creeley in the late twentieth century. After a public reading, he was asked, "Was that a real poem or did you make it up yourself?" Even Duchamp could not have put it better.

What's behind that seemingly naive question is the juggernaut of modernism. Does a mass of sounds organized by a composer qualify as music? Does a poet produce a poem simply because she's known to be a poet? Is a canvas that my five-year-old could make worth all that money—well, you get the drift. Eliot's poem is one among many seismic events that upended the simple means-end equation of the arts, the system that reassured the public that the qualities and characteristics of music, art, and poetry were generically fixed and therefore readily accessible to anyone with eyes, ears, and a modest education.

What Eliot made clear in both precept and practice is that modern poetry—and modern art in general—was difficult. And, more importantly, that the difficulty was inevitable, not optional. It reflected the seismic fault of modernity. Despite the wild-goose chases unleashed by Eliot's notes, the real difficulty is not intellectual. A new environment was teaching everyone to watch for motorized traffic, use a telephone, parse the grammar of cinematic jump cuts, negotiate railway schedules, and be borne aloft in airplanes. Modern life was a smorgasbord of bits and pieces in ceaseless motion. Eliot spoke the lingua franca of modernity. The assimilation of everyday life yielded the corporeal collage that Dutch artist Piet Mondrian transcribed in his essay "Le Grands Boulevards": "Negro head, widow's veil, Parisienne's shoes, soldier's legs, cart wheel, Parisienne's ankles, piece of pavement, part of a fat man, walking-stick nob, piece of newspaper, lamp post base, red feather."

The Waste Land is a paradigmatic collage poem, published when collage in the visual arts was being recognized as reflecting a natural aptitude of the harried metropolitan citizen: perception in a state of distraction, Walter Benjamin called it. This new perceptual repertoire was dimly registered in the mermaids of "Prufrock." The mermaids bring us back to Wagnerism, which provoked the arts to switch places in a vast game of musical chairs. The quotations from Wagner and all the other sources that fill Eliot's poem like sparkling bits of mosaic tile offer a troubling reassurance to the reader: you may not understand the poem, but you can stroke its fur as you listen to the mermaids' song.

Part Four

CHAPTER TEN

Parallax

In 1938 Cleanth Brooks and Robert Penn Warren published *Understanding Poetry*, a college textbook that reigned supreme for the rest of the century, with a fourth edition appearing in 1976. Both men had degrees from Vanderbilt, and they consolidated their outlook when they were Rhodes Scholars at Oxford. That outlook had come to be known as the New Criticism by the time *Understanding Poetry* was published. Brooks had published an essay on *The Waste Land* in 1937 that validated the poem's "organic unity" and, in doing so, was instrumental in making it a canonical centerpiece of higher education. New Criticism is known for advocating close reading, eventually coming under attack for minimizing biographical and historical context. Yet *Understanding Poetry* makes a grand portentous gesture toward History, capital H: "*The Waste Land* is a poem totally concerned with the breakup of civilization—not, to be sure, the physical breakup, with buildings crashing into the street or government offices burning, but a spiritual breakup."

Twenty years after *The Waste Land* was published, Eliot ventured some pertinent claims about reductive readings. "A poem may appear to mean very different things to different readers, and all of these meanings may be different from what the author thought he meant," he recounted in a lecture in Glasgow during the Second World War. "For instance, the author may have been writing some peculiar personal experience," he continued, "yet for the reader *The Waste Land* may become the expression of a general situation." He was, in effect, sanctioning the view of New Criticism, which had anointed him its honorary head.

In a lecture at the University of Minnesota in 1956, before an audience exceeding ten thousand, Eliot made a very different point worth heeding. To understand a poem, he proposed, we need to be aware of "what the poetry is aiming to be." The all-too-common question of poets and artists generally is What were you trying to say? But even when the medium is words—and words are inevitably presumed to be saying something—the art consists in what is *made*. And the mysteries of artistic creation are such that even the artist may have only the foggiest notion of what the work is "aiming to be." Much of how it gets there derives from preconscious, even irrational, resources. A poem ends up on the page. But it's not an utterance like a phone message or a telegram. In this respect, every poem is susceptible to Prufrock's refrain, "That is not what I meant at all."

After reading Cleanth Brooks's essay on *The Waste Land*, Eliot responded in 1937. "I think that this kind of analysis is perfectly justified," he allowed, adding a caveat: "so long as it does not profess to be a reconstruction of the author's method of writing." He then returns to the role of what he calls music: "Reading your essay made me feel, for instance, that I had been much more ingenious than I had been aware of, because the conscious problems with which one is concerned in the actual writing are more those of a quasi musical nature, in the arrangement of metric and pattern, than of a conscious exposition of ideas." Brooks, and the New Critics generally, placed great emphasis on the trope of irony—so much so that it became a crutch, a perennially handy way of terminating further investigation. In the case of *The Waste Land*, the term *collage* was avoided in discussions of method. How did all those discrete fragments hang together? Irony, it was said. But irony is intentional, and as Eliot told Brooks, his mind while composing his poem was elsewhere, underwater as it were with Wagner's Rhine Maidens.

Collage registers the apperceptual model Walter Benjamin called reception in a state of distraction. Now this, now that, the creative outlook darting between foreground and background. The paratactic succession of one thing after another in collage is not predicated on conceptual postulates. The postulates arise abruptly in response to stimuli—environmental provocations. Clickbait, a century before that term was invented. It's a misleading term insofar as it suggests a kind of unthinking, uninhibited reflex action. So it can be more meaningfully augmented with another more recent term, multitasking. The steady stream of nonsequential incommensurable items in *The Waste Land* requires multitasking on the part of a reader.

In the final section of the poem, "What the Thunder Said," a verse stanza begins with a question—"What is that sound high in the air"—though no question mark is given. Subsequent lines dimly sketch a chaotic assault on capital cities, followed by an image of a woman that is, in the most basic sense, a non sequitur.

What is the city over the mountains
Cracks and reforms and bursts in the violet air
Falling towers
Jerusalem Athens Alexandria
Vienna London
Unreal

A woman drew her long black hair out tight
And fiddled whisper music on those strings
And bats with baby faces in the violet light
Whistled, and beat their wings
And crawled head downward down a blackened wall

The mood summoned by this juxtaposition of domestic interiority and historical cataclysm evokes an eerie scene like those painted by Giorgio de Chirico, beloved of the Surrealists, anchoring the bat-scape in an urban milieu delegated to waste space by that dangling modifier *unreal*. That word is itself a fragment broken off an earlier evocation of the living dead:

Unreal City,
Under the brown fog of a winter dawn,
A crowd flowed over London Bridge, so many,
I had not thought death had undone so many.

This is a good example of what gripped readers, as the evocation of a familiar urban scene gives way to sudden twist: the living throng on their way to work become figures in the underworld. Much of *The Waste Land* is like this. A concrete scene or image appears, evoking a mood: something else is imminent, something glimpsed in peripheral vision. Perception in a state of distraction.

I've emphasized collage and parataxis as the basic tools underpinning Eliot's poem. *The Waste Land* was the poem that introduced a broad readership to collage as a reading experience, which was distinct from looking at visual collage. But it was not the first. It was preceded by *Paris*, a poem by Hope Mirrlees who, as it happens, was a friend of Eliot's (albeit after both their poems were published), and it was followed by Nancy Cunard's *Parallax*, a self-consciously post–Waste Land poem. There is yet another poet with whom Eliot forged a bond of solidarity, a major innovator in the use of collage, Marianne Moore. The rest of this chapter fills in their side of the story. Much has been made of Eliot's misogyny—in some of the Knopf *Poems* in 1920, in his treatment of Vivien—but *The Waste Land* was sui generis in ways that were helpful to women, whose literary efforts tended to be brusquely dismissed or, at best, marginalized as exceptions to the rule of male-dominated "tradition." It must be said that Eliot himself played a commanding role in the instantiation of *tradition* as a masculine prerogative, and he was a willing partner in the modernizing push associated with the "Men of 1914." But for women like Mirrlees, Cunard, Moore, and others, the very existence of an exception, an upstart like *The Waste Land*, enfranchised a potential space for the outsider.

*

London was a daunting place to be in September 1940 when the German Luftwaffe began a prolonged bombing campaign on the city, soon extended to other English cities as well. H. D. lived there throughout the war, during which she wrote three book-length poems. The trilogy begins right in the center of the devastation:

> An incident here and there,
> and rails gone (for guns)
> from your (and my) old town square

Yet H. D. found the experience invigorating, as if the vacancies of bombed buildings released revenants of the past, ghosts whirling up like mist from the rubble. "The past is literally blasted into consciousness with the Blitz," she wrote. She reported to an American friend, "The house next door was struck another night. We came home and simply waded through glass, while wind from now unshuttered windows made the house a barn, an unprotected dug-out. What does that sort of shock do to the mind, the imagination—not solely of myself, but of an epoch?"

After a month of the Blitz, T. S. Eliot moved to the countryside in Surrey, midway between southwest London and the South Downs. He rented lodging from Hope Mirrlees, living there with her mother and aunt on a farm that regularly accommodated nearly two dozen evacuees from the bombing raids. Old friends noticed how well he looked during his sojourn there (while he still made trips to the city for work, and as air-raid warden on the rooftop of the Faber office). He told Virginia Woolf it was the healthiest he'd been in years.

Mirrlees was an old friend, and she had been one of the few who was willing to endure Vivien during her prolonged withdrawal into mental fog. "She gave the impression of absolute terror, of a person who's seen a hideous goblin, a goblin ghost," Hope recalled for BBC Radio in the sixties.

> Her face was all drawn and white, with wild, frightened, angry eyes. An over-intensity over nothing, you see. Supposing you were to say to her, 'Oh, will you have some more cake?' she'd say: 'What's that? What do you mean? What do you say that for?' She was terrifying. At the end of an hour I was absolutely exhausted, sucked dry. And I said to myself: Poor Tom, this is enough! But she was his muse all the same.

Eliot consigned his "muse" to a mental institution in 1938, where she died in 1947.

Eliot had gotten to know Mirrlees when she was living with Jane Ellen Harrison in Paris in the early twenties, a friendship that continued when the couple moved back to London for Harrison's last years at the end of the decade. Eliot's essays make repeated reference to Harrison, who was a member of the school of Cambridge Ritualists to whom he felt much indebted. One of the articles reprinted in *The Sacred Wood* was "Euripides and Professor Murray," which acknowledged Gilbert Murray's valuable role as a scholar while railing against his translations of Greek tragedy. Murray was Harrison's close friend and colleague, to whom she dedicated her book *Themis: A Study of the Social Origins of Greek Religion* in 1912. Known even in her youth as the most brilliant woman in England, Jane carried her wisdom through to the end. Asked in old age whether she'd like to be young again, she replied: "You cannot be you—you that are—young again. You cannot unroll that snowball which is you: There is no 'you' except your life—lived."

Prefacing a second edition of *Themis* in 1927, Harrison could look back with satisfaction on its reputation as a challenge to received notions of ancient Greece. Early in her career she had been deeply informed by the latest findings in the fields of anthropology and sociology. These were new disciplines then, and they cast fresh light on the fertility rites not only of contemporary aborigines but of ancient Greek cults, which had long been mounted on the classical pedestals of eighteenth-century aesthetics privileging nobility and reason. Harrison, along with her Cambridge peers, knew that there was nothing rational about mythological consciousness. As Nietzsche had argued in *The Birth of Tragedy*, reason was precariously perched on a froth of irrational drives.

What set Harrison's perspective off from the general revisionary trend was her understanding of gender. The Olympian gods, she realized, were idealizations plucked from the teeming cauldron of older fertility cults and purified. "It is characteristic of an Olympian," she wrote, "as contrasted with a mystery-god like Dionysos, that his form is rigidly fixed and always human." But humans are animals, coexisting with other animals. To worship figures cleansed of human frailties and animal sapience results in a static world of "unmeaning perfection, incapable of movement or change." Harrison drew from Freud to suggest the Olympians were aligned with consciousness, while the fertility cults from which they derived were subconscious. And these cults, she found, had been matrilineal. Olympus blocked awareness of the earth mother at the center of life.

When Hope Mirrlees studied at Newnham College, Cambridge, she became a favored pupil of Jane Harrison. Both had considerable linguistic abilities, and during the war they were spending much of their time in Paris, learning Russian together and translating Slavic folktales. It was there in 1919 that Mirrlees wrote her long poem *Paris*. She had first visited the city in 1913, accompanied by a college friend who would soon marry Virginia Woolf's younger brother. Woolf avidly read Mirrlees's first novel, *Madeleine* (1919), writing to a friend, "It's all Sapphism so far as I've got—Jane and herself," she added, clarifying the couple's relationship.

Virginia was impressed by Hope's command of French and struck by her independence. She found her

> a very self conscious, wilful, prickly & perverse young woman, rather conspicuously well dressed & pretty, with a view of her own about books & style, an aristocratic & conservative tendency in opinion, & a corresponding taste for the beautiful & elaborate in literature.

"Hope Mirrlees," she wrote to a friend, is "a capricious young woman, but rather an exquisite apparition, scented, powdered, dressing for dinner, and very highly cultivated." A few days later she followed up with the news that Hope—"Jane Harrison's favorite pupil"—"has written a very obscure, indecent, and brilliant poem, which we are going to print."

Virginia did not mention that this poem would present a nearly insurmountable challenge to her typesetting and proofreading skills. Her diary for April 1920 registers the toll: "Half blind with writing notices, & corrections in 160 copies of Paris." She had to insert by hand "St." before John on the first page. Woolf's laborious work included lines spilling across the page with no regular stanzas, many capitalized words and phrases, much French, and even a few bars of music. Here's how it begins:

> I want a holophrase
> 　NORD-SUD
>
> 　ZIG-ZAG
> 　LION NOIR
> 　CACAO BLOOKER
>
>
> Black-figured vases in Etruscan tombs
> 　RUE DU BACK (DUBONNET)
> 　SOLFERINO (DUBONNET)
> 　CHAMBRE DES DEPUTES
>
>
> Brekekek coax coax we are passing under the Sein
> 　DUBONNET

The Scarlet Woman shouting BYRRH and deafening
St. John at Patmos

Vous descendez Madame?
QUI SOUVENT SE PESE BIEN SE CONNAIT
QUI BIEN SE CONNAIT BIEN SE PORTE

CONCORDE

I can't
I must go slowly

What's a holophrase? This linguistic term derives from Harrison's *Themis*. "Language, after the purely emotional interjection" she wrote, "began with whole sentences, *holophrases*, utterances of a relation in which subject and object have not yet got their heads above water but are submerged in a situation." She gives, as example, the Fuegian holophrase *mamihlapinatapai*, meaning "looking-at-each-other,-hoping-that-either-will-offer-to-do-something-which-both-parties-desire-but-are-unwilling-to-do." Even today, Harrison observes, "impulsive people . . . plunge into a statement of relations before they tell you who they are talking about." Gradually, in the evolution of language, the holophrase dissolves into parts of speech, nouns and verbs.

Harrison's suggestion that the holophrase is the expression of a "holopsychosis" suggests something about *Paris*, particularly in its inaugural role in the poem, indicating something wanted or desired. Mirrlees's holopsychosis involves a plunge into the great city in an attempt to synthesize it into a poem that has all the concentration of a holophrase. A way of not only saying *this and that* but somehow charging all the particulars with the capacities of verbs. Nouns as actions. In a way, she was doing with Paris what Walter Benjamin later attempted in his uncompleted Arcades project, focusing on Paris as the capital of modernity. Both Benjamin and Mirrlees approached even the tiniest bit of language, along with fugitive material evidence, as holophrastic clues. The poem ends with such a material trace in the figure of Ursa Major traced in asterisks. The stellar Great Bear is an oblique reference to the affectionate term Jane and Hope used for each other, and there's a photograph of the two women with Hope clutching a teddy bear.

Mirrlees wrote a preface to her 1919 novel *Madeleine*, in which she evokes a panorama of tiny materialized droplets as an absolute registration of life, much as if she's describing the atomic theories of the ancient Greek Democritus, whose vision was immortalized in Lucretius's epic poem *De rerum*

FIG. 10.1. Hope Mirrlees (left) and Jane Ellen Harrison.

natura. "Life is like a blind and limitless expanse of sky," she writes, "for ever dividing into tiny drops of circumstances that rain down, thick and fast, on the just and unjust alike. Art is like the dauntless, plastic force that builds up stubborn, amorphous substance cell by cell, into the frail geometry of a shell." As an accretion of such cells, *Paris* is a poem that avoids any first-person expression as well as any exposition that would so much as situate a presumed character in a determinate time and place. Nonetheless, it plunges readers into one Parisian locale after another, where they are obliged to absorb without forethought whatever comes to hand. The reader, in other words, is instantly submersed in the city as unceasing sensory phantasmagoria. It is, says scholar Sandeep Parmar, a "corporeal multiplicity of one."

As a Parisian promenade, the poem owes much to the *flânêrie* of Apollinaire and Cendrars.

> It is pleasant to sit on the Grand Boulevards—
> They smell of
> Cloacae
> Hot indiarubber
> Poudre de riz
> Algerian tobacco

Another formative influence, Mirrlees acknowledged, was Jean Cocteau's book-length poetic homage to aviator Roland Garros, *Le Cap de Bonne Espérance*. Although there are occasional product names in Cocteau's poem, it bears little resemblance to Mirrlees's scattershot barrage of discontinuities in *Paris*. But a measure of the parallel may be gleaned from an omnibus review of current French poetry by F. S. Flint, in which he makes passing reference to *Le Cap*, describing it as "a collection of images placed one against the other, with few of the ordinary connecting links of speech, it being left to the reader to form the fusion in his mind. If the fusion takes place you have the sensation of poetry, if not, you are bewildered." This characterization is even more applicable to *Paris*, and of course to *The Waste Land*.

The first and third books of poetry set by Virginia Woolf for Hogarth Press were Eliot's little pamphlet *Poems* in 1919 and *The Waste Land* in 1923. In between was *Paris* in 1920. Until recently, *Paris* was quite forgotten. Its reappearance prompts the question of whether it influenced *The Waste Land*. Mirrlees professed not to know whether Eliot had read it. But it seems unlikely he would not have seen this other poetry title by Hogarth Press. More to the point, though, is the length and method of Mirrlees's poem. In the edition Virginia Woolf typeset, the text is twenty pages followed by a page of notes. It is the most sustained collage poem in English prior to *The Waste Land*. But, with its diminutive print run, it's the very model of fugitive coterie publishing, likely to have been seen only by subscribers to Hogarth Press.

Paris did not fare as well as *The Waste Land*, in part because women were not esteemed on the same plane as men, particularly when it came to anything smacking of the avant-garde, as in the Dada reference in one of the few reviews:

> This little effusion looks at the first blush like an experiment in Dadaism; but there is method in the madness which peppers the pages with spluttering and incoherent statement displayed with various tricks of type. It seems meant by a sort of futurist trick to give an ensemble of the sensations offered to a pilgrim through Paris. But it is certainly not a "Poem," though we follow the author's guidance in classing it as such.

Such a response reflects establishment literary taste of the time, for which anything remotely out of the ordinary is festooned with descriptors like *trick* and *stunt* before being dismissively ushered offstage.

Paris may not be as cagey and "mature" as *The Waste Land*, but in hindsight it's a revealing weathervane. If Eliot had not carefully estimated his chances of success and applied himself accordingly, preparing the launchpad as it were with *Prufrock* and *The Sacred Wood*, *The Waste Land* wouldn't have stood a chance. Mirrlees's poem is more elliptical, its condensations more severe than Eliot's. Apart from its own merits, *Paris* is now welcome as a provocation to reading, much as *The Waste Land* was in 1922. Where the latter is overexposed, the unfamiliarity of *Paris* elucidates what Eliot's first readers had to contend with.

After *Paris* and *The Waste Land*, Hogarth Press published another long poem in 1925: *Parallax* by Nancy Cunard. Twenty pages long, like *Paris*, it's a very different poem, not least because Cunard revered Eliot's poetry and had been particularly smitten with *The Waste Land*. Reviews of *Parallax* frequently linked the two, not always to her detriment, even if one thought the poem "a rather delirious echo of Mr. T. S. Eliot's Waste Land." A more insightful reading was by Louise Morgan, who detected "an almost sensational repression" at work below the surface, "as if one were treading a clear swept, trimly bordered garden path around the crater of a volcano."

Virginia Woolf was intrigued by Nancy's demeanor, "with the startled honest eyes, & all the green stones hung about her." During one meeting, "she slipped into easy desperate-sounding chatter, as if she didn't mind saying everything—everything—had no shadows no secret places—lived like a lizard in the sun, & yet was by nature for the shade. And I should be re-reading her poem to choose a title." This suggests it may have been Virginia who named it "Parallax." In manuscript, Nancy called it "The Sempiternal Fool."

There was a certain notoriety to the literary productions of "Miss Cunard" because she published under her maiden name (though some reviewers persisted in calling her Mrs. Sidney Fairbairn in deference to her estranged husband). Her name was inescapably associated with society columns, as the Cunard Line had dominated transatlantic shipping routes since the 1840s.

FIG. 10.2. Cover of Nancy Cunard's *Parallax* (1925).

Despite her bluestocking background, she was an inveterate enthusiast of progressive art.

Nancy was in love with Pound during the years he lived in Paris, 1920–1926. They took a walking tour of southern France together in 1922. This was the troubadour country he knew well, and he had undertaken similar expeditions with Wyndham Lewis and with T. S. Eliot. Many of the poems in Cunard's *Sublunary* (1923) chronicle her affair with Pound, and the chronicle continues to inform *Parallax*. Their adventure was one of

> resumed love-songs and the rhythms of illusion.
> —And around me
> Legend of other times on dry gold background,
> Pitted with slow insinuations.

As the record of a personal search, it pursues something similar to Mirrlees's holophrase: "Midnight, aurora, daytime, all in one key." Its moods range from rueful reflection ("candle wasting at both ends") to hopeful expectations ("Have I not loved you better, loving again?"). It shares with *The Waste Land* the imprisoning metropole, "London, the hideous wall, the jail of what I am." By the end, "I have changed my prisons" where she finds herself confronted by "The articulate skeleton / In clothes grown one with the frame." The skeleton speaks, "Hail partner," and the poem ends "In doubt, in shame, in silence."

Cunard's poem has no notes, nor does it need them. Fleeting place-names like Genoa, Cortona, Aix, and Les Beaux indicate a Mediterranean itinerary, just as Battersea and Wimbledon place us in England. Aside from the title there are no words likely to propel a reader to the dictionary. Yet *Parallax* takes the liberty of being obscure, as Eliot's poem is obscure, with its investment in rapid transitions without explanation. In Cunard's case, the persistent forward movement is more clearly registered in emotional terms. The mind of the poem is rich with experiences, and such richness is not resolved into narrative. Rather, experience rises up, blending agitation and sweetness, remorse and expectancy all at once or at least in close proximity in an "old tattoo of journeys."

Parallax has an epigraph by Sir Thomas Browne that situates the title and helps frame the poem's register of experience. "Many things are known as some are seen, that is by Paralaxis, or at some distance from their true and proper being." As a title, *Parallax* suggests both theme and method. In astronomy, it refers to the way an object appears to change its position because of a change in the position from which it's viewed. Anything observed from a moving vehicle is subject to parallax, just as walking around a sculpture in order to view it from all sides is to submit it to parallax. But Browne's epigraph adds another dimension, in his evocation of things perceived anew "at some distance from their true and proper being." This suggests mental or emotional adjustments relative to relations perceived at a distance. Wordsworth's emotions recollected in tranquility offer one poetic model—calming the mind to get a clean perspective on things—but parallax for Cunard turns out to be a way of simultaneously being distant *and* at the center of emotional intensity, like the lizard Woolf saw in Cunard, shadow and sun combined.

Although Hope Mirrlees and Nancy Cunard could be counted among Eliot's friends, only one woman received unstinting backing from him: fellow American Marianne Moore. (Did he know they were both raised in St. Louis?) He arranged for the Faber publication of her *Selected Poems* in 1935 and wrote an introduction for it. He made the observation, applicable to his own experience, that "we have all to choose whatever subject matter allows us the most powerful and the most secret release; and this is a personal affair."

By the time Marianne was born in 1887, her father had already succumbed to the religious mania that landed him in mental care (at one point he carried out the biblical dictum about the offending hand by amputating his own). Nicknames found fertile soil in the Moore household, with mother Mary as Mole, brother Warner the Badger, and Marianne as Rat (these were from *The Wind in the Willows*, but there were others). Not only that: she was *Mister* Rat, making it disconcerting to find family letters using the male pronoun for Marianne.

After college at Bryn Mawr (H. D. was a classmate), Marianne lived with her mother until the latter's death in 1947. It was not a happy arrangement, but perhaps inevitable. Her mother was protective both of her own needs and of her daughter's frailty. Marianne was five feet four but her weight could drop as low as seventy-five pounds, mainly in response to stress. Her mother thought that letting her live on her own was too perilous. Ratty, as she called her, was "*too little* to be chased about by big cats." Even when she was in her forties and had a handsome salary as editor of *The Dial*, she was being claimed by her mother as a dependent on her tax return (Marianne dutifully turned over any income to her mother). As a friend observed in 1921, "Only a person of her intellectual robustness could have survived such a mother."

Apart from publications in the Bryn Mawr literary journals, Moore made her mark in the leading vanguard publications. Between 1915 and 1923 she published extensively in *Poetry*, *The Egoist*, *Others*, *The Little Review*, *The Dial*, *Contact*, *Broom*, and *Secession*. By the time her book *Observations* was published in 1924, she had published more than eighty poems in these and other journals, accruing a dedicated following.

Reviewing the *Others* anthology for 1917, Ezra Pound found the spirit of Laforgue alive "in the slightly acid whimsicalities," the "sinuosities and mental quirks" of Moore and Mina Loy. At Pound's prompting, Eliot reviewed the same collection in *The Egoist* and singled out Loy and particularly Moore for special notice. Pound was motivated to contact Moore to inquire about her person and her poems. Intrigued by what he surmised might be a personal disclosure about her race, "Are you a jet black Ethiopian Othello-hued," Pound asked, "or was that line in one of your *Egoist* poems but part of your general elaboration and allegory and designed to differentiate your color from that of the surrounding menagerie?" She obligingly corrected his supposition—she (like Mary Butts) was a flaming redhead—and admitted she knew nothing of Laforgue. Such influences as she could credit were Henry James, Blake, Hardy, and "the minor prophets."

Moore's first book, *Poems*, was issued by the Egoist Press in 1921. It was the surreptitious doing of H. D. and her wealthy partner Bryher, who had become friends with Marianne during a visit to New York. She was thrilled when it arrived unannounced in the mail, but also furious. "Darwin speaks of a variety of pigeon that is born naked without any down whatever. I feel like that Darwinian gosling," she promptly wrote Bryher. "You say I am stubborn. I agree and if you knew how much more than stubborn I am, you would blame yourself more than you do, on having put a thing through, over my head."

Eliot had offered to help Moore get published in April, and only three months later she was obliged to send him *Poems*, despite her previous insistence, that "for me to be published so, would merely emphasize the meagerness of my production." Disclosing Bryher's role in publishing the booklet, she allowed that "as the act of a friend it is a testimony of affection but if it were the act of an enemy, I should realize that it was an attempt to show how little I had accomplished." She continued to regard her work insufficient to make a volume. But *Poems* got her thinking. When Monroe Wheeler started a publication series with the moniker "Manikin," her new (and longest) poem "Marriage" made for a choice selection. The Manikin publications were pamphlets, but because Wheeler regarded Manikin as a periodical, it didn't count as a "book" to its author.

Meanwhile (the plot thickens) she had developed a relationship with Scofield Thayer, editor of *The Dial*. Having heard her read a poem at a party, he decided she must become a mainstay of the journal. They began meeting and dining together, and at some point he appears to have either proposed to Marianne or violated some propriety, and while she (and her mother) were incensed, Thayer persisted in getting her into the editorial fold of the journal. The trump card he played was the same that had procured "The Waste Land" for *The Dial*. He offered her the Dial Award to be announced at the end of 1924, which would entail publication of significant poems in the journal to be followed up by a book.

In three consecutive issues, *The Dial* published "Silence," "Sea Unicorns and Land Unicorns," and "An Octopus." These three plus fifty other poems were meanwhile typeset for *Observations*, which was to appear by Christmas. It was a rush job, compounded by the additional labor of producing notes, a novelty for a collection of poems. Thayer had asked about her use of quotations in one poem, to which she responded by providing extensive annotations. While assembling the manuscript he'd suggested using the notes, which she did while adding notes for most of the other poems as well. To top it off in a completely original flourish, she also provided an index. Eliot relished her notes, which he found "are always pertinent, curious, conclusive, delightful, and give no encouragement whatever to the researcher of origins." This was in emphatic contrast to his own notes for *The Waste Land*, which he later denounced as "the remarkable exposition of bogus scholarship that is still on view to-day."

Moore's notes were a tacit acknowledgment of difficulties in the poems, prompted perhaps by the ridicule heaped upon the Egoist Press pamphlet in the English press. Those poems, the *Times Literary Supplement* guffawed, were only "a clumsy prose . . . [which] give an adventitious effect to it by tricks of printing which only obscure her meaning." The reviewer dismissively concluded, "We have only devoted so much space to Miss Moore because her compositions have found their way into literary periodicals, and seem to represent the latest device for disguising a lack of inspiration by means of a superficial unconventionality." The wry dismissal was taken up in America by Louis Untermeyer (who else?): "While Miss Moore has elected to offer her highly intellectualized dissertations in the form of poetry, she is not, in spite of the pattern of her lines, a poet." Her work in *Poems*, he finds, are "essays in the disguise of verse." Harriet Monroe, having published her poems in *Poetry*, could not afford to be dismissive, but she was querulous in her mixed praise. "She shouts at our stupidity," she sensed. "And we yawn back at Miss Moore's omniscience." "What I do find in certain poems," she conceded, "is a brilliant array of subtly discordant harmonies not unlike those of certain ultra-modern composers." The most famous "ultra-modern composer" at that time was Leo Ornstein, whose piano composition *Suicide in an Airplane* provides the undertone of Monroe's appraisal.

As it happened, such demurrals were rare. Moore's work met with near-ecstatic reception by her peers. H. D. and Bryher, who were not known to be behind the publication of *Poems*, lost no time in their boosterism. H. D. in *The Egoist* proclaimed the poems "destined to endure longer, far longer than the toppling sky-scrapers, and the world of shrapnel and machine guns in which we live." Moore was a valiant American, no less, "fighting in her country a battle against squalor and commercialism." From Bryher: "The spirit is robust, that of a man with facts and countries to discover and not that of a woman sewing at tapestries." English poet Edith Sitwell found Moore enticingly strange. "I can see no trace of any influence," she wrote. "Beauty is not the first quality noticeable here, but a strangeness like that of negroid art." Nonetheless, "this book should be studied, for certainly she is among the most interesting American poets of the day."

Observations roused an even more clamorous welcome. Among other responses, it served as a way of emancipating the female poet from the stigma of being a "poetess." Eliot wrote that "one never forgets that it is written by a woman; but," he added, "one never thinks of this particularity as anything but a positive virtue." Another reviewer was astonished that "a book of poems by a woman should contain not a single 'love-poem' or poem of motherhood," and pronounced this to be "in itself singular." In her work, wrote Matthew Josephson in *Broom*, "there is no sob, no throwing back of the hair with disheveled hands. There is great mystery and great tranquility." Rather, "emotion in her is calcined to a thin ash." Richard Aldington captured the exposed posture of the male reader confronted with "a most menacing superiority; one is conscious of a clear piercing gaze and an unfavorable judgment of oneself somehow emanating from the pages. Instinctively one straightens one's tie and tries hard to rub up a claim to something more than insignificance. I always feel I ought to apologize for having the presumption to read Miss Moore's poems."

It was never a determination to intimidate that guided Moore's sense of poetic vocation. Her aesthetic sensibility encompassed everything from netsuke to baseball. She was ever alert to what steadfast attentiveness could yield, so her poems often seem stimulated by audacities beyond our reckoning. Paradigmatic, in this respect, is her great long poem "An Octopus," which is actually about Mount Rainier in Washington. She acknowledged among her sources "government pamphlets on our national parks," but the reader has to take the extra step of consulting the pertinent pamphlet, with its characterization of the glacier on the great volcanic peak as "an enormous frozen octopus stretching icy tentacles down every side."

FIG. 10.3. Marianne Moore, photographed for the Dial Award (1924).

Moore learned from modern painting that subject matter was not the focus but the instigation of an artwork. This was another legacy of Wagnerism, which had prompted expectations that musical qualities could emanate from painted surfaces and words on the page. Moore's unique contribution to this legacy was to disguise "music" in a thicket of grammatical cues lifted from a variety of mundane sources. Where Eliot sampled the classics, Moore poached marvels from the everyday effluvia of American life, from *Vogue* to *Scientific American*.

It would seem anomalous that Scofield Thayer thought so poorly of *The Waste Land* while he was so appreciative of similar collage strategies in Moore's poems. He admired her "use of quotations like Picasso's of newspapers," and thought it registered the "infringement of mechanical upon our life; thus even by the sea the noise of steamers etc. become part of aesthetic whole." Although Scofield was dismissive of modernism generally, he was a wealthy collector and prized his Picassos. He may also have thought Eliot's cut-and-paste from classical sources was pretentious, whereas Moore could hardly be accused of highbrow posturing with her clippings. And while Moore respected Eliot's achievement in *The Waste Land*, she found the poem macabre.

Observations has lately assumed the status of a masterwork of American poetry, and I emphasize the lateness. Much of the reason is Moore's lifelong fidget, her propensity to revise her poems. *Observations* was not reprinted in its original form until 2002. In the meantime, it was scaled down in the 1935 *Selected Poems*, which she kept revising until a 1951 *Collected Poems* presented a lifetime's work in a scant 150 pages (plus notes). Near the end of her life Moore produced a misleadingly titled *Complete Poems*, notorious for its cutthroat excisions. The prerogative of an author to so severely tamper with a body of work has few parallels. To some extent, her revisions reflected her determination to live up to the outsized expectations of her peers.

Moore's most famous poem, "Poetry," was subjected to the most drastic revisions. The only enduring continuity is provided by its archly poised opening: "I too, dislike it." In *Observations* it is twenty-nine lines (many overrun because of their length, extending the poem onto a second page). In its final version in 1967 it was pared down to three:

I, too, dislike it.
    Reading it, however, with a perfect contempt for it, one discovers in
    it, after all, a place for the genuine.

Moore began pruning right away. In the second edition of *Observations*, printed just a few months after the first, "Poetry" was already reduced to thirteen lines. In lines lost from then on (though not in the 1935 *Selected Poems* produced under the guidance of T. S. Eliot, where the original version is used), we relish one of the more famous images in modern poetry, which concludes a statement beginning with a quote from Yeats:

nor till the poets among us can be
    "literalists of
    the imagination"—above
        insolence and triviality can present

    for inspection, imaginary gardens with real toads in them, shall we have
        it.

Moore's poetry overall could be described as harboring real toads in imaginary gardens.

The index to *Observations* is a poetic composition in its own right, diligently deploying the alphabet from A to Z. A typical sequence (with an alphabetic oversight):

> shaving-brush, 78, 104
> Shiras, G., 98
> Shock, G., 102
> shorthand, 57
> SILENCE, 82, 105
> silence, wrap with, 29
> slight snake, 69
> smoothness, 88
> Smith, G. A., Ahasueras banquet, 78, 104; crashing itself out, 72, 102;
>   foam on its barriers, 72, 102; ocean of hurrying consonants, 72, 102;
>   slight snake, 69, 101

All the poem titles ("Silence" was one) appear in the index, with double entries for the poem and the note about it. Some sources get fulsome references when they recur in multiple poems, like G. A. Smith, author of the *Expositor's Bible*. The index is—like the poems themselves—a place to roam, until you find yourself in a thicket. The index entries, as Wescott wrote, are "an object lesson in the exploitation of an environment by a mind which, in relation to it, is eccentric."

It was the eccentricity that won readers over. Reading Marianne Moore is like entering a sixteenth-century cabinet of curiosities (*Wunderkammern*, as they were called in German), those charmed precincts housing everything from stuffed animals to precious stones, anatomical peculiarities and botanical marvels, juxtaposed by inscrutable criteria, taxonomically suggestive while avoiding system. William Carlos Williams got closest to this perception in his appraisal for *The Dial* in 1925. The dense materiality of Moore's poems, he realized, was a mode of thought, and "she occupies the thought to its end, and goes on." He revisited an analogy Van Vechten and Sherwood Anderson had used to describe Gertrude Stein:

> Miss Moore gets great pleasure from wiping soiled words or cutting them clean out, removing the aureoles that have been pasted about them or taking them bodily from greasy contexts. For the compositions which Miss Moore intends, each word should first stand crystal clear with no attachments; not even an aroma.

"This is new!" he exclaimed. "The quality is not new but the freedom is new, the unbridled leap."

It requires a leap of faith for the reader to undergo the submersion imposed by Moore's poems. The titles often prompt unhelpful expectations. "England" begins with English pastoral but quickly moves on to America; "Radical" refers to a carrot; "Black Earth" is a self-portrait in the guise of a hippopotamus. Other titles entice by most unusual means: "To Be Liked by You Would Be a Calamity," "Injudicious Gardening," "Diligence is to Magic as Progress is to Flight," "Those Various Scalpels," are examples. "In This Age of Hard Trying Nonchalance is Good And" gives the first line as title, as many do.

Despite the backing of Pound and Eliot, and despite her own increasingly public persona after the Second World War, Marianne Moore's poetry tended to be set apart from the prevailing story lines of modernism, particularly in the homosocial milieu of the New Critics. If she was mentioned, it was in passing. H. D. fitfully persisted as well, thanks largely to the exorbitant late works, the epic *Helen in Egypt* and smaller but still book-length poem *Hermetic Definition*, posthumously published in 1972. *Helen in Egypt* arrived just in time for H. D. to see it the day before she died in 1961.

The writings of Hope Mirrlees, Nancy Cunard, and Mary Butts were utterly forgotten. Reprint editions of the poems, edited by Sandeep Parmar, of Mirrlees (2011) and Cunard (2016) make available work nearly a century old. Among resurrections of forgotten women writers, no one has had greater success than Mina Loy, largely thanks to the editorial dedication of Roger Conover. Her book *Lunar Baedecker* was published by Robert McAlmon's Contact in Paris in 1923, which also issued William Carlos Williams's *Spring and All* the same year. Contact titles were fugitive publications when they appeared, so Williams's was little known until it was included in a volume of other scarcities, *Imaginations*, in 1970 (and not reprinted on its own until 2011). The equally small Jargon Press published Loy's *Lunar Baedeker and Time-Tables* in 1958, momentarily resuscitating a then long-forgotten poet, but it too quickly slipped out of sight. It was not until Jargon (again) published the formidable *Last Lunar Baedeker* (1982) that Loy resurfaced. Still, it would not be until 1996 that a commercial edition appeared, its title ingeniously trumping the "Last" as *The Lost Lunar Baedeker*.

There is one woman who never faded from view, even though the tastemakers of New Criticism spurned her. *The Autobiography of Alice B. Toklas* vaulted Stein into celebrity in 1934, landing her on the covers of *Time* magazine, *Saturday Review of Literature*, and the *New York Herald Tribune*. Carl Van Vechten's hefty compendium, *The Selected Writings of Gertrude Stein*, published the year she died in 1946, ensured that she remained before the public eye. But however influential Stein has been as a totem of Anglo-American modernism, she did not wield the studiously impersonal sort of authority cultivated by Eliot. She was a celebrity, while Eliot played the long game as editor of *The Criterion*, with unimpeachable yet bland authority. It was an act, as Pound recognized when he came up with the nickname Possum, befitting one dead in appearance only.

In 1927 Eliot's former publisher John Rodker published *The Future of Futurism*, which he reviewed under the snappy title "Charleston, Hey! Hey!" It was also ostensibly a review of *Composition as Explanation* by Gertrude Stein, though Eliot refrained from any appraisal. Instead, he concluded the review with what sounds like peevish dismissal:

[Stein's] work is not improving, it is not amusing, it is not interesting, it is not good for one's mind. But its rhythms have a peculiar hypnotic power not met with before. It has a kinship with the saxophone. If this is of the future, then the future is, as it very likely is, of the barbarians. But this is the future in which we ought not to be interested.

Little would one imagine from this that Eliot wanted to secure *Composition as Explanation* for *The Criterion* until he learned it was being published as a Hogarth pamphlet by Virginia Woolf. If Stein did not quite pass muster for him as "literature," her "hypnotic power" was arresting. In his Clark lectures of 1926 he suggested that, along with seventeenth-century metaphysical verse, Stein's work provided "an extremely valuable exercise for unused parts of the mind."

Eliot's manner of cultured pontification was tirelessly rehearsed both before and after the publication of *The Waste Land* stamped his reputation as someone whose every utterance merited attention. From 1923 until he was awarded the Nobel Prize in 1948, Eliot published over three thousand pages of critical prose, some of it in books but mostly in periodicals. By the time John Crowe Ransom announced *The New Criticism* in a book title in 1941, Eliot was widely regarded as its instigator, or at least its sanctioning authority. The interpretive agility prized by the New Criticism had been demonstrated by Cleanth Brooks's 1937 article on *The Waste Land*, serving as a kind of demonstration piece for the movement. Stein's work, needless to say, was immune to such exegetical horse whispering. To be serious about Stein, for nearly half a century after her death when the New Criticism prevailed, was tantamount to not being serious.

Eliot's alliance with the New Critics proved mutually beneficial. His eminence lent authority to the initiative that would dominate literary study during the Cold War boom years of higher education; and the interpretive protocols of close reading promoted by New Criticism ensured canonical status to Eliot's poetry and critical views. *The Waste Land* became a permanent fixture of the curriculum, but its uniqueness was obscured by the curatorial terms of appraisal—organic form, irony, and other fixations of the New Critics. It's only through the perspectives of poets outside the Anglo-American literary world like Seferis and Montale, or those within it but at its margins like the women I've profiled here, that Eliot's poem recovers its original strangeness. And its strangeness comes from collage, or, in more patently literary terms, from the simultanism of Apollinaire and Cendrars. As long as the focal plane of readers guided by New Criticism was predominately Anglo-American, a needed international perspective was ventured only by those like the Mexican poet Octavio Paz (another Nobel laureate), for whom *The Waste Land* was "the first great simultanist poem in English." In the year of its centenary, it's finally possible to see Eliot's poem emerging from a long-standing curatorial shadow, to rejoin a realm of modernist artifacts that were unabashedly confrontational, renegade, noncompliant, and full of zest.

CHAPTER ELEVEN

"Ezra Pound Speaking"

When it was published, *The Waste Land* was received as an exclamation point for the postwar mood. That mood was far from the superficial gaiety chronicled in tales of the so-called lost generation of Paris's Left Bank. *The Waste Land* set the tone. "The War bled the world white. It had to recover. While it was in that exhausted state a sort of weed-world sprang up and flourished. All that was real was in eclipse, so all that was unreal came into its own and ran riot for a season." When Wyndham Lewis wrote these reflections, he had gloomy forebodings of another world war. Thanks to the Great War, he observed, "artistic expression has slipped back again into political propaganda and romance, which go together. When you get one you get the other." He was still in England, resenting it, and could only look back wistfully, wondering about the squandered potential of his gang. But they had paled before "the really malefic 'Bloomsburies,' who with their ambitious and jealous cabal have had such a destructive influence upon the intellectual life of England." If the Great London Vortex had not been snuffed out by the war, he imagined that "a less sordid atmosphere would have prevailed. The writing and painting world of London might have been less like the afternoon tea-party of a perverse spinster."

Lewis greeted this tea party with characteristic pugnacity, but also with undimmed naïveté. It was pointless to rouse sleeping dogs by reprising *Blast*, so in 1921 he launched *The Tyro*. It was an attempt to make the case for abstract art and modernist tendencies more broadly. "During the last ten years," he wrote in an editorial, "writers and people in conversation have said: 'Cubism, Futurism, Vorticism, and all the rest of that revolutionary phase of art, is dead.'" *The Tyro* published articles by Eliot and others, and reproductions of the artists who'd been featured in *Blast*. It folded after two issues. Another periodical, *The Enemy*, followed, also short-lived. Lewis spewed forth a torrent of books between the wars, fiction and nonfiction, cantankerous and insightful. Lewis was filling in the picture and plugging the gap, as it were, of his proving ground: prewar.

Prewar had been commendable from the perspective of 1936. "Europe was full of titanic stirrings and snortings—a new art coming to flower to celebrate or announce a 'new age.'" For future generations, he predicted, the pioneers in the English scene "will stand out like monosyllabic monoliths— Pound, Joyce, Lewis" (Eliot being oddly omitted). But all that glorious effort—registered poignantly in his boast, "I was at its heart. In some instances I was *it*"—had stalled. Or worse than stalled, it was ancient history: "By the end of this century the movement to which, historically, I belong will be as remote as predynastic Egyptian statuary." "We are not only 'the last men of an epoch,'" as Lewis acknowledged they'd been called; "*We are the first men of a Future that has not materialized. We belong to a 'great age' that has not 'come off.'*" The lingering brushfires were on the verge of flickering out, and "all that is 'advanced' moves backwards, now, towards that impossible goal, of the pre-war dawn."

*

Like Lewis, Ezra Pound launched his own journal in 1927, pointedly named *The Exile*. It lasted for only four issues, and among its few claims to fame was its debut of Louis Zukofsky with "Poem Beginning 'The,'" its 330 numbered lines and notes identifying sources echoing *The Waste Land*. The final issue included "The Descent of Winter" by William Carlos Williams, a book-length prose/poem successor to *Spring and All*. Pound concluded the issue with a miscellany of "Data" listing publications, making approving references to the development of abstract cinema, extolling the genius of his friend Man Ray, casting a positive glance at Lenin, and suggesting that novelists turn their attention to "the *types* of humanity now permitted to govern America, congressmen, members of state assemblies, lobbyists etc." It was a harbinger of fixations that would swell over time.

In early 1921 Ezra and Dorothy Pound settled in Paris. As Sylvia Beach, proprietor of the bookshop Shakespeare & Co., later recalled, he said they'd left London "because the water was creeping up, and they might wake up some morning to find they had web feet." To Ford Madox Ford he admitted, "I daily ask myself why the hell I stayed in Eng. so long; and then comfort myself with the reflection that one cdnt/ have left during the war, and that I probably escaped as soon as possible."

As the Mauberley poem revealed, Pound had burned his English bridges. In part it was owing to what one correspondent called "his ingenuity of insult." John Quinn observed as early as 1917, "He is a powerful astringent. He may inflict pain, but his pain is salutary. It is wonderful how people who do not know him hate him. I sometimes think that opposition, even hatred, is the harvest he wants to gather." Ten years later,

FIG. 11.1. At the Jockey Club in Paris, 1923: American artist Man Ray is squatting at the left, with a bemused Mina Loy kneeling nearby. Next to her is Dadaist Tristan Tzara, flanked by Jean Cocteau, with Ezra Pound standing behind him. Standing directly behind Loy is Jane Heap, editor of *The Little Review*.

Ford Madox Ford (who changed his last name from Hueffer during the war) called Ezra "a swashbuckler of the Arts. I rather wish he was not." Ford thought him typically American in that "he stupefies himself with the narcotics of reform."

The next four years in Paris were a whirlwind. Pound promoted the career of American pianist and composer George Antheil, who brandished a pistol onstage before addressing the keyboard, and was busy writing ultra-modern, jazz-inflected compositions purporting to achieve some covenant with the fourth dimension. Pound published music reviews under the nom de plume William Atheling, wrote two operas, and began a relationship with violinist Olga Rudge that would last to the end of his life. Shortly after Ezra and Dorothy moved to Rapallo, Italy, in early 1925, Olga gave birth to Ezra's daughter Mary. After the fashion of many artists, like H. D. with her daughter, Perdita, the child was raised by others. The next year Dorothy had a son named Omar (not Ezra's) who was likewise sent to England for his upbringing.

This complex progeny faced a delicate challenge when Homer and Isabel Pound visited in 1928, then moved to Rapallo. Ezra decided that only his father would be privy to all the details. But the parents settled in with gusto, and when Zukofsky visited in 1935 he was housed with the elder Pounds and subjected to readings of Ezra's juvenilia by his adoring mother. Yeats and his wife also moved to Rapallo, soon followed by Richard Aldington and Ford Madox Ford. The Italian Riviera was becoming a successor colony to prewar London.

Despite the presence of friends and family, Pound's intellectual life followed increasingly esoteric paths, and his manner of assembling his ragpicker's motley of interests didn't make it easier on readers. The poet Archibald MacLeish, whom Ezra found too adhesive a follower of his and Eliot's example, complained that "the man has sheep herder's madness. I wish he would stick to Cantos." Pound thought he had a method. As he put it in *ABC of Economics*, "I am not proceeding according to Aristotelian logic, but according to the ideogramic method of first heaping together the necessary components of thought."

The telltale verb is *heaping*, which is more or less the method of the Cantos. As he revealed to the writer James T. Farrell in 1932, his epic consisted of "ANY bloody thing to excite curiosity." Earlier, in 1927, he had suggested a thematic structure to his father.

A. A. Live man goes down into world of Dead
C. B. The 'repeat in history'
B. C. The 'magic moment' or moment of metamorphosis, bust thru from quotidian into 'divine or permanent world'. Gods, etc.

A decade later, such deliberate counterpoint design could seem increasingly muddled by new installments of the poem. In his introduction to *The Oxford Book of Modern Verse* in 1936, Yeats found the "deliberate nobility" of Pound's work compromised "by its proper opposite, nervous obsession, nightmare, stammering confusion."

Not only the Cantos, but anything Pound wrote was afflicted by a kind of logorrhea compounded by his economic obsessions. "There are more questions in my head than I can set down with apparent coherence," he confessed to one correspondent. But the situation was not altogether new. In 1915 he'd confessed to Joyce that "my head is a squeezed rag." At that time he'd characterized himself as a typewriting machine; now twenty years later he saw himself "running top speed and likely to emit folly." He dashed off *Guide to Kulchur* in six weeks, chalking up about three thousand words a day—during which he was duplicating that tally on correspondence. *Cantos LII–LXXI* (1939) was written in little over a year.

His major expenditure was in postage. His letters were now almost entirely written in splutters of unorthodox spelling. "Bull Muss has DONE more, and distributed More to the PEEPUL than any yourpeeing govt." is a modest example, with the Mussolini reference playing on Bull Moose and its pun on urine. Old friends were exhausted by such antics. Yeats pleaded for plain English, and Ford protested, "Get the waiter at your hotel to write your letters for you." Pound was undeterred, dashing off daily bits of "EZthority" to the younger generation, who were only too glad to have his attention; and he began to think of his global ministrations as an "Ezuversity." A self-appointed enlightener, Ez was fulfilling the diagnosis famously rendered by Gertrude Stein: "He was a village explainer, excellent if you were a village, but if you were not, not." She adds that "Ezra also talked about T. S. Eliot. It was the first time any one had talked about T. S. at the house. Pretty soon everybody talked about T. S."

Ernest Hemingway, when asked how his old friend had come to be a supporter of Mussolini and the Fascist regime, replied that Pound's program of cultural renewal had fizzled in England, nor had it gained traction in France, so he ended up in Italy where he was appreciated. While this is a sensible time line, it's far from the whole story, though it does touch on Pound's preoccupation with schemes to "restart civilization"—the phrase he'd used to pitch Bel Esprit on behalf of Eliot. Pound had become interested in banking, social credit, and theories of capital while he was living in Paris. Having left behind the social whirl of the French capital, in Rapallo he gave free rein to his peeves, the oldest being his gripe about obtuse publishers. "The best writers of my generation," Pound reflected, were printed "by small organizations initiated for that purpose and in defiance of the established publishing business of their time." Business as usual, having no interest in whatever he regarded as "the best," was a crime against humanity. "Artists are the race's antennae. The effects of social evil show first in the arts," and, concluding this syllogism, "Most social evils are at root economic." Increasingly, Pound's indignation about this plight was seasoned with wrath. His Cantos swelled, absorbing the history of China, early American presidents, the wisdom of Confucius, the evils of usury. The poem became a contact print of his obsessions, as the earlier scheme of getting Eliot free of the bank ballooned to a quixotic ambition to emancipate culture from evil bankers, tarred by him as Jews. Long stretches of these Cantos can be tough going, though jolts of "luminous detail" continued to compel the respect of Pound's peers.

In the thirties, Pound's interests were all over the map. Not surprisingly, he was the author of *How to Read* (1931), followed up by *ABC of Reading* (1934);

but there was also *ABC of Economics* (1933). Collections of essays on literary subjects continued apace—*Make It New* (1934), *Polite Essays* (1937). He was also busy expanding his purview in *Guide to Kulchur* (1938), *Jefferson and/or Mussolini* (1935), and the economic pamphlets *Social Credit* (1935) and *What Is Money For* (1939). The stream of poetry, translations, and correspondence swelled. "The more I hear of the political, philosophical, ethical zeal and labors of the brilliant members of Pound's big brass band the more I wonder why I was ever let into it 'with my magic flute,'" James Joyce wondered. The astute musical analogy came naturally to the Irishman, who might have had a more lucrative career with his fine tenor voice. Another Irishman, the young Samuel Beckett, recognized the virtue of *Make It New* as "education by provocation." H. L. Mencken, an early supporter of Pound, wrote him reproachfully in 1937: "You made your great mistake when you abandoned the poetry business, and set up shop as a wizard in general practice."

Pound repeatedly sought an audience with Mussolini. Though it was granted only once, that was enough to send the poet over the moon. His next priority was to get back to America and set Roosevelt straight. Pound spent three months in his homeland in 1938, some of it wandering around congressional administrative buildings in search of legislators to harangue. Even before disembarking from his ship, he was met by reporters, eager to know his thoughts on Mussolini. "He has a mind with the quickest uptake of any man I know except Picabia," Pound said of the Fascist leader. But who was Mussolini being compared to? "Picabia is the man who ties the knots in Picasso's tail." This was Pound's way of acknowledging one of the key conspirators of Dada who had become a boon companion during his Paris years.

While in the States Pound was given an honorary degree at his alma mater, Hamilton College. There were also welcome opportunities to finally meet Marianne Moore and reconnect with old friends. Staying with E. E. Cummings, he was "gargling anti-semitism from morning till morning," the younger poet confided to a friend. "We don't know if he's a spy or merely schizo, but we do feel he's incredibly lonesome." His old pal Bill Williams wrote of his impressions during the visit: "I like him immensely as always, he is inspiring and has much information to impart but he gets nowhere with it." But, as he sadly noted, "the man is sunk, in my opinion, unless he can shake the fog of fascism out of his brain." For Pound himself, the trip seems to have fueled delusions, as he now fancied himself a grand operator in international diplomacy. It was only a short step to travesty.

Between October 1941 and July 1943, Pound made over a hundred broadcasts on Radio Rome as part of its *American Hour*, transmitted shortwave throughout Europe, Britain, the United States, and the Pacific. "Ezra Pound Speaking" was his byline. The program was broadcast twice a week and rebroadcast three times. He was paid 350 lire per talk (about $17 in the exchange rate of the time, or over $300 today), and once the war commenced and foreign assets were closed off, it was his primary source of income. He periodically went to Rome to record his program in batches.

The Italian government was pleased to have the support of a prominent American, with the added bonus that his delivery was entertaining. It was full of the regional accents that had crept into his correspondence, bending spelling nearly out of legibility. On the radio it worked. But there was some concern. A functionary in the Institute of Overseas Cultural Relations tried to warn Rome Radio: "There is no doubt in my mind that Ezra Pound is insane! He is a pleasant enough madman and he is certainly a friend of Italy, but . . ." Back in the States, William Carlos Williams heard from a bank teller that he'd been mentioned on air, and he was incensed. "What the hell right has he to drag me into his dirty messes?"

A month after the Japanese attack on Pearl Harbor in December 1941, Pound was introduced on air by a statement he drafted:

Rome Radio, acting in accordance with the fascist policy of intellectual freedom and free expression of opinion by those who are qualified to hold it, has offered Dr. Ezra Pound the use of the microphone twice a week. It is understood that he will not be asked to say anything whatsoever that goes against his conscience, or anything incompatible with his duties as a citizen of the United States of America.

Meanwhile, the American government's Foreign Broadcast Intelligence Service was listening in, making transcripts of the broadcasts. Nancy Cunard was one of those called upon to decipher the foreign words and phrases.

Transcribers had their work cut out for them. Forced to make guesses about names, Confucius became "confusion," and another Chinese sage, Mencius, morphed into the American writer Mencken. The difficulty was exacerbated by Pound's tendency to transfer the caterwauling raconteur style of his personal correspondence into public speech, with unannounced shifts of topic, and name-dropping as if everyone should recognize the personae, as in this example: "Gus Flaubert and I myself, and diverse others, includin' if you must go so far back, Mencius and Confucius, saw something worse than just one BAD idea, and that was the corruption of the whole and TOTAL means of communication of all ideas whatsoever. The corruption of language, the destruction of all precision in terminology." Pound liked Mallarmé's credo about purifying the language of the tribe. But little would have been clarified by reference to the French symbolist, and "Gus Flaubert" makes the novelist sound like a local pal.

Although Pound was intent on driving the message home even as he strayed from the ostensible topic, the broadcasts generally rebuked the United States for being suckered into a war he thought had been finagled by international financiers. He urged listeners to get busy researching the root cause: "If there is still some campus not yet invaded by the hosts of Belial and Jewry, not wholly squashed under the dung-flow from Wall Street and Washington, I suggest you start taking notes and figures." He thought Americans lacked historical perspective. "Note when American history went out of fashion. When the kids in the lower grades heard of Lenin and Marx and Trotsky, and not so much of Lincoln and Washington. Watch the gradual creep up of obscurantism."

He was often delusional in his claims, as when he ventured that he could have single-handedly thwarted the war with Japan if his native land had had the guts to send him on a mission to Tokyo. He assumed Fenollosa's trunk of Chinese poems and Noh plays afforded him special access to the Asian mind. One of the stranger moments came in the broadcast for March 8, 1942, when he recalls, "Twenty-five, 26, 27 years ago night life, or night dance clubs started in London. Looked diverting, nobody wondered WHY? Ole Frida started the cave of the calf, nobody thought any evil." Frida Strindberg, former wife of Swedish writer August Strindberg, opened the Cave of the Golden Calf, hiring Wyndham Lewis to decorate the place, which became a hotbed of Vorticist nightlife. But Pound inexplicably lurches into dark ponderings, dimly linked to his obsession with international finance. "Wake up one morning and find the spirit of England, immortal spirit of England's May Day, chained in a brothel. Just another hat trick, undermining, cutting away. Where did she get the money to do it?" he ominously wonders about Frida.

Expressions of disgust were richly registered, as he railed against "such dung heaps of perfumed pus as the Atlantic Monthly, and Harper's and Scribner's." He had a penchant for mocking politicians with an abandon that even Donald Trump could envy: President Wilson was "Woodrow codface," the English prime minister was "balloon-faced bumbustuous Churchill," and the BBC radio network was "the British Blurb Corporation" and "the Bloody Boobs Corporation," among other epithets.

Throughout, Pound believed his broadcasts were a forum for patriotism, a way of protesting the political derelictions of his native land. "To send boys from Omaha to Singapore to die for British monopoly and brutality is not the act of an American patriot," he said on February 19, 1942. He was also alert to the residual derelictions of American culture, the "small dirty meanness" of racism, among other things. "Anybody who will draw back a minute and look at the way people pick on minorities, can see what I mean."

By this point his teenage daughter, Mary, was staying with her mother, Olga, Pound's longtime mistress, near Rapallo, where the poet continued to live with his wife. Ezra proudly took her under his wing with pedagogic tasks, learning English and Greek, memorizing poetry, and translating his Cantos into Italian. (German was her first language, so both English and Italian were lessons in the paternal Ezuversity.) She also heard him rehearsing his radio talks, noticing that "it seemed as though he possessed two voices: one angry, sardonic, sometimes shrill and violent for the radio speeches; one calm, harmonious, heroic for Homer." Sometimes he read poetry on air, but mostly the anger prevailed, the hectoring grew apace, and vilification of Roosevelt as "Jewsfeldt" more hysterical and slanderously unhinged.

During a visit to the American Consulate in Rome to (unsuccessfully) renew his passport, he made a scene and departed by taunting the staff with a Fascist salute. In 1931 he'd started dating letters by the Fascist calendar, counting from 1922 as year one with Mussolini's march on Rome. Near the end of the decade he would sometimes sign letters "Heil Hitler" or with a swastika, and the anti-Semitism became more pronounced. He disavowed pogroms, only to take the big step of suggesting something like the "final solution" (about which he knew nothing): "If some man had a stroke of genius and could start a pogrom UP AT THE TOP, there might be something to say for it."

He was generating alarm back in America. The poet Eunice Tietjens raised the prospect of treason in the pages of *Poetry* in April 1942: "That it should be one of the poets who is thus playing Lord Haw-Haw, no matter how ineffectually, seems to cast a slur on the whole craft. In the name of American poetry, and of all who practice the art, let us hope that this is the end of Ezra Pound." A year later, on July 26, 1943, a federal grand jury indicted eight Americans residing abroad of treason. Pound was deemed "a person owing allegiance to the United States [who], in violation of his said duty of allegiance, knowingly, intentionally, willfully, unlawfully, feloniously, traitorously, and treasonably did adhere to the enemies of the United States." In 1944 a pamphlet called *The Black Badge of Treason* was published, attacking Pound and speculating whether it would be better for him to be executed or to die by his own hand.

In August 1943 Pound wrote a letter to the attorney general, Francis Biddle, in hopes of dismissing the indictment, explaining that "I have not spoken with regard to *this* war, but in protest against a system which creates one war after another, in series and system." In September, poet Archibald MacLeish (who held various high-level government positions during the war) expressed concern that the indictment could backfire and "confer the paraphernalia of martyrdom upon a half-cracked and extremely foolish individual." By September, the situation was dire, and in a journey of heroic desperation Pound walked the 450 miles from Rome to the Tirol, where his daughter was staying with the foster parents who had raised her. She was astonished, asking, "How did you get here, where from? And he pointed to his feet, red, full of blisters, his ankles swollen. 'I walked out of Rome.'" It was only then, in what he expected might be a final visit, that he revealed to Mary the existence of his wife, Dorothy, and her son Omar. These disclosures were a revelation to the teenager, and it was not until many decades later that even scholars grasped the complexities of Pound's personal life.

In a moment weirdly prophetic of his own looming future, Pound concluded his broadcast for January 29, 1943, "Whom God would destroy, he first sends to the bug house." "Bughouse" was what he consistently called St. Elizabeth's in Washington, DC, where he was confined from 1946 to 1958. But this is jumping ahead. First stop on his return journey to America was a military prison compound in Pisa.

In May 1944 Ezra and Dorothy were ordered out of the "prohibited area" in Rapallo and moved in with Olga up the nearby mountain in Sant'Ambrogio. They lived there for a year, the two woman who hated each other being forced to coexist. As the Fascist regime collapsed and American forces worked their way up the Italian Peninsula, Pound's delusions of grandeur began to affect his thinking. He fancied the Americans might welcome him as a font of valuable information, yet when he was apprehended in May 1945 he made a gesture of a noose tightening around his neck.

For a few weeks he was in the custody of the counterintelligence center in Genoa, where (surprisingly) an American journalist was permitted to interview him. On May 9, 1945, the *Chicago Sun* and *Philadelphia Record* featured the headline

Confucius and Kindred Subjects
Pound, Accused of Treason
Calls Hitler Saint, Martyr

Pound still harbored the grandiose idea that the president needed his advice. "If I am not shot for treason," he figured, "I think my chances of seeing Truman are good." The journalist was astonished that the American detainee, facing a charge of treason, was mainly preoccupied with Confucius. When apprehended, he had taken a Chinese dictionary and his copy of the ancient sage with him.

On May 24 he was transferred to the Disciplinary Training Center in Pisa, where various miscreants of the American military were detained. Those accused of murder and rape were held in cages. Pound was deemed the most dangerous of all, and he was placed in a cage with reinforced wire, unwalled on all sides, with a spotlight and a guard watching him at all times, and a few blankets for bedding on a concrete slab. After nearly a month in the cage the sixty-year-old was both physically and mentally broken, and he was removed to the medical compound. He spent the next five months there, with access to the unit's typewriter. While in the cage he had scrawled a few lines on a scrap of toilet paper, and now he embarked full throttle on another installment of Cantos. He could be heard humming away as he typed, sounding the cadences of his poem. He had found in the latrine a copy of *The Pocket Book of Verse* edited by Morris Speare, an improbable stimulus at a crucial moment, fertilizing his imagination with cadences from the past.

> That from the gates of death,
>   that from the gates of death: Whitman or Lovelace
>   found on the jo-house seat at that
> in a cheap edition! [and thanks to Professor Speare]
> hast'ou swum in a sea of air strip
>   through an aeon of nothingness,
> when the raft broke and the waters rose over me

The Homeric plight of Odysseus had been introduced in the first Canto, and now Pound was experiencing a similar challenge as "a man on whom the sun has gone down." He took on the name Odysseus uses to deceive the Cyclops, asking who's there: "Ou tis," he says, "No one." Another self-portrait: "As a lone ant from a broken ant-hill / from the wreckage of Europe, ego scriptor." Yet in the DTC in Pisa Pound finds himself not strictly alone but a member of a tribe, "we who have passed over Lethe." He even registers the execution of fellow prisoners. "If you can imagine the thoughts of a man condemned to death being X-rayed ten minutes before his execution," wrote the poet Eugenio Montale (who knew Pound), "then you will be able to form an idea of the *Pisan Cantos.*"

The Cantos were modeled on Dante's tripartite structure, and early Cantos written during the First World War were presumed to be the passage through Inferno. But Pound's compositional interpenetrations defied any clear separation of Hell, Heaven, and Purgatory. All were at hand all at once and most of the time. This propensity gave rise in *The Pisan Cantos* to repeated ruminations on the theme.

> I don't know how humanity stands it
>> with a painted paradise at the end of it
>> without a painted paradise at the end of it
> the dwarf morning-glory twines round the grass blade
> magna NUX animae with Barabbas and 2 thieves beside me

The dark night of the soul indicated in the Latin kept the captive mind fixated on paradise.

> Le Paradis n'est pas artificiel
>> but spezzato apparently
> it exists only in fragments unexpected excellent sausage,
>> the smell of mint, for example

Paradise is not artificial, but subject to breakage, returning in radiant moments. At other times, it's bound to its antithesis: "Le paradis n'est pas artificiel, / L'enfer non plus": paradise may not be artificial, but neither is hell. The guiding light, or thread—if any such thing can be imputed to these Cantos—came at the mercy of Confucius's *Analects*. It was a pointed, and poignant, question for a man in captivity, maybe nearing the end, with the cornucopia of the past all around him, interpenetrated with all the details of his present plight: "How is it far if you think of it?"

Pound was detained for so long because the military and FBI were busy assembling material for the prosecution of his case. He was finally flown back to the United States on November 16, 1945. Those accompanying him got the impression the poet was a crackpot. His American publisher, James Laughlin (who had started New Directions before the war at Pound's urging—"Nude Erections," Ezra punned), found Julien Cornell to handle the legal defense, and Cornell reported that the poet was "very wobbly in his mind and while his talk is entirely rational, he flits from one idea to another and is unable to concentrate even to the extent of answering a single question, without immediately wandering off the subject." This led Cornell to consider insanity as the best defense. As it happened, a series of witnesses for the prosecution took the same line, even though several of them recognized that Pound was hardly "insane," merely scattered and obsessed. One of them noted that if he was asked about his case, "Confucius and these other things seemed to get roped in."

While awaiting the jury trial, Pound was confined at St. Elizabeth's, a large (and overcrowded) federal asylum in Washington, DC. The doctor on his ward asked the poet what was wrong with him, and he replied, "All of Europe upon my shoulders." On January 4, 1946, he began to receive visits from Charles Olson, who had spent the war years working for the Office of Strategic Services, soon to be transformed into the CIA. Most recently he had been a high-ranking official in the Democratic National Committee. He was an aspiring poet and was also working on a book about Herman Melville, published as *Call Me Ishmael* in 1947. "Olson saved my life," Pound told his lawyer.

The visits could be trying for Olson. Even before meeting Pound, Olson had called him a scoundrel, but seeing him looking so worn-out in court, he wanted to be of help. So he was surprised at his first visit to find Pound fit and vigorous, his eyes "no longer hooded with hate," he innocently supposed. Olson found to his dismay that the vigor extended to his deplorable side, anti-Semitism and the rest. Furthermore, he harbored delusions. In January 1946, "He shot in something about 'I understand they think to send me to Japan. I could find out things, what the Russians are up to.'" In encounters extending over a few years, Olson saw Pound's "nerves turning like a wild speed-machine," with the result that "his mind bursts from the lags he sees around him." Simply put, "Ezra *is* a tennis ball, does bounce on, off, along, over everything. But that's the outside of him. Inside it's the same, but different, he bounces, but like light bounces."

Olson's diagnosis was prescient: "He does not seem to have inhabited his own experience. It is almost as though he converted too fast." There is a tantalizing comparison to be made between Pound's associative quickness and jazz great Charlie Parker, coming into prominence just as Pound was on trial. "Bird," as he was known, not only played faster than anyone; his solos were like the Cantos with his incessant split-second riffs on a whole medley of tunes from pop schmaltz to Stravinsky. A dual portrait could be written, illustrating the prophetic depravity of cognitive fast-forward in these two inimitable figures.

On February 15 the jury trial was convened, and all the evidence (mostly "expert opinion") of Pound's unfitness to stand trial resulted in a verdict corroborating that view. He was assigned to the custody of St. Elizabeth's until such time as he was deemed fit to stand trial for treason. He would remain there until 1958. Dorothy arrived and took lodging nearby. More and more visitors appeared, and throughout the next decade the Ezuversity was in session—and enrollment, measured by correspondence, was booming. The person characterized by *Time* magazine as "the ragbaggy old darling of the U. S. expatriate intelligentsia" had his forum. Somehow the setting was apt: one visitor was amazed that Pound was "oblivious of a white-headed man beside us who was stroking the radiator and talking to it as if it were a cat."

FIG. 11.2. Ezra Pound, *The Pisan Cantos* (1948).

In 1948 *The Pisan Cantos* was published by New Directions in America and Faber in England. (Ever since he joined the firm in 1925, Eliot had seen to it that Faber was the English publisher of Pound's poetry and literary prose.) The Faber edition was ten pages longer, continuing the long-standing differences between American and British texts, which deviated not only in the typography but at times in textual details. (Even the titles could vary: *Cantos XXXI–XLI* in England was *Eleven New Cantos* in America.) The American edition featured Gaudier-Brzeska's profile of the poet as a much younger man on the dust jacket. Soon a controversy even more intense than that surrounding Pound's indictment for treason would erupt, when the inaugural Bollingen Prize for poetry was awarded to *The Pisan Cantos*.

*

On September 26, 1948, T. S. Eliot celebrated his sixtieth birthday on board a liner crossing the Atlantic. He was on his way to Princeton University to take up a visiting fellowship at its Institute for Advanced Study, jovially signing letters as "Advanced Student." A few old acquaintances were there, but most people were too intimidated to approach the legendary poet. Eileen Simpson, wife of poet John Berryman, found him to be agreeably courteous. She was also astonished to find he could down five martinis without any change in aspect. This was inspirational news to a postwar generation of poets known for being blotto. He took the opportunity to visit Pound at St. Elizabeth's when he was invited to lecture at the Library of Congress. Then, in November, news came that he was the latest recipient of the Nobel Prize for literature. When Berryman congratulated him, he sighed and said, "The Nobel is a ticket to one's funeral. No one has ever done anything after he got it."

*

When Pound was taken into custody in Italy in 1945, his solitary and increasingly manic mission to "restart civilization" had become all-consuming. When he was arrested, he was an elderly, overworked autodidact with delusions of grandeur. It might seem that the Imagist crispness of "In a Station of the Metro" was far from the "ragbag" of the Cantos, but there was some continuity. Pound approached the epic scale of world civilization with the same self-assurance with which he'd picked a face out of the metro crowd. He made the snapshot ethos of Imagist haiku into a poetic principle: "dichten = condensare," composition is compression. But condensing a throng into an image is one thing; subjecting global currency practices to such compression is something else.

Pound was nevertheless a hero to many, particularly those who openly acknowledged their debt to his unfailing support, including Eliot, Lewis, H. D., and Hemingway, not to mention those who had passed away, like Yeats and Joyce. As patient number 58,102 at St. Elizabeth's, symbolically proximate to the nation's capital, Pound was news that stayed news in the worst way. Because he was a clearinghouse for the divergent avenues by which poetry had become modernized (not strictly *modernist*), he was impossible to avoid: the simple mechanics of literary history required a layover at Pound Central. But there were some—Louis Untermeyer, for instance, Eliot's old nemesis—who seized on the political controversy to dismiss the poetry outright.

The literary alarm bells began ringing in 1946, shortly after the treason charges were put on hold and Pound was consigned to St. Elizabeth's. William Rose Benét and Conrad Aiken's *Anthology of Famous English and American*

Poetry was due to be reprinted by Random House when the publisher decided Pound should be dropped from the collection because of his political views. Aiken was distressed, and the matter was resolved only after W. H. Auden, a Random House mainstay and ascendant crown prince of modern poetry, threatened to find another publisher unless Pound's work was retained.

Another controversy, behind the scenes, concerned an introduction to Pound's *Selected Poems* being prepared for New Directions. John Berryman selected the poems, and Rolfe Humphries was writing the introduction. But it foundered on his reference to Pound's anti-Semitism: "There will be no allusion to jews or to mental condition or the whole deal is off," the poet insisted. Humphries, for his part, objected to a *supervised* introduction, maintaining that his admiration for the poetry could be reasonably balanced by qualms about the poet's political positions. Pound, exasperated, thought Humphries was "NUTS about free speech. He can free speech anywhere save in PERMANENT form in an introd/ where it is irrelevant." After all, Pound's troubles began with his radio broadcasts, and as he liked to say, free speech without free radio speech is nothing. Though few would agree that biographical and contextual considerations are irrelevant, especially in Pound's case, *Selected Poems* was issued without an introduction.

During these negotiations the controversy regarding the Bollingen Prize erupted. Under the auspices of the Library of Congress, the prize was awarded to *The Pisan Cantos* in February 1949. This was the first (and last) poetry award sponsored by the US government. In 1943, while MacLeish was librarian of Congress, he appointed Allen Tate as consultant in poetry (a role later elevated to poet laureate). Tate, in turn, proposed that the library appoint a board of advisers on literary matters. Tate's successors—and subsequent board members—were Robert Penn Warren, Louise Bogan, Karl Shapiro, Robert Lowell, and Léonie Adams, who held the office in 1948–1949. These six were supplemented for deliberations on the Bollingen Prize by Aiken, Auden, Eliot, Theodore Spencer, Katherine Anne Porter, Willard Thorp, Paul Green, and Katherine Garrison Chapin. Chapin was married to Francis Biddle, the attorney general to whom Pound had written after Biddle filed the indictment for treason, and he urged his wife to oppose any initiative to award the prize to Pound.

Shapiro was in a vexed position, having published *Trial of a Poet and Other Poems* in 1947, before *The Pisan Cantos* appeared. The title poem, nearly thirty pages long, is clearly about Pound.

> He sat down with masters, he furthered them
> In heroic efforts, indefatigably seeking

What the age demanded
And finding the forms that the age deserved.

Is this that man so broken,
Sitting now in a plain chair, slumped over,
With lowered eyes and beard unpointed . . .

The speakers in the poem are the Poet, Public Officer, Doctor, Priest, and a Chorus of Poets. The chorus speaks the lines above and laments the ignominy of seeing one of its own go over to the dark side. "Thus we become / Like children in a nightmare on a dead street / Who hear a monster behind and cannot scream." Yet the Chorus of Poets recognize even madness as a mission: "you were sent by us as a scout / To explore the ore of the horror ahead."

The Poet is given a grandiose speaking role, albeit in prose, that goes on for ten pages.

> *Poet.*   A poet in our times is a semibarbarian in a civilized community. He lives in the days that are past. The march of his intellect is like that of a crab, backward. The highest inspirations of poetry are resolvable into three ingredients: the rant of unregulated passion, the whine of exaggerated feeling, and the cant of factitious sentiment.

(Quotation marks are inserted at the beginning of every prose line.) Shapiro cannot resist the temptation, in the end, to ventriloquize his own views in the mouth of the Poet. The Poet takes the place of the judge, and concludes his sentence, "I condemn the prisoner to be known hereafter as a dull poet and the lapdog of his age."

The committee was a veritable all-star team of the poetry world, and when they met for deliberations in November 1948, its star caliber was heightened by the recent announcement that Eliot would be receiving the Nobel Prize. His departure for Sweden to accept the award was little more than a week later. The starstruck Bogan was tickled to see the great man sharpening his pencil with a penknife during the meeting. Talk about an elephant in the room! This, after all, was the man addressed near the beginning of the first Pisan Canto: "yet say this to the Possum: a bang, not a whimper, / with a bang, not with a whimper"—reprising Eliot's conclusion to "The Hollow Men." Shapiro observed at the time that Eliot's presence "perhaps inhibited open discussion." As the lone Jew on the committee, he also felt the other members tiptoed around the awkward issue of Pound's anti-Semitism. After the final vote tally, Shapiro grew increasingly outspoken about "an act of intellectual arrogance which has no parallel in literary history."

Other nominees for the prize were the second installment of William Carlos Williams's *Paterson*, Randall Jarrell's *Losses*, and *A Green Wave* by Muriel Rukeyser. These last two didn't stand a chance, given the competition, and there were only three votes for Williams—by Shapiro, Chapin, and Aiken, who had always been wary of Pound. Even before the first meeting, everyone seems to have felt the final result was a foregone conclusion. The votes were tallied in February (several by mail, including Eliot's), and the committee issued its award to Pound with a statement to the effect that this was strictly decided on the basis of literary merit. The prevailing exegetical protocols of the New Criticism provided a tacit justification for keeping politics and poetry segregated.

"Pound, in Mental Clinic, Wins Prize for Poetry Penned in Treason Cell" was the *New York Times* headline. The controversy was taken up across the country in newspapers, journals, and magazines. Pound, with swelled head, mocked the "Bubble-Gum" prize as "Bollingen's bid for immortality." The prize was named for the recently convened foundation, the initial purpose of which was to promulgate the works of psychoanalyst C. G. Jung (Bollingen was the name of his Swiss summer home). The Bollingen Series went on to become one of the most distinguished publishing programs in the postwar decades, and the separately administered prize was taken up by Yale University Library, where it continues to thrive, with an increasing propensity in recent decades to recognize poets in the Poundean lineage (including Gary Snyder, Robert Creeley, Susan Howe, Charles Wright, Nathaniel Mackey, Charles Bernstein, and Mei-Mei Berssenbrugge).

The most bilious assault on the honor to Pound was by the poet Robert Hillyer, who published two articles in *Saturday Review of Literature* in 1949. The title of the first, "Treason's Strange Fruit," played on the title of Billie Holiday's chastening 1939 song about lynching. It was followed by "Poetry's New Priesthood," an indictment of New Criticism for having nurtured the apolitical attitudes that made the award to Pound possible. Hillyer went overboard in linking Pound's fascism with Nazi sympathies he imputed to Jung's circle, a charge he was forced to retract. His was a paranoid account of a cabal consisting of past and present Fellows of the Library of Congress, the New Critics and their literary quarterlies, and aluminum tycoon Paul Mellon (who had funded the Bollington Foundation). Taken together, Hillyer charged, they were launching "the mystical and cultural preparation for a new authoritarianism."

The damage was done, but there was more to the damage. Quite by accident, Malcolm Cowley found out that the editors of *Saturday Review* had engineered the whole controversy to pump up circulation. "It was a great success," he was told. "We thought it would give us three exciting issues but it went on for six." Eliot suspected as much, and he was not alone. The magazine even printed a letter to the editor by a reader who charged, "Your articles on Ezra Pound and the Bollingen Fellows should make you the darling of the House Committee of Un-American Affairs. If ever a publication took over the technique of guilt by association and thorough smearing of reputations you are it."

The Bollingen committee members rebutted the *Saturday Review* as incitement to mob rule. It was no less authoritarianism than fascism, they charged, boosting a "standard-brand positive Americanism as a test for literary worth." In the ensuing wrangle the journals favorable to the New Criticism were forced to defend the award, while a range of others across the political spectrum from right to left denounced it (from *Masses and Mainstream* to *Catholic World, Partisan Review, Atlantic*, and *Time*). The consensus was that the government had been played by a gang of wily insiders in the literary racket. Even the insanity diagnosis Pound had received came under fire from Dr. Fredric Wertham, the Bellevue psychiatrist who had recently launched a campaign against comic books that led to congressional investigations and the eventual self-policing of the industry under the Comic Books Code.

The Pisan Cantos took on an unwitting epic dimension inasmuch as it occupied a confluence of volatile issues in America at a time of increasing anxiety about foreign or "un-American" influence in the culture at large. The book itself was an object lesson in the right person being in the right place at the right time, while dramatizing the pitfalls of being colossally wrong. Insofar as the controversy remained resolutely focused on the poet, it failed to address the precarious situation of poetry in America. In 1949 Muriel Rukeyser published *The Life of Poetry*, and while she avoided mention of Pound, she could have been thinking of the Bollingen affair when she wondered, "What is the fear of poetry? To a great extent it is a fear produced by a mask, by the protective structure society builds around each conflict."

Much indignation was stirred up by the prize, but indignation and opportunism quickly became comrades in arms. A red herring in the Pound case was based on a literal reading of the treason clause, meaning he had imparted secrets to the enemy. This was presumptuous, for Pound had no access to secrets in any sense of the word, and anyone privy to the transcripts would see that his inflammatory rhetoric (as his defense lawyer said) "reminded me of the way Wall Street bankers and lawyers used to talk." Pound's own take on the matter was repeatedly deployed in *The Pisan Cantos*: no free speech without free radio speech.

Archibald MacLeish is known for his dictum "A poem should not mean / But be," from "Ars Poetica" in his 1926 collection *Streets in the Moon*. But a variant in the poem is more pertinent to his defense of Pound: "A poem should be equal to: / Not true." In 1950 he published *Poetry and Opinion*, a booklet about the Bollingen controversy, in which he made a telling point about the double standards that had dogged the debate. "Only by demonstrating that it is the *function of poetry itself* to communicate right ideas about these things," he suggested, "can you argue that wrong ideas invalidate the poetry." Another poet, Richard Eberhart, thought, "Fifty years will remove the politics and leave the poetry"—a misguided prognosis intended as consolation to New Directions publisher James Laughlin.

"Is modern poetry a tale told by an Eliot, full of Pound and fury, signifying Williams?" This clever quip is by Peter Viereck, political scientist and poet whose career was played out on the wrong side of Cold War liberalism in politics, and the wrong side of Eliot & Co. in poetry. He was warned by an influential editor who, "while privately agreeing, said I must stop criticizing what he called 'the Pound-Eliot-Tate establishment,' or I would 'no longer be publishable.'"

The P-E-T establishment was a fault line revealed by the Bollingen affair, which was its first seismic event. Long before it wielded such influence, it was a partnership, the terms of which were spelled out by Pound to Eliot: "You let *me* throw the bricks through the front window. You go in at the back door and take the swag." As long as Eliot was the all but crowned head of Anglo-American letters—a position he held for over forty years until his death in 1965—he was a staunch supporter of Pound, whose reputation was insured by the Bank of Eliot like an FDIC security deposit. The New Criticism served in effect as the talent and booking agency of the enterprise, and the Bollingen controversy revealed how ably its adherents could operate as spin doctors as they downplayed politics in favor of aesthetics. The text was the thing, and the life was off limits in the hallowed halls of GI Bill higher education.

The New Critical establishment would be in charge of reputations. Having set the protocols of literary study, it had work to do managing the poetry that would serve as The Right Stuff. Pound, the person, was "saved" as an accidental by-product of that supreme P-E-T value, Poetry. But in a society where the particulars of poetry mattered as little as the specific contents of packaged foods, the symbolic value of Poetry was more important than actual poems (and, except in fraught instances, poets themselves). Pound was "saved" for poetry in the double sense the philosopher Hegel celebrated in the German verb *aufheben*, meaning both to preserve and to cancel. Pound knew the formula: "No comment from the Bug House."

No comment didn't mean silence. Beginning with Olson's visit in 1946 there was a steady stream of visitors. Among the poets was a veritable honor roll of those who would monopolize kudos and commandeer many prizes in the next two decades: Robert Lowell, Elizabeth Bishop, John Berryman, Randall Jarrell, W. S. Merwin, and James Dickey, as well as those like Olson who were more openly partisan as Poundians, including Robert Duncan, Louis Zukofsky, and Paul Blackburn. And of course Pound's generational friends and supporters paid their respects, from Eliot and Tate to MacLeish and Marianne Moore. Scholars came knocking as well, with Marshall McLuhan, his student Hugh Kenner, Guy Davenport, A. Alvarez, and Samuel Hynes among them.

In time, the Ezuversity burgeoned like a mushroom colony after rain. "It was the world's least orthodox literary salon," writes Daniel Swift in *The Bughouse*, "convened by a fascist, held in a lunatic asylum, Tuesdays and Thursdays, Saturdays and Sundays, 2 until 4 p.m." Unorthodox, yes, but not strictly literary. Pound's prewar fixations on social credit, international banking, and other issues resumed as various cranks, acolytes, and traffickers in conspiracy theories began filling his mailbox and, when possible, visiting in person. One of them, Eustace Mullins, wrote a book about Pound and much later developed a website. "Mullins died in 2010, but he has a curiously vibrant, well-curated online afterlife," Swift found. "One click: from Pound's broadcasts to white supremacist websites. Another click and I am told that vitamin B3 can cure AIDS and acne and schizophrenia. One more click and I am back to Mullins and on through him to Pound."

"Ezra Pound, the American, is a glass-house, with all the furnishings of his mind visible." This description by John Cournos, from his autobiography in 1935, was a retrospective glimpse of his old London friend. It would become more and more evident during the years in Italy, and literally broadcast around the world on Rome Radio. Even the "bughouse" could double as the glass-house. But despite the swell of visitors and a cascade of international correspondence, the question of Pound's ultimate fate lingered. By 1955 when he turned seventy and had been in custody for a decade, some began to consider his fate.

MacLeish, who was a lawyer, began to test the waters, contacting Frost, Eliot, and Hemingway to endorse the prospect of springing the old poet. In the summer of 1957 he wrote Hemingway, reporting that he'd finally gotten up the nerve to visit Pound at St. Elizabeth's in December 1955. "What I saw made me sick and I made up my mind I wouldn't rest till he got out. Not only for his sake but for the good name of the country: after ten years it was beginning to look like persecution and if he died there we'd never wash the stain out." His visit with the old poet resulted in a testy correspondence. MacLeish objected to Pound's blinkered view of politics. "Why don't you read anything except what you do read?" he asked in exasperation. "You have founded a whole position on an almost complete ignorance of your own country and its too late to do anything about it." In the end, MacLeish glimpsed the humanity behind the bluster: "Your information may be horse-crackers but your heart is sound."

Hilda Doolittle kept up with the news from afar in Switzerland, where her doctor encouraged her to write memoirs as therapy. She was coming to terms with old age by revisiting her youth, in which Ezra had been so vital a part. The memoir's title, *End to Torment*, is a reference to Pound's release. "We have gone through some Hell together, separately," H. D. reflected. What was shared was tribal. "It is the *feel* of things rather than what people do. It runs through all the poets, really, of the world. One of *us* had been trapped. Now, one of *us* is free. But we, the partisans of world-thought, of the myth, shiver apprehensively. What now?" The tribe was suggested in a French headline: "*Ezra Pound, le Mallarmé U. S. ne mourra pas chez le fou*" (Ezra Pound, the American Mallarmé, will not die among the insane).

There had been obstacles to engineering the release. Even as MacLeish was making headway, and Frost was greasing the wheels with high-level functionaries in the government, Pound was in the news again. One of his devotees, John Kasper, had become a prominent segregationist, eventually landing a term in federal prison for bombing a desegrated school in Nashville. MacLeish and his team knew they had to bide their time until Kasper faded from the news cycle. It was not until April 1958 that the charge of treason was dropped, and Pound was free to go. Returning to Italy in July, the sweaty and unrepentant poet was photographed on shipboard demonstrating the fascist salute in proudly vulgar defiance.

It's characteristic of Pound to have soiled his emancipation this way. The most famous passage in *The Pisan Cantos* is the "Libretto" of Canto LXXXI. It has long been prized as a glorious recitative of self-reckoning, with its haunting refrain, "Pull down thy vanity." It had a deep effect on friends and family (it was the first of the Pisan sequence he sent to Dorothy and Olga from the DTL at Pisa). "Never have I seen Mamile [Olga] cry so unrestrainedly as when she read Canto 81," Mary recalled. MacLeish, who considered *The Pisan Cantos* a botch, insisted that "it contains one passage any living poet might have been proud to write."

> The ant's a centaur in his dragon world.
> Pull down thy vanity, it is not man
> Made courage, or made order, or made grace,
>   Pull down thy vanity, I say pull down,
> Learn of the green world what can be thy place
> In scaled invention or true artistry,
> Pull down thy vanity

For many readers, it's as if the words were an embodied sob. And yet (with Pound there's always a "yet") the passage is ambiguous. Sob, but also snarl. To whom is the reproach addressed? I heed the counsel of Richard Sieburth: "Pound's verse is richest when moving within its own space of self-contradiction." The "Libretto" is like a searchlight touching all horizons, from repentance to indignation, confession to defiance. Soon after his return to Italy in 1958, the impertinent restless energy subsided, and the surviving shell of Ezra Pound was overtaken by silence.

CHAPTER TWELVE

Significant Emotion

Directing his first film in 1929, with the support of the Surrealists and collaboration of Salvador Dalí, Luis Buñuel told the lead actor in *Un Chien Andalou*, "Stare out the window and look as if you're listening to Wagner." That's the disconcerted, slightly pained look you can see before he gazes at the street below and sees a crowd gathered around a severed hand, a hand swarming with ants. In 1936, Wyndham Lewis noted with some perplexity a newspaper headline, "Wagner is still the big box-office noise." When H. D. saw the front page of the *New York Times* for April 19, 1958, with its photo of Pound on his release from the bughouse, she was reminded of Wotan, presiding deity of Wagner's Ring. She had been pondering the early days of their relationship as "Ishilda and the Tristram with the harp."

The passwords of Wagnerism still hung in the air. In 1926 Hart Crane was cocky enough to think he'd overthrown Eliot as he worked on his long poem *The Bridge*. He saw it unfolding under a different patrimony. "Rimbaud was the last great poet that our civilization will see—he let off all the great cannon crackers in Valhalla's parapets, the sun has set theatrically several times since while Laforgue, Eliot and others of that kidney have whimpered fastidiously."

Valhalla, the home of the gods in Wagner's Ring cycle, is a citadel of artistic striving. Even Pound was not immune. In a short statement, "Ikon," published in 1913, he disclosed something unexpected behind Imagism. "It is in art the highest business to create the beautiful image," he imagined, writing under the sway of Yeats.

And if—as some say, the soul survives the body . . . then more than ever should be put forth the images of beauty, that going out into tenantless spaces we have with us all that is needful—an abundance of sounds and patterns to entertain us in that long dreaming; to strew our path to Valhalla; to give rich gifts by the way.

Despite anchoring his beatific vision against the backdrop of Wagnerism, he was wary of that milieu "when each art tried to lean on some other. Notably painting, sculpture and music leant heavily on bad literature."

A decade later, Pound had refined his instincts into principles. "There are two aesthetic ideals, the Wagnerian," he observed, in which "you confuse the spectator by smacking as many of his senses as possible at every possible moment." The other ideal, associated with Brancusi, Lewis, and Vorticism, was intent on "focusing the mind on a given definition of form, or rhythm, so intensely that it becomes not only more aware of that given form, but more sensitive to all other forms." This refinement, this corporeal tutor, offers "a scaling of eye-balls, a castigating or purging of aural cortices, a sharpening of verbal apperceptions."

Unsurprisingly, Pound's musical orientation was premodern, even medieval. "Wagner, a great musician," he allowed, "produced a sort of pea soup," and "Debussy distilled it into a heavy mist, which the post-Debussians have dessicated into a diaphanous dust cloud." Pound abjured the piano for the ease with which it could stack up chords, emitting orchestral soup, clotting the melodic continuity of single note sequences. Despite his concerns about Wagner, the Cantos deployed the leitmotif pioneered in the Ring cycle to signal themes associated with particular characters and events. Pound didn't acknowledge it, but he practiced it, just as the Cantos sustain in their own way the Wagnerian "endless melody."

Of all the grand enterprises in modern poetry, nothing can rival the Cantos in terms of scope and dimension, written as it was over a period of fifty years, exceeding a thousand pages. "An epic is a poem including history," Pound wrote. And while the Cantos touches on many mythological themes and episodes, its determination to "include" history is dominant. There is no more patently Wagnerian poem from the twentieth century than the Cantos. Wagner and Pound make improbable bedfellows. But in art, improbabilities often take on a life of their own. Historical contemporaries are not a peer group for the artist. Once we realize, with Pound, that "we do not all of us inhabit the same time," affinities ripen. And as the saying goes, time will tell.

Consider a performance of Richard Wagner's *Parsifal*. As you settle into your seat, you look over the program notes, likely to address the Grail legend that inspired the composer. Now imagine a different approach: instead of the usual background information you get the text of "The Waste Land." As the lights dim and the stage curtain opens, the music begins, and, as it unfolds, all that you see and hear is filtered through the words that begin with the cruelty of April, coursing through temptations and disappointments, scenarios of enticement and sterility, ending unresolved in fragments shored against ruin.

*

In *Wasteland: A History*, architectural historian Vittoria Di Palma suggests that "wasteland is defined not by what it is or what it has, but by what it lacks." As a consequence, "the emptiness that is the core characteristic of the wasteland is also what gives the term its malleability, its potential for abstraction." This arresting observation has some bearing on Eliot's poem (although not discussed in the book, it provides an epigraph). *The Waste Land* is a malleable text, susceptible not so much to abstraction as to supposition. It's like a coloring book with boldly delineated objects in which readers can fill in the colors as they please. The farmer's trousers can be red or black, the ground green or brown. A woman can be Vivien Eliot or someone else, and the presumed speaker may be Tiresias or Eliot himself.

One of the ways of capitalizing on such speculative attributions was parody. Samuel Hoffenstein published "The Moist Land" in January 1923, a mere two months after *The Waste Land* itself. Not quite as long as the original, it runs to ten pages in four sections ("The Demobilization of the Fleet," "A Three-Handed Game of Pinochle," "Death by Hooch," "Thunder and Lightning"). Much of the parody refrains from spoofing particular lines from the poem, until the ending:

> *Amo amas amat amabo amabimus*
> *Huius huiius huius—O mea culpa*
> There's never anything to say though I should say
> The less the more. The blue parrot's fainted.
> God bless you all. Paracelsus is drunk again.
> Daddy. Damdaddy. Damdaddy
>
> Shanty shanty shanty.

"The Moist Land" was reprinted in *Year In, You're Out* (1930), in which Hoffenstein also takes on Hart Crane, Edna St. Vincent Millay, Carl Sandburg, and others in an assortment best characterized by the title of one, "Couplets, Rare, Medium, and Well-Done."

Also published in 1923 was "The Dry Land" by Christopher Ward, a Prohibition title.

In the highlands, where the Revenooer dozes
Where the old, kind men have rosy noses—
O the Moonshine's *right*
In my old Kentucky home!

Here we find Eliot's "jug jug jug" supplemented by "bottles / And demi-johns." Ward relishes the calendrical opportunity that launches Eliot's poem—"April is the foolishest month, bringing / The First of April"—and he includes notes. "Mr. Eliot's poem will elucidate the difficulties of my poem much better than my notes can do; and I recommend it," he adds, "because my poem will seem more lucid by contrast."

In 1931 the English poet Herbert Palmer published *Cinder Thursday* (1931), a book-length poetic pastiche of, but not limited to, Eliot's moods and modes (the first section offers "*apologies to T. S. Eliot, Laura Riding, Gertrude Stein and certain Imagists*"). The title mocks *Ash Wednesday*, which also provides the manner of the poem exhibiting Eliot's newfound religious turn:

I refuse to be taken in by *The Waste Land*,
I refuse to pretend that I am not taken in.
I refuse to praise what I think I freely understand,
A hoax,
The most stupendous literary hoax since Adam,
Yet in some abysmal way creative,
Even in its disintegration . . .
God! what a mousetrap!

James Joyce, a seasoned mimic, registered his own pastiche in a letter chronicling a vacation in the south of France in 1925.

Rouen is the rainiest place getting
Inside all impermeables, wetting
Damp marrow in drenched bones.

. . .

I heard mosquitoes swarm in old Bordeaux
So many!
I had not thought the earth contained so many
   (Hurry up, Joyce, it's time!)

His parody ends by morphing Eliot's triple Shantih into "Shan't we? Shan't we? Shan't we?"

Parody doesn't quite apply to Martin Rowson's graphic novel *The Waste Land* (1990), which runs the original through the sieve of a detective plot à la Raymond Chandler. Chandler's Marlowe (Chris, a nod to Eliot's passion for Elizabethan revenge tragedies) is the gumshoe going "down those mean streets and up rats' alley." Two epigraphs from *The Long Goodbye* make reference to a "pale blonde" reading *The Waste Land* and another quoting "Prufrock." Characters from other poems populate the narrative (Sweeney, Baedeker) along with those named in *The Waste Land* (Tiresias is a drag queen). Idaho Ez shows up furtively from time to time, and in one scene Pound, Eliot, and Lewis form a trio in Hari Krishna garb with shaved heads. Crowd scenes hustle up a retinue of modernists, from Yeats, Conrad, and Stein to Eliot biographer Peter Ackroyd, as well as Hollywood stars Sidney Greenstreet, Mary Astor, and others who starred in films of novels by Chandler and Dashiell Hammett. Richard Wagner appears next to seagulls screeching, "Weiala weia!!" Marlowe's office ("Marlowe & Fisher") is adjacent to the publishing firm Faber & Faber. The Holy Grail stands in for the Maltese Falcon, and there's a "wiseguy" on a barstool: "He do the police in different voices!" A cartoon cat delivers the famous benediction with a lisp, "Thantih Thantih Thantih Thuckers!!"

Rowson hews most closely to the original in a note, strictly adhering to Eliot except for the words I've underlined:

> Not only the title but the plan and <u>much</u> of the incidental symbolism of <u>this book were</u> suggested by <u>Mr. T. S. Eliot's poem</u> . . . Indeed, so deeply am I indebted, <u>Mr. Eliot's poem</u> will elucidate the difficulties of the <u>book</u> much better than my notes can do; and I recommend it (apart from the great interest of the <u>poem</u> itself) to any who think such elucidation of the <u>book</u> worth the trouble.

Rowson's book could not be published intact in the UK, where the Eliot estate forbade quoting from the poem, though even in the American edition there are more allusions than quotes. In fact, the conspicuous hybridity of *The Waste Land* itself provides a perfect template for Rowon's send-up. "Eliot's serious rag-tomfoolery" is a heavyweight presence in Steven Tracy's *Hot Music, Ragmentation, and the Bluing of American Literature*, where it deftly slips into a rapport with African American blues and jazz legacies.

This is what caught the attention of African American undergraduate and aspiring jazz trumpeter Ralph Ellison in 1935, whose encounter with

Eliot's poem shifted his focus from music to literature. His novel *Invisible Man* reads like a player piano scored to Eliot's poem, in the key of "St. Louis Blues." "*The Waste Land* seized my mind," Ellison acknowledged with a forceful verb. "I was intrigued by its power to move me while eluding my understanding. Somehow its rhythms were often closer to those of jazz than were those of the Negro poets," he noticed; "its range of allusion was as mixed and as varied as that of Louis Armstrong."

Invisible Man is not a parody of *The Waste Land*, but its parodic elements suggest Ellison's kinship with a poem that often has invited parody as a show of affection, as when Allen Tate wrote "The Chaste Land" with a fellow undergraduate. What parodies reveal is that Eliot forged a distinctive idiom, one that flowed from his remark that his poetic line punctuates itself. As reviewers noted, it has a music all its own—a music that resists the conventions of musicality but is nonetheless like a pop song burrowing into your head. "Fear in a handful of dust" sounds portentous, of course, but it's an unshakable image—one that Rowson uses in the cover of his graphic novel, with the poet's knobby fingers proffering the dust.

These parodies and responses, ranging over a considerable span of time, register a sense of familiarity as well as quizzical interest in what Eliot's poem is. The charge of hoax was quickly dispelled by the magnitude of its reception, after which it was unseemly to accuse it of being the most "insubordinate" of poems. But its "rag-tomfoolery" lingered—despite the portentous Grail theme and the "mumbo jumbo" of what was derided as a "parade of pompous erudition." A century after its publication, *The Waste Land* has long been canonical, a centerpiece of higher education and a perennial shorthand for modernism. But is it a masterpiece?

There's a prodigious body of scholarship on *The Waste Land*, and even more on *Ulysses*, but the term *masterpiece* is rarely if ever used, even by the keenest admirers of Eliot and Joyce. In fact, the term derives from an artisanal context: the medieval chef d'oeuvre singled out as the artifact that elevated its maker from apprentice to master. But while most would regard *Ulysses* as a prodigious step beyond *Dubliners* and *A Portrait of the Artist as a Young Man*, and *The Waste Land* a transformative gesture surpassing "Prufrock," their authors were not workshop apprentices, nor did they regard their earlier works as training exercises, preparatory to accreditation.

Even if *The Waste Land* is (or isn't) a masterpiece, can it be called classic? Gertrude Stein punned her way into an indelible definition of the classic in "Composition as Explanation," the essay Eliot wanted for *The Criterion*. "Those who are creating the modern composition authentically are natu-

FIG. 12.1. Cover artwork for *The Waste Land* by Martin Rowson (HaperCollins, 1990).

rally only of importance when they are dead," Stein reasoned, "because by that time the modern composition having become past is classified and the description of it is classical. That is the reason why the creator of the new composition is an outlaw until he is a classic." By the same punning principle, she discerned the role of the masterpiece distinguishing entity from identity. In the act of creation, she says, identity is beside the point. The work itself, the entity, prevails. Furthermore, the masterpiece is gratuitous, a gift, not a transaction: "A master-piece has essentially not to be necessary, it has to be that is it has to exist but it does not have to be necessary it is not in response to necessity as action is because the minute it is necessary it has in it no possibility of going on."

The transit from outlaw to classic better approximates the significance accorded *Ulysses* and *The Waste Land* than any talk about masterpieces. But, to heed Stein's point about masterpieces, the notoriety surrounding their initial appearance was clouded by presumptions of necessity. If *The Waste Land* was welcomed as a registration of postwar ennui, and *Ulysses* (in Eliot's view) gave orderly shape to the "immense panorama of futility and anarchy which is contemporary history," this implied that they offered expedient solutions to a pressing problem. This was the view of the New Critics, who deplored anarchic modernity and sought solace in the responses of Eliot, Joyce, and others who, they felt, could no longer in good faith conform to older artistic codes when responding to the alleged futility of modern life. Responding to a derelict world, they thought, art itself had to go off the rails. Damaged art reflected damaged life.

The cultural and aesthetic assumptions the New Critics brought to Eliot's poem have dissipated, but the question of applicability still hangs in the air. It's muted somewhat in the case of anything canonical, which is tantamount to being famous for being famous. Richard Wagner boldly thought his mythologically generative music dramas could be world historical, transformative, and redemptive. *The Waste Land* deployed some of the same mythic material and summoned a grand vision of collapse alleviated only by a grace note of supplication (shantih), but it had no big mission statement. If anything, given the strained circumstances in which it was written, the clerk typist's sordid dismissal of her lover would best apply: "Well now that's done: and I'm glad it's over."

*

The Waste Land, along with other works by the "Men of 1914" like Joyce's *Ulysses* and Pound's Cantos, prompted W. B. Yeats's speculation that they absorbed "a deluge of experience breaking over us and within us," blending swimmer and waves into a single substance. Another way of putting it is to say that the works solicit the reader as collaborator. When early readers confessed that they could no longer distinguish Eliot's poem from their own thoughts and memories, they were in effect admitting that Eliot had captured "the physiology of our sensations." This reveals much about the poem itself (which, after all, was compared to dreams as well as clouds in their phantasmagorical mutations): it was neither a philosophical venture nor a grand hypothesis; it was more like a tone poem, as Aiken recognized. Hearing it induced the "resonant happiness" Curtius recalled, even if it resisted paraphrase and taunted the understanding.

Ezra Pound spoke of his "ideogramic method" as a ragbag, its contents conjoined like bits of metal clutched by a magnet in the "radiant node or cluster" of the vortex. In the magnetic vortex, the heap hangs together paratactically, one thing next to another. A larger purview, a sense of orientation and purpose, is not strictly under the control of the writer or artist. The Jugendstil designer August Endell anticipated, in 1897, the advent of something more than a stylistic change: "We're witnessing the onset of a completely new art, an art with forms that designate nothing and depict nothing and recall nothing," one that he supposed would have an impact similar to that of music. When Curtius found happiness in *The Waste Land*, he associated it with the poem's musicality, by which he meant something like Endell's "new art."

As Pound developed the ideogramic method in his early Cantos, he was unknowingly honing himself for the editorial ministrations he applied to *The Waste Land*, which was a surreptitious demonstration of his method.* Pound also developed an intertextual procedure in "Homage to Sextus Propertius" that helped him recognize continuities in Eliot's poem between written and quoted material. He was developing skills of layering, whereas

---

* The first outing of Pound's epic was "Three Cantos of a Poem of Some Length" in the American edition of his collection *Lustra* in 1917. Groups of three or four Cantos appeared in issues of *Poetry* (July and August 1917), *Future* (February 1918), and *The Dial* (in three issues 1920–1922). The first Cantos in *Lustra* did not end up in the poem, but earlier versions of what stayed appeared in Pound's collections *Quia Pauper Amavi* (1919) and *Poems 1918–1921* (1921). Although a diligent reader might have been prepared by Pound's *Cantos* for Eliot's *The Waste Land*, the less attentive were unlikely to think of Pound and Eliot as poets embarked on parallel paths. After 1922, apart from a final appearance in *The Dial* and a group in Eliot's *Criterion*, the Cantos would be available only in more and more fugitive little journals. The general public did not have access to the poem until 1933 with American and British editions of *A Draft of Thirty Cantos*, and by then *The Waste Land* had settled in as an obliterating forerunner, it seemed. Three previous groups of Cantos in book form were limited to deluxe editions of two hundred or fewer copies.

what writers more commonly attend to is sequencing. Sequencing is hypotactic: building up an argument, making consecutive sentences add up in a rhythm of progression. Reaching a conclusion, offering an overview. By contrast, layering is paratactic, though that doesn't mean a miscellany. Pound was training himself as a craftsman of ligatures, becoming the *miglior fabbro* Eliot anointed him in 1925 when he first supplied the dedication to *The Waste Land*.

Pound and Eliot seem not to have been aware of Hope Mirrlees's *Paris*. If they had, they might have seized upon the "holophrase" she adapted from Jane Harrison, who defined it as the utterance "of a relation in which subject and object have not yet got their heads above water but are submerged in a situation." A heaping together, really: ideogram seasoned by Mina Loy's terms, intensity and immensity. Eliot perceived in Gertrude Stein's bath of words cleansed of all prior usage a "peculiar hypnotic power." Loy saw them as "an intercepted cinema of suggestion," itself a suggestive enough phrase that it applies to Eliot as well—*The Waste Land*, that holophrase, speaking the language of the listening eye.

When Pound first read Eliot's poems in manuscript, he was impressed that his fellow American had modernized himself. It was a lesson Pound himself had only recently realized he needed to engage "the living tongue," thanks to that guffaw of Ford Madox Ford. Thus commenced Imagism: direct treatment without ornament, delivered in natural speech rhythms. These precepts hardly seem revolutionary now, but at the time they threw down a gauntlet.

Imagism, in its diminutive scale, was a decisive step in what physicist H. L. Hinton valued as "unlearning." He understood that everything we learn builds up a hard shell of impenetrability. Learning something new doesn't mean that the old useless stuff just drops away. It needs to be actively dislodged by unlearning. What Pound realized was that prevailing poetic practices had left poetry tongue-tied, as it were. Poets emitted strings of syllables at a certain tempo like parrots reciting key words. He knew it was an excrescence but didn't know how to divest himself of the voice-over that insinuated "poetry" as a universal value, albeit a value recognizable only in certain (by 1910 predominately maudlin) performances. And then Eliot appeared.

Eliot "modernized" himself by fluidly handling plain speech. Actual speech, when deployed by Victorian predecessors like Tennyson, was in dialect. So when *Prufrock and Other Observations* ventured normative locutions of everyday palaver, some thought the contents were observations, not poems. Consider "Morning at the Window," with its portrait of despondent housemaids. A reader in 1917 might have acknowledged the imagistic proficiency while also noting a lack of versification, and avoidance of rhyme:

> The brown waves of fog toss up to me
> Twisted faces from the bottom of the street,
> And tear from a passer-by with muddy skirts
> An aimless smile that hovers in the air
> And vanishes along the level of the roofs.

Readers passed over such subtleties of social document in favor of "La Figlia che Piange," which Eliot was frustrated to find becoming acceptable to old-school readers, who relished its singsong refrain "weave, weave the sunlight in your hair."

Eliot was, in effect, doing what Eugenio Montale later professed as his own mission with respect to Italian poetry, wringing the neck of eloquence. It's an expression that, unlike anything in Imagism, admits that renovation is aggressive. Symons made the same point more innocuously when he observed that Laforgue was dispensing with the "privileges of poetry"—by which I take him to mean the privilege of exempting poems from performing any other function than sounding like other poems. Riding and Graves sensed the persistence of such conformity when they distinguished a "'poetical' period" from a "psychological period," when a certain "freakishness" prevails—like being subjected to the drawn-out doubts and hesitations of J. Alfred Prufrock for pages on end.

Unlearning, wringing the neck of eloquence, dispensing with the privileges of a poetical period: these were all attendant features of even so rudimentary an aspiration as direct treatment of the subject, whether objective or subjective. It was similar in its way to Richard Wagner's endless melody, banishing the highlighted moments invested in aria so that the music could offer a continuously immersive experience. Concentrating on the task at hand, then, could swell to the immense panorama of the Wagnerian Ring cycle, or narrow to the "direct treatment" in two lines of Pound's "In a Station of the Metro."

These efforts were put in distinctly nineteenth-century terms by Remy de Gourmont when he characterized Symbolism as "individualism in literature, liberty in art." The equation took a turn soon after the fin de siècle when Apollinaire realized that Cubism was not a mimetic but a conceptual art. It was then but a short step for Marcel Duchamp to unveil the R. Mutt urinal, and by naming it *Fountain* create a "new thought for that object" (even earlier he had dubbed a standard-brand snow shovel *In Advance of the Broken Arm*). Mix and match, then relish the incongruities. It was the principle of slapstick, in which a pristine banker in a top hat encounters a banana peel. Charlie Chaplin, like the poet envisioned by Marianne Moore, was a literalist of the imagination.

The Waste Land emerged after all these initiatives, ways of framing the modernist push. New York publisher Alfred Knopf thought the poem "great fun," an expression that places it against the backdrop of popular culture. As Burton Rascoe realized, Eliot's poem was like Gershwin's *Rhapsody in Blue*, mixing "classico-heroic themes with barrel-house wails of sorrow with a brooding overtone of lost loveliness." If Eliot was an uncanny clown to some, he was also walking a tightrope over an abyss, as his friend Richard Aldington saw. He didn't specify what the abyss might be, but Eliot himself was heedful of the tightrope as, with mechanical exactitude, he placed one foot in front of the other, day after day, year after year.

"In my beginning is my end," Eliot wrote in "East Coker," the second of his *Four Quartets*. A beginning can be estimated in various ways, not all of them beholden to the personal *I*, although behind any one of the precipitating portals another *I* stands revealed. It's there in Rimbaud's memorable "*I* is an other." Is there any more palpable and prominent exponent of that realization than T. S. Eliot? How is J. Alfred Prufrock not the literal transcription of Rimbaud's dictum? Prufrock enabled a Harvard undergraduate to fidget with his self-doubts in the guise of another, somebody who said "I," only it wasn't him. Generations of playwrights and novelists had done the same. Melville begins *Moby-Dick* with three bare words, "Call me Ishmael." "The Love Song of J. Alfred Prufrock" begins with misleading joviality, "Let us go then, you and I." The "I" in question, it's soon evident, is an unappealing companion.

There's another scenario in which Rimbaud's phrase applies. Where else is the discovery that "I is someone else" more forcefully revealed than in the interpersonal carnal embrace? No wonder the degree of trepidation involved defines a biological threshold. Even if the occasion itself is not momentous, it reveals the precariousness of whatever is deemed to have been so. It puts an *I* on the line, nudges "I" into inescapable intimacy with an other—one who is also another I. Eliot made that leap in 1914 when he married in order to "solve" the nagging problem of his "inexperience."

The Waste Land is a poem that could have had other titles. "He Do the Police in Different Voices" was one. A plausible alternative might have been Rimbaud's *A Season in Hell*, which Eliot knew well. In 1958 H. D. copied down an observation by Edmund Wilson. "Of no other poem," he remarked of *The Waste Land*, is it more true "that the artist is a kind of prison from which the works of art escape." Once it escaped, the poem had a life of its own, one increasingly at odds with the directions taken by its author in his remaining forty-three years.

The precepts in the Sanskrit terms to which *The Waste Land* builds (generosity, compassion, restraint) were the fruit of Eliot's study of Eastern religions at Harvard. He converted to the Anglican Church in 1927 but had an affinity with Buddhism. The trauma that precipitated his long poem compelled him to seek relief from domestic trauma. It didn't work out that way, but the poem nurtures the hope of peace and benediction. His final years were a time of public eminence, personal happiness (he married his secretary, Valerie, in 1957), and declining health. But there was more, much more, than met the eye.

*

On January 2, 2020, a sealed autobiographical statement by T. S. Eliot was opened and made public. It was dated November 1960, five years before the poet's death, and revised in 1963. It was provoked when Eliot's friend Emily Hale deposited his correspondence with her at Princeton University Library. The letters were to be unsealed fifty years after her death, and Eliot—not pleased, but legally helpless—left instructions that his statement be opened the same day.

"It is painful for me to have to write the following lines," he begins. "I cannot conceive of writing my autobiography." Eliot had famously argued for impersonality as a virtue, extolling "the objective correlative" as the adequate expression of emotion—or, in his case, trauma. Restraint was his métier. But now he had to confess, or at least elucidate. Emily Hale had not responded in kind when he declared his love for her in 1914, shortly before he left for Germany and England on a traveling fellowship from Harvard.

In the 1960 statement, Eliot suggested that any explanation for his doomed marriage to Vivien Haigh-Wood would be unintelligible to others. He admitted that at the time he still believed himself to be in love with Miss Hale. Or, he allowed, he may have been motivated to resurrect that belief when, soon after the vows, the marriage devolved into "misery." In fact, as he goes on to recount, the marriage was itself a desperate attempt to correct the course of his life. He was pursuing a graduate degree in philosophy when he met Vivien, but had "a gnawing doubt, which I could not altogether conceal from myself, about my choice of a profession."

Certain sentences and phrases from Eliot's 1960 statement have been in circulation since they were quoted by his second wife in her introduction to the 1971 edition of *The Waste Land* manuscripts. The full text of the paragraph from which those extracts were drawn is a carefully scripted dissimulation:

> My meeting with Pound changed my life. He was enthusiastic about my poems, and gave me such praise and encouragement as I had long since ceased to hope for. I was happier in England, even in wartime, than I had been in America: Pound urged me to stay in England and encouraged me to write verse again. I think that all I wanted of Vivienne was a flirtation or a mild affair: I was too shy and unpracticed to achieve either with anybody. I believe that I came to persuade myself that I was in love with her simply because I wanted to burn my boats and commit myself to stay in England. And she persuaded herself (under the influence of Pound) that she would save the poet by keeping him in England. To her, the marriage brought no happiness: the last seven years of her life were spent in a mental home. To me, it brought the state of mind out of which came *The Waste Land*. And it saved me from marrying Emily Hale.

There was no such marital prospect in 1915, and it was not until separating from Vivien (sometimes spelled Vivienne) that Eliot resumed contact with Emily, which resulted in the correspondence from 1932 to 1947 she bequeathed to Princeton. He then offers what is now known to be a phenomenally misleading conclusion.

> Emily Hale would have killed the poet in me: Vivienne was nearly the death of <u>me</u>, but she kept the poet alive. In retrospect, the nightmare agony of my seventeen years with Vivienne seems to me preferable to the dull misery of the mediocre teacher of philosophy which would have been the alternative.

The existential mortification is palpable, as is his gratitude that the poet found a way to persist, even at the expense of the man.

As he fabricated this version of events, Eliot was well aware of what would be discovered in 2020 when Hale's archive was made public. It consists of several thousand pages of typed letters, unremitting in their declaration of love. So astounding and consistent is the ardor in the letters—chronicled with scrupulous discernment by Frances Dickey in publications and blogs—as to beggar all previous suppositions about the relationship. Biographers have had little to work with in their estimation of what Emily Hale meant to Eliot. The unsealed archive offers too vast a revelation to elaborate here, and in any case *The Waste Land* precedes by a decade the period of Eliot's correspondence with Hale. Inasmuch as it does have a part to play in the present book, its significance can be found in a passage that one biographer cites from the notebooks of Henry James.

In February 1895 James jotted down an idea for a story (one that remained unwritten, though variants can be found in tales like "The Great Good Place" and "The Beast in the Jungle"). The subject is "the man of genius who, in some accursed hour of his youth, has bartered away the fondest vision of that youth and lives ever afterwards in the shadow of the bitterness of the regret." James imagines, as seed for a tale, "the fancy of his *recovering* a little of the lost joy, of the Dead Self, in his intercourse with some person, some woman, who knows what that self was, in whom it still lives a little. This intercourse is his real life." As James realizes with emphasis: "*She is his Dead Self: he is alive in her and dead in himself.*" In this citation, Lyndall Gordon has excised James's fiddling estimations of what will and will not work for a story, distilling a model applicable to Eliot that is uncannily prescient of what the letters to Hale have finally revealed.

*

American reception of *The Waste Land* was more discerning, and welcoming, than that in England. But it was not universal. In his midcentury autobiography, William Carlos Williams was still incensed by the poem: "Eliot had turned his back on the possibility of reviving my world. And being an accomplished craftsman, better skilled in some ways than I could ever hope to be, I had to watch him carry my world off with him, the fool, to the enemy." As a cultural nativist, Williams was skeptical of his friend Pound's Eurocentrism, which he saw more dangerously personified by Eliot. When *The Waste Land* appeared, Williams lamented that it had set American poetry back fifty years. It wasn't just the poem, but the pose. Eliot was "so slimy," he thought, in his "affectation of authority, an offensive leaking from above so that the water is polluted."

Williams misconstrued the booty he imagined Eliot betraying to the enemy. He thought *The Waste Land* catastrophic because it contravened the celebration of the local, the receptive crucible of culture, culture as opposed to that abstraction, "civilization." Williams was following the cultural nativism of Van Wyck Brooks in *America's Coming-of-Age* (1915) and Waldo Frank's *Our America* (1919), to which Williams himself added *In the American Grain* (1925). "It has been to place myself as the offshoot of an unerudite locality that my major struggle has taken form," he reflected in 1929.

Williams was a friend of artists, applauding those who resisted Paris, stayed home, and found American subjects. He prized Alfred Stieglitz's galleries, 291 and An American Place. His anti–Waste Land book *Spring and All* was dedicated to Charles Demuth, and other painter friends of the poet were Arthur Dove, Marsden Hartley, Charles Sheeler, and Stuart Davis, who provided the frontispiece illustration to Williams's stream of consciousness *Kora in Hell: Improvisations* (1920). The young artist wrote of *Kora*, "To me it suggests a development toward word against word without any impediments of story, poetic beauty or anything at all except word clash and sequence."

The interests, lives, and works of artists overlapped with those of the poets. Williams relished such contacts and edited the little magazine *Contact*. His contacts included Mina Loy, Marianne Moore, Wallace Stevens, and, across the Atlantic, H. D. and Pound. Marianne Moore, "her red hair plaited and wound twice about the fine skull," Williams recalled, "was our saint—if we had one—in whom we all instinctively felt our purpose come together to form a stream. Everyone loved her." It was reciprocal. "In his effort to 'annihilate half truths,' Dr Williams is hard, discerning, implacable and deft," Moore appreciatively enumerated. "Discerning the world's hardness, his reply is the reply of Carl Sandburg's boll weevil to threats of sand, hot ashes and the river: 'That'll be ma HOME! That'll be ma HOME!'" His was not Whitman's barbaric yawp; the model for Williams's poetic vision was the medical case history. No detail was beneath attention. "I like most my ability to be drunk with a sudden realization of value in things others never notice," he wrote in an omnibus questionnaire for the final issue of *The Little Review*.

There was progeny. A group of (mostly) New York poets took Williams and Pound as rudder for Objectivism: Louis Zukofsky, George Oppen, Charles Reznikoff, Carl Rakosi, Lorine Niedecker. Williams's *Autobiography* reprints the bulk of a recently published manifesto, "Projective Verse," written by Charles Olson during the time he was visiting Pound in the bughouse. Olson soon became rector of Black Mountain College in North Carolina, looking out over idyllic Lake Eden east of Asheville. Founded by Bauhaus refugees in 1933, during Olson's tenure it was a crucible of activities mingling the arts, a rekindling of the old Wagnerian dream. John Cage composed and as pianist accompanied dances by Merce Cunningham. Painters were in abundance, including Robert Rauschenberg, Cy Twombly, Franz Kline, Willem and Elaine de Kooning. Olson was joined by fellow poets Robert Duncan and Robert Creeley. Black Mountain poets had alliances with the Beats, foremost of whom was Allen Ginsberg, who'd known Williams since he was a teenager. Williams wrote the preface to Ginsberg's *Howl* (1956). Taken by some at the time as a rebuke to *The Waste Land*, with hindsight it was clearly an idiomatic update of Eliot's vision.

Thanks in part to Ginsberg, Olson, and others, Williams's nativism prevailed. Eliot, as Williams saw, took poetry into the classroom, but except in rare cases he didn't take the poets with him. Imagine them, instead, gathering in an increasingly lively and swelling group on a veranda outside a lecture hall, its glum silence barely touched by a slow, measured "High Anglican asbestos voice." Williams is out there in the hubbub, heeding the very different voices of a world he saw abandoned by Eliot.

The late poet C. D. Wright, introducing a facsimile reprint of Williams's scarce 1923 book *Spring and All*, evokes his determinedly earthy localism: "The pediatrician from Rutherford discharged the symbolic heap of myth and metaphor; adjusted his focal length to light up cast-off, common things; dug his heels into American dirt and passed directly into the moment." This, as Wright vividly renders it, is exactly the "primary impetus, the elementary principle of all art, in the local conditions" that Williams thought thwarted by *The Waste Land*. What the New Jersey doctor failed to appreciate was that Eliot too was immersed in his own local conditions. After all, London and Grail legends can be every bit as compelling as the American Arcadia.

In the last decade of Williams's life—he died in 1963, two years before Eliot—American poetry entered a divisive phase. Raw versus cooked was one way of framing it. It was a time of anthology wars, each side fielding ranks of contenders, with little overlap between them. Eventually this adversarial sensibility faded. Prizes routinely reserved for one side became less predictable. The mistake all along was the thought of winners and losers. Eliot was favored by those, like the New Critics, envious of his authority. Pound was the acknowledged master of others who could harbor no illusions of his personal authority. He withdrew from the frenetic activity he'd sustained through the years of incarceration, and found himself appalled in the mirror of self-reflection. "I am no longer particularly pleased with my past life, and the moments of extreme blindness and insensitivity have been PHEnomenal," he allowed. As decades passed, the flaws of both poets were there for all to see. The poetry remains. And as Pound outlived all his old companions, the Cantos dimmed out into "drafts and fragments," where he too adopted the telling line from *The Waste Land*:

> From time's wreckage shored,
>> these fragments shored against ruins

*

What does it mean that poetry can emerge from such imponderable depths of dissimulation as revealed by Eliot's letters to Emily Hale? Old news, it would seem, at least to those cognizant of the serpentine path from stimulus to artistic response. The benign visage of an artist's muse obscures the churn of unidentifiable resources an artist works with. Eliot's marital misery isn't a key to *The Waste Land*, but it can sensitize us to its free-floating air of distress. Eliot did not have Paul McCartney hovering nearby, telling Jude to take a sad song and make it better. He had his sherpa, Ezra Pound, who abided by *make it better* but left the sadness intact. There was a poem to be made, apart from any private travails.

Eliot's relationship with Emily Hale was resumed nearly a decade after *The Waste Land*, several years after his religious conversion, and only after he saw no way forward with Vivien. His poems continued to reflect his theory of the objective correlative, that poetry expressed whatever needed expression by fugitive resources. For the poet, *I* was always other. In "Tradition and the Individual Talent" Eliot resorted to a chemical analogy for what he extolled as depersonalization ("the action which takes place when a bit of finely filiated platinum is introduced into a chamber containing oxygen and sulphur dioxide"). The person who suffers, Eliot explained, has "not a 'personality' to express, but a particular medium, which is only a medium and not a personality, in which impressions and experiences combine in peculiar and unexpected ways."

The Waste Land was a demonstration piece of how peculiar and unexpected the combinations could be. However much his relationship with Emily Hale informs *The Four Quartets* like a submerged emotional and autobiographical Atlantis, *The Waste Land* is governed by what he called "*significant* emotion, emotion which has its life in the poem and not in the history of the poet." The simultanism, parataxis, and collage aspects of the poem were not a subterfuge to obscure the personal; they were the expedient means to produce a poem, a poem that instantly communicated "significant emotion" to those who knew nothing of Eliot the man, a poem in which even the question of who speaks is variable.

In 1939–1940, T. S. Eliot wrote "East Coker," in which he extended the collage aspect of *The Waste Land* not by quotation, but by shifting registers of speech. After a courtly seventeen lines beginning section II, he breaks the spell.

That was a way of putting it—not very satisfactory:
A periphrastic study in a worn-out poetical fashion,
Leaving one still with the intolerable wrestle
With words and meanings.

The theme of linguistic deficiency returns in section V.

So here I am, in the middle way, having had twenty years—
Twenty years largely wasted, the years of *l'entre deux guerres*—
Trying to learn to use words, and every attempt
Is a wholly new start, and a different kind of failure
Because one has only learnt to get the better of words
For the thing one no longer has to say, or the way in which
One is no longer disposed to say it. And so each venture
Is a new beginning, a raid on the inarticulate
With shabby equipment always deteriorating
In the general mess of imprecision of feeling,
Undisciplined squads of emotion.

These emotional squads point to something deeper than word-craft. In 1947, Eliot tantalizingly drew marriage into the compass of what this passage furtively addressed. "For, just as a poet can never be sure that he knows how to write poetry, but must constantly start as if afresh, so, I think, married people must always regard each other as a mysterious person whom they are gradually getting to know, in a process which must go on to the end of the life of one or the other." Vivien died in 1947. It was a time of reckoning—not only with words.

Yet the words continued to dwell on a presence persisting in the vacancy.

The unattached devotion which might pass for devotionless,
In a drifting boat with a slow leakage,
The silent listening to the undeniable
Clamor of the bell of the last annunciation.

The slow leakage had finally capsized the marital boat. When Eliot went to America in 1933 with invitations for numerous appearances, he used the occasion of his prolonged absence as a practical way to distance, and separate, himself from Vivien. She continued to beseech, haunt, and provoke from afar for four more years until she was committed to an asylum, at the bequest of her husband and her brother.

In "Little Gidding" Eliot narrates an encounter with "a familiar compound ghost / Both intimate and unidentifiable." Composite it may be, but the ghost of his French friend Jean Verdenal (plausibly, though Eliot suggested it was "myself at the age of seventeen or thereabouts") revives to administer a kind of malediction, in which the poet confronts

> . . . the rending pain of re-enactment
> Of all that you have done, and been; the shame
> Of motives late revealed, and the awareness
> Of things ill done and done to others' harm
> Which once you took for exercise of virtue.

The use of the second person does not diminish the confessional urgency of this passage. The life of the poet prevailed, but the man behind the mask was still breathing, forever in awe of what the thunder said:

> . . . the communication
> Of the dead is tongued with fire beyond the language of the living.

ACKNOWLEDGMENTS

Thanks are due to my agent, Andrew Stuart, for his quick read, eagle eye, and steady support through two books now. The Princeton University Press editorial dream team not only enriched the book but made its publication a memorable experience. Anne Savarese's clairvoyant editorial touch led me to welcome solutions time and again. Lauren Lepow's eagle eye saved many a blunder, and her phrasal suggestions were so astute and plentiful as to warrant some kind of credit as coauthor. James Collier's timely handling of pictorial challenges was an immense relief. Before these folks ever saw the manuscript, Suzi Wong patiently annotated printouts, helping me focus amidst a compressed compositional schedule in a pandemic year. This is the fruit of our shared lifetime in and around poetry.

The resources of the Helen S. Lanier endowment have played an enabling role in all my scholarly publications and activities over the past twenty years, and this book could not have been undertaken without such beneficence. I'm also grateful to Nicholas Allen's trusty stewardship of the Willson Center for Arts and Humanities at the University of Georgia, thanks to which I carved out much needed time to write *What the Thunder Said*.

REFERENCES

INTRODUCTION

Page

1   **king of the cats**: Foster 2:616 n. 69

3   **the first piece**: Eliot, *Poems* 374

5   **I say: a flower**: Mallarmé, *Divagations* 210

7   **To me it was only**: Crawford 423

9   **a new art color**: Joyce, *Ulysses* 5

10   **the rhythm of the steppes**: Eliot, *Prose* 2:370

11   **The winter evening**: Eliot, *Poems* 15

12   **the most important**: Eliot, *Poems* 74

13   **These are *my* humours**: Montaigne 167

13   **a new universe**: Adams 381

14   ***I* is someone else**: Rimbaud 304

14   **the soul must be**: Rimbaud 307

14   **the poet is truly**: Rimbaud 309

14   **Our 'own' times**: Forster 66

14   **I was present**: Lewis, *Blasting* 30

14   **The world is giving**: Marc and Kandinsky 260

15   **about the war**: Lewis, *Blasting* 1

15   **This book is Art**: Lewis, *Blasting* 67

15   **You will be astonished**: Lewis, *Blasting* 4

15   **still adjusted**: Lippmann 3

15   **we have to describe**: Lippmann 95

15   **Infinity, show us**: Gibson 20

16   **I have seen the eternal**: Eliot, *Poems* 8

16   **thousand sordid images**: Eliot, *Poems* 16

16   **Every street lamp**: Eliot, *Poems* 18

16   **The morning comes**: Eliot, *Poems* 15

16   **I am moved**: Eliot, *Poems* 16

17   **You mightn't think**: Eliot, *Poems* 595

18   ***Without a Mask***: Reverdy 25

18   **the immense panorama**: Eliot, *Prose* 2:478

18   **the present consists**: Eliot, *Prose* 2:482

18   **if you hunt**: Baker 70

19   ***Sprachvermögen***: Wagner, *Oper* 336

19   ***unendlichen Sehnens***: Wagner, *Kunstwerk* 88

19   **that which he does**: Wagner, *Essays* 24

19   **It is the musician**: Wagner, *Essays* 40

19   **In Wahrheit**: Wagner, *Schriften* 130

20   **the meaning is merely**: Eliot, *Prose* 2:184

20   **felt he was witnessing**: Baring 195–196
20   **omnianonymous**: Kramer 278

CHAPTER ONE. WAGNERISM

Page
23   **love torturing itself**: Eliot, *Poems* 236
23   ***Frisch weht der Wind***: Eliot, *WL* lines 31–34
23   ***Oed und leer***: Eliot, *WL* line 42
24   **Weialala leia**: Eliot, *WL* lines 277–278, repeated 290–291
24   **It would be difficult**: Eliot, *Prose* 2:745
24   **his critical intelligence**: Eliot, *Prose* 4:744
24   **a minor survivor**: Eliot, *March Hare* 388
24   **In his time**: Yeats, *Essays* 111
24   **I believe that**: Yeats, *Essays* 191
24   **The arts by brooding**: Yeats, *Essays* 187
25   **Du mußt dein Leben**: Rilke, *New* 204
25   **Just look at these**: Nietzsche, *Case* 19
25   **I only attack things**: Liébert 53
25   **messiah of a new age**: Beckson 277
26   **the work of Wagner**: Duncan, *Art* 105
27   **Other men are lenses**: Emerson 616
28   **was not always**: Huneker, *Overtones* 66
28   **Wagner seems to have**: Large and Weber 21
28   **Wagner's operas are**: Martin 101
28   **Be assured that I**: Dolan 234
28   **The Wagnerite must**: Zuckerman 30
28   **For the Wagnerian**: Hartford 58
28   **who assured me**: Hartford 56
28   **deeds of music**: Shaw-Miller 249 n. 1
28   **the site had to exist**: Ross, *Wagnerism* 42
28   **No matter where**: Large and Weber 293
29   **One could not walk**: Koss 48
29   **Cutlets, baked potatoes**: Hartford 53
29   **The town is packed**: Köhler, *Nietzsche* 114
29   **faith in the 'Art Work**: Hartford 88
29   **The coiffures**: Turbow 144
29   **the cheap seats**: Beckson 289
29   **in spite of**: Blissett 53
29   **The word Bayreuth**: Blissett 71
29   **Young men dressed**: Furness 138 n. 70
30   **in which the French**: Debussy 66
30   **Parsifal will long remain**: Huneker, *Overtones* 107
30   **in an unnatural**: Köhler, *Wagner* 163
30   **one of the few**: Huckel xi
30   **in rapt pleasure**: Wilde 112
30   **it is the music of**: Symons, *Plays* 300–301
30   **The music creeps**: Huneker, *Overtones* 199
30   **a master of thrilling**: Huneker, *Overtones* 330
30   **At no time before**: Kennaway 63
30   **symptom of the times**: Kennaway 68
31   **Are you particularly**: Kennaway 89

31   **On every side**: Richardson 121
31   **so internal, so organic**: Proust 206
31   **hypnotism of Bayreuth**: Cocteau 39
32   **Nietzsche's touch**: Gilman 59
32   **he always did**: Gilman 52
32   **a pell-mell**: Sokoloff 216
32   **Certainly those were**: Nietzsche, *Letters* 180
32   **I was indescribably**: Nietzsche, *Letters* 180
32   **The best and loftiest**: Nietzsche, *Letters* 53
32   **My thoughts always**: Nietzsche, *Letters* 66
33   **On every page**: Prideaux 99
33   **This is the book**: Cosima Wagner, *Diaries* 1:447
33   **in it one sees**: Cosima Wagner, *Diaries* 1:354
33   **with solemn feelings**: Cosima Wagner, *Diaries* 1:446
33   **Dear friend**: Wagner, *Letters* 787–788
33   **Strictly speaking**: Wagner, *Letters* 809
34   **He is one of those**: Köhler, *Nietzsche* 101
34   **the entire loafing**: Prideaux 151
34   **Wagner as a *writer***: Nietzsche, *Untimely* 247
34   **not the prophet**: Cate 227
34   **all those who attend**: Nietzsche, *Untimely* 198
34   **He who gives**: Nietzsche, *Untimely* 197
35   **class of rich idlers**: Förster-Nietzsche 272
35   **Frequent thoughts**: D'Iorio 30
35   **monument of rigorous**: D'Iorio 68
35   **and had the inner**: Nietzsche, *Letters* 168
35   **When we left**: Young, *Nietzsche* 224
35   **whose cold and precise**: Cosima Wagner, *Diaries* 1:931
36   **more likely to listen**: Cosima Wagner, *Diaries* 1:989
36   **the honeymoon**: D'Iorio 11
36   **to the father**: D'Iorio 71
36   **I have long been**: Prideaux 169
36   **When, in the privacy**: Köhler, *Nietzsche* 156
36   ***belief* that my altered**: Prideaux 235
36   **Wagner was by far**: Prideaux 235
36   **I cannot go there**: Gilman 130
37   **in Nietzsche evil**: Köhler, *Nietzsche* 131
37   **It was my lead**: Köhler, *Nietzsche* 81
37   **I find the whole man**: Köhler, *Nietzsche* 157
37   **It has been practically**: Nietzsche, *Letters* 167
37   **Absurd as it seems**: Nietzsche, *Unpublished* 318
37   **Wagner gets rid of**: Nietzsche, *Unpublished* 323
37   **immoderate, eccentric**: Nietzsche, *Unpublished* 319
37   **entirely unrestrained**: Nietzsche, *Unpublished* 331
37   **something of the almost**: Nietzsche, *Human* 5
38   **As soon as we climb**: Nietzsche, *Human* 101
38   **Wagner's stage**: Nietzsche, *Case* 27
38   **When a musician**: Nietzsche, *Case* 20
38   **a talent for lying**: Nietzsche, *Case* 17
38   **the greatest mime**: Nietzsche, *Case* 20
38   **this old magician**: Nietzsche, *Case* 8
38   **I am the child**: Nietzsche, *Case* 3
38   **I was one of**: Nietzsche, *Case* 8

38	**The effect of Wagner**: Nietzsche, *Case* 32
38	**If you want to be**: Nietzsche, *Case* 240
38	*Wagner est une*: Nietzsche, *Case* 13
38	**total transformation**: Nietzsche, *Case* 17
38	**Wagner's art is sick**: Nietzsche, *Case* 13
39	**Sickness itself**: Nietzsche, *Case* 13
39	**Oh, the rattlesnake-pleasure**: Nietzsche, *Case* 13
39	**perhaps provides**: Nietzsche, *Case* 28
39	**I was *violently* ill**: Nietzsche, *Letters* 208
39	**the emotivity**: Gilman 194
39	**the break with Wagner**: Gilman 50
39	**He died of Wagner**: Gilman 127
40	**Ever since Wagner**: Nietzsche, *Contra* 401
40	**the most fanatic**: Nietzsche, *Contra* 390
40	**Regarding artists**: Nietzsche, *Contra* 396
40	**My objections**: Nietzsche, *Contra* 389
40	**Ariadne, I love you**: Nietzsche, *Letters* 346
40	**I have begun to be**: Nietzsche, *Letters* 342
40	**I hold, quite literally**: Nietzsche, *Letters* 339
40	**Dear Professor**: Nietzsche, *Letters* 346
41	**I am just having**: Nietzsche, *Letters* 346
41	**It was my wife**: Köhler, *Nietzsche* 176
41	**My Wagner mania**: Nietzsche, *Letters* 180
42	**sexual psychopath**: Nordau 500
42	**imbecile**: Nordau 94
42	**mystically degenerate**: Nordau 300
42	**a madman, with flashing**: Nordau 416
42	**Nietzsche wrote his most**: Nordau 452–453
42	**Wagnerism is the most**: Nordau 213
43	**craving for revolt**: Nordau 171
43	**Richard Wagner is**: Nordau 171
43	**let us imagine**: Nordau 541
43	**Can any one with**: Anon., *Regeneration* 208
43	**The psychological foundation**: Simmel 325
44	**Its own new**: Nordau 40
44	**I could prove**: Shaw 326
44	**What in the name of**: Shaw 326

CHAPTER TWO. THE FOREST OF SYMBOLS &
THE LISTENING EYE

Page

45	**a reprobate rake**: Nordau 231
45	**so many of**: Ross, *Wagnerism* 155–156
45	**he loves disease**: Nordau 294
45	**mediocre writers**: Quenoy 44
45	**a joy almost sensual**: Starkie 493
46	**the final cry**: Baudelaire, *Letters* 146
46	**deeply-pondered**: Baudelaire, *Painter* 133
46	**I admit that I am**: Baudelaire, *Painter* 138
46	**La nature est**: Baudelaire, *Oeuvres* 11
47	**Nature is**: Baudelaire, *Flowers* 23

47 **I like that young man**: Jullian, *Dreamers* 193
47 **One authority reported**: Gautier 8
47 **As for living**: Villiers 170
47 **a bundle of energy**: Grey 232
47 **Now smiling ear to ear**: Grey 234
47 **what a piano**: Raitt 89
48 **R. set his head on fire**: Köhler, *Wagner* 579
48 **Could it have been**: Wagner, *Letters* 859
48 **the only ray of love**: Köhler, *Wagner* 582
48 **Ma Judith**: Wagner, *Lettres* 93
48 **Nowhere does reflected**: Gregor-Dellin 445
48 **This marvelously organized**: Gregor-Dellin 498–499
48 **the most intoxicating**: Sokoloff 252
49 **with the crazy ambition**: Quenoy 89
49 **in the discreetly lit**: Bloch 122
49 **I'm off to vespers**: Bloch 114
50 **Mallarmé left the concerts**: Bloch 114
50 **prodigious occasions**: Mallarmé, *Divagations* 163
50 **verse is being tampered**: Mallarmé, *Divagations* 183
50 **volatile dispersal**: Mallarmé, *Divagations* 185
50 **truly extraordinary spectacle**: Mallarmé, *Oeuvres* 2:697
50 **Music joins Verse**: Mallarmé, *Divagations* 207
50 **I say: a flower**: Mallarmé, *Divagations* 210
51 **Le temple enseveli**: Mallarmé, *Collected* 72
51 **The buried temple**: Mallarmé, *Poems in Verse* 171
51 **The buried temple empties**: Mallarmé, *Collected* 72
51 **the buried temple shits**: Mallarmé, *Azure* 54
51 **I would rather**: Mallarmé, *Collected* 121
51 **prismatic subdivisions**: Mallarmé, *Collected* 121
51 **they are joined**: Mallarmé, *Collected* 123
54 **I was looking**: Valéry 309
54 **I was *now***: Valéry 311
54 ***spatial* reading**: Valéry 312
54 **Verse is an incantation**: Mallarmé, *Divagations* 264
55 **there were many ways**: Farr 18
55 **is it speech half asleep**: Farr 15
55 **The more closely**: Pierrot 122
55 **All art is**: Yeats, *Essays* 18
55 **One is furthest**: Yeats, *Essays* 162
55 **a literature in which**: Symons, *Studies* 101
55 **to prolong the moment**: Yeats, *Essays* 159
56 **The essence of art**: Valency 72
56 **l'homme-affiche de l'au-délà**: Jullian, *Esthètes* 86
57 **the visible is only**: Rapetti 30
57 **deeds made visible**: Shaw-Miller 249 n. 1
57 **a musical sensation**: Thomson, "Arcadia" 59
57 **music revealed itself**: Lloyd 148
57 **all the divine**: Maeterlinck 214
57 **We all live**: Maeterlinck 179
58 **I have grown**: Maeterlinck 105–106
58 **to bring to birth**: Maeterlinck 168
58 **It is idle**: Maeterlinck 4
58 **I feel myself**: Rilke, *Images* 91

58   **The artist's function**: Rilke, *Prose* 22
59   **savage god**: Yeats, *Autobiography* 210
60   **a sphinx-like**: Friedman 151
60   **What is the meaning**: Gourmont 10
60   **We now *hear***: Mallarmé, *Selected* 39
60   **orange motif**: Vaughan 38
61   **musical sensations**: Gauguin 145
61   **polichrophilharmonique**: Vaughan 41
61   **that curious game**: Yeats, *Essays* 236
61   **the sound of an hour**: Mallarmé, *Divagations* 59
61   **To look is to listen**: Weber 39
61   **in a picture gallery**: Wagner, *Prose* 1:121
61   **This is what we are**: Duncan, *Speaks* 50
62   **symphony of spiritual love**: Rudorff 144
62   **The affair came off**: Huneker, *Unicorns* 218, 224, 226
63   **through music and color**: Mattis 219
63   **sonar-chromatic**: MacDonald 9
63   **In its relation**: Heyman 7
63   **Would you have your**: Heyman 50
64   **almost continuous**: Scott, *Music* 133
64   **those spiritual intelligences**: Scott, *Music* 109
64   **with its millions**: Scott, *Music* 109
64   **color, music, perfume**: Scott, *Music* 134
64   **the boys of sour**: Scott, *Music* 136
64   **undesirable obsessing**: Scott, *Music* 136
64   **Only dissonances**: Scott, *Music* 136–137
64   **Why limit our**: Scott, *Modernism* 61
65   **Unlearning is one**: Scott, *Modernism* 25
65   **the pathos of**: Dahlhaus 38
66   **we like to hear**: Schopenhauer 2:451
66   **We can regard**: Schopenhauer 1:262
66   **Music is as *immediate***: Schopenhauer 1:257
66   **We could just as well**: Schopenhauer 1:262–263
66   **we ourselves are now**: Schopenhauer 2:451
66   **only music can express**: Wyzéwa 249
66   **one is, so to speak**: Albright 6
66   **Each man is**: Laforgue, *Selected* 195
66   **a few gay spirits**: Nietzsche, *Letters* 22
66   **I saw my future**: Bely 3
67   **With phrases as**: Steinberg 41
67   **the colors of the**: Steinberg 209
67   **degree of incessant**: Scott, *Modernism* 66
67   **we are not just**: Endell 147
68   **a whole Pleiades**: Gauguin 31

CHAPTER THREE. BECOMING MODERN

Page
69   **Il n'y a plus**: Apollinaire, *Oeuvres II* 945, *Selected* 229
69   **Avant d'entrer**: Apollinaire, *Oeuvres poétiques* 140
70   **Picasso studies**: Apollinaire, *Cubist* 13
70   **not an imitative art**: Apollinaire, *Cubist* 25

70   **These young painters**: Apollinaire, *Cubist* 18
70   **Most of the new**: Apollinaire, *Cubist* 13
70   **Bing bang bong**: Apollinaire, *Calligrammes* 53, 55
71   **Lyricism is only**: Apollinaire, *Selected* 231
71   **catalogues, posters**: Shattuck 215
71   **a freedom hitherto**: Apollinaire, *Selected* 228
71   **ringmaster of the arts**: Shattuck 196
71   **made you listen**: Shattuck 205
72   **theoretical and practical**: Shattuck 223
72   **To my way of thinking**: Shattuck 225
73   **Hors d'oeuvres**: Shattuck 293
73   **a sort of sur-realism**: Apollinaire, *Oeuvres II* 865
73   **It fills the same role**: Shattuck 169
73   **The first time**: Satie 101
73   **before writing a work**: Shattuck 114
73   **OKLAHOMA, *20 janvier***: Cendrars, *Complete* 267
74   **Poetry isn't in**: Cendrars, *Complete* 373
74   **Dis Blaises**: Cendrars, *Complete* 240
74   **His eye goes from**: Cendrars, *Modernities* 100
74   **He is the only man**: Cendrars, *Modernities* 97
74   **written in blood**: Cendrars, *Selected* viii
75   **more marvelous than**: Cendrars, *Modernities* 25
75   **the optimistic pessimism**: Cendrars, *Modernities* 91
75   **From Paris has spread**: Dos Passos 165
75   **lost in the labyrinth**: Cendrars, *Modernities* 4
75   **you are part of**: Cendrars, *Modernities* 4
76   **Seated in my rocking chair**: Cendrars, *Modernities* 5
76   **but as an aura**: Cendrars, *Sky* 61
77   **Limbs fly**: Cendrars, *Modernities* 12–13
77   **I have the sense**: Cendrars, *Modernities* 14
77   **The only poet**: Hemingway 81
77   **the idea came**: Baudelaire, *Paris* ix
77   **Which of us**: Baudelaire, *Paris* ix–x
77   **It was, above all**: Baudelaire, *Paris* x
78   **le triomphe**: Jacob, *Cornet* 16
78   **balancing the elements**: Jacob, *Dice* 247
78   **Style is considered**: Jacob, *Cornet* 15–16
79   **complexity in form**: Jacob, *Dice* 1
79   **emotional ensemble**: Clarke 2:75
80   **She rose in moonlight**: Aiken, *Divine* 5
80   **I flatly give myself**: Aiken, *Divine* 287
80   **Poems can be written**: Fletcher, *Preludes* x
81   ***Street Magic***: Storer 30
81   **It is certain**: Storer 114
81   **most of the good**: Storer 107
81   **vers-librists**: Storer 110
82   **you can do almost**: Storer 110
82   **I want to speak**: Hulme 49
82   **spilt religion**: Hulme 62
82   **new verse resembles**: Hulme 56
82   **Damn it all**: Pound, *Collected* 42
82   **gymnastic personality**: Cummings 79
83   **the first to teach me**: Rainey 4

83   **it was several years**: Eliot, *Letters* 1:212
83   **slang and astronomy**: Symons, *Symbolist* 59
83   **En vérité**: Laforgue 130–133
83   **The old cadences**: Symons, *Symbolist* 57

CHAPTER FOUR. THE SCHOOL OF IMAGES

Page
87   **the genial proprietor**: Nelson 132
88   **a horrible agglomerate**: Carpenter 113
88   **the new Montana**: Pound, *Parents* 177
88   **a bit of a**: Goldring 48
88   **dressed in imitation**: Carr 417
88   **most negligently**: Carr 252
88   **happily cuckoo**: Norman 26
89   **His appearance was**: Cunard, *Hours* 123–124
89   **the large velvet**: Anderson 243
89   **jerky manner**: Carpenter 229
89   **difficult to distinguish**: Carpenter 263
89   **a galvanized agile**: Saunders 367
89   **an inebriated kangaroo**: Carr 214
89   **Ezra danced**: Carr 404
89   **Ezra has a *wonderful***: Carr 404
89   **As the music grew**: Crosby 265
90   **How could they**: Pound, *Dorothy* 3
90   **Ezra never seemed**: Carr 403
90   **more charming**: Carr 324
90   **and I had about**: Pound, *Parents* 170
90   **Yeats has found**: Longenbach 17
91   **rather remarkable**: Homberger 38
91   **Detestable person**: Pound, *Letters* 17
92   **a thread of true**: Homberger 44
92   **foolish archaisms**: Homberger 58
92   **'ellum' for 'elm'**: Homberger 56
92   **vague large promise**: Homberger 50
92   **no new book**: Homberger 54–55
92   **the turbulent opacity**: Homberger 61
92   **still interesting**: Homberger 62
92   **he has produced**: Homberger 78
92   **only very rarely**: Homberger 81
92   **the heavy incrustations**: Homberger 83
92   **linguistic fancy dress**: Homberger 84
92   **few new poets**: Homberger 63
92   **shocking vigor**: Homberger 71
92   **boudoir tinkle**: Homberger 73
93   **Make-strong old**: Pound, *Personae* v
93   **Go, my songs**: Pound, *Collected* 97
93   **Come, my songs**: Pound, *Collected* 108
93   **Come, my songs, let us**: Pound, *Collected* 103
93   **I have gone**: Pound, *Collected* 103
94   **flabby lemon**: Carr 126

94 **displayed me trapped**: Pound, *Selected Prose* 432

94 **almost alone among**: Pound, *New Freewoman* (September 1, 1913): 113

94 **luminous detail**: Pound, *Poetry and Prose* 1:49

94 **May I for my own**: Pound, *Collected* 76

95 **no one cares to**: Pound, *Poetry and Prose* 1:58

95 **for good fellowship**: Pound, *Collected* 268

95 **The old star-eaten**: Pound, *Collected* 270

95 **beauty like a scented**: Pound, *Collected* 270

95 **A touch of cold**: Pound, *Collected* 269

95 **School of Images**: Pound, *Collected* 268

96 **Can you teach**: Pound, *Letters* 9

96 **an over-elaborate**: Pound, *Letters* 10

96 **a sort of *rigor***: H. D., *End* 35

96 **You are clear**: H. D., *Sea* 24

97 **first kisses**: H. D., *End* 3–4

97 **We sway with**: H. D., *End* 12

97 **Two girls in love**: Guest 26

97 **H. D. Imagiste**: H. D., *End* 18

97 **almost insane relish**: Aldington 134

97 **I have never known**: Aldington 111

98 **one of the 'Imagistes'**: *Poetry* (November 1912): 65

98 **Her sketches from**: *Poetry* (January 1913): 135

98 **the Elimination of**: Carr 754

98 **Direct treatment of**: Flint, *Poetry* (March 1913): 199

98 **If you are using**: Pound, *Poetry* (March 1913): 205

98 **Go in fear**: Pound, *Poetry* (March 1913): 201

99 **Let the candidate**: Pound, *Poetry* (March 1913): 202

99 **An 'Image' is that**: Pound, *Poetry* (March 1913): 200

99 **I don't know that**: Pound, *Letters* 11

99 **I mate with my free**: Pound, *Poetry* (April 1913): 1

100 ***In a Station***: Pound, *Poetry* (April 1913): 12

100 **Vurry Amur'k'n**: Pound, *Letters* 14

100 **my dazzling friend**: Frost 97

100 **And then there is**: Frost 105–106

100 **has the good sense**: Pound, *Poetry and Prose* 1:138

100 **I don't mind**: Frost 110

100 **they are better**: Frost 110

101 **the most generous**: Frost 238

101 **I want to be a poet**: Frost 154

101 **I turned me**: Drinkwater 79

101 **Ezra was a citizen**: Aldington 110

101 **the Georgians caress**: Eliot, *Prose* 1:679

102 **I have just met**: Gould 117

102 **stands, or I should**: Pound, *Letters* 38

103 **It would be much**: Pound, *Letters* 78

103 **foremost member**: Pound, *Letters* 43–44

103 **You have only yourself**: Damon 274–275

103 **Amygisme**: Gould 177

103 **Nearly anyone is ready**: Pound, *Poetry and Prose* 1:275

103 **I once saw**: Pound, *Poetry and Prose* 1:280

103 **The image is not**: Pound, *Poetry and Prose* 1:283

103 **expressionism, neo-cubism**: Pound, *Poetry and Prose* 1:282

104   **accelerated impressionism**: Pound, *Poetry and Prose* 1:275
104   **a new Futurist**: *Pound/Joyce* 26
104   **that wretched little**: Carr 746
105   **on a Hulme basis**: Pound, *Little* 155
105   **before August, 1912**: Carr 480
105   **You deserve all**: Carr 767
105   **about four years**: Pound, *Poetry* (October 1914): 29–30
105   **and alternately bless**: Pound, *Dorothy* 161
105   **demon saleswoman**: Carr 568
105   **the most national**: Carr 809
105   **hippopoetess**: Carr 671
106   **When we invented**: Smith 46
106   **Spectric connotes**: Morgan and Knish x
106   **Spectrism if you must**: Smith 24
106   **If I were only**: Morgan and Knish 56
106   **If I should enter**: Morgan and Knish 45
107   **The theme of a poem**: *Others* 3, no. 5 (January 1917): 2
107   **The Imagists, suicidally**: Smith 23
107   **takes a challenging**: Smith 23
107   **to poetry what Cubism**: Smith 30
107   **deification of Whim**: *Documents* 22
107   **essentially epileptic**: *Documents* 43
108   **a clever hoax**: *Documents* 45
108   **We are in an anaemic**: Watson 177
108   **When one leaves**: Watson 175
108   **for the elimination**: Burgess, *The Bookman* 35 (March 1, 1912): 15
108   **And yet, these diabobs**: Burgess, *Unabridged* 14
109   **a tomcat on**: Smith 32
109   **phosphorescent / plumbing**: Morgan, *Pins.* Poems in the unpaginated booklet are ordered alphabetically by last names of the subjects.

CHAPTER FIVE. PIG CUPID

Page
110   **supremely stupid**: Lewis, *Blasting* 90
110   **a bigger *Blast***: Lewis, *Blasting* 90
110   **the ringleader**: King 58
110   **What is all this**: Lewis, *Blasting* 24
111   **moralism, feminism**: Rainey, Poggi, and Wittman 51
111   **enormous desire**: Ross, *Wagnerism* 23
111   **a flamboyant personage**: Goldring 64
113   **Marinetti declaimed**: Wees 98
113   **full of force**: Ross, *Georgian* 37
113   **as a Futurist picture**: O'Keeffe 139
113   **You are a futurist**: Lewis, *Blasting* 37
113   **Wyndham Lewis pigsty**: Woolf, *Letters* 2:527
113   **an orang-outan**: Eliot, *Prose* 1:720
113   **the thought of the modern**: Eliot, *Prose* 1:747
113   **I had never seen**: Hemingway 109
114   **all this organized**: Lewis, *Blasting* 35
114   **I might almost**: Lewis, *Blasting* 57

114 **WE WHISPER IN YOUR EAR**: *Blast* 1, 19
114 **The Art-Instinct**: *Blast* 1, 33
115 **cowboy songster**: Lewis, *Blasting* 280
115 **I discovered beneath**: Lewis, *Blasting* 278
115 **Ezra's boyscoutery**: Lewis, *Blasting* 254
115 **The whole effect**: Cork 171
115 **the incongruity between**: Cork 172
115 **Shut up, you understand**: Epstein, *Autobiography* 56
115 **modern man can live**: Pound, *Machine* 79
116 **One can still think**: Pound, *Machine* 58
116 **they do not stir**: Pound, *Machine* 59
116 **The immaculate**: Loy, *Lost* 80
116 **unfounded relationship**: Burke 82
117 **was able to understand**: Stein, *Autobiography* 162
117 **A sap that is that**: Stein, *Selected* 466
117 **The days are wonderful**: Stein, *Selected* 465
117 **the house is full**: Rudnick 95
117 **in sympathy with**: Burke 177
117 **like a cinema**: Burke 170
118 **psycho-synthesis**: Burke 146
118 **He is one of the most**: Burke 157
118 **you can say that Marinetti**: Burke 178
118 **for twenty years added**: Burke 180
118 **caught in the machinery**: Burke 165
118 **Of course being the most**: Burke 188
119 **Gertrude Stein is doing**: Rudnick 70
119 **There is no Life**: Loy, *Camera Work* 46 (April 1914): 18
119 **helpless, ecstatic**: Rhoades, *Camera Work* 46 (April 1914): 18
120 **DIE in the Past**: Loy, *Camera Work* 45 (January 1914): 13
120 **Knick-knacks**: Loy, *Camera Work* 45 (January 1914): 15
120 **We shout the obscenities**: Loy, *Camera Work* 45 (January 1914): 15
120 **He had said one**: Burke 166
120 **MAY your egotism**: Loy, *Last* 273
121 **FORGET that you live**: Loy, *Last* 272
121 **TODAY is the crisis**: Loy, *Last* 273
121 **Pig Cupid**: Loy, *Lost* 53
121 **THE Futurist can**: Loy, *Last* 273
121 **The skin-sack**: Loy, *Lost* 53
121 **Let them clash together**: Loy, *Lost* 66
122 **a crescendo & transcendo**: Burke 185
122 **a peculiar kind**: Burke 208
122 **You have no idea**: Burke 187
122 **unaffiliated group**: Burke 197
122 **falsetto radicalism**: Burke 197
122 **LET the Universe**: Loy, *Last* 273
122 **suffering the ethereal**: Emerson 459
123 **one must in fact**: Loy, *Last* 295
123 **Curie / of the laboratory**: Loy, *Lost* 94
123 **What I feel now**: Burke 187
123 **I was connected up**: Loy, *Last* 289
123 **the plastic static**: Loy, *Last* 289
123 **to track intellection**: Loy, *Last* 297

123   **a literature reduced**: Loy, *Last* 291
123   **intercepted cinema**: Loy, *Last* 293
123   **It is the variety of**: Loy, *Last* 292
124   **to work smashing**: Williams, *Essays* 163
124   **brooding over each word**: H. D., *Bid Me* 163
124   **one who cares for**: Curnutt 171
124   **none of the words**: Riding 189
124   **process of disintegration**: Loy, *Last* 293
124   **a subconscious muddle**: Loy, *Lost* 173
124   **cymophanous sweat**: Loy, *Lost* 64
124   **immediate agamogenesis**: Loy, *Lost* 47
125   **the carnose horologe**: Loy, *Lost* 83
125   **Etiolate body**: Loy, *Lost* 65
125   **the theoretic elastic**: Loy, *Lost* 20
125   **Her eliminate flesh**: Loy, *Lost* 98
125   **the inebriate regret**: Loy, *Lost* 98
125   **Diurnally variegate**: Loy, *Lost* 38
125   **raw caverns**: Loy, *Lost* 78
125   **Omniprevalent Dimension**: Loy, *Lost* 72
125   **gong / of polished**: Loy, *Lost* 79
125   **pulverous pastures**: Loy, *Lost* 77
125   **Street lights footle**: Loy, *Lost* 72
125   **Accoupling / of the masculine**: Loy, *Lost* 44
125   **quotidienly passed**: Loy, *Lost* 36
125   **flapped friezily**: Loy, *Lost* 27
125   **Poetry is prose**: Loy, *Lost* 157
125   **broiling shadows**: Loy, *Lost* 43
125   **ilix aisles**: Loy, *Lost* 76
125   **shampooed gigolos**: Loy, *Lost* 95
125   **bed-ridden monopoly**: Loy, *Lost* 54
125   **the heinous absurdity**: Loy, *Lost* 62
125   **Our eyelashes polish**: Loy, *Lost* 72
125   **The Effectual Marriage**: Loy, *Lost* 36
126   **yellow candles**: Longworth 469
126   **cigarette of literature**: Burke 185
126   **the new little journal**: Longworth 471
126   **lascivious revelation**: Loy, *Lost* 6
127   **drops repeated words**: Van Vechten, "How to Read Gertrude Stein," *The Trend* 7,
          no. 5 (August 1914): 556
127   **It would be a pity**: Gallup 96
127   **Food Descending**: Rasula, *Destruction* 112
127   **We immediately fell**: Rasula, *Destruction* 122
128   **Having been lucky**: Cabanne 15
128   **enormously lazy**: Cabanne 72
128   **every day in plumbers'**: Wood, *The Blind Man* 2 (May 1917): 5
130   **What a wonderful**: Rasula, *Destruction* 148
130   **Je suis brute**: Kouidis 10
130   **become masters of**: Loy, *Lost* 283
130   **To what end**: Loy, *Lost* 165
130   **Put yourself at**: Loy, *Last* 276
130   **advocates the fulfillment**: Loy, *Last* 281
131   **Cravan / colossal**: Loy, *Last* 96

CHAPTER SIX. ENTER ELIOT

Page
132   **solitary volcano**: Pound, *Parents* 233
132   **He is a headlong**: Foster 1:475
132   **practiced it without**: Aldington 105
132   **In 1912 Ezra**: Aldington 105
132   **He helps me**: Longenbach 19
132   **her face was made**: Foster 2:6
132   **It is possible that**: Pound, *Literary Essays* 215
133   **The petals fall**: Pound, *Collected* 119
134   **busted into**: Pound, *Parents* 336
134   **Rihaku flourished**: Pound, *Cathay* 4
134   **the personal hatred**: Pound, *Cathay* 32
134   **like a door**: *Pound/Ford* 25
134   **By the North Gate**: Pound, *Collected* 143
135   **March has come**: Pound, *Collected* 141
135   **There is no end**: Pound, *Collected* 146
135   **the inventor of Chinese**: Pound, *Selected* xvi
135   **it will be called**: Pound, *Selected* xvii
135   **If Pound's translations**: Bush 1
136   **I don't think I have**: Carpenter 344
136   **Out with it**: Pound, *Collected* 231
136   **Now set forth**: Ruthven 101
136   **carefully went through**: Pound, *Letters* 179
136   **My job was**: Pound, *Letters* 149
136   **Propertius Soliloquizes**: Carpenter 330
136   **I may perhaps avoid**: Pound, *Letters* 231
136   **Personae and Portraits**: Pound, *Umbra* 128
136   **when he can get into**: Lewis, "Simpleton" 89–90
137   **Pound has always**: Raffel 113
137   **intellectual eunuch**: Lewis, "Simpleton" 90
137   **He is never happy**: Lewis, "Simpleton" 63
137   **Impatient tireless**: Eliot, *Letters* 1:49
137   **The stuff I sent**: Eliot, *Letters* 1:63
137   **I was jolly well**: Pound, *Letters* 40
137   **The devil of it**: Eliot, *Letters* 1:63
137   **He is the only**: Pound, *Letters* 40
138   **Pound is rather**: Eliot, *Letters* 1:63
138   **Let us go then**: Eliot, *Poems* 5
138   **I have seen the eternal**: Eliot, *Poems* 8
139   **one of those who**: Symons, *Symbolist* 62
139   **a very self-conscious**: Symons, *Symbolist* 58
139   **when I am formulated**: Eliot, *Poems* 7
139   **charmingly sophisticated**: Eliot, *Letters* 1:105
139   **Our marriage was hastened**: Eliot, *Letters* 1:117
139   ***lived* through material**: Eliot, *Letters* 1:138
139   **sans doute**: Eliot, *Letters* 1:24
139   **vous laissent**: Eliot, *Letters* 1:29
139   **once handsome**: Eliot, *WL* line 321
140   **I owe her**: Eliot, *Letters* 1:119

140   **I was very**: Eliot, *Letters* 1:ix
140   **I have been going**: Eliot, *Letters* 1:82
140   **a symbol of the Paris**: Eliot, *Prose* 4:417
140   **I should be better**: Eliot, *Letters* 1:82
140   **I terrified**: Eliot, *Letters* 1:105
140   **how much they owed**: Eliot, *Letters* 1:77
140   **such a genuine**: Huxley 156
141   **it is almost entirely**: Murray 92
141   **the 'spoilt kitten'**: Morrell 96
142   **filled with a strange**: Dempsey 22
142   **You had never given**: Dempsey 29
142   **I might have had**: Dempsey 29
142   **I felt after E.O.**: Dempsey 73
142   **girls with arms**: Dempsey 139
142   **an ambiance**: Pearson 239
142   **I expected her**: Russell 61
143   **pseudo-honeymoon**: Clark 311
143   **I want to give her**: Clark 311
143   **Anyhow I don't think**: Monk 440
143   **I don't really understand**: Clark 313
143   **impulses of cruelty**: Russell 64
143   **Mrs T. S. Eliot's**: Waugh, *Diaries* 731
143   **unwise perhaps**: Eliot, *Letters* 1:120
144   **I was fond of them both**: Russell 9
144   **crucible of dysfunction**: Seymour-Jones 4
144   **two highly nervous**: Goldstein 100
144   **It has been nerves**: Eliot, *Letters* 1:157
144   **The headaches are**: Crawford 246
144   **I have absolute**: Eliot, *Letters* 1:153
144   **he is no longer**: Eliot, *Letters* 1:129–130
144   **naif determination**: Symons, *Makers* 83
145   **the unmetrical, incoherent**: Symons, *Makers* 70
145   **everyone knows**: Rainey 14
145   **there is a small**: Rainey 14
145   **an American who**: Seymour-Jones 42
145   **It is the final perfection**: Eliot, *Prose* 1:648
146   **a polished, cultivated**: Crawford 307
147   **We've been having**: Woolf, *Letters* 2:296
147   **conviction of his humbug**: Woolf, *Letters* 2:296
147   **Bloomsbuggars**: Carpenter 244
147   **The more I see**: Woolf, *Letters* 2:572
147   **But at my time**: Woolf, *Letters* 3:38–39
147   **We know what**: Goldstein 173
147   **a washed out**: Woolf, *Diary* 1:262
147   **overwhelmingly cultured**: Huxley 117
147   **as haggard**: Huxley 140
147   **Eliot has created**: Huxley 140
147   **The Undertaker**: Seymour-Jones 144
147   **Where does his queer**: Morrell 101–102
148   **Pale, marmoreal**: Woolf, *Diary* 2:90–91
148   **A mouth twisted**: Woolf, *Diary* 2:77
148   **I am disappointed**: Woolf, *Diary* 2:140
148   **sardonic, guarded**: Woolf, *Diary* 2:187

148   **He is a consistent**: Woolf, *Diary* 2:67–68
148   **the sinister & pedagogic**: Woolf, *Diary* 2:302
148   **peevish, plaintive**: Woolf, *Diary* 2:238
148   **He elaborates & complicates**: Woolf, *Diary* 2:238
148   **poor dear Tom**: Woolf, *Letters* 3:457–458
148   **some notoriety**: Eliot, *Letters* 1:369
148   **I often feel that 'J.A.P.'**: Eliot, *Letters* 1:165–166
149   **His 'poems' will hardly**: Grant 73
149   **interesting experiments**: Grant 74
150   **Polyphiloprogenitive**: Eliot, *Poems* 49
151   **Clutching piaculative**: Eliot, *Poems* 49
151   **between the idea**: Butts, *Journal* 264
151   **fatally handicapping**: Brooker 21
151   **writing nothing**: Brooker 21
151   **immense enjoyment**: Eliot, *Letters* 1:252 n.4
151   **When the syllables**: Unger 5
151   **Mr. Eliot's English**: Brooker 37
152   **Weird and Brilliant Book**: Brooker 41
152   **documents that would**: Brooker 47
152   **vein that tempts**: Brooker 45
152   **a species of mordant**: Brooker 46
152   **He is now the uncanniest**: Brooker 44
152   **Mr. Eliot is about**: Brooker 35
152   **has given us**: Brooker 35
152   **jazz poetry**: Brooker 35
155   **too too too**: Carpenter 354
155   **an attempt to condense**: Carpenter 370
155   **I'm no more**: Carpenter 365
155   **For three years**: Pound, *Collected* 205
155   **Non-esteem of**: Pound, *Collected* 220
156   **I never mentioned**: Pound, *Collected* 212
156   **The age demanded**: Pound, *Collected* 206
157   **Eliot's a wild**: Aldington 219
157   **For God's sake**: Aldington 219
157   **Ezra's form of defense**: Aldington 105
157   **There died a myriad**: Pound, *Collected* 208
157   **Died some**: Pound, *Collected* 208
157   **that quality that makes**: Carpenter 364

CHAPTER SEVEN. "MY NERVES ARE BAD TONIGHT"

Page
161   **the Men of 1914**: Lewis, *Blasting* 251–252
161   **to embalm**: Eliot, *Prose* 1:609
161   **the historical sense**: Eliot, *Wood* 49
161   **It is not true**: Eliot, *Prose* 2:66
162   **the odd distinction of being**: Eliot, *Prose* 2:68
162   **The only way to take**: Eliot, *Prose* 2:69
162   **the distinction of believing**: Eliot, *Prose* 2:69
162   **one two three**: Butscher 45
162   **elaborate lunacies**: March and Tambimuttu 21
163   **he was oldish**: Aiken, *Jig* 14

163   **I am spread**: Aiken, *Jig* 19
163   **The widths of puddles** Aiken, *Jig* 108
163   **I do not know**: Aiken, *Jig* 101
163   **Who am I?**: Aiken, *Jig* 120
163   **We lift our faces**: Aiken, *Jig* 121
163   **Till human voices**: Eliot, *Poems* 9
163   **That was a somber**: Aiken, *Jig* 17
163   **How the devil**: Aiken, *Letters* 109
163   **T. S. E. had underlined**: Aiken, *Letters* 109
164   **Have you tried**: Aiken, *Letters* 109
164   **Was I the fool**: Aiken, *Letters* 110
164   ***Not with a bang***: Eliot, *Poems* 84
164   **There was an address**: Pearson 166
165   **Yes . . . it is interesting**: Spindler 85
165   **the greatest success**: Eliot, *Prose* 2:369
165   **interpenetration and**: Eliot, *Prose* 2:370
165   **the rhythm of**: Eliot, *Prose* 2:370
165   **three offensive letters**: Eliot, *Letters* 1:770
166   **one remains always**: Crawford 324
166   **seemed a man playing**: Goldstein 39
166   **He gives you the creeps**: Gordon 253
166   **he uses violet**: Goldstein 106
166   **amazed to notice**: Pearson 239
166   **seemed anxious**: Pearson 238
166   **heap of broken**: Eliot, *WL* line 22
166   **I had greatly overdrawn**: Eliot, *Letters* 1:584
166   **cottage for neurasthenics**: Eliot, *Letters* 1:581
166   **neuropathic aristocracy**: Epstein, *Poesie* 58
166   **an *imperfect physiology***: Epstein, *Poesie* 83
166   **It is not a question**: Epstein, "New" 10
167   **Spatial speed**: Epstein, "New" 10
167   **Waste lands become**: Epstein, "New" 3
167   **neurotic carnality**: Crawford 390
167   **Our civilization**: Eliot, *Prose* 2:381
167   **One must look**: Eliot, *Prose* 2:382
167   **Tom Eliot has had**: Aiken, *Letters* 65
167   **chief drawback**: Goldstein 33–34
168   **reads more like**: Gold 524 n. 35
168   **disjointed narration**: Gold 531
168   **Vittoz may not**: Gold 533
168   **mental activity of women**: Beard 96
169   ***American nervousness***: Beard 176
169   **All our civilization**: Beard 97
169   **Modern nervousness**: Beard 138
169   **our one great**: Schuster 7
169   **Have we lived**: Schuster 42
170   **contagious diagnosis**: Pietikainen 6
170   **a cacophony of complaints**: Rabinbach 154
170   **not simply a malady**: Rabinbach 160
171   **higher orders**: Drinka 190
171   **neurasthenic circles**: Lutz 6
171   **vast army of**: Schuster 49
171   **muscular Christianity**: Schuster 122

172   **Herr Ober**: Grosz 20
172   **Waiter! A glass**: Killen 218
172   **What is happening**: Pietikainen 1
172   **when classicism says**: Everdell 100
172   **the invention of motion**: Benjamin, *Illuminations* 137
172   **seasickness on dry land**: Benjamin, *Illuminations* 130
172   **a quickened, multiplied**: Pater 153
173   **Have you ever been**: Eliot, *Letters* 1:546
173   **it must be remembered**: Eliot, *Letters* 1:788
173   **We have all to choose**: March and Tambimuttu 218
173   **in a trance**: Crawford 398
173   **I placed before him**: Carpenter 405–406
174   **Caro mio**: Pound, *Letters* 169
174   **Complimenti**: Pound, *Letters* 169
174   **These are the poems**: Pound, *Letters* 170
174   **About enough**: Pound, *Quinn* 206
174   **Eliot's *Waste Land***: Pound, *Letters* 180
175   **Studies in European**: Dempsey 52
175   **and I must confess**: Eliot, *Letters* 1:651
176   **queer duck**: Dempsey 98
176   **mortuaries for**: Dempsey 64
176   **With many apologies**: Dempsey 71
176   **the very heart**: Dempsey 70
176   **gentleman of some**: Dempsey 70
176   **intellectual sewer**: Dempsey 185
176   **If Eliot's long poem**: Dempsey 106
177   **such matter as**: Goldstein 284
178   **restart civilization**: *Pound/Williams* 109
179   **Flowed up the hill**: Eliot, *WL* line 66
179   **If it is stated**: Eliot, *Letters* 1:712

CHAPTER EIGHT. "I HAVE HEARD THE MERMAIDS SINGING"

Page
180   **In the days when**: Eliot, *Prose* 1:537
181   **As she laughed**: Eliot, *Poems* 26
181   **exercises continuously**: Muir 644
181   **As a poet**: Muir 646
181   **everything is underlined**: Muir 646
182   **Eliot weighed**: March and Tambimuttu 219
183   **objective correlative**: Eliot, *Wood* 100
185   **The horror**: Eliot, *Poems* 323. The full passage Eliot originally intended as epigraph was: "Did he live his life again in every detail of desire, temptation, and surrender during that supreme moment of complete knowledge? He cried in a whisper at some image, at some vision,—he cried out twice, a cry that was no more than a breath—'The horror! the horror!'"
186   **Eliot is a mighty**: Brooker 349
186   **a hodge-podge**: Grant 170
186   **a parade of pompous**: Clarke 2:81
186   **deliberate mystification**: Clarke 2:124
186   **a phantasmagoric**: Clarke 2:94
186   **the altar of some**: Clarke 2:118

186   **one of the most**: Clarke 2:102

186   **waste paper**: Clarke 2:120

186   **a dandy**: Grant 185

187   **it is an erudite**: Rascoe, *New York Tribune* (November 3, 1922): sec. 5, p. 8

187   **the human soul**: Brooker 79

187   **a cadaver**: Clarke 2:85

187   **A poem that has**: Clarke 2:118

187   **discovers that after all**: Clarke 2:125

187   **these fragments**: Eliot, *WL* line 430

187   **a vagrant string**: Clarke 2:113

187   **a collection of flashes**: Clarke 2:65

187   **boiling in the nozzle**: Brooker 78

187   **cross-section**: Brooker 78

187   **kaleidoscopic, profuse**: Clarke 2:92

187   **enters the crowd**: Baudelaire, *Painter* 9

187   **One may easily**: Gorman 64

188   **kaleidoscopic movement**: Clarke 2:81

188   **I am compelled**: Clarke 2:124

188   **which is to take**: Clarke 2:125

188   **a grunt would serve**: Grant 192

188   **the apotheosis**: Clarke 2:96

188   **If it is a plan**: Grant 159

188   **it is a condition**: Clarke 2:94

188   **originally consisted of**: Grant 161

188   **in perpetual want**: Clarke 2:110

188   **rhythm of alteration**: Clarke 2:79

189   **the bidding of**: Grant 183

189   **this poem actually is**: Clarke 2:89

189   **a sound of high**: Clarke 2:122

189   **We 'accept' the poem**: Grant 161

189   **agonized outcry**: Grant 170

189   **Sometimes it turns**: Clarke 2:73

189   **Eliot's jumble**: Clarke 2:81

189   **It is rumored**: Brooker 104

190   **a group of us**: Brooker 97

190   **mingling of willful**: Clarke 2:82

190   **Eliot has written**: Clarke 2:74

190   **at present it is**: Brooker 117

190   **have occasioned a display**: Clarke 2:81

190   **Saint Pauls**: Colum 361

190   **group-criticism**: Colum 361

190   **assimilative mind**: Colum 362

191   **The novel is a form**: Eliot, *Prose* 2:478

191   **mythical method**: Eliot, *Prose* 2:479

191   **a continuous parallel**: Eliot, *Prose* 2:478

191   **his imitator Mr Ezra**: Clarke 2:75

192   **Practically the whole**: Loy, *Stories* 257

192   **We hope not**: Grant 136

192   **the absence of any**: Clarke 2:82

192   **undoubtedly the literary**: Eliot, *Letters* 2:170

192   **considerable 'spoofing'**: Eliot, *Letters* 2:74

192   **I do not like a poem**: Eliot, *Letters* 2:74–75

192   **its natural sequence**: [mother] Eliot, *Letters* 2:124

192	**merely a kind of**: Eliot, *Letters* 2:11
192	**un étrange monde**: Eliot, *Letters* 2:276
193	**loves to make**: Clarke 2:72
193	**broken blank verse**: Cox and Hinchliffe 60
193	**the method is that**: Cox and Hinchliffe 61
194	**I am much excited**: Wilson, *Letters* 94
194	**nothing more or less**: Wilson, *Letters* 94
194	**the chief difficulty**: Spindler 77
194	**I assure you**: Spindler 78
194	**The problem is what**: Spindler 107
194	**if only we were surrounded**: Spindler 107
194	**If only we can contrive**: Spindler 204
195	**Eliot is tubercular**: Spindler 80
195	**What do you think**: Crane 105
195	**has been more influenced**: Crane 114–115
195	**I take Eliot**: Crane 114–115
195	**has outclassed Baudelaire**: Crane 114–115
195	**You will profit**: Crane 90
195	**Having absorbed him**: Crane 90
195	**by the Eliotish**: Underwood 76
195	**I look forward to**: Underwood 73
196	**Have you been struck**: Ransom 116
196	**if there were to be held**: Rickword 180
196	**Eliot has been able**: Rickword 180
196	**even 'Satanism'**: Raffel 21
196	**Blank day after day**: Auden 388
197	**chiefly important**: Cox and Hinchliffe 58
197	**After luncheon**: Waugh, *Brideshead* 33
197	**made it possible**: Sharpe 292
197	**the provincial England**: Sharpe 291
197	**If it is a natural**: Sharpe 292
197	**However sheltered**: Brearton 160
197	**paddle along**: Stallworthy 115
198	**the poet who had taken**: March and Tambimuttu 79
198	**enabled us to know**: March and Tambimuttu 78
198	**the modern world**: March and Tambimuttu 234
198	**we were like new-born**: Connolly 227
198	**The stranger who**: March and Tambimuttu 38
198	**He is a cosmopolitan**: Unger 5
198	**So deeply has Eliot's**: March and Tambimuttu 42
198	**I feel, like most**: March and Tambimuttu 35
198	**It is impertinent**: Empson 89
199	**How did we schoolboys**: March and Tambimuttu 146
199	**What we wanted**: March and Tambimuttu 147
199	**To have painted**: March and Tambimuttu 151
199	**I ran with the pack**: Friede 224
200	**Am I cuckoo**: Aiken, *Letters* 156
200	**There's nothing melancholy**: Aiken, *Letters* 185
200	**T. S. Eliot, with his ear**: Butts, *Journal* 275
200	**new imagination**: Butts, *Journal* 95
200	**Eliot's intellectual classicism**: Blondel 430
201	**There is no road**: Butts, *Journal* 198 n. 9
201	**I have not got it**: Butts, *Journal* 248

201   **the frog that jumps**: Moore, *Letters* 298
202   **Why catch up**: Blondel 248
202   **There's more divine**: Blondel 63
202   **Polyandry**: Butts, *Journal* 108
202   **I think that I am**: Butts, *Journal* 110
202   **the first man**: Butts, *Journal* 133
202   **Go away & flirt**: Butts, *Journal* 137
202   **The mind of the priests**: Butts, "Pythian Ode," *Transatlantic Review* 2, no. 3 (1924): 235
202   **'My nerves are bad**: Eliot, *WL* lines 111–114
203   **The ivory men**: Eliot, *Waste Land Facsimile* 13
203   **Pressing lidless**: Eliot, *WL* line 138
203   **You know I am ill**: Crawford 415
203   **Glad this awful year**: Crawford 343
203   **She spoke to him**: Seymour 389
203   **In the last ten**: Eliot, *Letters* 2:627
203   **To her the marriage**: Rainey 8

CHAPTER NINE. OTHER VOICES

Page
204   **April is the cruelest**: Eliot, *WL* lines 1–4
204   **Avril est**: Eliot, "La terre mise à nu" 174
204   **April ist**: Eliot, "Das wüste Land" 362
204   **Abril es el mes**: Eliot, *Tierra Baldía* 13
205   **Abril es el mes**: Eliot, "El Paramo" 15
205   **April är**: Eliot, "Det öde Landet" 25
205   **Aprile è**: Eliot, "La Terra Desolata" 29
205   **brings the sailor**: Eliot, *WL* lines 221–223
205   **heimwärts drängt**: Eliot, "Das wüste Land" 368
206   **Su poema**: Eliot, *Tierra Baldía* 9
206   **miraculous economy**: Eliot, *Tierra Baldía* 7
206   **Allusion in Mr. Eliot's**: Cox and Hinchliffe 52
206   **O O O O**: Eliot, *WL* line 128
206   **dieser Fetzen**: Eliot, "Das wüste Land" 365
206   **ages and styles**: Curtius 359
207   **even on the first**: Curtius 357
207   **The only common**: Akitoshi
208   **What seas**: Eliot, *Poems* 107
208   **He tells me**: Seferis, *Poems* 43
208   **I wanted to test**: March and Tambimuttu 132
208   **chilled ashes**: Seferis, "Eliot" 150
208   **it sculpts silence**: Seferis, "Eliot" 154
208   **the epic of a pivotal**: Seferis, "Eliot" 152
209   **The difficulty inherent**: Seferis, "Eliot" 157
209   **foreign elements**: Seferis, "Eliot" 159
209   **These days there are**: March and Tambimuttu 134
209   **After the outburst**: March and Tambimuttu 127
209   *an inner reading*: Montale, *Second* 179
210   **Like the cubist**: Montale, *Second* 181

210   **its music carried me**: March and Tambimuttu 120
210   **He is the discoverer**: Curtius 399
210   **the sense of an interior**: March and Tambimuttu 192
210   **not an absence**: March and Tambimuttu 247–248
210   **music of ideas**: Cox and Hinchliffe 53
210   **The poetry got into**: March and Tambimuttu 45
210   **He sang it & chanted**: Woolf, *Letters* 2:178
211   **The mood of 1924**: Rascoe, *We Were* 233
211   **this was no poem**: Eliot, *Prose* 6:314
211   **Fümms bö**: Schwitters 52
211   **I know that a poem**: Eliot, *Prose* 6:321
211   **despite its intensity**: Spender, *World* 146
211   **had to invent**: Riding and Graves 50
211   **Eliot is one of**: Montale, *Second* 173
211   **the line punctuates**: Goldstein 181
212   **Once, after having**: Spender, *Eliot* 206
212   **The most real horror**: Ross, *Wagnerism* 489
212   **is at least in part**: Ross, *Wagnerism* 493
212   **Eliot's Wagner nostalgia**: Ross, *Wagnerism* 489
212   **a bomb in**: Slonimsky 157
212   **methodische Negation**: Slonimsky 149
212   **the cruelest of**: Slonimsky 153
212   **emancipation of dissonance**: Schoenberg 260
213   **gadji beri**: Riha 68
214   **Jingle. Bloo**: Joyce 256
214   **There are two aesthetic ideals**: Pound, *Antheil* 44
214   **an unconscious exercise**: Schopenhauer 1:256
214   **a growing discredit**: Babbitt 47
214   **Datta. Dayadhvam**: Eliot, *WL* lines 401, 411, 418
214   **beating obedient**: Eliot, *WL* lines 421–422
215   **a new naturalism**: Butts, *Journal* 382
215   **a poem in which**: Yeats, *Vision* 4
215   **Certain typical**: Yeats, *Wheels* 73
216   **is like the chameleon**: Brooker 25
216   **the reading public**: Riding and Graves 79
216   **gets its excitement**: Riding and Graves 89
216   **The appearance of freakishness**: Riding and Graves 90
216   **afraid of the infringements**: Riding and Graves 99
216   **puts in a personal**: Riding and Graves 109
217   **does not want to understand**: Riding and Graves 106
217   **the plain reader**: Riding and Graves 136
217   **warned against**: Eliot, *Prose* 4:689
217   **is groping for some**: Riding and Graves 47
217   **a newly created**: Riding and Graves 118
217   **a declaration of**: Riding and Graves 124
217   **not only from episode**: Riding and Graves 50
218   **Tactile reception**: Benjamin, *Work* 40
218   *Reception in distraction*: Benjamin, *Work* 40 41
218   **By contrast**: Benjamin, *Work* 40
218   **the act of finding**: Stevens 174
220   **Was that a real**: Creeley title
220   **Negro head**: Mondrian 126

CHAPTER TEN. PARALLAX

Page

223   *The Waste Land* is a poem: Brooks and Warren 306
223   A poem may appear: Eliot, *Prose* 6:314
223   what the poetry is: Eliot, *Prose* 8:128
224   That is not what I: Eliot, *Poems* 8
224   I think that this kind: Winchell 165–166
224   What is that sound: Eliot, *WL* line 366
224   What is the city: Eliot, *WL* lines 371–381
225   Unreal City: Eliot, *WL* lines 60–63
226   An incident: H. D., *Walls* 7
226   The past is literally: Robinson 2
226   The house next door: Carr 868
226   She gave the impression: Gordon 286–287
227   You cannot be you: Wade 192
227   It is characteristic: Harrison xx–xxi
227   unmeaning perfection: Harrison xxi
228   It's all Sapphism: Wade 168
228   a very self conscious: Woolf, *Diary* 1:248
228   a capricious: Woolf, *Letters* 2:383
228   has written a very: Woolf, *Letters* 2:385
228   Half blind with writing: Woolf, *Diary* 2:33
228   I want a holophrase: Mirrlees 3
229   Language, after the purely: Harrison 473–474
229   looking-at-each-other: Harrison 474
229   impulsive people: Harrison 474
229   holopsychosis: Harrison 475
230   Life is like a blind: Briggs 266
230   corporeal multiplicity: Mirrlees xxxvii
230   It is pleasant: Mirrlees 9
231   a collection of images: Flint 10
231   This little effusion: Mirrlees xxxix
232   a rather delirious: Chisholm 98
232   an almost sensational: Chisholm 99
232   with the startled: Woolf, *Diary* 2:320
232   she slipped into: Woolf, *Diary* 2:320
233   resumed love-songs: Cunard, *Poems* 115
233   Many things are known: Cunard, *Poems* 99
233   Midnight, aurora: Cunard, *Poems* 100
233   candle wasting: Cunard, *Poems* 102
233   Have I not loved you: Cunard, *Poems* 110
233   London, the hideous: Cunard, *Poems* 104
233   I have changed: Cunard, *Poems* 114
233   The articulate skeleton: Cunard, *Poems* 115
233   Hail partner: Cunard, *Poems* 115
233   In doubt, in shame: Cunard, *Poems* 115
233   old tattoo of journeys: Cunard, *Poems* 105
234   at some distance: Cunard, *Poems* 99
234   we have all to choose: Eliot, *Prose* 5:233
234   *too little* to be chased: Leavell 162
234   Only a person of her: Leavell 223

235   **in the slightly acid**: Gregory 26
235   **Are you a jet black**: Pound, *Letters* 143
235   **the minor prophets**: Moore, *Letters* 123
235   **Darwin speaks**: Moore, *Letters* 164
235   **for me to be published so**: Moore, *Letters* 152
236   **are always pertinent**: Eliot, *Prose* 8:127
236   **the remarkable exposition**: Eliot, *Prose* 8:127
236   **a clumsy prose**: Gregory 32
236   **We have only devoted**: Gregory 33
236   **While Miss Moore**: Gregory 47
236   **essays in the disguise**: Gregory 49
236   **She shouts at**: Gregory 37
236   **What I do find**: Gregory 39
237   **destined to endure**: Gregory 20
237   **fighting in her country**: Gregory 21
237   **The spirit is robust**: Gregory 36
237   **I can see no trace**: Gregory 34
237   **this book should be**: Gregory 35
237   **one never forgets**: Eliot, *Prose* 2:498
237   **a book of poems**: Gregory 74
237   **there is no sob**: Gregory 40
237   **a most menacing**: Gregory 75
237   **government pamphlets**: Moore, *Observations* 107
237   **an enormous frozen**: Leavell 217
238   **use of quotations**: Dempsey 110
239   **I too, dislike it**: Moore, *Prose* 36
239   **nor till the poets**: Moore, *Selected* 53
240   **shaving-brush**: Moore, *Observations* 118
240   **an object lesson**: Gregory 50
240   **she occupies the thought**: Williams, *Essays* 126
240   **Miss Moore gets**: Williams, *Essays* 128
241   **This is new**: Williams, *Essays* 131
242   **[Stein's] work is not**: Eliot, *Prose* 3:29
242   **an extremely valuable**: Eliot, *Prose* 2:682
243   **the first great simultanist**: Paz 133

CHAPTER ELEVEN. "EZRA POUND SPEAKING"

Page
244   **The War bled**: Lewis, *Blasting* 18
244   **artistic expression**: Lewis, *Blasting* 252
244   **the really malefic**: Lewis, *Blasting* 279
244   **During the last ten**: Lewis, *The Tyro* 2 (1922): 3
244   **Europe was full**: Lewis, *Blasting* 255–256
245   **I was at its heart**: Lewis, *Blasting* 257
245   **By the end**: Lewis, *Blasting* 256
245   **We are not only**: Lewis, *Blasting* 258
245   **all that is 'advanced'**: Lewis, *Blasting* 258
245   **the *types* of humanity**: Pound, *Exile*
245   **because the water**: Carpenter 378–379
245   **I daily ask myself**: Carpenter 378–379
245   **ingenuity of insult**: Raffel 86

245 **He is a powerful**: Reid 272
246 **a swashbuckler**: Raffel 98
247 **the man has sheep**: Carpenter 468
247 **I am not proceeding**: Pound, *Selected Prose* 209
247 **ANY bloody thing**: Carpenter 478
247 **A. A. Live man**: Pound, *Parents* 625
247 **deliberate nobility**: Yeats, *Oxford Book* xxv
247 **There are more questions**: Pound, *Letters* 262
247 **my head is a squeezed**: *Pound/Joyce* 44
247 **running top speed**: Carpenter 508
248 **Bull Muss**: Carpenter 492
248 **Get the waiter**: Carpenter 557
248 **EZthority**: Carpenter 525
248 **He was a village**: Stein, *Autobiography* 246
248 **restart civilization**: *Pound/Williams* 109
248 **The best writers**: Pound, *Selected Prose* 197
248 **Artists are**: Pound, *Selected Prose* 199
249 **The more I hear**: *Pound/Joyce* 234
249 **education by provocation**: Carpenter 526
249 **You made your**: Raffel 108
249 **He has a mind**: Norman 358
249 **gargling anti-semitism**: Carpenter 559
249 **I like him immensely**: Williams, *Letters* 184
250 **There is no doubt**: Carpenter 585
250 **What the hell**: Williams, *Autobiography* 316
250 **Rome Radio**: Pound, *Radio* xiii
250 **Gus Flaubert**: Pound, *Radio* 92
251 **If there is still**: Pound, *Radio* 93
251 **Note when American**: Pound, *Radio* 93
251 **Twenty-five**: Pound, *Radio* 57–58
251 **such dung heaps**: Pound, *Radio* 91
251 **Woodrow codface**: Pound, *Radio* 21
251 **balloon-faced**: Pound, *Radio* 42
251 **the British Blurb**: Pound, *Radio* 25
251 **the Bloody Boobs**: Pound, *Radio* 26
251 **To send boys**: Pound, *Radio* 43
252 **small dirty meanness**: Pound, *Radio* 387
252 **it seemed as though**: Carpenter 602
252 **Jewsfeldt**: Carpenter 568
252 **If some man had**: Pound, *Radio* 115
252 **That it should be one**: Carpenter 611
252 **a person owing**: Carpenter 620
253 **I have not spoken**: Norman 389
253 **confer the paraphernalia**: MacLeish, *Letters* 317
253 **How did you get here**: Rachewiltz 185
253 **Whom God would destroy**: Pound, *Radio* 27
253 *Confucius and Kindred*: Carpenter 650
254 **If I am not shot**: Carpenter 652
254 **That from the gates**: Pound, *Pisan* 80.661–667
254 **a man on whom**: Pound, *Pisan* 74.193
254 **As a lone ant**: Pound, *Pisan* 76.208–209
254 **we who have passed**: Pound, *Pisan* 74.842
254 **If you can imagine**: Montale, *Essays* 134

255   **I don't know how humanity**: Pound, *Pisan* 74.389–393
255   **Le Paradis**: Pound, *Pisan* 74.457–460
255   **Le paradis**: Pound, *Pisan* 76.249–250
255   **How is it far**: Pound, *Pisan* 79.148
255   **Nude Erections**: *Pound/Ford* 163
255   **very wobbly**: Carpenter 702
256   **Confucius and these other**: Carpenter 721
256   **All of Europe**: Swift 33
256   **Olson saved my life**: Carpenter 734
256   **no longer hooded**: Olson 36
256   **He shot in something**: Olson 61
256   **nerves turning**: Olson 97
256   **his mind bursts**: Olson 97
256   **Ezra *is* a tennis ball**: Olson 100
256   **He does not seem**: Olson 99
257   **the ragbaggy**: Carpenter 716
257   **oblivious of a white-headed**: Carpenter 776
258   **The Nobel is**: Simpson 73
258   **dichten = condensare**: Pound, *ABC* 77
259   **There will be no allusion**: Witemeyer 81
259   **He sat down**: Shapiro, *Trial* 57
260   **Thus we become**: Shapiro, *Trial* 60
260   **you were sent**: Shapiro, *Trial* 68
260   **A poet in our times**: Shapiro, *Trial* 71
260   **I condemn**: Shapiro, *Trial* 78
260   **yet say this**: Pound, *Pisan* 74.9–10
260   **perhaps inhibited**: Shapiro, "Case" 519
261   **an act of intellectual**: Shapiro, *Defense* 29
261   **Pound, in Mental Clinic**: *New York Times* (February 20, 1949): front page
261   **Bollingen's bid**: Carpenter 793
261   **the mystical and cultural**: McGuire 214
262   **It was a great**: Leick 32
262   **Your articles on Ezra**: Leick 33
262   **standard-brand**: Fellows 13
262   **What is the fear**: Rukeyser 44
262   **reminded me**: Carpenter 596
263   **no free speech**: Pound, *Pisan* 74.42
263   **A poem should not**: MacLeish, *Street* 38
263   **Only by demonstrating**: MacLeish, *Opinion* 35
263   **Fifty years**: Moody 3:279
263   **Is modern poetry**: Viereck 228
263   **while privately agreeing**: Viereck 235
263   **You let *me* throw**: Carpenter 264 n.
264   **No comment**: Carpenter 793
264   **It was the world's least**: Swift 10
264   **Mullins died**: Swift 178–179
264   **Ezra Pound, the American**: Cournos 235
265   **What I saw**: MacLeish, *Letters* 397
265   **Why don't you read**: MacLeish, *Letters* 379
265   **Your information**: MacLeish, *Letters* 385
265   **We have gone through**: H. D., *End* 26
265   **It is the *feel***: H. D., *End* 44
265   ***Ezra Pound, le Mallarmé***: H. D., *End* 35

265   **Never have I seen**: Rachewiltz 257
265   **it contains one passage**: MacLeish, *Letters* 345
265   **The ant's a centaur**: Pound, *Pisan* 81.144–150
265   **Pound's verse**: Pound, *Pisan* xxxiv

CHAPTER TWELVE. SIGNIFICANT EMOTION

Many of the quotations in this chapter have been cited earlier in the book and documented in references for previous chapters.

Page
267   **Stare out the window**: Ross, *Wagnerism* 595
267   **Wagner is still**: Lewis, *Blasting* 264
267   **Ishilda**: H. D., *End* 42
267   **Rimbaud was**: Crane 261
267   **It is in art**: Pound, *Poetry and Prose* 1:203
268   **when each art**: Pound, *Antheil* 42
268   **There are two**: Pound, *Antheil* 44
268   **a scaling of**: Pound, *Antheil* 44–45
268   **Wagner, a great**: Pound, *Antheil* 40
268   **endless melody**: Rasula, *Shiver* 222–247
268   **An epic is**: Pound, *Make* 19
268   **we do not all**: Pound, *Make* 19
269   **wasteland is defined**: Di Palma 3
269   *Amo amas*: Hoffenstein 117
270   **In the highlands**: Diepeveen 127
270   **April is the foolishest**: Diepeveen 125
270   **Mr. Eliot's poem**: Diepeveen 130
270   *apologies to T. S.*: Palmer 11
270   **I refuse to be**: Palmer 17
270   **Rouen is the rainiest**: Ellmann 572
271   **down those mean streets**: Rowson's book is unpaginated
271   **Eliot's serious**: Tracy 191
272   *The Waste Land* **seized**: Ellison 203
272   **Those who are creating**: Stein, *Masterpieces* 27
274   **A master-piece**: Stein, *Masterpieces* 86
274   **Well now that's done**: *WL* line 252
277   **The brown waves**: Eliot, *Poems* 21
277   **weave, weave the sunlight**: Eliot, *Poems* 28
278   **In my beginning**: Eliot, *Poems* 185
278   **Of no other**: H. D., *End* 56
279   **It is painful**: Eliot, *Prose* 8:596
279   **a gnawing doubt**: Eliot, *Prose* 8:597
280   **My meeting with Pound**: Eliot, *Prose* 8:597–598
280   **Emily Hale would**: Eliot, *Prose* 8:598
281   **the man of genius**: Gordon 401
281   **Eliot had turned**: Williams, *Autobiography* 174
281   **so slimy**: Williams, *Letters* 225
281   **It has been**: Williams, "Statement" 98
282   **To me it suggests**: Tashjian 62
282   **her red hair**: Williams, *Autobiography* 146
282   **In his effort**: Moore, *Prose* 57

282   **I like most**: Williams, "Questionnaire" 87
283   **High Anglican**: Pearson 359
283   **The pediatrician**: Williams, *Spring* xii
283   **I am no longer**: Bacigalupo 250
284   **From time's wreckage**: Pound, *Drafts* 11
284   **the action which takes**: Eliot, *Prose* 2:108
284   **not a 'personality'**: Eliot, *Prose* 2:110
284   ***significant* emotion**: Eliot, *Prose* 2:112
285   **That was a way**: Eliot, *Poems* 187
285   **So here I am**: Eliot, *Poems* 191
285   **For, just as**: Eliot, *Prose* 7:17 n. 8
285   **The unattached devotion**: Eliot, *Poems* 195
286   **a familiar compound**: Eliot, *Poems* 204
286   **myself at the age**: Eliot, *Poems* 1013
286   **the rending pain**: Eliot, *Poems* 205
286   **the communication**: Eliot, *Poems* 202

Ackroyd, Peter. *T. S. Eliot*. London: Hamish Hamilton, 1984.

Adams, Henry. *The Education of Henry Adams*. Edited by Ernest Samuels. Boston: Houghton Mifflin, 1973.

Aiken, Conrad. *The Jig of Forslin*. Boston: Four Seas, 1916.

———. *The Pilgrimage of Festus*. New York: Knopf, 1923.

———. *The Divine Pilgrim*. Athens: University of Georgia Press, 1949.

———. *Selected Letters of Conrad Aiken*. Edited by Joseph Killorin. New Haven, CT: Yale University Press, 1978.

Akitoshi, Nagahata. "The Reception of Ezra Pound and T. S. Eliot in Japan." In *Oxford Research Encyclopedias* online (March 28, 2018).

Albright, Daniel, ed. *Modernism and Music: An Anthology of Sources*. Chicago: University of Chicago Press, 2004.

Aldington, Richard. *Life for Life's Sake: A Book of Reminiscences*. New York: Viking, 1941.

Anderson, Margaret. *My Thirty Years' War*. New York: Knopf, 1930.

Anonymous. *Regeneration: A Reply to Max Nordau*. London: Constable, 1895.

Apollinaire, Guillaume. *Oeuvres poétiques*. Edited by Marcel Adéma and Michel Décaudin. Paris: Gallimard, 1965.

———. *Selected Writings*. Translated by Roger Shattuck. New York: New Directions, 1971.

———. *Calligrammes: Poems of Peace and War (1913–1916)*. Translated by Anne Hyde Greet. Berkeley: University of California Press, 1980.

———. *Oeuvres en prose complètes*. Vol. 2. Edited by Pierre Caizergues and Michel Décaudin. Paris: Gallimard, 1991.

———. *The Cubist Painters*. Translated by Peter Read. Berkeley: University of California Press, 2002.

Auden, W. H. *Poems: Volume II, 1940–1973*. Edited by Edward Mendelson. Princeton, NJ: Princeton University Press, 2022.

Babbitt, Irving. "Humanism: An Essay at Definition." In *Humanism and America: Essays on the Outlook of Modern Civilization*, edited by Norman Foerster, 25–51. New York: Farrar & Rinehart, 1930.

Bacigalupo, Massimo. *Ezra Pound, Italy, and The Cantos*. Clemson, SC: Clemson University Press, 2020.

Baker, Nicholson. *The Anthologist*. New York: Simon & Schuster, 2009.

Baring, Maurice. *C*. Oxford: Oxford University Press, 1986.

Baudelaire, Charles. *The Painter of Modern Life and Other Essays*. Translated by Jonathan Mayne. London: Phaidon, 1964.

———. *Paris Spleen*. Translated by Louise Varèse. New York: New Directions, 1970.

———. *Oeuvres complètes*. Vol. 1. Edited by Claude Pichois. Paris: Gallimard, 1975.

———. *Selected Letters*. Translated by Rosemary Lloyd. Chicago: University of Chicago Press, 1986.

———. *The Flowers of Evil*. Translated by Nathan Brown. Zagreb: MaMa Multimedia Institute, 2021.

Beard, George M. *American Nervousness*. New York: Putnam, 1881.

Beckson, Karl. *London in the 1890s: A Cultural History*. New York: Norton, 1992.

Bely, Andrei. *The Dramatic Symphony*. Translated by Roger and Angela Keys. New York: Grove Press, 1986.

Benjamin, Walter. *Illuminations*. Edited by Hannah Arendt. Translated by Harry Zohn. New York: Schocken, 1969.

―――. *The Work of Art in the Age of Its Technological Reproducibility and Other Writings on Media*. Edited by Michael W. Jennings, Brigid Doherty, and Thomas Y. Levin. Translated by Edmund Jephcott et al. Cambridge, MA: Harvard University Press, 2008.

Blissett, William F. "George Moore and Literary Wagnerism." *Contemporary Literature* 13, no. 1 (Winter 1961): 52–71.

Bloch, R. Howard. *One Toss of the Dice: The Incredible Story of How a Poem Made Us Modern*. New York: Liveright, 2017.

Blondel, Nathalie. *Mary Butts: Scenes from the Life*. Kingston, NY: McPherson, 1998.

Brearton, Fran. *Incorrigibly Plural: Louis MacNeice and His Legacy*. Manchester, UK: Carcanet Press, 2014.

Briggs, Julia. "Hope Mirrlees and Continental Modernism." In *Gender in Modernism: New Geographies, Complex Intersections*, edited by Bonnie Kime Scott, 261–270. Urbana: University of Illinois Press, 2007.

Brooker, Jewel Spears, ed. *T. S. Eliot: The Contemporary Reviews*. Cambridge: Cambridge University Press, 2004.

Brooks, Cleanth, and Robert Penn Warren. *Understanding Poetry*. 4th ed. New York: Holt, Rinehart and Winston, 1976.

Burgess, Gelett. *Burgess Unabridged: A New Dictionary of Words You Have Always Needed*. New York: Stokes, 1914.

Burke, Carolyn. *Becoming Modern: The Life of Mina Loy*. New York: Farrar, Straus and Giroux, 1996.

Bush, Christopher. "Introduction 'From the Decipherings.'" In Ezra Pound, *Cathay: A Critical Edition*, edited by Timothy Billings, 1–13. New York: Fordham University Press, 2019.

Busoni, Ferruccio. *Esthetics of New Music*. Translated by Th. Baker. In *Three Classics in the Aesthetic of Music*, 73–102. New York: Dover, 1962.

Butscher, Edward. *Conrad Aiken: Poet of White Horse Vale*. Athens: University of Georgia Press, 1988.

Butts, Mary. *Ashe of Rings*. London: Wishart, 1933.

―――. *The Journal of Mary Butts*. Edited by Nathalie Blondel. New Haven, CT: Yale University Press, 2002.

Cabanne, Pierre. *Dialogues with Marcel Duchamp*. Translated by Ron Padgett. New York: Viking, 1971.

Carpenter, Humphrey. *A Serious Character: The Life of Ezra Pound*. Boston: Houghton Mifflin, 1988.

Carr, Helen. *The Verse Revolutionaries: Ezra Pound, H. D. and the Imagists*. London: Jonathan Cape, 2009.

Cate, Curtis. *Friedrich Nietzsche*. London: Hutchinson, 2002.

Cendrars, Blaise. *Selected Writings*. Edited by Walter Albert. New York: New Directions, 1966.

―――. *Modernities and Other Writings*. Edited by Monique Chefdor. Translated by Esther Allen. Lincoln: University of Nebraska Press, 1992.

―――. *Complete Poems*. Translated by Ron Padgett. Berkeley: University of California Press, 1992.

―――. *Sky: Memoirs*. Translated by Nina Rootes. New York: Paragon House, 1992.

Chisholm, Anne. *Nancy Cunard: A Biography*. New York: Knopf, 1979.

Clark, Ronald W. *The Life of Bertrand Russell*. New York: Knopf, 1976.

Clarke, Graham, ed. *T. S. Eliot: Critical Assessments*. 4 vols. London: Christopher Helm, 1990.

Cocteau, Jean. *Oeuvres complètes*. Vol. 9. Paris: Marguerat, 1946.

Colum, Mary M. "Modernists." *The Literary Review* 3, no. 18 (January 6, 1923): 361–362.

Connolly, Cyril. *The Selected Works of Cyril Connolly*. Vol. 1, *The Modern Movement*. Edited by Matthew Connolly. London: Picador, 2002.

Cork, Richard. *Wild Thing: Epstein, Gaudier-Brzeska, Gill*. London: Royal Academy of Arts, 2009.

Cournos, John. *Autobiography*. New York: Putnam, 1935.

Cox, C. B., and Arnold P. Hinchliffe, eds. *The Waste Land: A Casebook*. London: Macmillan, 1968.

Crane, Hart. *The Letters of Hart Crane, 1916–1932*. Edited by Brom Weber. New York: Hermitage House, 1952.

Crawford, Robert. *Young Eliot: From St. Louis to The Waste Land*. New York: Farrar, Straus and Giroux, 2015.

Creeley, Robert. *Was That a Real Poem or Did You Just Make It Up Yourself*. Santa Barbara, CA: Black Sparrow Press, 1976.

Crosby, Caresse. *The Passionate Years*. London: Alvin Redman, 1955.

Crowder, Henry. *As Wonderful As All That?* Navarro, CA: Wild Trees Press, 1987.

Cummings, E. E. *Selected Letters*. Edited by F. W. Dupee and George Stade. New York: Harcourt, Brace, 1969.

Cunard, Nancy. *Parallax*. London: Hogarth Press, 1925.

———. *These Were the Hours: Memories of My Hours Press, Réanville and Paris, 1928–1931*. Edited by Hugh Ford. Carbondale: Southern Illinois University Press, 1969.

———. *Selected Poems*. Edited by Sandeep Parmar. Manchester: Carcanet Press, 2016.

Curnutt, Kirk, ed. *The Critical Responses to Gertrude Stein*. Westport, CT: Greenwood Press, 2000.

Curtius, Ernst Robert. *Essays on European Literature*. Translated by Michael Kowal. Princeton, NJ: Princeton University Press, 1973.

Dabney, Lewis M. *Edmund Wilson: A Life in Literature*. New York: Farrar, Straus and Giroux, 2005.

Dahlhaus, Carl. *The Idea of Absolute Music*. Translated by Roger Lustig. New York: Cambridge University Press, 1989.

Damon, S. Foster. *Amy Lowell: A Chronicle, with Extracts from Her Correspondence*. Boston: Houghton Mifflin, 1935.

Dawson, N. P. "Enjoying Poor Literature." *Forum* 69 (March 1923): 1371–1379.

Debussy, Claude. "Monsieur Croche the Dilettante Hater." In *Three Classics in the Aesthetics of Music*, 1–71. New York: Dover, 1962.

Dempsey, James. *The Tortured Life of Scofield Thayer*. Gainesville: University Press of Florida, 2014.

Dickey, Frances. "May the Record Speak: The Correspondence of T. S. Eliot and Emily Hale." *Twentieth-Century Literature* 66, no. 4 (December 2020): 431–462.

Dickey, Frances, and John Whittier-Ferguson. "Joint Property, Divided Correspondents: The T. S. Eliot–Emily Hale Letters." *Modernism/modernity* online, volume 5, cycle 4 (January 29, 2021).

Diepeveen, Leonard, ed. *Mock Modernism: An Anthology of Parodies, Travesties, Frauds, 1910–1935*. Toronto: University of Toronto Press, 2014.

D'Iorio, Paolo. *Nietzsche's Journey to Sorrento: Genesis of the Philosophy of the Free Spirit*. Translated by Sylvia Mae Gorelick. Chicago: University of Chicago Press, 2016.

Di Palma, Vittoria. *Wasteland: A History*. New Haven, CT: Yale University Press, 2014.

Documents of the 1913 Armory Show: The Electrifying Moment of Modern Art's American Debut. Tucson, AZ: Hol Art Books, 2009.

Dolan, Therese. *Manet, Wagner, and the Musical Culture of Their Time*. London: Ashgate, 2013.

Dos Passos, John. *Orient Express*. New York: Harper, 1927.

Drinka, George Frederick. *The Birth of Neurosis: Myth, Malady and the Victorians*. New York: Simon and Schuster, 1984.

Drinkwater, John. "The Fires of God." In *Georgian Poetry 1911–1912*, 75–83. London: Poetry Bookshop, 1912.

Duncan, Isadora. *The Art of the Dance*. Edited by Seldon Cheney. New York: Theatre Arts, 1928.

———. *Isadora Speaks*. Edited by Franklin Rosemont. San Francisco: City Lights, 1981.

Eliot, T. S. "La terre mise à nu." Translated by Jean de Menasce. *L'Esprit* 1 (May 1926): 174–194.

———. "Das wüste Land." Translated by E. R. Curtius. *Neue Schweizer Rundschau* 20, no. 4 (April 1927): 362–377.

———. *The Sacred Wood: Essays on Poetry and Criticism*. 2nd ed. London: Methuen, 1928.

———. "El Paramo." Translated by Enrique Munguía, Jr. *Contemporáneos* 26/27 (July–August 1930): 15–32.

———. *Tierra Baldía*. Translated by Angel Flores. Barcelona: Editorial Cervantes, 1930.

———. "La Terra Desolata." Translated by Mario Praz. *Circoli: Rivista di Poesia* 4 (July–August 1932): 27–57.

———. "Det öde Landet." Translated by Karin Boye and Erik Mesterton. *Spektrum* 2, no. 2 (February 1932): 25–44.

———. "Jałowa Ziemia." Translated by Czesław Miłosz. *Twrczosc* 2, no. 10 (October 1946): 5–20.

———. *The Waste Land: A Facsimile and Transcript of the Original Drafts Including the Annotations of Ezra Pound*. Edited by Valerie Eliot. New York: Harcourt, Brace, 1971.

———. *Inventions of the March Hare: Poems 1909–1917*. Edited by Christopher Ricks. San Diego, CA: Harcourt, Brace, 1996.

———. *The Waste Land: Authoritative Text, Contexts, Criticism*. Edited by Michael North. New York: Norton, 2001.

———. *The Letters of T. S. Eliot*. Vol. 1, *1898–1922*. Edited by Valerie Eliot and Hugh Haughton. Rev. ed. London: Faber and Faber, 2009.

———. *The Letters of T. S. Eliot*. Vol. 2, *1923–1925*. Edited by Valerie Eliot and Hugh Haughton. London: Faber and Faber, 2009.

———. *The Poems of T. S. Eliot*. Vol. 1, *Collected and Uncollected Poems*. Edited by Christopher Ricks and Jim McCue. Baltimore: Johns Hopkins University Press, 2015.

———. *The Complete Prose of T. S. Eliot*. Edited by Ronald Schuchard. 8 vols. Baltimore: Johns Hopkins University Press, 2021.

Ellison, Ralph. *Collected Essays*. Edited by John F. Callahan. New York: Modern Library, 1995.

Ellmann, Richard. *James Joyce: New and Revised Edition*. New York: Oxford University Press, 1982.

Emerson, Ralph Waldo. *Essays and Lectures*. New York: Library of America, 1983.

Empson, William. *Collected Poems*. New York: Harcourt, Brace, 1949.

Endell, August. *Vom Sehen: Texte 1896–1925 über Architektur, Formkunst und "Die Schönheit der großen Stadt."* Edited by Helge David. Basel: Birkhäuser, 1995.

Epstein, Jacob. *Epstein: An Autobiography*. New York: Dutton, 1963.

Epstein, Jean. *La Poésie d'aujourd'hui: Un nouvel état d'intelligence*. Paris: Sirène, 1921.

———. "The New Conditions of Literary Phenomena." *Broom* 2, no. 1 (April 1922): 3–10.

Everdell, William. *The First Moderns: Profiles in the Origins of Twentieth-Century Thought*. Chicago: University of Chicago Press, 1997.

Farr, Florence. *The Music of Speech, Containing the Words of Some Poets, Thinkers and Music-Makers Regarding the Practice of the Bardic Art Together with Fragments of Verse Set to Its Own Melody*. London: Elkin Mathews, 1909.

Fellows in American Letters of the Library of Congress. *The Case Against the* Saturday Review of Literature. Chicago: Modern Poetry Association, 1949.

Fletcher, John Gould. *Preludes and Symphonies*. New York: Macmillan, 1930.

Flint, F. S. "Some Modern French Poets (A Commentary, with Specimens)." *The Monthly Chapbook* 4, no. 1 (October 1919): 1–40.

Ford, Ford Madox. *Thus to Revisit: Some Reminiscences.* New York: Octagon, 1966.

Forster, E. M. *The Prince's Tale and Other Uncollected Writings.* Edited by P. N. Furbank. London: André Deutsch, 1998.

Förster-Nietzsche, Elizabeth, ed. *The Nietzsche-Wagner Correspondence.* Translated by Caroline V. Kerr. London: Duckworth, 1922.

Foster, R. F. *W. B. Yeats, A Life: I. The Apprentice Mage.* New York: Oxford University Press, 1997.

———. *W. B. Yeats, A Life: II. The Arch-Poet.* New York: Oxford University Press, 2003.

Friede, Donald. *The Mechanical Angel: His Adventures and Enterprises in the Glittering 1920's.* New York: Knopf, 1948.

Friedman, Donald, ed. *An Anthology of Belgian Symbolist Poets.* Translated by Donald Friedman. New York: Peter Lang, 2003.

Frost, Robert. *The Letters of Robert Frost.* Vol. 1, *1886–1920.* Edited by Mark Richardson and Robert Faggen. Cambridge, MA: Harvard University Press, 2014.

Furness, Raymond. *Wagner and Literature.* Manchester University Press, 1982.

Gallup, Donald, ed. *The Flowers of Friendship: Letters Written to Gertrude Stein.* New York: Knopf, 1953.

Gauguin, Paul. *The Writings of a Savage.* Edited by Daniel Guérin. Translated by Eleanor Levieux. New York: Viking, 1978.

Gautier, Judith. *Wagner at Home.* Translated by Effie Dunreith Massie. New York: John Lane, 1911.

Gibson, Michael. *Symbolism.* Translated by Chris Miller. Köln: Taschen, 1999.

Gilman, Sander L., ed. *Conversations with Nietzsche: A Life in the Words of His Contemporaries.* Translated by David J. Parent. New York: Oxford University Press, 1987.

Gold, Matthew K. "The Expert Hand and the Obedient Heart: Dr. Vittoz, T. S. Eliot, and the Therapeutic Possibilities of 'The Waste Land.'" *Journal of Modern Literature* 3, no. 4 (Summer 2000): 519–533.

Goldring, Douglas. *South Lodge: Reminiscences of Violet Hunt, Ford Madox Ford and the English Review Circle.* London: Constable, 1943.

Goldstein, Bill. *The World Broke in Two: Virginia Woolf, T. S. Eliot, D. H. Lawrence, E. M. Forster, and the Year That Changed Literature.* New York: Picador, 2018.

Gordon, Lyndall. *T. S. Eliot: An Imperfect Life.* New York: Norton, 1999.

Gorman, Herbert S. "The Waste Land and the Younger Generation." *Literary Digest International Book Review* (April 1923): 47–48, 64.

Gould, Jean. *Amy: The World of Amy Lowell and the Imagist Movement.* New York: Dodd, Mead, 1975.

Gourmont, Remy de. *The Book of Masks.* Translated by Jack Lewis. Boston: Luce, 1921.

Grant, Michael, ed. *T. S. Eliot: The Critical Heritage.* Vol. 1. London: Routledge & Kegan Paul, 1982.

Gregor-Dellin, Martin. *Richard Wagner: His Life, His Work, His Century.* Translated by J. Maxwell Brownjohn. San Diego, CA: Harcourt, Brace, Jovanovich, 1983.

Gregory, Elizabeth, ed. *The Critical Response to Marianne Moore.* Westport, CT: Praeger, 2003.

Grey, Thomas S., ed. *Richard Wagner and His World.* Princeton, NJ: Princeton University Press, 2009.

Grosz, George. *Pass Auf! Hier Kommt Grosz: Bilder, Rhythmen und Gesänge, 1915–1918.* Edited by Wieland Herzfelde and Hans Marquardt. Leipzig: Philipp Reclam, 1981.

Guest, Barbara. *Herself Defined: The Poet H. D. and Her World.* New York: Doubleday, 1984.

H. D. *Sea Garden.* London: Constable, 1916.

———. *The Walls Do Not Fall.* Oxford: Oxford University Press, 1944.

————. *End to Torment: A Memoir of Ezra Pound*. Edited by Norman Holmes Pearson and Michael King. New York: New Directions, 1979.

————. *Bid Me to Live*. Redding Ridge, CT: Black Swan, 1983.

Harrison, Jane Ellen. *Themis: A Study of the Social Origins of Greek Religion*. 2nd ed. Cambridge: Cambridge University Press, 1927.

Hartford, Robert, ed. *Bayreuth: The Early Years*. London: Gollancz, 1980.

Hemingway, Ernest. *A Moveable Feast*. New York: Scribner, 1964.

Heyman, Katherine Ruth. *The Relation of Ultramodern to Archaic Music*. Boston: Small, Maynard, 1921.

Hoffenstein, Samuel. *Year In, You're Out*. New York: Liveright, 1930.

Homberger, Eric, ed. *Ezra Pound: The Critical Heritage*. London: Routledge & Kegan Paul, 1972.

Huckel, Oliver. *Parsifal, A Mystical Drama by Richard Wagner, Retold in the Spirit of the Bayreuth Interpretation*. New York: Crowell, 1903.

Hulme, T. E. *The Collected Writings of T. E. Hulme*. Edited by Karen Csengeri. Oxford: Clarendon Press, 1994.

Huneker, James. *Overtones: A Book of Temperaments*. New York: Scribner, 1904.

————. *Unicorns*. New York: Scribner, 1917.

Huxley, Aldous. *Letters of Aldous Huxley*. Edited by Grover Smith. New York: Harper and Row, 1969.

Jacob, Max. *Le Cornet à dés*. Paris: Gallimard, 1945.

————. *The Dice Cup (Le Cornet à dés)*. Translated by Michael Rosenthal. N.p.: Legible Books, 2019.

Joyce, James. *Ulysses*. New York: Vintage Books, 1990.

Jullian, Philippe. *Esthètes et Magiciens: L'art fin de siècle*. Paris: Perrin, 1969.

————. *Dreamers of Decadence: Symbolist Painters of the 1890s*. Translated by Robert Baldick. New York: Praeger, 1971.

Kennaway, James. *Bad Vibrations: The History of the Idea of Music as a Cause of Disease*. Burlington, VT: Ashgate, 2012.

Killen, Andreas. *Berlin Electropolis: Shock, Nerves, and German Modernity*. Berkeley: University of California Press, 2006.

King, James. *The Last Modern: The Life of Herbert Read*. New York: St. Martin's Press, 1990.

Köhler, Joachim. *Nietzsche and Wagner: A Lesson in Subjugation*. Translated by Ronald Taylor. New Haven, CT: Yale University Press, 1998.

————. *Richard Wagner: The Last of the Titans*. Translated by Stewart Spencer. New Haven, CT: Yale University Press, 2004.

Koss, Juliet. *Modernism after Wagner*. Minneapolis: University of Minnesota Press, 2010.

Kouidis, Virginia M. *Mina Loy: American Modernist Poet*. Baton Rouge: Louisiana State University Press, 1980.

Kramer, Lawrence. *Musical Meaning: Toward a Critical History*. Berkeley: University of California Press, 2002.

Laforgue, Jules. *Selected Writings of Jules Laforgue*. Edited and translated by William Jay Smith. New York: Grove Press, 1956.

————. *Essential Poems and Prose*. Translated by Patricia Terry. Boston: Black Widow Press, 2010.

Large, David, and William Weber, eds. *Wagnerism in European Culture and Politics*. Ithaca, NY: Cornell University Press, 1984.

Leavell, Linda. *Holding On Upside Down: The Life and Work of Marianne Moore*. New York: Farrar, Straus and Giroux, 2013.

Leick, Karen. "Ezra Pound v. *The Saturday Review of Literature*." *Journal of Modern Literature* 25, no. 2 (Winter 2001–2002): 19–37.

Lewis, Wyndham. "The Revolutionary Simpleton." *The Enemy* 1 (January 1927): 25–295.

————. *Blasting and Bombardiering*. London: Eyre & Spottiswoode, 1937.

Liébert, Georges. *Nietzsche and Music*. Translated by David Pellauer and Graham Parkes. Chicago: University of Chicago Press, 2004.

Lippmann, Walter. *Public Opinion*. New York: The Free Press, 1965.

Lloyd, Rosemary. *Mallarmé: The Poet and His Circle*. Ithaca, NY: Cornell University Press, 1999.

Longenbach, James. *Stone Cottage: Pound, Yeats and Modernism*. New York: Oxford University Press, 1988.

Longworth, Deborah. "The Avant-Garde in the Village: *Rogue* (1915)." In *The Oxford Critical and Cultural History of Modernist Magazines*, vol. 2, *North America 1894–1960*, edited by Peter Brooker and Andrew Thacker, 465–482. Oxford: Oxford University Press, 2012.

Loy, Mina. *The Last Lunar Baedeker*. Edited by Roger L. Conover. Highlands, NC: Jargon Society, 1982.

———. *The Lost Lunar Baedeker*. Edited by Roger L. Conover. New York: Farrar, Straus and Giroux, 1996.

———. *Stories and Essays*. Edited by Sara Crangle. Champaign, IL: Dalkey Archive, 2011.

Lutz, Tom. *American Nervousness 1903: An Anecdotal History*. Ithaca, NY: Cornell University Press, 1991.

MacDonald, Hugh. "Alexander Scriabin—Towards the *Mysterium*." Liner notes, Alexander Scriabin, *Preparation for the Final Mystery* (Decca audio CD, 1999).

MacLeish, Archibald. *Street in the Moon*. Boston: Houghton Mifflin, 1926.

———. *Poetry and Opinion: The Pisan Cantos of Ezra Pound, a Dialogue on the Role of Poetry*. Urbana: University of Illinois Press, 1950.

———. *Letters of Archibald MacLeish, 1907 to 1982*. Edited by R. H. Winnick. Boston: Houghton Mifflin, 1983.

Maeterlinck, Maurice. *The Treasure of the Humble*. New York: Dodd, Mead, 1897.

Mallarmé, Stéphane. *Selected Prose Poems, Essays, and Letters*. Translated by Bradford Cook. Baltimore: Johns Hopkins University Press, 1956.

———. *Collected Poems*. Translated by Henry Weinfield. Berkeley: University of California Press, 1994.

———. *Oeuvres complètes*. Vol. 2. Edited by Bertrand Marchal. Paris: Gallimard, 2003.

———. *Divagations*. Translated by Barbara Johnson. Cambridge, MA: Harvard University Press, 2007.

———. *The Poems in Verse (Poésies)*. Translated by Peter Manson. Oxford, OH: Miami University Press, 2012.

———. *Azure: Poems and Selections from the "Livre."* Translated by Blake Bronson-Bartlett and Robert Fernandez. Middletown, CT: Wesleyan University Press, 2015.

Marc, Franz, and Wassily Kandinsky, eds. *The Blaue Reiter Almanac*. Edited by Klaus Lankheit. Translated by Henning Falkenstein. New York: Viking, 1974.

March, Richard, and Tambimuttu, eds. *T. S. Eliot, A Symposium*. New York: Henry Regnery, 1949.

Martin, Stoddard. *Wagner to "The Waste Land": A Study of the Relationship of Wagner to English Literature*. Totowa, NJ: Barnes & Noble Books, 1982.

Mattis, Olivia. "Scriabin to Gershwin: Color Music from a Musical Perspective." In *Visual Music*, 211–227. New York: Thames and Hudson, 2005.

McGuire, William. *Bollingen: An Adventure in Collecting the Past*. Princeton, NJ: Princeton University Press, 1982.

Mirrlees, Hope. *Collected Poems*. Edited by Sandeep Parmar. Manchester: Carcanet Press, 2011.

Mondrian, Piet. *The New Art—The New Life: The Collected Writings of Piet Mondrian*. Edited and translated by Harry Holtzman and Martin S. James. Boston: G. K. Hall, 1986.

Monk, Ray. *Bertrand Russell: The Spirit of Solitude*. London: Jonathan Cape, 1996.

Montaigne, Michel de. *The Complete Essays*. Translated by M. A. Screech. New York: Penguin, 1991.

Montale, Eugenio. *Selected Essays*. Translated by G. Singh. Manchester: Carcanet, 1978.
———. *The Second Life of Art: Selected Essays*. Edited and translated by Jonathan Galassi. New York: Ecco Press, 1982.
Moody, A. David. *Ezra Pound, Poet: A Portrait of the Man and His Work*. Vol. 3, *The Tragic Years, 1939–1972*. Oxford: Oxford University Press, 2015.
Moore, Marianne. *Observations*. New York: Dial Press, 1924.
———. *Selected Poems*. London: Faber and Faber, 1935.
———. *The Complete Prose of Marianne Moore*. Edited by Patricia C. Willis. New York: Viking, 1986.
———. *The Selected Letters of Marianne Moore*. Edited by Bonnie Costello, with Celeste Goodridge and Cristanne Miller. New York: Knopf, 1997.
Morgan, Emanuel. *Pins for Wings*. New York: The Sunwise Turn, 1920.
Morgan, Emanuel, and Anne Knish. *Spectra: A Book of Poetic Experiments*. New York: Mitchell Kennerley, 1916.
Morrell, Ottoline. *Ottoline at Garsington: Memoirs of Lady Ottoline Morrell, 1915–1918*. Edited by Robert Gathorne-Hardy. London: Faber, 1974.
Muir, Edwin. "Mr. T. S. Eliot." *The Nation and Athenaeum* (August 29, 1925): 644–646.
Murray, Nicholas. *Aldous Huxley: A Biography*. New York: St. Martin's Press, 2002.
Nelson, James G. *Elkin Mathews: Publisher to Yeats, Joyce, Pound*. Madison: University of Wisconsin Press, 1989.
Nietzsche, Friedrich. *Selected Letters of Friedrich Nietzsche*. Edited and translated by Christopher Middleton. Chicago: University of Chicago Press, 1969.
———. *Unpublished Writings from the Period of Unfashionable Observations*. Translated by Richard T. Gray. Stanford, CA: Stanford University Press, 1995.
———. *Untimely Meditations*. Edited by Daniel Breazeale. Translated by R. J. Hollingdale. New York: Cambridge University Press, 1997.
———. *The Case of Wagner; Twilight of the Idols; The Antichrist; Ecce Homo; Dionysus Dithyrambs; Nietzsche contra Wagner*. Translated by Carol Diethe et al. Stanford, CA: Stanford University Press, 2021.
———. *Human, All Too Human II and Unpublished Fragments from the Period of Human, All Too Human II (Spring 1878–Fall 1879)*. Translated by Adrian Del Caro et al. Stanford, CA: Stanford University Press, 2021.
Nordau, Max. *Degeneration*. 2nd ed. New York: Appleton, 1895.
Norman, Charles. *Ezra Pound: A Biography*. Rev. ed. London: Macdonald, 1969.
O'Keeffe, Paul. *Some Sort of Genius: A Life of Wyndham Lewis*. London: Jonathan Cape, 2000.
Olson, Charles. *Charles Olson and Ezra Pound: An Encounter at St. Elizabeths*. Edited by Catherine Seelye. New York: Grossman, 1975.
Palmer, Herbert E. *Cinder Thursday*. London: Ernest Benn, 1931.
Pater, Walter. *The Renaissance: Studies in Art and Poetry*. Edited by Adam Phillips. Oxford: Oxford University Press, 1986.
Paz, Octavio. *Children of the Mire: Modern Poetry from Romanticism to the Avant-Garde*. Translated by Rachel Phillips. Rev. ed. Cambridge, MA: Harvard University Press, 1991.
Pearson, John. *The Sitwells: A Family's Biography*. New York: Harcourt, Brace, 1978.
Pierrot, Jean. *The Decadent Imagination 1880–1900*. Translated by Derek Coltman. Chicago: University of Chicago Press, 1981.
Pietikainen, Petteri. *Neurosis and Modernity: The Age of Nervousness in Sweden*. Boston: Brill, 2007.
Pound, Ezra. *Personae*. London: Elkin Mathews, 1909.
———. *Cathay*. London: Elkin Mathews, 1915.
———. *Gaudier-Brzeska*. London: John Lane, 1916.
———. *Quia Pauper Amavi*. London: The Egoist, 1919.
———. *Hugh Selwyn Mauberley*. London: Ovid Press, 1920.
———. *Umbra: The Early Poems of Ezra Pound*. London: Elkin Mathews, 1920.

———. *Poems 1918–1921*. New York: Boni and Liveright, 1921.

———. *A Draft of XVI Cantos*. Paris: Three Mountains Press, 1925.

———. *Antheil and the Treatise on Harmony*. Chicago: Pascal Covici, 1927.

———. *A Draft of the Cantos 17–27*. London: John Rodker, 1928.

———, ed. *The Exile* 4 (Autumn 1928)

———. *A Draft of XXX Cantos*. Paris: Hours Press, 1930.

———. *Selected Poems*. Edited by T. S. Eliot. London: Faber and Faber, 1933.

———. *ABC of Reading*. London: Routledge, 1934.

———. *Make It New*. London: Faber and Faber, 1934.

———. *The Letters of Ezra Pound, 1907–1941*. Edited by D. D. Paige. New York: Harcourt, Brace, 1950.

———. *Literary Essays*. Edited by T. S. Eliot. New York: New Directions, 1954.

———. *Pound/Joyce: The Letters of Ezra Pound to James Joyce, with Pound's Essays on Joyce*. Edited by Forrest Read. New York: New Directions, 1957.

———. *Collected Shorter Poems*. London: Faber and Faber, 1962.

———. *Drafts & Fragments of Cantos CX–CXVII*. New York: New Directions, 1968.

———. *Selected Prose 1909–1965*. Edited by William Cookson. London: Faber and Faber, 1973.

———. *"Ezra Pound Speaking": Radio Speeches of World War II*. Edited by Leonard W. Doob. Westport, CT: Greenwood Press, 1978.

———. *Pound/Ford: The Story of a Literary Friendship*. Edited by Brita Lindberg-Seyersted. New York: New Directions, 1982.

———. *Ezra Pound and Dorothy Shakespear, Their Letters: 1909–1914*. Edited by Omar Pound and A. Walton Litz. New York: New Directions, 1984.

———. *The Selected Letters of Ezra Pound to John Quinn, 1915–1924*. Edited by Timothy Materer. Durham, NC: Duke University Press, 1991.

———. *Ezra Pound's Poetry and Prose: Contributions to Periodicals*. Vol. 1, *1902–1914*. Edited by Lea Baechler, A. Walton Litz, and James Longenbach. New York: Garland, 1991.

———. *Machine Art and Other Writings: The Lost Thought of the Italian Years*. Edited by Maria Luisa Ardizzone. Durham, NC: Duke University Press, 1996.

———. *Pound/Williams: Selected Letters of Ezra Pound and William Carlos Williams*. Edited by Hugh Witemeyer. New York: New Directions, 1996.

———. *The Pisan Cantos*. Edited by Richard Sieburth. New York: New Directions, 2003.

———. *Ezra Pound to His Parents: Letters 1895–1929*. Edited by Mary de Rachewiltz, A. David Moody, and Joanna Moody. New York: Oxford University Press, 2010.

Pound/The Little Review. The Letters of Ezra Pound to Margaret Anderson: The Little Review Correspondence. Edited by Thomas L. Scott and Melvin J. Friedman, with the assistance of Jackson R. Bryer. New York: New Directions, 1988.

Prideaux, Sue. *I Am Dynamite! A Life of Nietzsche*. New York: Tim Duggan Books, 2018.

Proust, Marcel. *In Search of Lost Time*. Vol. 5, *The Captive; The Fugitive*. Translated by C. K. Scott Moncrieff and Terence Kilmartin. Revised by D. J. Enright. New York: Modern Library, 1993.

Quenoy, Paul du. *Wagner and the French Muse: Music, Society, and Nation in Modern France*. Bethesda, MD: Academica Press, 2011.

Rabinbach, Anson. *The Human Motor: Energy, Fatigue, and the Origins of Modernity*. New York: Basic Books, 1990.

Rachewiltz, Mary de. *Discretions*. Boston: Little, Brown, 1971.

Raffel, Burton. *Possum and Ole Ez in the Public Eye: Contemporaries and Peers on T. S. Eliot and Ezra Pound, 1892–1972*. Hamden, CT: Archon Books, 1985.

Raine, Kathleen. *Autobiographies*. London: Skoob, 1977.

Rainey, Lawrence. *The Annotated Waste Land with Eliot's Contemporary Prose*. New Haven, CT: Yale University Press, 2005.

Rainey, Lawrence, Christine Poggi, and Laura Wittman, eds. *Futurism, An Anthology*. New Haven, CT: Yale University Press, 2009.

Raitt, A. W. *The Life of Villiers de l'Isle-Adam*. Oxford: Clarendon Press, 1981.

Ransom, John Crowe. *Selected Letters of John Crowe Ransom*. Edited by Thomas Daniel Young and George Core. Baton Rouge: Louisiana State University Press, 1985.

Rapetti, Rodolphe. "Landscapes and Symbols." In *Van Gogh to Kandinsky: Symbolist Landscape in Europe 1880–1910*, 17–38. New York: Thames & Hudson, 2012.

Rascoe, Burton. "A Bookman's Day Book." *New York Tribune* (November 3, 1922), sec. 5, p. 8.

———. "A Bookman's Day Book." *New York Tribune* (January 14, 1923), 22–23.

———. *We Were Interrupted*. Garden City, NY: Doubleday, 1947.

Rasula, Jed. *Destruction Was My Beatrice: Dada and the Unmaking of the Twentieth Century*. New York: Basic Books, 2015.

———. *History of a Shiver: The Sublime Impudence of Modernism*. New York: Oxford University Press, 2016.

Reid, B. L. *The Man from New York: John Quinn and His Friends*. New York: Oxford University Press, 1968.

Reverdy, Pierre. *Prose Poems*. Translated by Ron Padgett. Brooklyn, NY: Black Square, 2007.

Richardson, Joanna. *Judith Gautier: A Biography*. London: Quartet Books, 1986.

Rickword, Edgell. *Essays and Opinions, 1921–1931*. Edited by Alan Young. Cheadle, Cheshire, UK: Carcanet New Press, 1974.

Riding, Laura. *Contemporaries and Snobs*. New York: Doubleday, Doran, 1928.

Riding, Laura, and Robert Graves. *A Survey of Modernist Poetry*. London: Heinemann, 1927.

Riha, Karl, and Waltraud Wende-Hohenberger, eds. *Dada Zürich: Texte, Manifeste, Dokumente*. Stuttgart: Philipp Reclam, 1992.

Rilke, Rainer Maria. *Selected Works*. Vol. 1, *Prose*. Translated by G. Craig Houston. New York: New Directions, 1967.

———. *The Book of Images*. Translated by Edward Snow. Rev. ed. New York: North Point Press, 1994.

———. *New Poems*. Translated by Joseph Cadora. Port Townsend, WA: Copper Canyon Press, 2016.

Rimbaud, Arthur. *Complete Works: Selected Letters*. Translated by Wallace Fowlie. Chicago: University of Chicago Press, 1966.

Robinson, Matte. *Astral H. D.: Occult and Religious Sources and Contexts for H. D.'s Poetry and Prose*. New York: Bloomsbury Academic, 2016.

Ross, Alex. *Wagnerism: Art and Politics in the Shadow of Music*. New York: Farrar, Straus and Giroux, 2020.

Ross, Robert H. *The Georgian Revolt 1910–1922: Rise and Fall of a Poetic Ideal*. Carbondale: Southern Illinois University Press, 1965.

Rowson, Martin. *The Waste Land*. New York: HarperCollins, 1990.

Rudnick, Lois Palken. *Mabel Dodge Luhan: New Woman, New Worlds*. Albuquerque: University of New Mexico Press, 1984.

Rudorff, Raymond. *Belle Epoque: Paris in the Nineties*. London: Hamilton, 1972.

Rukeyser, Muriel. *The Life of Poetry*. New York: Current Books, 1949.

Russell, Bertrand. *The Autobiography of Bertrand Russell*. Vol. 1. Boston: Little, Brown, 1967.

Ruthven, K. K. *A Guide to Ezra Pound's* Personae *(1926)*. Berkeley: University of California Press, 1969.

Satie, Erik. *A Mammal's Notebook: Collected Writings of Erik Satie*. Edited by Ornella Volta. Translated by Antony Melville. London: Atlas Press, 1996.

Saunders, Max. *Ford Madox Ford: A Dual Life*. Vol. 1, *The World before the War*. Oxford: Oxford University Press, 1996.

Schoenberg, Arnold. *Style and Idea: Selected Writings*. Edited by Leonard Stein. Translated by Leo Black. Berkeley: University of California Press, 1984.

Schopenhauer, Arthur. *The World as Will and Representation*. 2 vols. Translated by E.F.J. Payne. New York: Dover, 1966.

Schuster, David G. *Neurasthenic Nation: America's Search for Health, Happiness, and Comfort, 1869–1920*. New Brunswick, NJ: Rutgers University Press, 2011.

Schwitters, Kurt. *Poems, Performance Pieces, Proses, Plays, Poetics*. Edited and translated by Jerome Rothenberg and Pierre Joris. Philadelphia: Temple University Press, 1993.

Scott, Cyril. *The Philosophy of Modernism—Its Connection with Music*. London: Waverley, 1917.

———. *Music: Its Secret Influence throughout the Ages*. Wellingborough, Northamptonshire, UK: Aquarian Press, 1973.

Seferis, George. *Collected Poems*. Translated by Edmund Keeley and Philip Sherrard. Rev. ed. Princeton, NJ: Princeton University Press, 1995.

———. "Introduction to T. S. Eliot." Translated by Susan Matthias. *Modernism/modernity* 16, no. 1 (January 2009): 146–160.

Seymour, Miranda. *Ottoline Morrell: Life on the Grand Scale*. New York: Farrar, Straus and Giroux, 1992.

Seymour-Jones, Carole. *Painted Shadow: The Life of Vivienne Eliot*. New York: Nan A. Talese, 2002.

Shapiro, Karl. *Trial of a Poet and Other Poems*. New York: Reynal & Hitchcock, 1947.

———. "The Case of Ezra Pound." *Partisan Review* 16, no. 5 (1949): 518–520.

———. *In Defense of Ignorance and Other Essays*. New York: Random House, 1960.

Sharpe, Tony, ed. *W. H. Auden in Context*. Cambridge: Cambridge University Press, 2012.

Shattuck, Roger, *The Banquet Years: The Origins of the Avant Garde in France: 1885 to World War I*. Rev. ed. New York: Vintage Books, 1968.

Shaw, George Bernard. *Major Critical Essays: The Quintessence of Ibsenism, The Perfect Wagnerite, The Sanity of Art*. London: Constable, 1947.

Shaw-Miller, Simon. *Visible Deeds of Music: Art and Music from Wagner to Cage*. New Haven, CT: Yale University Press, 2002.

Simmel, Georg. *On Individuality and Social Forms: Selected Writings*. Edited by Donald N. Levine. Chicago: University of Chicago Press, 1971.

Simpson, Eileen. *Poets in Their Youth: A Memoir*. New York: Vintage Books, 1983.

Slonimsky, Nicolas. *Lexicon of Musical Invective: Critical Assaults on Composers since Beethoven's Time*. New York: Norton, 2000.

Smith, William Jay. *The Spectra Hoax*. Middletown, CT: Wesleyan University Press, 1961.

Sokoloff, Alice Hunt. *Cosima Wagner: Extraordinary Daughter of Franz Liszt*. New York: Dodd, Mead, 1969.

Some Imagist Poets: An Anthology. Boston: Houghton Mifflin, 1915.

Some Imagist Poets 1916: An Annual Anthology. Boston: Houghton Mifflin, 1916.

Spender, Stephen. *T. S. Eliot*. New York: Viking, 1976.

———. *World within World: The Autobiography of Stephen Spender*. New York: St. Martin's Press, 1994 [1951].

———. *New Selected Journals 1939–1995*. Edited by Lara Feigel and John Sutherland, with Natasha Spender. London: Faber, 2012.

Spindler, Elizabeth Carroll. *John Peale Bishop: A Biography*. Morgantown: West Virginia University Library, 1980.

Stallworthy, Jon. *Louis MacNeice*. London: Faber, 1995.

Starkie, Enid. *Baudelaire*. New York: Penguin Books, 1971.

Stein, Gertrude. *The Autobiography of Alice B. Toklas*. New York: Harcourt, Brace, 1933.

———. *What Are Masterpieces*. Los Angeles: Conference Press, 1940.

———. *Selected Writings*. Edited by Carl Van Vechten. New York: Random House, 1946.

Steinberg, Ada. *Word and Music in the Novels of Andrey Bely*. Cambridge: Cambridge University Press, 1982.

Stevens, Wallace. *The Palm at the End of the Mind: Selected Poems and a Play*. Edited by Holly Stevens. New York: Vintage Books, 1990.

Storer, Edward. *Mirrors of Illusion*. London: Sisley's, [1908].

Swift, Daniel. *The Bughouse: The Poetry, Politics, and Madness of Ezra Pound*. New York: Farrar, Straus and Giroux, 2017.

Symons, Arthur. *Plays, Acting and Music: A Book of Theory*. London: Constable, 1909.

———. *Studies in Seven Arts*. London: Martin Secker, 1924.

———. *The Symbolist Movement in Literature*. New York: Dutton, 1958.

Symons, Julian. *Makers of the New: The Revolution in Literature, 1912–1939*. New York: Random House, 1987.

Tashjian, Dickran. *William Carlos Williams and the American Scene, 1920–1940*. New York: Whitney Museum of American Art, 1978.

Thomson, Belinda. "Parisianism." In *Toulouse-Lautrec and la Vie Moderne: Paris 1880–1910*, edited by Phillip Dennis Cate, 21–26. New York: Skira Rizzoli, 2013.

Thomson, Richard. "Arcadia Contested." In *Van Gogh to Kandinsky: Symbolist Landscape in Europe 1880–1910*, edited by Richard Thomson et al., 41–65. New York: Thames & Hudson, 2012.

Tracy, Steven C. *Hot Music, Ragmentation, and the Bluing of American Literature*. Tuscaloosa: University of Alabama Press, 2015.

Turbow, Gerald D. "Art and Politics: Wagnerism in France." In *Wagnerism in European Culture and Politics*, edited by David Large and William Weber, 134–166. Ithaca, NY: Cornell University Press, 1984.

Underwood, Thomas A. *Allen Tate: Orphan of the South*. Princeton, NJ: Princeton University Press, 2000.

Unger, Leonard, ed. *T. S. Eliot: A Selected Critique*. New York: Rinehart, 1948.

Untermeyer, Louis. *From Another World: The Autobiography of Louis Untermeyer*. New York: Harcourt, Brace, 1939.

Valency, Maurice. *The End of the World: An Introduction to Contemporary Drama*. New York: Oxford University Press, 1980.

Valéry, Paul. *Leonardo, Poe, Mallarmé*. Translated by Malcolm Cowley and James R. Lawler. Princeton, NJ: Princeton University Press, 1972.

Van Vechten, Carl. "How to Read Gertrude Stein." *The Trend* 7, no. 5 (August 1914): 553–557.

Vaughan, Gerard. "Maurice Denis and the Sense of Music." *Oxford Art Journal* 7, no. 1 (1984): 38–48.

Viereck, Peter. *Archer in the Marrow: The Applewood Cycles of 1968–1984*. New York: Norton, 1987.

Villiers de l'Isle-Adam. *Axel*. Translated by Marilyn Gaddis Rose. Dublin: Dolmen Press, 1970.

Wade, Francesca. *Square Haunting: Five Writers in London between the Wars*. New York: Tim Duggan Books, 2020.

Wagner, Cosima. *Cosima Wagner's Diaries*. Vol. 1, *1869–1877*. Edited by Martin Gregor-Dellin and Dietrich Mack. Translated by Geoffrey Skelton. New York: Harcourt, Brace, Jovanovich, 1978.

———. *Cosima Wagner's Diaries*. Vol. 2, *1878–1883*. Edited by Martin Gregor-Dellin and Dietrich Mack. Translated by Geoffrey Skelton. New York: Harcourt, Brace, Jovanovich, 1980.

Wagner, Richard. *Das Kunstwerk der Zukunft*. Leipzig: Wigand, 1850.

———. *Prose Works*. Vol. 1, *The Art-Work of the Future, Etc.* Translated by William Ashton Ellis. London: Kegan Paul, Trench, Trübner, 1892.

———. *Sämtliche Schriften und Dichtungen*. Vol. 7. Leipzig: Breitkopf und Härtel, 1912.

———. *Three Wagner Essays*. Translated by Robert L. Jacobs. London: Eulenburg, 1979.

———. *Selected Letters of Richard Wagner*. Edited and translated by Stewart Spencer and Barry Millington. New York: Norton, 1988.

———. *Oper und Drama*. Edited by Klaus Kropfinger. Stuttgart: Reclam, 1994.

Wagner, Richard and Cosima. *Lettres à Judith Gautier*. Edited by Léon Guichard. Paris: Gallimard, 1964.

Watson, Steven. *Strange Bedfellows: The First American Avant-Garde*. New York: Abbeville Press, 1991.

Waugh, Evelyn. *Brideshead Revisited: The Sacred and Profane Memories of Captain Charles Ryder*. Boston: Little, Brown, 1946.

———. *The Diaries of Evelyn Waugh*. Edited by Michael Davie. London: Weidenfeld and Nicholson, 1976.

Weber, Max. *Essays on Art*. New York: Rudge, 1916.

Wees, William C. *Vorticism and the English Avant-Garde*. Toronto: University of Toronto Press, 1972.

Wilde, Oscar. *The Picture of Dorian Gray*. 2nd ed. Edited by Michael Patrick Gillespie. New York: Norton, 2007.

Williams, William Carlos. "Questionnaire." *The Little Review* 12, no. 2 (May 1929): 87–88.

———. "A Tentative Statement." *The Little Review* 12, no. 2 (May 1929): 95–98.

———. *Selected Essays*. New York: Random House, 1954.

———. *Selected Letters*. Edited by John C. Thirlwall. New York: McDowell, Obolensky, 1957.

———. *The Autobiography*. New York: New Directions, 1967.

———. *Spring and All*. New York: New Directions, 2011.

Wilson, Edmund. *Axel's Castle: A Study in the Imaginative Literature of 1870 to 1930*. New York: Scribner's, 1931.

———. *Letters on Literature and Politics, 1912–1972*. Edited by Elena Wilson. New York: Farrar, Straus and Giroux, 1977.

Winchell, Mark Royden. *Cleanth Brooks and the Rise of Modern Criticism*. Charlottesville: University Press of Virginia, 1996.

Witemeyer, Hugh. "The Making of Pound's 'Selected Poems' (1949) and Rolfe Humphries' Unpublished Introduction." *Journal of Modern Literature* 15, no. 1 (Summer 1988): 73–91.

Woolf, Virginia. *The Question of Things Happening: The Letters of Virginia Woolf*. Vol. 2, *1912–1922*. Edited by Nigel Nicolson. London: Hogarth Press, 1976.

———. *A Change of Perspective: The Letters of Virginia Woolf*. Vol. 3, *1923–1928*. Edited by Nigel Nicolson. London: Hogarth Press, 1977.

———. *The Diary of Virginia Woolf*. Vol. 1, *1915–1919*. Edited by Anne Olivier Bell. New York: Harcourt, Brace, 1977.

———. *The Diary of Virginia Woolf*. Vol. 2, *1920–1924*. Edited by Anne Olivier Bell, assisted by Andrew McNeillie. New York: Harcourt Brace, 1978.

Wyzéwa, Téodor de. "Descriptive Music." Translated by Jennifer Day. In *Music in European Thought 1851–1912*, edited by Bojan Bujic, 247–250. Cambridge University Press, 1988.

Yeats, W. B. *Wheels and Butterflies*. London: Macmillan, 1934.

———, ed. *The Oxford Book of Modern Verse 1892–1935*. Oxford: Oxford University Press, 1936.

———. *The Autobiography of William Butler Yeats*. New York: Macmillan, 1953.

———. *A Vision*. New York: Macmillan, 1956.

———. *Essays and Introductions*. New York: Macmillan, 1961.

Young, Julian. *Friedrich Nietzsche: A Philosophical Biography*. New York: Cambridge University Press, 2010.

Zuckerman, Elliott. *The First Hundred Years of Wagner's 'Tristan.'* New York: Columbia University Press, 1964.

INDEX